W9-BZH-943

The
PerformanceStat
Potential

INNOVATIVE GOVERNANCE IN THE 21ST CENTURY

ANTHONY SAICH
Series editor

This is the seventh volume in a series that examines important issues of governance, public policy, and administration, highlighting innovative practices and original research worldwide. All titles in the series will be copublished by the Brookings Institution Press and the Ash Center for Democratic Governance and Innovation, housed at Harvard University's John F. Kennedy School of Government.

The PerformanceStat Potential

A Leadership Strategy for Producing Results

Robert D. Behn

ASH CENTER FOR DEMOCRATIC GOVERNANCE
AND INNOVATION
John F. Kennedy School of Government
Harvard University

BROOKINGS INSTITUTION PRESS
Washington, D.C.

Copyright © 2014
ASH CENTER FOR DEMOCRATIC
GOVERNANCE AND INNOVATION
Harvard University

All rights reserved. No part of this publication may be reproduced or transmitted in any form or by any means without permission in writing from the Brookings Institution Press, 1775 Massachusetts Avenue, N.W., Washington, D.C. 20036, www.brookings.edu.

The Brookings Institution is a private nonprofit organization devoted to research, education, and publication on important issues of domestic and foreign policy. Its principal purpose is to bring the highest quality independent research and analysis to bear on current and emerging policy problems. Interpretations or conclusions in Brookings publications should be understood to be solely those of the authors.

Library of Congress Cataloging-in-Publication data is available.
ISBN 978-0-8157-2527-5

Digital printing

Printed on acid-free paper

Typeset in Adobe Garamond

Composition by Cynthia Stock
Silver Spring, Maryland

To

MARK

My favorite second baseman and
My favorite backpacking partner

Contents

Appendixes

Acknowledgments: Years in the Making, a Cast of Thousands

From Baltimore to Brisbane, New York to New Orleans, Washington, D.C., to Washington State, public officials have been generous with their insights and patience. To them, my thanks.

"A large acquaintance with particulars often makes us wiser
than the possession of abstract formulas, however deep."
WILLIAM JAMES, Harvard University[1]

"One good example is worth a thousand theories"
LAWRENCE SUMMERS, Harvard University[2]

Years in the making? Literally. On February 9, 2001, I was at Boston Police Headquarters to observe its Crime Analysis Meeting (which, over the years evolved into the city's CompStat). Three months later, I was in Lowell, Massachusetts, for its CompStat session. Then, on October 9, 2003, I was in Baltimore's city hall for my first CitiStat meetings, which focused on the Department of Recreation and Parks and the Bureau of Water and Wastewater. Three months later, I was back in Baltimore to again observe CitiStat and these two agencies. I was hooked.

A cast of thousands? Absolutely. Over a decade, I investigated three dozen different efforts to employ the PerformanceStat leadership strategy. (See list below.) And in this process, I have interviewed, chatted with, and observed thousands of people. They were tolerant of my presence and gracious in offering their ideas, reflections, and insights. I have presented preliminary versions of these chapters at a number of meetings of scholars and public executives. And I frequently used these materials in the Performance Leadership course that I teach at the Kennedy School and in numerous executive education programs and seminars both at the School and elsewhere. Those who listened have provided me with a lot of feedback that have modified, improved, and sharpened the ideas presented here.

In my research, I have visited, observed, or held extensive discussions with the three dozen agencies and jurisdictions that were employing, seeking to employ, or thinking they were employing a PerformanceStat leadership strategy. These include:

CompStats in Boston; Los Angeles; Lowell, Mass.; Queensland, Australia, plus New York City's TrafficStat.

City, County, and State AgencyStats: NYC Department of Children's Services (ChildStat), NYC Department of Correction (TEAMS), NYC Human Resources Administration (JobStat and VendorStat), NYC Department of Probation (STARS), Los Angeles County Department of Public Social Services (DPS-STAT), Los Angeles County Department of Mental Health (STAT), Rhode Island Department of Education (EdStat), Ohio Department of Job and Family Services (PerformanceCenter), and Wisconsin Department of Children and Families (KidStat).

Federal AgencyStats: Food and Drug Administration (FDA-Track), Federal Emergency Management Agency (FEMAStat), Department of Housing and Urban Development (HUDStat), Department of the Treasury (Quarterly Performance Reviews), Department of Veterans Affairs (Monthly Performance Reviews).

JurisdictionStats: Aberdeen (Scotland, CitiStat), Atlanta (ATLStat), Baltimore (CitiStat), Columbus (Ohio, Columbus*Stat), Hartford (HartStat), King County (Washington, KingStat), Louisville (LouieStat), Maryland (StateStat), New Orleans (BlightStat), Newark (ReentryStat), PalmBay (PalmStat),Philadelphia (PhillyStat), Providence (ProvStat), Rotterdam (The Netherlands, MaasStat), San Francisco (SFStat), Somerville (SomerStat), Syracuse (SyraStat), Warren (Michigan, CitiStat), Washington, D.C. (CapStat), Washington State (GMAP).

Following is a partial list of people who contributed in some way to this book. I say partial because I was never able to write down the names of all those who spoke at a PerformanceStat session or who commented on a presentation (and thus contributed to my understanding of the workings of this strategy). Partial because my memory doesn't permit me to recall the names of all of those with whom I did talk. Thus, what follows fails to adequately acknowledge every member of this PerformanceStat cast of thousands—including chief executives, middle managers, front-line supervisors, and scholars (let alone students and executive-education participants). Inevitably, I may have inadvertently left some people off this list. To them (or to those whose names I have misspelled), I apologize.

David Abbott, Mark Abramson, Tara Acker, Jacob Aguilar, Jennifer Ahn, Amiee Albertson, Alphonzo Albright, Greg Allen, Nicholas Altieri, Christina Altmayer, Alan Altshuler, Eloise Anderson, Susan Angell, Phil Ansell, John

Antonelli, Kenneth Apfel, Kendra Amaral, Constance Ament, Louise Appleton, Arcelio Aponte, Robin Arnold-Williams, Paul Arns, David Ashley, Amy Astle-Raaen, Douglass Austin, Shannon Avery

Tasha Bahal, Sara Bahler, Amy Baker, Jessie Baker, Eugene Bardach, Anthony Barksdale, James Barry, Alison Battaglia, Susan Battle-McDonald , Phineas Baxandall, Frederick Bealefeld, George Beard, Gregory Beaverson, Charlie Beck, Jody Becker-Green, William Beiersdorfer, Peter Beilenson, Larisa Benson, William Berger, Jill Berry, Michael Bezanson, Jim Blakeman, Beth Blauer, Sherry Bodine, Pool Boersma, Jenifer Boss, Bruce Botka, Leigh Botwinik, Fredi-Ellen Bove, Anthony Braga, William Bratton, Daniela Bremmer, Patricia Brennan, Jonathan Breul, Terri Bright, Katie Brillantes, Jonathan Brock, Connie Brown, Dustin Brown, Philip Browning, Russ Brubaker, Denise Burgin, Mark Bussow

Mary Campbell, Robin Campbell, Pamela Cardillo, Christopher Carlson, Robin Carmichael, Edward Carrasco, Timothy Carroll, Stephen Carruth, Roxanne Carter, Andrea Castaneda, Sylvia Chasco, Samuel Clark, Dan Clement, David Cicilline, Frank Cirivello, John Coffey, Christine Cole, Nani Coloretti, Steven Conry, Belinda Conway, John Corrigan, Mark Cranston, Kimberly Cregeur, Thomas Criman, Evangeline Cummings, Joseph Curtatone

Albert D'Attilio, Lisa Danzig, Alicia Darensbourg, Greg Davies, Edward Davis, Joseph Dear, Jorrit de Jong, Dominic Del Pozzo, Joseph DeMartino, Gail Dershewitz, Swati Desai, Carolyn Dias, Ralph Di Fiore, Joseph Dillon, John Dixon, Dick Doane, Robert Doar, David Dolinsky, John Donahue, Kevin Donahue, Leif Dormsjo, Matthew Driscoll, Robert Dunford, Jane Dunham

Adel Ebeid, Amy Edwards, Dory Edwards, David Edwards, David Eichenthal, Michael Enright, Brian Epps, Charles Euchner, John Evangelista

Mary-Beth Fafard, Robert Farmer, Duriya Farooqui, Michael Farrell, Andrew Feldman, Lee Feldman, Michael Fisher, Tom Fitzsimmons, Jan Flory, Kimberly Flowers, Lisa Foehr, Todd Foglesong, Susan Fojas, Caroline Fooshee, Fiona Forster, Paul Foster, Chris Fox, Alfred Foxx, Andrew Frank, Mark Freeman, Andrew French, Mark Friedman

James Gaffey, Francisco Galarza, Matthew Gallagher, John Gamage, Lisa Garabedian, Kwevin Giangola, Amber Gillum, Lorene Gilmore, Philip Ginsburg, Deborah Gist, Marcus Glasper, Alan Glassman, Paul Glock, Jeff Godown, Stephen Goldsmith, Sheryl Goldstein, Greg Gomez, Peter Grace, Helene Grady, Lisa Graham, Carol Grant, Gineen Gray, Elise Greef, Clark Greene, Richard Greenwald, Darryl Griffen

Daniel Hadley, Judy Hall, Sherri Hall, Doug Hamilton, Susan Hann, Marsha Hanna, Arlene Happach, Darryl Harrison, James Hartley, Jean Hartley, Frank Hartmann, Nikki Hatch, Harry Hatry, Natalie Helbig, Larry Hellman,

Nick Hernandez, Gabriela Herrera, Gerry Hertzberg, Carter Hewgley, Charles Hewitt, Anthony Heywood, Iris Hill, William Hilton, Stephanie Hirsch, Jason Hoak, Carole Holland, Barry Holman, Cindi Holmstrom, Martin Horn, Elspeth Hough, Arnold Howitt, Jessica Hu, Ronald Hunt, Howard Husock

Michael Jacobson, Anita Jennings, Richard Jennings, Ingrid Johnson, Queen Jones

John Kamensky, David Kaufman, Robin Kay, Steven Kelman, Chad Kenney, Karen Kent, Donald Kettl, Thatcher Kezer, Timothy Kiang, Jennifer Kistler, Natalie Knight, Bill Knowles, Lonsdale Koester, Peter Kolesnik, Andrew Kopplin, Hope Koprowski, Karalyn Kratowicz, Justin Kray, Matthew Krieger, Robert Kuzma

Catherine Lamb, Michael Lambert, Gary Lanigan, Judith LaPook, Andrew Lauland, Donald Leatherwood, Karen Lee, Richard Leinhardt, Dutch Leonard, Richard Levy, Jon Lewis, Jeffrey Liebman, Russell Linden, Daniel Linskey, Dan Lioi, Stephen Lisauskas, Kimberly Liston, David Luberoff, Douglas Lumpkin

Kristen Mahoney, Mike Maier, Tim Malin, Lindsay Major-Ringgold, Marcia Marsh, Clive Martlew, Robert Maruca, John Mattingly, Gary Maynard, Miguel Matos, Mark McAteer, Yvonne McDonald, Kevin McGuire, Colin McKay, Laura Meixell, Shelley Metzenbaum, David Michel, Christopher Mihm, David Milne, Ken Mokrzycki, Julio Molleda, Gary Moore, Daro Mott, Mark Moore, Catherine Motz, Ravio Murnieks, William Murphy, Amanda Myers-Hauss

Richard Negrin, James Newman, Spencer Nichols, Sara Norman, Michael Nutter

Mark Olivera, Fred Olson, Martin O'Malley, Bernard O'Rourke, Donna Owens

Peter Panagi, David Panagore, Frances Pardus-Abbadessa, William Parent, Roger Parris, Ruth Parsons, James Pearsol, Joe Perez, Jose Perez, Andrea Phillips, Joseph J. Pilat, Robert Pipik, Jessie Poli, Lowell Porter, Michael Powell, Victor Prince, Jim Proce, Stefan Pryor

Paul Rakosky, Stephanie Rawlings-Blake, Michael Reese, Alaina Restivo, Trent Rhorer, Bryan Richardson, Barbara Riley, Gary Robinson, Todd Rogers, Brian Roulin, Valerie Russo

Joel Sacks, Jay Sakai, Jose Sanchez, Bryna Sanger, Eva Santos, Tony Saudek, Michael Scagnelli, Elliot Schlanger, Rebecca Schwei, Joe Scialfa, David Scott, Valerie Scott-Oliver, Pedro Segarra, Ronojoy Sen, Richard Serino, Joshua Sharfstein, Steven Sharkey, Suzanne Sherman, Stephen Shipman, Sameer Sidh, Heidi Sieck, Jonathan Sikorski, John Simmons, Raymond Singleton, Deborah Smith, Patricia Smith, Steven Smith, Mary Ann Snider, Arianne Spaccarelli, Francis Spangenberg, Malcolm Sparrow, Sheryl Spiller, Phillip Stafford, Cheryl Stephani, Peg Stevenson

Daniel Tangherlini, Janetta Taylor, Neva Terry, Eric Thomas, Simon Thomas, Christopher Thomaskutty, David Thornburg, John Timoney, Paul Trause, John Trott, Jeffrey Tryens, Jason Turner, Joyce Turner

Valentina Ukwuoma

Bas van der Pool, Matthew Vanderbyl, Andrew Vetter, Doreen Vetter, Chris Vein

Kevin Walsh, Richard Walsh, John Wanchick, Kevin Ward, Michael Ward, Joyce Washington, Mary Washington, Dave Watkins, Peggy Watson, Melissa Wavelet, Katie Weaver Randall, Michael Webb, Jason Weinstein, Heather Weston, Chuck Wexler, Richard White, Michael Wilhelm, Ronald Wilhelmy, Brian Willett, Jolanda Williams, Tracy Williams, Julie Wilson, Morley Winograd, Oliver Wise, Guy Worley

Jason Yarborough, Lynnette Young

Janet Zars, David Zlowe, Ashley Zohn

Many colleagues and friends read draft chapters and provided useful feedback. Three, however, read the entire manuscript and provided detailed comments and suggestions. I paid attention to all of their comments, and even followed up on their suggestions. To Eugene Bardach, Donald Kettl, and Jeffrey Liebman I owe a special thanks.

Harvard's Kennedy School of Government is "committed to solving real world public problems," while seeking to ensure the "transparent engagement" of its faculty. Thus, in the spirit of full disclosure, I should report that I was provided some assistance in the development of BayStat by the City of Palm Bay, Florida, and of FEMAStat by the Federal Emergency Management Agency—assistance for which I was compensated.

Finally, I should thank my family—Judy, Mark, Liz, Alex, and Clare—who tolerated the days I spent traveling to visit another PerformanceStat ("Again?") or hiding in my garret office (rewriting another paragraph again and again). Now they—plus all those mentioned above—can stop asking: "When's the book going to be done?"

Preface

U.S. government can't seem to accomplish anything.
JIM ALGIE, Owen Sound Sun Times, Ontario[1]

Programmes work in limited circumstances and for the realist, the discovery
of these scope conditions is the main task of review and synthesis.
RAY PAWSON, University of Lees[2]

"Why does poor performance get so much attention in public policy?" This question has been raised by Åge Johnsen of Oslo and Akershus University College. He noticed "the preoccupation with poor performance" of government, the "dysfunctional effects of performance measurement," and "the strategy of naming, blaming and shaming" the poor performers. Johnsen does point out that this focus on poor performance—on data revealing (or simply suggesting) that a public organization is performing badly—"may improve decision making and facilitate policy innovation, enhance transparency and administrative control as well as facilitate responsiveness and democratic accountability." But he also notes that this "negativity bias" may encourage public officials to engage in a strategy of "blame avoidance," and to do so "in spite of the 'learning from best practice' rhetoric."[3]

Yet despite all this negative focus on poor performance, some public executives have shunned blame avoidance and, instead, are actively and explicitly seeking to improve the performance of government. They aren't trying to jump to the top of the performance mountain. Instead, they seek to ratchet up performance, one notch at a time, learning as they go.

Some of these public executives are explicitly attempting to employ a "PerformanceStat" leadership strategy. Others may be using a strategy that—even though they have never heard of CompStat or CitiStat or PerformanceStat—contains some or even many of its core concepts. Some have carefully observed what others are doing and then have consciously sought to adapt what they saw to their own organization and circumstances. Others have learned about the strategy indirectly and have endeavored to (re)invent it for their own organization. All have experimented, trying different things to learn what is effective in achieving the results they seek to produce next.

None of these strategies is identical. Each has been adapted from core leadership principles and key operational components. How they work depends on both the specifics of the strategy and the specifics of the situation. Nevertheless, there are many underlying commonalities.

This book is an effort to identify these commonalities, to define what they are, to explain their significance, and to describe how they work—or at least how they might work in specific circumstances. I have organized the book in the following (obviously logical) structure:

—In chapters 1 and 2, I introduce several different examples of Performance-Stat and explore how different people have described them.

—Then, in chapter 3, I present the core leadership principles and key operational components of this leadership strategy.

—In chapter 4, given the debate about CompStat's effects, I review the potential causes for the significant reductions in crime across the United States.

—In chapters 5 and 6, I examine two key aspects of any effective performance-leadership strategy: a focus on achieving specific public purposes, and combining responsibility with discretion to accomplish specific results.

—Next, in chapter 7, I provide several examples of such accomplishments achieved using different PerformanceStat strategies (though other chapters contain more examples).

—Over the next six chapters, 8 through 13, I survey other important aspects of this leadership strategy: data, analysis, meetings, feedback and follow-up, the human and organizational competences, and learning and adaptation.

—In chapter 14, I discuss the need for public executives to understand how any strategy they employ might work.

—Then, in chapter 15, I suggest how, through 16 specific behaviors of the leadership team, a PerformanceStat strategy can affect the behavior of people and organizations.

—Finally, in chapter 16, I emphasize the necessity of the leadership team making a full commitment to improving performance and producing results.

I hope you find this logic as compelling as I do. Okay: I simply hope you find that it works.

1

CompStat and Its PerformanceStat Progeny

How and why was the original PerformanceStat leadership strategy adopted and adapted by many different public agencies and government jurisdictions?

Jack [Maple] is the smartest man I've ever met on crime.
WILLIAM BRATTON, Police Commissioner of New York City[1]

Whenever anything is being accomplished, it is being done,
I have learned, by a monomaniac with a mission.
PETER DRUCKER, Claremont Graduate University[2]

One night in the winter of 1994, Jack Maple was sitting in Elaine's—an expensive, four-star restaurant and celebrity hangout on the Upper East Side of Manhattan—drinking. As befits any urban legend, the reports on what he was drinking differ. As Maple remembered the night, he was on his third glass of champagne.[3] Maple's boss, William Bratton, recalled that he too was in Elaine's that night and insisted that Maple, because he knew that he "might get called to a crime scene at any time," usually drank multiple cups of double espresso.[4]

Regardless of whether Maple was inspired by the grape or the bean, the dozen words that he scrawled on a napkin that evening have been engraved on the minds of numerous public executives who seek to improve performance and produce better results:

1. Accurate and timely intelligence
2. Rapid deployment
3. Effective tactics
4. Relentless follow-up and assessment

These are "the four principles"[5] of CompStat, the leadership strategy developed in the New York City Police Department by Commissioner Bratton, Deputy Commissioner Maple, and their NYPD colleagues.[6] Their purpose? To improve the department's performance, and thus to produce better results. Specifically, when Bratton became NYPD's commissioner, he committed himself and his organization to reducing the city's crime by 10 percent in the first year, 25 percent over two years, and 40 percent over three years.[7]

The "CompStat Craze"

Indeed, in New York City, crime did drop. It dropped significantly. George Mason University's David Weisburd and Stephen Mastrofski and their colleagues have called CompStat "a major innovation in American policing."[8] To George Kelling of the Manhattan Institute and William Sousa of Rutgers University, "Compstat was perhaps the single most important organizational/administrative innovation in policing during the latter half of the 20th century."[9] William Walsh of the University of Louisville labeled it "an emerging police managerial paradigm."[10] Dall Forsythe, now at New York University, called it an "effective management innovation."[11] Mark Moore of Harvard has described it as "an important administrative innovation in policing."[12] Indeed, in 1996, Harvard University's Kennedy School of Government honored NYPD's CompStat with an Innovation in American Government Award.[13]

As in any field of human endeavor, an innovation that proves successful (or merely appears to be successful) is disseminated through professional networks and informal channels to others who adopt and adapt it.[14] By 1999, five years after Maple first scribbled down his four principles on Elaine's napkin, a third of the 445 police agencies in the United States with more than 100 sworn officers that responded to a survey reported that they had "implemented a CompStat-like program," and another quarter of these agencies said that they were planning to do so.[15] This "Compstat Craze," as Christopher Swope called it in *Governing* magazine,[16] was certainly a broad and rapid diffusion of this innovation throughout the policing profession.[17]

Moreover, as police departments across the United States—and around the world—created their own versions of CompStat, they found Maple's four points worth saluting. In the Los Angeles Police Department, where Bratton served as police chief from 2002 to 2009, "the elements of CompStat consist of four distinct principles."[18] To the Philadelphia Police Department, "the philosophy behind COMPSTAT is deceptively simple. It is based on four principles which have proven to be essential ingredients of an effective crime-fighting strategy."[19]

In Columbia, South Carolina, the police department introduced Maple's ideas about CompStat using almost exactly the same words: "four principles which have proven to be key ingredients of an effective crime-fighting strategy."[20] In Escondido, California, the police department reported that "the CompStat process is based on four crime fighting strategies."[21] The Minneapolis Police Department used a different name, CODEFOR (for Computer Optimized Deployment—Focus On Results), but still emphasized the same "four elements essential to crime control."[22]

Big-city police departments are not, however, the only ones using the CompStat approach.[23] Numerous departments in small cities and towns have also adopted this leadership strategy; they too have emphasized the importance of Maple's four principles. Sandy Springs, Georgia (population 100,000), simply called them "the elements." In West Vancouver, British Columbia (population 42,000), the police department listed them as "the four principles." To the police in Shawnee, Oklahoma (population 29,000), they are "four key principles." Burlington Township, New Jersey (population 20,000), called them "essential principles." Warwick Township, Pennsylvania (population 12,000), echoed Philadelphia, describing them as "four principles which have proved to be essential ingredients of an effective crime-fighting strategy."[24]

Moreover, CompStat and Maple's four principles have been adopted not only to fight crime but also to reduce traffic accidents. And they have been employed not only by municipal police departments but also by police agencies at the state and provincial levels.

In the Canadian province of Manitoba, the Winnipeg Police Service created the term "CrimeStat";[25] the name may be different, but "the philosophy is built on [the same] four principles."[26] In the State of Washington, the Highway Patrol named its approach "Accountability Driven Leadership," which "embraces many of the principles of COMPSTAT."[27] In Australia, policing is the responsibility not of the municipalities but of the states, all of which created their own versions of CompStat (each with its own distinct name): Queensland named it Operational Performance Reviews; New South Wales, Operations Crime Reviews; Tasmania, Management Group Performance Reviews; Western Australia, Organisational Performance Reviews; and South Australia, Performance Outcomes Reviews.[28] Only Victoria calls it "COMPSTAT." Not surprisingly, the Queensland Police Service reports that its Operational Performance Reviews are "based on the [same] four key elements."[29]

In 1998 the NYPD created TrafficStat for the purpose of "reducing crashes, injuries, and fatalities, and increasing public safety."[30] Others did the same. Troop C of the Louisiana State Police, based in Houma, created its own TrafficStat "composed of four components."[31] In Canada, one of the components of the traffic safety program of the Ontario Provincial Police is "result driven policing," which is based on principles that include Maple's four.[32]

For all of these police agencies, the purpose of creating their own version of CompStat is the same as the NYPD's: To improve performance and thus to produce better results, specifically, to reduce crime (and traffic accidents).

How, however, do Maple's four principles do that? *How* could they do that?

"Compstatmania": From CompStat to AgencyStat

Police departments were not the only public agencies to adopt CompStat. In what the *Gotham Gazette* called "Compstatmania,"[33] other public agencies in New York City—public agencies that had no responsibility for crime or traffic—also sought to adapt the NYPD's leadership strategy. Obviously, however, each agency had to adapt the concept to its own needs to improve its performance and thus to produce better results (whatever that agency's specific results might be). The New York City Department of Parks and Recreation launched ParkStat.[34] The Human Resources Administration created JobStat, as well as VendorStat, Homecare VendorStat, HASAStat (for HIV/AIDS Services Administration), and MAPStat (for Medicaid).[35] The city's Administration for Children's Services established ChildStat. Even the Off-Track Betting Corporation created BET-STAT.[36] Honest!

Not all of these "children of CompStat," as the *Gotham Gazette* labeled them, had the suffix "Stat" in their name. For example, the city's Department of Correction created TEAMS, which stands for Total Efficiency Accountability Management System. Essentially, this is CorrectionStat. Similarly, the Department of Probation created STARS, for Statistical Tracking, Analysis and Reporting, or what might be called ProbationStat. The city's Housing Authority created APTS, for Authority Productivity Tracking System; think of this as HousingStat. The Department of Transportation called its version DOTMOVE.

Each of these New York City departments was seeking to improve performance—and thus achieve better results. Each of these public agencies sought to adapt the CompStat leadership strategy to its own purposes. Now the city didn't just have policing's CompStat. A variety of different city agencies had their own "AgencyStat."[37]

During the years that Bratton and Maple developed CompStat, Rudolph Giuliani was New York City's mayor.[38] Thus it is not surprising that when Giuliani ran for president in 2008, he promised to create CompStat-like programs in the federal government—FedStat, BorderStat, TerrorStat, and GAPStat. In the process, Giuliani invoked Maple's principles: CompStat, he told the press, "is all about: accurate and timely intelligence, effective tactics, rapid deployment of personnel and resources, and relentless follow-up and assessment."[39]

Actually, several units of the U.S. government had already created their own AgencyStats. For the San Diego district of the U.S. Border Patrol, it was, indeed, BorderStat. And the Environmental Protection Agency called its version EPAStat.

Then, in December 2010, Congress passed and President Barack Obama signed the GPRA Modernization Act.[40] The original GPRA, the 1993 Government Performance and Results Act, had been designed to "improve Federal program effectiveness" and to "help Federal managers to improve service delivery."[41] Yet, it had not produced much improvement. Consequently, the GPRA Modernization Act, often referred to as the GPRA Mod Act, required federal agencies to conduct "quarterly priority performance reviews."

Even before the 2010 legislation the Food and Drug Administration had developed FDA-Track, the Department of Housing and Urban Development had established HUDStat, the Federal Emergency Management Agency was in the process of launching FEMAStat, and the Department of the Treasury was conducting quarterly performance reviews (though without a clever name). Now, Congress had apparently instructed all the agencies of the U.S. government to create something similar to NYPD's CompStat.[42]

Yet could CompStat help the FDA or HUD or FEMA produce their quite different results?

CitiStat: From CompStat to JurisdictionStat

In the fall of 1999, Martin O'Malley, a city councilor in Baltimore, was campaigning for mayor in a city with a lot of problems. From 1990 to 2000, the city had lost almost 85,000 residents, nearly one-eighth of its 1990 population. More than one in five residents lived below the poverty level, and 14 percent of the housing units were vacant. Moreover, Baltimore had a notoriously high crime rate.

Thus, O'Malley asked Jack Maple to help him create CompStat in Baltimore. But as they drove around the city, Maple kept asking why they couldn't apply the CompStat leadership strategy to other aspects of city government. O'Malley demurred, but Maple kept insisting. The result was CitiStat, the first effort to adapt this leadership strategy to improve the performance of an entire governmental jurisdiction. And Maple's four principles were central to how O'Malley's leadership team thought about and created CitiStat.

Indeed, O'Malley remembers, "ComStat tenets immediately became our four basic tenets of CitiStat."[43] In Baltimore, these official "tenets" of CitiStat—which has been continued and expanded by O'Malley's two successors as mayor, Sheila Dixon and Stephanie Rawlings-Blake—are quite similar to Maple's original four points. A decade after its creation, the "CitiStat Tenets" were on the wall of the CitiStat room and the CitiStat website:

—Accurate and Timely Intelligence Shared by All
—Rapid Deployment of Resources
—Effective Tactics and Strategies
—Relentless Follow-up and Assessment[44]

Under Dixon, Baltimore explicitly recognized its debt to both Maple and CompStat:

CitiStat's Tenets were developed from the tenets created by Jack Maple for New York City's ComStat—a strategy that uses timely and accurate crime data to inform policing efforts. CitiStat uses the same tenets to provide timely, reliable services to Baltimore's residents.[45]

And Rawlings-Blake continued the acknowledgment: "The CitiStat Office follows four main tenets. Those tenets were originally developed by Jack Maple."[46]

Indeed, in the early years of the twenty-first century, CitiStat became the hot new thing. Journalists described it as a "Baltimore success story,"[47] a "pioneering innovation in across-the-board, eye-on-the-sparrow management,"[48] a "great success,"[49] "acclaimed,"[50] "much-emulated,"[51] a program that "may represent the most significant local government management innovation of this decade."[52] In 2004, CitiStat won, again from Harvard's Kennedy School, one of the awards for Innovation in American Government.[53]

In Baltimore, CitiStat has become an institution. It is how Mayors O'Malley, Dixon, and Rawlings-Blake ran the city. CitiStat was not a nice little add-on. It became central to their management of city government. CitiStat was the leadership strategy that these three mayors employed to ensure that city agencies were focused on their priorities—on improving specific aspects of their performance.

CompStat had not only evolved into AgencyStat. It had also evolved into JurisdictionStat. Yet exactly how could Maple's four principles improve the performance of an entire government?

The "Pilgrimages" of "Urbanistas"

Then, just as police chiefs had flocked to watch NYPD's CompStat, reported Charles Bens of Best Practices Consulting, "mayors began to show up in Baltimore to learn more about the CitiStat miracle."[54] Neal Peirce, a columnist with the *Washington Post* Writers Group, noted that "the CitiStat model is spreading."[55]

TABLE 1-1. Some of the U.S. Municipalities That Have Sought
to Employ a Version of CitiStat

City	Name for Its CitiStat
Atlanta, Ga,	ATLStat
Brookhaven, N.Y.	ServiceStat
Bridgeport, Conn.	CitiStat
Buffalo, N.Y.	CitiStat
Columbus, Ohio	Columbus*Stat
Fort Lauderdale, Fla.	FL2Stat
Hartford, Conn.	HartStat
Louisville, Ky.	LouieStat
Minneapolis, Minn.	Results Minneapolis
Mobile, Ala.	CitiSmart
New Orleans, La.	NOLAStat
North Hempstead, N.Y.	TownStat
Philadelphia, Pa.	PhillyStat
Providence, R.I.	ProvStat
Richmond, Va.	RichmondWorks
Rockford, Ill.	RockStat
San Francisco, Calif.	SFStat
Springfield, Mass.	CitiStat
St. Louis, Mo.	CitiView
Syracuse, N.Y.	SyraStat
Washington, D.C.	CapStat

Observed Sam Allis, a columnist for the *Boston Globe,* "Mayors and urbanis-
tas from across the country visit Baltimore, and most return home believers."[56]
O'Malley's "urban innovations—primarily CitiStat," reported *Time* magazine,
"have brought other curious mayors on pilgrimages to Baltimore."[57]

Many of these believers created their own version of CitiStat. Primarily they
did so in large cities with the capacity to develop an analytical staff to organize
and examine "accurate and timely intelligence" (table 1-1). Nevertheless, several
small municipalities also decided they could make effective use of this leadership
approach (table 1-2).

Moreover, at least three counties—Montgomery and Prince George's Counties
in Maryland and Cuyahoga County in Ohio—have created their CountyStat.[58]
In addition, King County, Washington, established its own KingStat, while
neighboring Snohomish County created SnoStat. The CitiStat leadership strategy

TABLE 1-2. Some of the Small U.S. Municipalities That Have Sought to Employ a Version of CitiStat

Municipality	Population	Name for Its CitiStat
Palm Bay, Fla.	100,000	PalmStat
Somerville, Mass.	75,000	SomerStat
Union Township, N.J.	54,000	CitiStat
Amesbury, Mass.	9,000	AmesStat

has even spread beyond the borders of the United States: The London Borough of Barnet created FirstStat, and in the Netherlands, Rotterdam created MaasStat (named for the Maas River, which flows through the city).

In 2005, when Christine Gregoire became governor of Washington, she initiated the first use of this leadership approach for an entire state, calling it GMAP, for Government Management, Accountability and Performance. And in 2007, when Martin O'Malley became governor of Maryland, he established StateStat.

Not all of those jurisdictions that launched, with much enthusiasm and publicity, their own version of CitiStat have continued to employ the strategy. New mayors decided they didn't want to use their predecessor's approach. And many chief executives failed to comprehend how expensive an effective PerformanceStat is—expensive not in terms of their financial budget but expensive in terms of their most valuable asset: their own time and the time of their leadership team. Moreover, to too many chief executives, "CitiStat" was little more than a data dashboard on which they posted some performance measures; they had no analysis, no meetings, no feedback, and no follow-up. They posted some data on the web and congratulated themselves on being part of the performance-management avant-garde.

Certainly, not all of these CitiStats and CountyStats have truly exploited the potential of the PerformanceStat leadership strategy to produce results.

Maple's Principles Invade the Public-Management Culture

Before he was twenty-one, Jack Maple was a cop. He began his career with the New York City Transit Police, and at twenty-seven he became its youngest detective. In 1990, when Bratton moved from Boston, where he was superintendent of the Metropolitan District Police, to head New York's Transit Police, Maple sent him a ten-page plan. Soon they were talking about Maple's ideas—"He had a million of them," Bratton wrote—and soon Maple was implementing them.[59]

Two years later, when Bratton returned to Boston to be superintendent in chief of its police department, he took Maple with him. And when Bratton returned to New York in January 1994 to be the NYPD's commissioner, he made Maple his deputy commissioner for crime-control strategies. At the core of Maple's crime-control efforts was the CompStat leadership strategy.

In the subsequent decades, Maple's influence has been felt even outside policing, even outside New York and Baltimore. For example, Mobile, Alabama, noted that its CitiSmart is based on Maple's "4 tenets."[60] In Union Township, New Jersey, Mayor Clifton Peoples Jr. wrote about his version of CitiStat: "The core principles of the system include: accurate and timely intelligence; rapid deployment of resources; effective tactics and strategies; and relentless follow-up and assessment."[61] When Governor Gregoire signed the legislation establishing GMAP, she noted that it "brings together accurate and timely intelligence, effective tactics and strategies, rapid deployment of resources and relentless follow-up and assessment."[62]

In Scotland, the Improvement Service, in an analysis of performance strategies, added only a few words to Maple's principles and Baltimore's tenets, and asserted:

Four Tenets constitute the foundation of Citistat.

1. Accurate and Timely Intelligence
2. Effective Tactics and Strategies
3. Rapid Deployment of Resources
4. Relentless Follow-Up and Assessment[63]

Moreover, Maple's four principles have been reiterated and expanded in a variety of government reports, scholarly articles, and popular publications. The Worcester, Massachusetts, Regional Research Bureau discussed them in detail in its report titled *CompStat and CitiStat: Should Worcester Adopt These Management Techniques?*[64] The Economy League of Greater Philadelphia concluded that "the success of the CitiStat model of municipal management is built on four pillars."[65] In a research paper, *Local Criminal Justice Board Effectiveness,* the Ministry of Justice in the United Kingdom reported:

A proven performance management model, conceived by Jack Maple and applied to police organisations and non-crime pubic services across North America can be applied to the LCJB [Local Criminal Justice Board] context. The key features of the model are: . . . .[66]

You guessed it: the same four.

Moreover, Maple's four principles have been reiterated and expanded in a variety of reports and books—not just those by Maple and Bratton. You can find them in *Intelligence-Led Policing*, by Jerry Ratcliffe of Temple University;[67] *The CompStat Paradigm*, by Vincent Henry of Long Island University;[68] *Using Performance Data for Accountability*, by Paul O'Connell of Iona College;[69] *What Every Chief Executive Should Know*, by Jon Shane at John Jay College;[70] and *Securing the City*, by Christopher Dickey of *Newsweek*.[71] With CompStat, argues Dean Dabney of Georgia State University, "police operations are guided by four core management principles."[72]

Even as a variety of public agencies and government jurisdictions adapted the CompStat approach to improve their own performance, they too stressed the same four concepts. Today Maple's mantra can be found on the walls of government buildings, in the publications and on the websites of public agencies, in presentations by public officials,[73] in the publications of professional associations, in journal articles and presentations by academics,[74] in books on criminology,[75] in the marketing materials of firms selling information technology,[76] and on the PowerPoint slides of management consultants.[77]

And yet . . . *how* can the dozen words that Maple wrote on Elaine's napkin improve the performance of such a diversity of public organizations?

"'Stat' Fever"

In January 2007, thirteen years after the NYPD first started creating CompStat, Ellen Perlman wrote an article in *Governing* magazine titled "'Stat' Fever." No longer was it just CompStat in some police departments. No longer was it just AgencyStat in New York City. No longer was it just CitiStat in some cities and StateStat in a couple of states. A variety of agencies and jurisdictions had created a variety of such leadership strategies. Indeed, while focusing on several examples, including Baltimore's CitiStat and Washington's GMAP, Perlman reported that "the idea has caught on in many other jurisdictions."[78]

To denote collectively all of these different adaptations of NYPD's Comp-Stat—and to capture the core leadership principles and key operational components that provide this strategy with the *potential* (but only the *potential*) to improve the performance of public agencies and governmental jurisdictions—I have coined the word "PerformanceStat."[79]

What, however, is this PerformanceStat? *How* can it help a public agency produce results? *How* can it help a government jurisdiction improve its performance?

Maple's four principles suggest that improving performance in the public sector is hardly complicated, though the evidence to the contrary is significant.[80] Furthermore, Maple's principles offer little operational guidance. What exactly is CompStat, let alone PerformanceStat? Can there really be such magic in Jack Maple's four principles?

The trouble with Maple's words is that they fail to clarify what CompStat is—let alone what an AgencyStat or JurisdictionStat might be. They are unobjectionable, yet uninformative. They suggest—or permit others to infer—that CompStat or CitiStat or PerformanceStat is a simple system that can be easily employed throughout the public sector. So does the proliferation of offices, procedures, meetings, databases, and websites with the suffix -Stat.

In reality, PerformanceStat is a complex *leadership strategy.* It *can* prove effective, but only if an organization's leadership team adapts it creatively, analytically, persistently. Some of the AgencyStats and JurisdictionStats mentioned have produced some specific improvements in results. Some have failed to have any meaningful impact. Some are merely data dashboards. Some are serious efforts to exploit the PerformanceStat potential—to specify purposes to be achieved, to analyze how and why performance is improving or not, and to motivate individuals and teams to make the operational changes necessary to achieve specific performance targets. Others are little more than MimicStat. And Maple's four principles are of little help in distinguishing among them.

Still, Elaine's napkin has certainly obtained an iconic immortality.[81] On August 4, 2001, at age 48, Jack Maple died.[82] Yet, Jack Maple lives.

2

Searching for PerformanceStat

What do people who have created or observed something that looks like a PerformanceStat think it is?

CitiStat, Buffalo's long-awaited computerized accountability system, was launched Friday.
BRIAN MEYER, Reporter, *Buffalo News[1]*

Washington state will institute for all agencies a computerized accountability system.
EDITORIAL, *The Columbian*, Vancouver, Washington[2]

"Performancestat" covers all of the CompStats, CitiStats, and other variants and adaptations of NYPD's original performance strategy. Some of these are "AgencyStats," designed to improve the performance of a single public agency. Others are "JurisdictionStats," designed to improve performance throughout an entire government. Every one is an effort to employ and adapt (if only implicitly) the ideas underlying NYPD's CompStat. Some, such as other cities' CompStats, are direct descendants of the original—carefully modeled after a visit to One Police Plaza in lower Manhattan. Similarly, many CitiStats are based on visits to Baltimore. Still others were created without any site visit—simply based on descriptions offered in academic treatises, popular articles, conference presentations, and consultants' advice.

Every CompStat is an adaptation of the original. Some were created by expatriates from the ranks of NYPD's mid-1990s leadership team. (*Governing* labeled them "Bratton's Brigade."[3] *City Journal* called them "The NYPD Diaspora."[4]) Even these CompStats were adaptations. They had to be.

When John Timoney left NYPD, where he had been William Bratton's chief of department, to become police chief in Philadelphia, he developed his own CompStat. When he later moved to Miami, he again employed the strategy. Neither version was identical to NYPD's. Neither could be. Neither the department nor the circumstances were the same. The purpose remained constant: To reduce crime. Twice, however, Timoney had to adapt the principles he had learned and helped develop in New York to new circumstances and challenges. Twice, he had to think through specifically what he would try to accomplish and how he would design CompStat to help him do it. Even NYPD's CompStat of today is different from the 1994 original; it too has evolved as the department learned and adapted.

Every PerformanceStat is an adaptation. There is no one single Performance-Stat. Every one is different. If you have seen one PerformanceStat, you have seen one PerformanceStat. So what is CompStat? Or CitiStat? Or PerformanceStat?

Scrutinizing Maple's Principles

Unfortunately, Jack Maple's four principles do not contain the answers. They do not adequately describe or sufficiently explain NYPD's CompStat. Neither do they adequately describe or sufficiently explain Baltimore's CitiStat. They are inadequate for understanding the variety of AgencyStats and JurisdictionStats. Not even a police department can create its own CompStat by using Maple's four principles—its 12 words—as the sole design manual. Elaine's napkin is not an operational guide for an effective performance strategy.

For someone who knows nothing about the strategy—who has never observed a CompStat meeting, who has never been given a briefing on CompStat, who has never read a detailed description or explanation of CompStat—Maple's four principles reveal little. They create no mental image. What does "effective tactics" really mean? What kind of tactics? What makes them effective? How can some-one distinguish an effective tactic from an ineffective one?

Those who have been working within a CompStat framework may implicitly appreciate what Maple's words mean in their own department. In any organiza-tion, a few words can evolve to codify a specific concept as captured by an illus-trative story. "Relentless follow-up" could remind everyone in NYPD of one time when Maple followed up very relentlessly with a particular precinct commander on a particular problem.

No one is opposed to Maple's principles. Who is against "timely and accu-rate intelligence"? Nevertheless, the four simply do not provide the practical blueprint—let alone the philosophical fundamentals—that a police department's leadership team needs to create its own CompStat. They certainly provide little practical guidance for the leadership team of an entire jurisdiction or a different kind of public agency. They do not even suggest *how* "relentless follow-up" might help to produce results.

Not that Maple's four principles are wrong. They just aren't that illuminat-ing. They capture some important ideas about PerformanceStat, particularly the emphasis on intelligence (for example, data) and follow-up. Yet they don't explain everything. If you want to understand the workings of CompStat—if you want to create your own CompStat (or another PerformanceStat)—Maple's principles aren't enough.

Indeed, Maple's principles leave much unanswered about *how* they might work to reduce crime. They don't explain the behavioral philosophy underlying this leadership strategy. They don't explain the cause-and-effect interactions among the components of the strategy. They don't capture the subtle things that the leaders do to motivate performance. They don't capture the tacit knowledge that these leaders have developed yet find difficult to explain in mere words.

This ambiguity—and the confusion it creates—means that not every attempt to employ this performance strategy takes advantage of all of its core leadership principles and key operational components let alone produces any significant improvements in performance. Not everything with the Stat suffix is for real.[5]

Decoding Elaine's Napkin

Still, many participants, observers, and analysts have tried—some succinctly, some expansively—to explain variants of the CompStat strategy. Maybe Elaine's napkin is a modern-day Rosetta Stone. Maybe one of these savants is a twenty-first-century Jean-François Champollion who can decipher its hidden meaning.[6] Maybe with someone's help, we can appreciate the deep significance and clear instructions of Maple's principles.

Jerry Ratcliffe argued that "CompStat is easy to define."[7] For, he explains, "the crime reduction mechanism of CompStat involves four principles," repeating Maple's phrases. Still what, exactly, did Ratcliffe think CompStat is? He called it "a police managerial accountability mechanism."[8] This description offers some conceptual underpinnings—it is about accountability[9]—but little operational guidance.

Jon Shane wrote: "The essence of the Compstat process is to 'collect, analyze, and map crime data and other essential police performance measures on a regular basis and hold police managers accountable for their performance as measured by these data.'"[10] It's about accountability—plus data and maps.

The Queensland Police Service offered a slightly more detailed explanation of its Operational Performance Review (OPR):

> [The] OPR process allows the Commissioner to hold regular, performance-focussed meetings to review each District's activities with Regional and District Managers and other members of the Senior Executive, in a formal positive environment. Review meetings continue to take place with

individual districts on an annual basis, each participating in sequence over a 6 month period. In addition to the formal meetings at Police Headquarters, the Commissioner visits regions some six months later to follow up on issues identified.[11]

This description is quite operational. It suggests that Queensland's OPR is primarily about "performance-focussed *meetings*" combined with field visits for *follow-up*.

In the *New York Times,* one reporter called NYPD's CompStat a "breakthrough computer program" and Baltimore's CitiStat "a pioneering innovation in an across-the-board, eye-on-the-sparrow management."[12] The Center for Evidence-Based Corrections at the University of California referred frequently to the "COMPSTAT system," describing it as a "strategic control system" and "management system" and called Baltimore's CitiStat a "data-driven, strict accountability performance measurement system."[13] To Dean Dabney, the "'Compstat model' or 'Compstat-aligned organization' refer to a strategic management model of policing"; it is an "innovative management system"—"a strategic control system built around four core principles."[14] Indeed, many observers have used the words "CompStat" and "system" in lock-step sequence.

Joel Samaha of the University of Minnesota wrote that CompStat "consists of five components: computerized crime-mapping technology, a management style, response tactics, follow-up, and accountability." What exactly is this "management style"? Samaha never quite defined it, though he emphasized: "Under COMPSTAT, power over discretionary decision making shifted down to precinct commanders." And although Samaha referred to CompStat as a "program" and a "tool," he recognized that it is more than a mere system—that it requires significant management and real leadership.[15]

Not everyone who uses the phrase "CompStat system" is suggesting that it is solely about computers or that it does not require purposive leadership.[16] Mayor Rudolph Giuliani, testifying before Congress, frequently used the phrase "COMPSTAT system," though he introduced it as "an innovative style of police management."[17] And April Pattavina of the University of Massachusetts at Lowell wrote:

> CompStat is a comprehensive system to manage police operations. It consists of holding patrol commanders accountable for all problems and issues in their respective geographic areas, meeting regularly with top command to develop strategies and tactics to address problems, implementing the strategies rapidly and convincingly, and following up to determine whether or not the new strategies were effective.[18]

Accountability; meetings; computer systems; data and maps; problems, tactics, and strategies; implementation; follow-up; effectiveness. We're learning more.

Comprehending CitiStat

How about CitiStat? Again, numerous participants and observers have sought to describe and explain Baltimore's approach.

Journalists have portrayed CitiStat in various ways: the *Baltimore Sun* described it as "statistics-driven," a "new high-tech program for government efficiency,"[19] "O'Malley's signature method for ensuring that government services are delivered efficiently."[20] To *The Star* of Windsor, Canada, it is "a computer program."[21] The *Buffalo News* called it "a computer tracking system"[22] and a "high-tech accountability system."[23] The *Daily Standard* labeled it "a computerized accountability program."[24] The *Irish Times* called it an effort "to replace a culture of delay and avoidance with a culture of accountability and results, monitored by technology."[25] Accountability with computers.

As with "Compstat," the words "CitiStat" and "system" are often used in tandem. "CitiStat is a performance management system" reported the Scottish Executive.[26] To *The Guardian* of London, it is "a system of decision-making for improved performance management."[27] An article in the *Stanford Social Innovation Review* described it as "a system for collecting data from each of the city's departments, poring over the data with department heads every other week, setting goals based on the data, and then holding city officials responsible for meeting those goals."[28] A decisionmaking system. Goals with responsibility.

Many journalists have emphasized the holding-people-accountable aspect of CitiStat. *The Guardian* described it as a way "to allow politicians to put non-performing officials on the spot,"[29] while to the *Times* of London, CitiStat is "a specially designed performance-review meeting" in "a special 'confrontation room.'"[30] Others portrayed Citistat meetings more vividly: "The mayor now hauls civil service chiefs into City Hall every month and forces them to explain their performance," reported *Scotland on Sunday;* "the officials ride the gauntlet, hating every minute."[31] The *New York Times* offered a similar portrait: "some department supervisors seemed to writhe like medical interns fumbling for the city's pulse,"[32] while Neal Peirce described "the probing" as "excruciatingly specific and penetrating."[33] The *Baltimore Sun* pictured a city manager at one meeting "looking as if he needs a cigarette and blindfold."[34] "The managers who are forced to go through these inquisitions are less than thrilled," observed *Governing;* they "often emerge from the sessions red-faced and embarrassed before their peers."[35] In the *Boston Globe,* Sam Allis reported a conversation overheard before the start of one meeting: "'I just finished puking,' jokes one department staffer on his way out of the men's room."[36] An article in the *National Civic Review* called CitiStat "Performance Measurement with Attitude."[37] Performance. Confrontation. Embarrassment. And more accountability.

Academics, consultants, and civic organizations have also examined CitiStat. Lenneal Henderson of the University of Baltimore called it "a bold and unprecedented effort to raise the performance," "a highly successful innovation in the management of city government" and of city agencies, and an effort "to immediately improve the performance and accountability of city agencies."[38] The Abell Foundation characterized it as a "well-directed, energetic hands-on, no-nonsense, no-delay response mechanism designed to deal promptly and effectively with citizen complaints."[39] The Abrahams Group described it as "how Baltimore manages for results," as "an accountability tool," and as "a groundbreaking use of digital technology."[40] In *City Journal,* Fred Siegel and Van Smith, wrote that CitiStat "applies rapid data-gathering and analysis to all city agencies" and "introduces transparency and accountability into a city notoriously unfamiliar with either."[41] Perri 6 of the University of Birmingham has described CitiStat as an "adversarial style of decision making,"[42] as "a highly confrontational" system complete with "a 'star chamber' room for frequent grilling of chief officers on their performance."[43] Innovation. Data. More accountability. More confrontation.

So CitiStat is about accountability—with confrontation, writhing, and embarrassment. Plus meetings with transparency. Also computers and technology, data and analysis. Plus goals and effectiveness.

Penetrating PerformanceStat

How do people describe and explain other versions of this leadership strategy?

In 2005, the Los Angeles County Department of Public Social Services created DPSSTATS for "DPSS Total Accountability, Total Success." To the department, it is:

> an innovative management tool that creates a forum for Executive Management and key managers across the Department to review current and comprehensive data so that swift, effective decisions could be made to enhance the Department's operations to better serve the more than 2 million residents of Los Angeles County that are served by this Department.[44]

Further, the Department's two-page fact sheet for DPSSTATS described its meetings, performance measures, slides, data book, and follow-up.[45]

Swati Desai of the Nelson A. Rockefeller Institute of Government served for many years as director of the Office of Policy and Program Analysis in New York City's Human Resources Administration, with lead responsibility for JobStat. She has called it "a performance management tool." But Desai went on to explain that JobStat "clarifies objectives, facilitates ongoing monitoring, promotes learning, and commands accountability."[46]

In *Leading Across Boundaries,* Russell Linden argued that an effective PerformanceStat has six "key characteristics." It:

—Focuses middle and senior managers on achievement of certain agreed-upon goals.

—Makes heavy use of data to assess performance and inform decisions.

—Includes regular, structured meetings where senior leaders question agency managers about recent performance and outcomes, and managers discuss what they are learning and how they are working together to achieve the outcomes.

—Emphasizes persistent follow-up and produces action plans for improvement after each meeting.

—Is managed by a small unit that tracks and analyzes agency performance between meetings.

—Provides a disciplined approach to senior-level decision making.[47]

In Washington state, Governor Christine Gregoire's office described its Government Management, Accountability and Performance (GMAP) program as "a tool set designed to hold state government and agency leadership accountable to customers, taxpayers, and citizens for the quality, efficiency, and effectiveness" of state agencies based on "seven principles":

1. Engage the leader(s) at the top of the organization. GMAP stresses the personal presence of senior managers and others needed to make decisions.
2. Do not measure for measurement's sake. This is a waste of resources. . . . Effective measures require clarity on:
    a. what programs and services expect to influence, and
    b. how agencies will use measures to manage programs and get results.
3. Develop and use timely and accurate performance data to set targets and inform decisions.
4. Reward candor in identifying and diagnosing performance barriers and creativity and commitment to overcoming them. It is OK to identify

missed targets. It is even more important to know why you missed targets and to have a plan to address barriers to meeting them.

5. When the data indicates needed action, quickly and clearly specify what needs to be done, who will do it, and when it will be done. . . .

6. Persistent follow-up and clear accountability. Agency leadership should relentlessly follow up on commitments made in action plans. They should also monitor results over time to verify change is real and sustainable.

7. Create a continuous learning environment.[48]

Now we have a little conceptual enlightenment and a little more operational guidance—some help in understanding *how* PerformanceStat might work and who has to do what to make it effective.

Accountability or Computers, or Both

Many of these descriptions emphasize that PerformanceStat is about "accountability." Or maybe it's about computers.

—PerformanceStat can be conceptualized as an *accountability mechanism:* We need to hold those lazy subordinates accountable (for doing what we told them to do). From this perspective, data become a weapon to dramatize subordinates' inadequacy or incompetence.

—PerformanceStat can be conceived as a *computerized database:* We need data that subordinates could use to somehow improve their performance. From this perspective, data are collected and stored somewhere—with the hope that someday someone will look at and somehow use them.

—Or, sometimes it can be about both: A "computerized accountability system."

When Buffalo launched its CitiStat, the *Buffalo News* called it a "computerized accountability system."[49] The *St. Louis Post Dispatch* used the same phrase to describe CitiView (St. Louis's version of CitiStat).[50] *New Orleans CityBusiness* used these exact three words to describe that city's CompStat.[51] When Washington launched GMAP, *The Columbian* (of Vancouver, Washington), did so too.[52]

Computers and accountability: Either of these two words helps the neophyte categorize the concept. You can put it in your technology box: "I get it. It's about putting numbers in a computerized data base." Or, you can put it in your "accountability" box: "I get it. It's about punishing those who screw up."[53]

Unfortunately, these simplifications distort what the executives who are struggling to improve performance are doing. Holding people accountable—punishing the screw-ups—isn't enough. Technology isn't enough either. Nor are data. Data are essential. How else can you learn whether or not performance is improving? And reproving the indolent—and removing the incompetents—is necessary too. Neither, however, is sufficient. Not even close.

Still, the journalists' focus on accountability is quite predictable. The blindfolds. The last cigarette. The puking. Great copy.

Moreover, focusing on accountability—the punishment of the clueless and nefarious—suggests that the inability to improve performance simply derives from a few people's misfeasance or malfeasance: If you identify and eliminate the clowns, performance will quickly improve. If only it were that easy. If only it were clear what data were needed and how to analyze them. If only it were evident how to conduct an effective meeting. If only it were easy to motivate those who survive the purge. If only it were obvious *how* to improve performance.

Obviously, it isn't easy. If it were, couldn't public executives who are trying to improve performance simply copy some organization's data system and accountability model?

PerformanceStat is more than data and accountability—much more.

The Search for the "System," the "Model," the "Tool"

"What is it?" For any PerformanceStat, the answer is—all too often—a "system." Perhaps a "model." Maybe a "tool" or a "mechanism." All very mechanistic. Easy to replicate.

Union, New Jersey's Mayor Clifton Peoples called CitiStat "an accountability tool."[54] Silvia Gullino of Kingston University in London described it as an "innovative e-government *tool*."[55] To the U.S. Government Accountability Office, CitiStat is "an accountability *tool*."[56] To the Center for American Progress, CitiStat is a "*model*," "a data-tracking and management *tool*," "a data-driven management *system*."[57] The Economy League of Greater Philadelphia called CitiStat "a simple operations management *tool*," "a database *system*," and "an accountability *tool*."[58] Montgomery County, Maryland, labeled its CountyStat "a Results-Based Accountability *System*."[59] The Auditor General of Scotland concluded that "the Citistat *tool* can improve performance management."[60] The Highland Health Board, the National Health Service's regional unit in Northern Scotland, proposed to establish "bi-monthly scrutiny through the citistat *mechanism*."[61] [All italics added!]

In 2006, New York City's Administration for Children's Services launched ChildStat. But, what, exactly, was "ChildStat"? The *New York Times* explained that it was "modeled after the Police Department's management system, Comp-Stat,"[62] which helped people who knew about CompStat, though they might have wondered how a "management system" designed for policing would work in child welfare.

Indeed, how can a journalist explain something as complicated as a real, functioning PerformanceStat? At the *New York Times,* a series of six different reporters answered this question by using a few, well-established code words that sound impressive but contain little real information. Over half a decade, a reader of the *New York Times* would learn that ChildStat was: "a data system,"[63] "a new effort to track the most vulnerable families,"[64] "a computerized system,"[65] "a data collection and tracking system,"[66] "a case review system,"[67] and "an accountability program."[68] None of these journalistic abridgements adequately describes ChildStat. No effective PerformanceStat can be explained meaningfully in a dozen words.

The Necessity of Leadership

Thinking of CompStat or CitiStat or ChildStat as a "system" or "model" is attractive. Either word implies—or permits others to infer—that there exists a straightforward technological procedure that, if followed properly, will produce miraculous results. It suggests that you can set up such a "system" in your organization, push the start button, and walk away. Your "system" will function wonderfully on automatic pilot.

Unfortunately, because of the ubiquity of the "system" metaphor, many efforts to create a PerformanceStat miss something. Indeed, despite their use of the ***Stat suffix, not all the efforts to produce results listed in chapter 1 were capable of realizing the PerformanceStat potential. For they missed something important: the intangible but essential role of leadership.

This leadership isn't invisible. A visitor can see it at any PerformanceStat meeting—but only if the visitor knows what to look for. The first-time visitor, however, is striving just to understand a conversation complicated by a flock of acronyms flying overhead. The visitor cannot decipher the subtle issues underlying the discussion or appreciate the nature of the leadership.

Beneath the system metaphor lies the assumption that the organization is the proper unit of analysis. The agency has to get its performance system right. The jurisdiction has to employ the proper performance model. In fact, however, the relevant unit of analysis is the leadership team. In trying to understand any effective PerformanceStat, too many people seek to catalog the *explicit components of the organization's system.* Thus, they fail to appreciate the *leadership team's subtle, tacit behaviors.* An organization may have dutifully copied all the visible pieces of a "performance model"; yet this system will have little impact without real—consistent and persistent—leadership. (These leadership behaviors are examined in detail in chapter 15.)

Of course, some do benefit from convincing the world that CompStat (or CitiStat) is indeed a system—particularly, some kind of computerized system. These people are prepared to sell you such a "system." For example, there is "a new version of the legendary COMPSTAT system, now powered by Oracle." Want to guess who sponsored this "Special Report" in *Government Technology* describing "Oracle integration technology"?[69] The Results Leadership Group calls its ResultsStat™ a "tool" and "a management model similar to CompStat and CitiStat."[70] And you will not be surprised to learn that the Worldwide Law Enforcement Consulting Group (staffed by some NYPD veterans) "can construct a 'Comp-Stat' style management system for your Department and also provide the training necessary for your personnel to acclimate themselves to the system."[71]

PerformanceStat is more than a system or a model—much more. Performance-Stat is a leadership strategy. In any organization, improving performance requires real leadership.

Explaining This Elephant

Most descriptions of PerformanceStat resemble the classic portraits of an elephant offered by six blind men. One upon grabing an ear said an elephant was "very like a fan." Another who felt the tusk concluded that the animal was "very like a spear."[72] Similarly, for PerformanceStat, one commentator grabs the technology ear and observes: "PerformanceStat is 'very like' a computer system." Another, grasping the accountability tusk, concludes: "PerformanceStat is 'very like' an accountability system." None has completely examined this "elephant," so none fully comprehends it. Still, each can latch onto a big, familiar piece.

Moreover, even if you have studied an entire elephant, it is still difficult to describe such an animal to someone who has never seen one. You would have to resort to similes—describing the most visible features by comparing them to other familiar objects. "It's big, like a dinosaur, but doesn't have scales. It has very big ears—you know, sorta like, a big fan. . . ."

Of course, everyone knows what an elephant is. Even young children know; they learn about elephants from books, at a zoo, or on television. Yet, how would you describe an elephant in words? My dictionary offers the following definition:

Any of a family (Elephantidae, the elephant family) of thickset usu. extremely large nearly hairless herbivorous mammals that have a snout elongated into a muscular trunk and two incisors in the upper jaw developed esp. in the male into large ivory tusks and that include two living forms and various extinct relatives: as a: a tall large-eared mammal (*Loxodonta africana*) of tropical Africa—called also *African elephant;* b: a relatively small-eared mammal (*Elephas Maximus*) of forest of southeastern Asia—called also *Asian elephant, Indian elephant.*[73]

Not every informative. Indeed, if you really need to explain an elephant to someone, you would not use *words.* You would use a *picture.* My dictionary does precisely this.

Anyone seeking to explain CompStat, or CitiStat, or any other PerformanceStat faces the same challenge. Words do not capture the concept. And there aren't any useful pictures.

What is CompStat? What is CitiStat? How do you describe this elephant? You can start with the pieces—the computer ear, accountability tusk. But what about the weird concept of the follow-up trunk? What's this all about? How does it work? What is it for?

Moreover, like an elephant, PerformanceStat is more than a collection of its anatomical parts. It isn't just computers, accountability, and meetings. None of these components are novel. How, however, does the whole thing work? Imagine having to explain how an elephant works. What's with this trunk thing? Is it really functional? What does it accomplish? How?

And what's going on inside? Even if you are not blind, you can't see what is happening inside an elephant. You could assume that elephant lungs work like human lungs. In fact, not exactly.[74]

Finally, don't forget to explain how elephants live—with solitary males exiled from the females, who live in small matriarchal herds. No individual piece is incomprehensible, yet how do these individual pieces function together to create an animal? How do the individual animals function together to create a living herd? How do these herds function together to create a surviving species? How can you explain PerformanceStat so that people will comprehend not just the individual pieces, but also *how* this leadership strategy might work to improve performance?

Any effort to describe both an individual elephant and a herd of elephants has an advantage: Much (but not everything) is out in the open. You can head into the bush with a guide, or hover over the grasslands in a helicopter, and observe what individuals and herds are doing. Moreover, their individual and collective behavior will not be idiosyncratic to a specific elephant or a particular herd. There will be some differences among them, but elephant behavior will fall into some standard, explicable patterns.[75]

Yet even if we could trace the ancestry of every PerformanceStat back to NYPD's CompStat, we would discover a number of mutations along the hereditary path—mutations significant enough to obscure some of the ancestry. Other than the ***Stat label, how might we identify the core leadership principles and key operational components of the PerformanceStat strategy?

The Difference between Naming and Knowing

When Richard Feynman, the Nobel-winning physicist, was a boy, his father took him on long walks in the woods. Feynman's father could tell him the name of the brown-throated thrush in English—and also in Portuguese, Italian, Chinese, and Japanese. Nevertheless, Feynman's father would emphasize: "When you've finished with all that"—when you know the bird's name in multiple languages—"you'll know absolutely nothing about the bird."[76]

Later in life, Feynman recalled that his father "knew the difference between knowing the name of something and knowing something."

In science, the failure to make this distinction is called the "nominal fallacy."[77] It is the assumption that because you have named something you understand it—that the name itself explains it. For public executives, this is a nasty problem. They are constantly admonished to employ some new management tactic that someone else has made work somewhere else: change management, performance measures, a balanced scorecard, data mining, customer relationship management, a blue ocean strategy, employee engagement, benchmarking, strategic alignment, lean thinking. . . . Public executives are constantly told to use this or that latest idea.

Any of these concepts might help an organization. But merely stating the name and advising someone to use it is silly. By themselves, the names "CompStat," CitiStat," and "PerformanceStat" explain nothing. Zero!

Neither do Jack Maple's four principles. *How* does "relentless follow-up" help to produce results? And does it make a difference if this follow-up is not aggressively relentless but just seriously persistent? If so, why?

A police executive can know all of the code words and still know nothing about *how* CompStat might reduce crime or what to do to create performance-improving, results-producing CompStat in another police agency. And certainly these words provide little guidance for an executive who seeks to adapt the CompStat approach outside the world of policing.

PerformanceStat is not just one thing—or even four things. To produce results, a leadership team has to engage in a variety of behaviors. Producing results in any organization is a complex undertaking. And giving a name to this complexity of behaviors is not enough.

Naming is not the same as knowing.

3

Clarifying PerformanceStat

What core leadership principles and key operational components do effective PerformanceStat strategies have in common?

We can know more than we can tell.
MICHAEL POLANYI, chemist and philosopher[1]

There is no new thing under the sun.
ECCLESIASTES[2]

What exactly is CompStat? Or CitiStat? How could anyone recognize an effective PerformanceStat? How could anyone tell whether something that a governmental jurisdiction or a public agency claimed was its very own, apparently unique, performance-enhancing, results-producing "SomethingStat" was the real thing? Or merely mindless mimicry? What gives a PerformanceStat leadership strategy the *potential* to produce results?

If the leadership team of a governmental jurisdiction or public agency wanted to create its own adaptation of this performance strategy, what should it do? What are the core leadership principles and key operational components that it would need to employ? How might these principles and components interact to create the *potential* to produce real results? What principles are core? What components are key? What looks nice but is actually irrelevant? How can the leadership team effectively employ the core principles? How much does it need to adapt the operational components?

—The conceptual question is: How do the leadership principles underlying a PerformanceStat strategy have a causal impact on organizational performance?

—The practical question is: How does the leadership team use the operational components to put into practice the underlying leadership principles?

Defining PerformanceStat

Unfortunately, too many of the agencies and jurisdictions that have created a SomethingStat (which they claim is a progeny of Compstat) are mere mimicries. They miss one or more of the key operational components—let alone the core leadership principles. They fail to appreciate how their own leadership behaviors can have a cause-and-effect impact on results. Consequently, their SomethingStat lacks the true *potential* to improve performance.

To identify those adaptations that have the potential to make an impact on performance, I have evolved the following definition of PerformanceStat:

> A jurisdiction or agency is employing a PerformanceStat *leadership strategy* if, in an effort to achieve specific *public purposes,* its leadership team *persists* in holding an ongoing series of *regular, frequent, integrated meetings* during which the chief executive and/or the principal members of the chief executive's leadership team plus the director (and the top managers) of different subunits use *current data* to *analyze* specific, previously defined aspects of each unit's recent *performance;* to provide *feedback* on recent progress compared with *targets;* to *follow up* on previous decisions and commitments to produce *results;* to examine and *learn* from each unit's efforts to improve *performance;* to identify and solve *performance-deficit* problems; and to set and achieve the next *performance targets.*

This definition reflects what I have learned from observing and investigating, comparing and contrasting three dozen efforts to create something similar to CompStat or CitiStat. (See the acknowledgments.) Obviously, not all of these efforts contained all of these features. Still, the prototypes I have seen—be it CompStat in Los Angeles or CitiStat in Baltimore—did combine all of these features, though not in precisely the same way or to the same degree.

This definition is long. Yet, it is not all that constraining. It could apply to a public agency and its AgencyStat or to a governmental jurisdiction and its JurisdictionStat. It could apply to a variety of public-sector performance strategies created without any knowledge of CompStat or CitiStat. It could apply to leadership strategies that public executives were using before William Bratton or Jack Maple first put on the badge. In contrast, the MimicStats lack one or more of these principles and components. They may have created no targets, provided no feedback, held no meetings, or demonstrated no persistence.

For example, creating a data warehouse of performance measures and posting a data dashboard on the Internet may generate attention. But without any critical analysis, this data dump will fail to reveal the organization's performance deficits. Without the meetings, it will fail to foster an analytical discussion about how to eliminate these deficits. Without using the data to provide feedback on progress, managers who are seeking to eliminate these deficits will never learn what is working and what isn't.

This definition is also boring—complex, not simple. It contains a multitude of principles and components that cannot be captured by a simple metaphor. It lacks the dramatic flair of the three-word phrase: "computerized accountability system." It is long, not short. It suggests that, to realize the *potential* of PerformanceStat, the leadership team has to do a lot of work. Damn.

Conceptually, however, this definition does emphasize several core leadership principles:

—The leadership team that is using the PerformanceStat strategy focuses on achieving specific *public purposes.*

—It seeks to eliminate or mitigate its current *performance deficit(s)* by achieving specific *performance targets.*

—It *collects* and *analyzes* current (not last year's) *data* that relate to these purposes, help reveal whether performance is improving, and provide insight into differences and changes in its performance.

—It establishes a rhythm and routine to the organization's focus on performance through a series of *regular, frequent, integrated meetings* in which the key executives and managers *analyze the data, follow up* on previous agreements, provide *feedback* on progress, seek to *learn* what is and isn't working, and decide what slight modifications or significant changes they should make in their current strategies.

—Through all this, the leadership team *persists* in its emphasis on improving performance so as to achieve specific public purposes.

Operationally, this definition emphasizes that, when designing and employing its PerformanceStat, the members of the leadership team need to:

—specify the public *purpose* they are trying to achieve;
—decide what *data* they will collect;
—*analyze* these data to identify performance deficits and improvements;
—create performance *targets* for the organization and its subunits;
—determine how and when they will conduct regular, frequent, integrated *meetings* and who will attend;
—provide *feedback* on progress compared with targets;

—build *operational capacity*—including both analytical capacity in a small, central staff and in the subunits plus leadership and managerial capacity throughout;

—create a regular process to *follow up* on problems identified, solutions proposed, and decisions made at the meetings; and

—remain *persistent*.

When doing all this, the leadership team will need to think carefully about how to adapt these principles and components to their specific purposes and particular circumstances.

All this is hardly revolutionary. You can find these principles and components in any management book. Don't effective public executives automatically—instinctively—do these things? What is so different?

Nothing. Yet everything. It's like the elephant; even the trunk is familiar once you think of it as a very elongated nose. The PerformanceStat potential lies not in any of the individual components but in their synergy—in the creativity, energy, and persistence with which the leadership team combines the various components of the strategy. An elephant is more than a collection of trunk and tusks, ears and lungs; all of these pieces have to work together to support an elephant's big body, while the big body is necessary to support the pieces. These pieces have to work together in synergy to create a living, functioning animal. The same is true for the components of any PerformanceStat; the components have to work together in synergy to create a result-producing strategy.

Moreover, public executives who are truly exploiting the PerformanceStat potential are doing so not as a sideline, not as yet another in a string of management fads. They are dedicated to using their PerformanceStat to make their organization work—to ensure that it improves performance, produces results, and thus achieves its purposes.

For each PerformanceStat, these components will be unique. No two versions of this leadership strategy are identical. Sometimes the differences are obvious. Sometimes they are subtle—missed even by a seasoned professional who makes only one quick visit.

Still, as *Ecclesiastes* explains, "There is no new thing under the sun."[3]

The Performance Deficit

A "performance deficit" is a significant aspect of an organization's work that needs improvement. It can occur any place along its value chain—from inputs, to activities and processes, to outputs, to outcomes—places where the organization is doing an inadequate job. If an organization could eliminate (or, at least, mitigate) one of its key performance deficits, performance would improve.

A particular, well-specified performance deficit provides the focus that an abundance of performance measures dilutes. It specifies a significant problem that the organization needs to fix. It drives the organization to collect the relevant data necessary to characterize the problem's key features, to do the analytical thinking necessary to determine its causes, and to make the operational improvements necessary to eliminate or mitigate it. By specifying a performance deficit, plus a target for fixing it, the leadership team establishes a priority—creating a basis for measuring and motivating its own performance.

Every organization—for-profit, nonprofit, public—has performance deficits, multiple performance deficits. How, however, does an organization identify its key performance deficits? Even a business firm, which sells goods or services in a competitive market, may not find this an easy question to answer. Sales are going down; but why? It may not be obvious. The customers may not like the product, but what exactly about the product do they not like? Moreover, even if the product's deficiency is clear, it may not be obvious where along the firm's value chain (from initial design to final quality control) lie the key performance deficits.

For an automobile manufacturer that is producing cars whose quality customers rate as inferior, a critical performance deficit might be the design of the car's interior or the design of the production line. It might be the quality of the steel the firm is buying or defects in the ignition system a vendor is supplying. It might be inadequate training of key personnel or sloppy work on the production line. Multiple performance deficits could contribute to the inferior quality. The firm needs to identify the key ones and fix them.

Performance deficits are revealed through the analysis of data. But what data? Sales volume and sales revenues are down. These are data. But such sales data don't answer the question: *Why* are sales down? Perhaps a customer survey reveals the product has a reputation for breaking down quickly? But *why?* The firm still needs to analyze data on inputs, activities, and processes to identify the performance deficits that are contributing to its poor outcome: low sales.

In the public sector, deciding what data to collect and analyze starts with purpose: What is the organization trying to accomplish? The organization's leadership team needs to choose data that help keep everyone focused on the purpose of their work. Moreover, the leadership team needs current data that provide insights into its performance deficits: *Why* are we not achieving our objectives? And it needs such data frequently. To improve performance, end-of-the-year data are useless. Do current data exist? If not, the organization needs to begin collecting them.

Then, the organization can use these data—particularly during its Performance-Stat meetings—to dramatize these performance deficits and to obligate each reporting unit to pay attention to its own performance deficits.[4]

Some public agencies get some kinds of data only annually. High-school graduation rates are important, but no school system gets data on them monthly. But a school system could identify key performance deficits—something that has a causal connection to graduation rates, something happening earlier in the value chain, something about which it could get data quarterly or even daily. Something like: truancy.

Researchers from Johns Hopkins and the Philadelphia Education Fund followed a cohort of students who entered the sixth grade in Philadelphia in 1996. The found that of the students who attended school 80 percent of the time or less in the sixth grade, only 13 percent graduated on time. And only 4 percent more graduated a year later.[5] This correlation does not prove causation; yet it is easy to understand what a causal connection *might* be.

Thus, if a school system has a high truancy rate—if this is a key performance deficit—it might choose to create some kind of TruancyStat with a target of cutting truancy in half in six months. The longer-term public purpose, however, is to drive up graduation rates—which can only be measured years later. The ultimate public purpose is, of course, to improve the students' future social and economic lives.[6]

Why the Cops—and NYPD in Particular—Had It Easy

Why policing? Why New York City? Why did the New York Police Department (NYPD) invent CompStat? Why wasn't a state Environmental Protection Agency first with "EnviroStat"? Why wasn't the South African Department of Transport first with "TransportStat"? Why wasn't the World Health Organization first with "HealthStat"?

Any public organization could have created the first PerformanceStat. Bratton and Maple did not invent (or stumble upon) some kind of forbidden knowledge that was hidden from other public executives. Still, I think it was easier for a police executive in New York City to figure out how to put the pieces together.

There are seven reasons why a police agency might be more apt to create a coherent strategy for improving performance:

1. *The operational purpose is politically clear.* There is general agreement— among police professionals, elected officials, and citizens—about what

should be accomplished, what the key indicators are, and which way they should move. Crime rates should go down. Arrest rates should go up. There is little ideological debate.[7]

2. *Data are automatically collected daily.* Police agencies—in the normal course of business—collect data related to performance. These include data on (a) crimes reported, (b) arrests, (c) the circumstances and details of each crime and arrest, (d) convictions, (e) sentences (including suspended sentences), and (f) officers who failed to appear at trials. None of these measures is a perfect outcome measure; nevertheless, each does capture important aspects of performance.

3. *Historical, baseline data are available.* Police agencies have been collecting such data for decades. They have a long time-series of data from which to analyze progress.

4. *A first-order analytical tool can reveal performance deficits.* Police agencies have a simple, first-order analytical tool for identifying patterns that reveal important performance deficits: dots on a map. Whether these dots mark robberies or burglaries, they can reveal patterns suggesting where to concentrate resources. To observe these patterns, no statistics course is required.[8]

5. *Focused efforts can produce a relatively quick impact and useful feedback.* Police agencies can often produce results (as revealed in changes in the data) quicker than other public agencies. Unlike those responsible for improving the education of children or the health of citizens, the police can, within years or even months, produce meaningful improvements in outcomes and learn from them.

6. *All police executives start as beat cops.* They have learned the business from the street level up. When a police executive asks a question at a CompStat meeting, he or she can distinguish—more easily than many other public executives—between answers that demonstrate thought, work, and commitment and ones that are evasive, careless, or dishonest. They are not easily deceived by subordinates. Furthermore, because they know the policing culture quite intimately, they may be able to figure out how to create a more results-oriented culture.

7. *The roll call can deliver the message to the front line.* In any organization, any new initiative is met with skepticism, particularly from middle managers and front-line workers: "How long will this 'fad' last?" In all large (or medium-size) organizations, the leadership team cannot easily get its message to the front line. The police, however, have a built-in way to do this: Three times every day, the cops begin their shifts at roll call—an ideal

opportunity for managers to deliver and repeat their message. (In the first month after John Timoney became police commissioner in Philadelphia, he attended roll call in every district: "The roll calls were quite valuable for me in getting my message out directly to the troops.")[9]

In addition, there are two reasons why the police department in New York City would have had an easier time than other police departments making this leadership strategy work:

8. *Multiple subunits facilitate comparison, motivation, and learning.* Police agencies are typically organized into geographic subunits, such as precincts. This permits the leadership team to compare the performance of these subunits, to use such comparisons to hold managers responsible for producing results, to *motivate* the managers of these subunits, to encourage subunits to experiment with different tactics, and to *learn* what works from the high performers. Moreover, the more subunits the agency has, the greater its ability to make relevant comparisons. NYPD has 76 precincts; for every precinct there exists another, similar precinct with which comparisons of performance, as revealed by the data, are legitimate and relevant. In New York, no precinct commander can get away with the standard bureaucratic excuse: "You don't understand, we're different."

9. *Size plus managerial discretion creates personnel flexibility.* New York City is big. It covers over 300 square miles and in 1994 had approximately 7.5 million residents (with another 1.5 million commuting into the city to work). It requires a large police force. When NYPD created CompStat, it had roughly 35,000 police officers. In making personnel assignments, NYPD's commissioner is constrained by civil service rules, collective bargaining requirements, and union contracts. Still, the commissioner has significant flexibility in assigning middle managers and thus the ability to replace ineffective managers with more proven (or more promising) ones. Thus, the commissioner can reward effective managers by giving them significant assignments and punish (if only symbolically) the underperformers. In a smaller police department with only a few precincts, or with more constraining civil-service or collective-bargaining laws, the top police executive might lack the flexibility to reassign middle managers. (At NYPD, the commissioner selects all deputy inspectors, inspectors, assistant chiefs, deputy chiefs, and bureau chiefs. In Philadelphia, Timoney had only two appointments: his two deputy commissioners.)[10]

Yes, when Bratton and Maple created CompStat, they never had it "easy." But, compared with the challenge of inventing something like PerformanceStat in other public agencies, they had it "easier."

Still, police departments are not the only public organizations that possess such advantages. Larisa Benson, who served as the first director of Washington State's Government Management, Accountability and Performance (GMAP), observed that the state's Liquor Control Board was having trouble with on-time delivery from some vendors. This is a performance objective that is easy to measure, for which there are no political opponents, and for which improvement could be produced quite quickly. The Liquor Control Board had many of the advantages that NYPD possessed. Yet it had not been exploiting them to improve on-time delivery. Only when the state created its GMAP strategy, did the Board employ a similar approach. The Liquor Control Board *could have* invented OnTimeDeliveryStat before NYPD created CompStat. Yet, it *did not*. The existence of favorable conditions does not guarantee that the public executives will recognize how to exploit them.

The Challenge of Designing MentalHealthStat

Compared with the police, public executives in mental health do not have it easy. Improving performance in mental health is significantly different from improving performance in policing—and more challenging too.

Yes, in mental health, the purpose is clear. For example, the first "goal" of the Los Angeles County Department of Mental Health is to:

> Enhance the quality and capacity, within available resources, of mental health services and supports in partnership with clients, family members, and communities to achieve *hope, wellness, recovery and resiliency* [emphasis added].[11]

Sounds reasonable. It is rather vague (though most strategic plans are hardly paragons in the precision of purpose). This purpose does, however, reflect what the mental health community thinks such an organization should accomplish. Certainly, all of us wish that our friends and family have "hope," "wellness," "resiliency," and, when necessary, "recovery" too. No interest group opposes these purposes.

Still, compared with police, mental health has much less operational clarity. How would such a department know when its performance has improved? Along what dimension should it measure its clients' "hope"? What should be its target for "resiliency"? What kind of "wellness" should it produce? Certainly, mental health workers don't complete a person's "recovery" with the same objective finality as police officers do when they wrap up an investigation with an arrest.[12] Bratton and Maple would not find this easy.

Like all public agencies, the Los Angeles County Department of Mental Health (DMH) collects a variety of data on the citizens whom it serves: input data, process data, output data, and even some outcome data. None of these, however, capture broad and continuing public interest. None summarize DMH's performance as well as does NYPD's weekly crime data. Moreover, the numerous mental health agencies in the U.S. lack the kind of baseline data that the police have generated as they produced their Uniform Crime Reports.[13]

Moreover, DMH does not possess any kind of first-order analytical tool—nothing equivalent to NYPD's dots on a map—that can give quick insights into what it might do to produce better results. Certainly DMH lacks a proven methodology that can have a relatively quick impact. Nor do mental health managers have a simple built-in communication mechanism—nothing like the roll call—with which to consistently and convincingly deliver their message to their "troops."

How would Los Angeles County know whether its mental health agency had accomplished something? Anything? What needs to go up? What needs to go down? Even if you focus on just one of DMH's four purposes, this isn't obvious. How might anyone measure hope, or wellness, or recovery, or resiliency? How might anyone know if any of these four characteristics had gone up for a specific individual or for the county? It's not even like asking people how safe they feel.

When the members of the leadership team at the Los Angeles County Department of Mental Health set out to create their own MentalHealthStat—they called theirs "Strategies for Total Accountability and Total Success" or "STATS"—they couldn't just copy CompStat from NYPD or the Los Angeles Police Department. They had to adapt the principles and components to address their own, unique performance deficits and to accomplish their own, specific purposes.

Intelligent Adaptation or Mindless Mimicry?

Many public agencies and government jurisdictions with their own Something-Stat fail to employ one or more of the core principles or key components of PerformanceStat. They may have established performance measures but do little more than post them on a dashboard. They may have no specific performance targets. They may hold no meetings, or hold them erratically. Or the meetings may be merely show-and-tell. They may provide little or no feedback. They may include little or no follow-up. If so, they are failing to capitalize on the full PerformanceStat *potential.*

To police executives who have employed the CompStat approach, such versions are disparaged as "CompStat Lite."[14] Maple called them "knock-off versions," in which people "just sit in a circle and chat about the intelligence."[15] When Timoney moved from Philadelphia to Miami, he concluded that all he inherited was "faux CompStat" (particularly because it involved little follow-up).[16] When Sylvester Johnson replaced Timoney in Philadelphia and modified that city's CompStat, some criticized it as "CompStat Lite"; one of the department's former deputies called it "LoveStat."[17] Similarly, in Denver, a former member of the city council labeled the city's version "Compstat lite."[18]

Any public executive can easily mimic the visible components of PerformanceStat. They can collect data, hold meetings, projects maps on screens, and announce that they have created their own, brilliant version of the latest management fashion. They can portray themselves as avant-garde executives. But unless they are purposeful and persistent, unless they are serious and resolute, and—perhaps most importantly—unless they intelligently adapt this leadership strategy's core principles and the key components to their own purposes, they will create nothing but FadStat. PerformanceStat has the *potential* to produce results—but only if this complex strategy is employed with creative subtlety in the adaptation of its leadership principles and with thoughtful diligence in the implementation of its operational components, always with a focus on achieving the organization's purposes.[19]

Always Start with Purpose

The reason for creating any PerformanceStat is to achieve specific public purposes by producing results. Thus, the leadership team of any agency or jurisdiction that chooses to employ the strategy needs to start with a specific public purpose—whether it is reducing crime or "improving and making a difference in the lives of Los Angeles County residents diagnosed with mental illness."[20]

Next, what are the organization's key performance deficits? The leadership team also needs to identify what is inhibiting performance. A performance deficit could be found in an administrative procedure or in a managerial system. It could be the result of informal pressures, diffuse priorities, multiple mandates, and counterproductive practices. Or a performance deficit could be created by the behavior of people who work in the organization or by the (lack of) leadership of its executives.

So what targets to eliminate or mitigate what key performance deficits should who achieve by when? When the leadership team decides to create its own

PerformanceStat, it needs to design its operational specifics to identify and focus on these deficits and targets.

Some organizations use the word "goal." Often, however, a "goal" is a vague, generalized aspiration: "Make the city safe." The word "target" has more specificity: "Reduce crime by 10 percent this year." As Governor Christine Gregoire emphasized at one GMAP session, "a target has a number and a date in it."[21]

Only after the members of the leadership team have made these basic choices—purpose; performance deficit; target—can they craft the rest of their performance strategy. They can't start with data. They can't start with meetings. They have to start with purpose. Only then can they decide what performance deficit(s) to fix next and how they will know when they have succeeded.

Establishing Their Own Accountability

In 1994, when Bratton became NYPD's commissioner he set three targets: Reduce crime by 10 percent in the first year, by another 15 percent in the second year, and by a total of 40 percent over three years.[22] CompStat was the strategy Bratton employed to produce these results. Any public executive can use a PerformanceStat strategy to improve his or her *own* performance.

But be careful. In creating their own, truly serious PerformanceStat, public executives are committing *themselves*—certainly internally, perhaps externally, and thus quite publicly—to making meaningful, specific, targeted improvements in results. This explicit, visible commitment creates a self-imposed discipline. It drives the executive and the leadership team to spend their own time concentrating on activities, tasks, and projects that will directly produce the specified results.

Through their PerformanceStat, a leadership team also seeks to discipline the rest of the organization. A well-crafted PerformanceStat provides everyone in the organization with an overarching purpose and specific targets for deciding how they should spend their own time. Moreover, the central PerformanceStat staff is charged not merely with *critiquing* the performance of subunits, but also with *helping* these units to learn and improve.

Line managers, however, may view the central PerformanceStat staff as intrusive meddlers. Moreover, given all the political and bureaucratic constraints around which they must navigate, and given all the other demands on their time, line managers may resent demands for actual results. They may conclude that PerformanceStat is putting their professional and personal reputations on the line. This is all true.

For the leadership team, however, this is doubly true. By creating their own targets, public executives explicitly and consciously put their own professional and personal reputations even more on the line. They have established the basis for their own accountability.

Holding Others Accountable

The most visible component of any PerformanceStat is the meeting. In the room, the organization's leadership team inquires about the performance of each subunit. Frequently, the subunit manager stands at a podium in the center of the room, surrounded by the leadership team, subordinates, peers, and visitors. Everyone's eyes are focused on the person at the podium. Even if there is no podium, even if the subunit's manager and key subordinates sit at a table facing the leadership team, everyone in the room recognizes who has primary responsibility for answering the questions. Little wonder that visitors report that PerformanceStat meetings are held in "a special 'confrontation room,'" in "a 'star chamber' room." Little wonder the word mostly frequently used to describe PerformanceStat is "accountability."

Nevertheless, PerformanceStat offers a distinct contrast with most policies and practices created to improve government's performance. These efforts have been primarily designed to *force others* to improve their performance. Neither the Government Performance and Results Act that the U.S. Congress enacted in 1993[23] nor the new, improved "modernization" that it passed in 2010[24] is designed to improve the performance of Congress. Rather, the first purpose of the original legislation is to "improve the confidence of the American people in the capability of the Federal Government, by systematically holding Federal agencies accountable for achieving program results." It dramatized what government's focus on performance has come to mean: holding *someone else* accountable.[25]

Over the past several decades, much of government's attention to performance has consisted primarily of auditing and evaluation—efforts by independent units to determine whether some other unit of government (but not their own) is performing well, adequately, or poorly. Governments today are full of auditors, evaluators, inspectors general, and other outsiders who seek to measure and critique the performance of *other* organizations and *other* officials. Michael Power of the London School of Economics and Political Science has called this "the audit explosion" and critiqued "the audit society."[26]

These approaches to improving performance are based—implicitly, at least—on what psychologist Frederick Herzberg called the KITA theory of motivation.[27] They offer little help, guidance, or training for public managers who want to produce results. Indeed, they appear to make the opposite assumption: Public managers do not want to improve performance. So it makes no sense to help them, at least not until you have "motivated" them by beating them up for their past failures and promising to beat them up even more for their future failures. (KITA, in case you hadn't guessed, is Herzberg's acronym for Kick In The Ass.)

What PerformanceStat Is Not—and Is

PerformanceStat is not a jurisdiction-wide reform. It is not a new performance regime. It is not a performance template. It is not an external (or even internal) audit. PerformanceStat is not a demand for agencies to produce new performance reports. It is not another set of transparency requirements. It is not a demand for others to improve their (inadequate) performance. PerformanceStat is not an attempt to force those idiots to shape up.

PerformanceStat is not about *them.* PerformanceStat is about *us:*

PerformanceStat is a leadership strategy that *we* are using to improve *our own* performance—and to do it now.

PerformanceStat is an internal effort to achieve public purposes by producing better results.[28]

First, however, the members of the leadership team have to decide what purpose they are trying to achieve and thus what results they should try to produce.

The Challenge of Understanding and Explaining Tacit Knowledge

Explicit knowledge can, by definition, be conveyed in words and equations, blueprints and manuals, instructions and rules. Tacit knowledge cannot. As the chemist and philosopher Michael Polanyi observed, "We can know more than we can tell."[29]

Individually, the components of PerformanceStat are relatively easy to explain. Who collects what data and how? For this component there can exist a formal system. Who conducts the meeting and how? There isn't any "system" for such meetings (though millennia ago, humans on the African savannas did invent the tribal meeting—and thus created a practice for subsequent generations to adapt and employ). Still, an interested observer can sit in, take notes, and afterward ask questions about what happened and why—about particular exchanges that looked important or puzzling. Of course, it is a little more difficult to observe accountability—unless accountability means the verbal rebuke, official demotion, or complete termination of a failing subordinate. If you want to understand the follow-up, you can do so. But you aren't going to grasp it by attending one meeting; to appreciate the value of the follow-up you have to observe several meetings.

Explaining the collective enterprise, however, is more challenging. What do the meetings accomplish? Individually? Collectively? What did this specific meeting accomplish? *How* did the meeting accomplish this? *How* did this meeting help improve performance? Do you really need so many meetings? Why? Why are you collecting these data? Why not those data? Who pays attention to the data? *How* does all this affect front-line workers? Aren't they the ones who will ultimately produce the results? Why aren't they in the room? *How* does your PerformanceStat affect them?

The knowledge to answer these questions exists. Some people have it. If, after a month or a quarter of employing their PerformanceStat, results improve, they can be dismissed as lucky. But if they have proven successful multiple times—if they have been able to establish a trend of consistently improving results—luck is an inadequate explanation. Someone must be doing something.

Still, conveying this tacit knowledge is extremely challenging.[30] This difficulty helps explain why so many management books are so simplistic. They consist primarily of vague proverbs that offer no more guidance to a perplexed executive seeking to improve performance than Sir Isaac Newton's equations of motion offer to a child trying to ride a bicycle.[31]

For the child learning to ride a bike, the good news is that instruction comes from a trusted master who offers a veteran's support, provides nimble guidance with a steady hand, and exercises wise discretion about when to let go. Unfortunately, few public executives benefit from such support, guidance, or discretion in letting go.

Obviously, mastering the tacit knowledge necessary to improve an organization's performance is more challenging than mastering the tacit knowledge necessary to ride a bicycle. All bicycles are essentially the same; once you have learned to ride one bicycle, you can ride them all.

Every public agency, however, is different. This year, every public agency is different—perhaps quite different—from last year's version of that very same agency. Thus, the tacit knowledge that proved so effective last year might be counterproductive this year.

Teaching someone to ride a bicycle is like teaching someone to exercise leadership. There is no manual. The knowledge that you have accumulated cannot be captured in words or formulas. You know a lot, but you cannot explain this knowledge. You cannot really *teach* it.

In fact, you have never really *taught* anyone to ride a bicycle. You certainly did not deliver a lecture on how Newton's equations explain a bicycle's motion.[32]

Instead, you *helped* someone to *learn*. You provided guidance—some useful (but hardly precise) hints that permitted your pupil to *learn* the tacit knowledge required to ride a bicycle. This tacit knowledge has been passed down from generation to generation without the help of books or equations, but simply through the thoughtful guidance by a series of experienced mentors.

Someday, perhaps, we will have created some knowledge about leadership and management that can be explicitly codified in words and equations. Until then, we need to do the next best thing: Experienced public executives should help their aspiring colleagues learn the tacit knowledge necessary to ride off successfully, without anyone holding on.

Human Yearning for Simple Explanations

"Bad money drives out the good." This truth is universally known as Gresham's Law—named for Sir Thomas Gresham, who is famous for six words he never said and for an idea he did not invent. Over four centuries ago, however, Gresham did make this point in a letter to Queen Elizabeth I: If government mints both good coins (with lots of silver) and bad coins (with less silver), the public will hoard the good coins—driving them out of circulation.

George Akerlof, winner of the Nobel Prize in economics, applied this idea to another aspect of economic life: the market for used cars. When you go to buy a used car, you lack some important information: Is this car a good one or a lemon? And you are worried: You might end up paying too much for a car that has a serious problem. The seller knows about this problem, of course, but you don't. You find it difficult to distinguish between a good used car and a bad one.

What to do? Because you don't want to be cheated, you are only willing to pay the lemon price, not the good-car price. Thus, explains Akerlof, "there is an incentive for sellers to market poor quality merchandise," since they won't get full value for good merchandise. This reduces both the quality and number of used cars available for sale.[33] (Why sell your used car when you can't get fair value for it?) The existence of bad used cars drives out the good ones.

A similar idea might apply to the intellectual market for leadership strategies. Some leadership strategies are simple—easy to explain, easy to understand, easy to implement. Others are complex—quite difficult to explain and understand. Moreover, in new circumstances, complex strategies require subtle adaptations.

The simple strategies are based primarily on explicit knowledge—ideas that can be easily specified in words. The complex strategies require tacit knowledge—a subtle appreciation of how the various aspects of the strategy interact to generate the desired human and organizational behavior. Unfortunately, many managers cannot ascertain which ones are effective and which ones are not. Thus, given that they can't decide which of the many available strategies are most effective, they choose the simpler ones. From this distinction emerges "Gresham's Law of Leadership Strategies":

> Simple leadership strategies drive out the complex.[34]

Or, to specify this relationship in a less pithy but more complete way:

> Simple, easily explained, easily comprehended, explicit-knowledge descriptions of a leadership strategy drive out a subtle, complicated, tacit-knowledge appreciation for the *potential* of a complex leadership strategy to influence human and organizational behavior in ways that improve performance.

Gresham's Law of Leadership Strategies actually comes in two slightly different versions: (1) We humans prefer simple leadership strategies to complex ones. (2) We also prefer simple explanations of complex leadership strategies to their subtle and complicated reality.

This all-too-human preference for the simple over the complex affects the behavior of public executives who have developed a sophisticated, subtle, complex leadership strategy: They are forced to explain their intricate ideas in simplistic terms. Effective public executives want to be appreciated. They want to be acknowledged for what they have accomplished. Such recognition is their primary reward. To benefit from this esteem opportunity,[35] however, they are forced to describe their complex strategy with a stylized simplicity that degrades its value to others.

Other public managers can readily replicate this easily described "model"—this explicit-knowledge "best practice." Indeed, their organization might even realize some short-term benefits. After all, even the stylized version of a complex strategy may include an important if elementary tactic that (if the organization has never utilized it) can have an impact. Or, a struggling yet basically motivated organization could benefit from the placebo effect. The organization will, however, have missed an opportunity to understand and adapt the subtle, tacit features of the strategy that can help to continually ratchet up performance.

H. L. Mencken, the sage of Baltimore, once observed: "There is always an easy solution to every human problem—neat, plausible, and wrong."[36] Certainly any serious performance challenge is a human problem—and an important one too. Yet, we humans favor strategies that are easy and neat.

As Thomas Gresham might have put it: Easy and neat leadership strategies drive out the subtle and complex.

4

Distinguishing CompStat's Impact

What kind of results—what reductions in crime—can be attributed to New York's CompStat?

> We have become more skeptical about what government can do, but these positive changes, at least in crime, suggest that we have become too skeptical.
> NATHAN GLAZER, Harvard University[1]

> The question "Does CompStat work?" makes about as much sense as the question "Does surgery work?"
> MARK KLEIMAN, University of California[2]

In the 1990s, crime in the United States "fell sharply,"[3] "dropped precipitously,"[4] "plummeted."[5] This decline was "very rapid,"[6] "unique, unexpected, dramatic,"[7] "remarkable,"[8] "sudden, unexpected,"[9] "unprecedented."[10] Criminologists, civic leaders, even the police were surprised by "the crime 'bust' of the 1990s."[11] Franklin Zimring of the University of California called it *The Great American Crime Decline.*[12] Steven Levitt of the University of Chicago and Stephen Dubner (Levitt's colleague of *Freakonomics* fame) asked: "Just where did all those criminals go?"[13]

From 1990 to 2000, the U.S. murder rate (per 100,000 residents) dropped by 41 percent, from 9.4 to 5.5. The violent-crime rate (again, per 100,000 residents) also dropped significantly, from 730 in 1990 to 507 in 2000, or by 31 percent.[14] (See table 4-1.)

During the 1990s, something significant seemed to be happening in the United States—and even more so in New York City.[15] The city's murder rate dropped from 30.7 to 8.4—or by 73 percent. Its violent-crime rate was also down from 2,384 to 945—or by 61 percent (double the national decline).

In New York City, the total number of murders dropped from 2,245 in 1990 to 673 in 2000—or by 70 percent. This decline compares with a 34-percent

TABLE 4-1. The Decline in Crime Rates in the United States and New York City, 1990–2000[a]

Percent

	1990 Crime rates		2000 Crime rates		Change in crime rates 1990 to 2000			
					Absolute change		Percent change	
Jurisdiction	Murder	Violent crimes	Murder	Violent crimes	Murder	Violent crimes	Murder	Violent crimes
United States	9.4	730	5.5	507	–3.9	–223	–41	–31
New York City	30.7	2,384	8.4	945	–22.3	–1,450	–73	–61

Source: FBI, Uniform Crime Reports, prepared by the National Archive of Criminal Justice Data (http://bjs.ojp. usdoj.gov/dataonline/).

a. Violent crimes include murder, rape and sexual assault, robbery, and assault. Crime rates are per 100,000 residents.

nationwide drop in the number of murders, and a 30-percent drop in the rest of the country (outside the city). Of the 1990–2000 drop in U.S. murders, 1,572 of the total decline of 7,852—or 20 percent—occurred in New York City. (See table 4-2.) Over the same period, of the U.S. drop in violent crimes of nearly 400,000, approximately 100,000—or 25 percent—occurred in the city.

New York City was a significant contributor to the great American crime decline of the 1990s. What—if anything—did CompStat have to do with it?

Nothing Works

Indeed, did CompStat have *anything* to do with it? Did CompStat have *any effect* on New York City's crime? After all, the not-very-subtle assumption of both social science and social policy is: "Nothing works."

The social-science assumption that nothing works is imbedded in the null hypothesis. When the question is whether something has an effect (for example, Does CompStat reduce crime?), social science assigns the burden of proof to the effect. Unless someone can produce convincing evidence of an effect, the null hypothesis is the default winner: It does *not* work. There could be a very real effect—an effect obscured by inadequate data, an effect that the best social scientists cannot detect. Still, unless the research conclusively reveals that an effect does exist, it doesn't. That's the rule.

The social-policy assumption that nothing works emerged in the 1970s from an effort to determine what works to rehabilitate criminals and reduce recidivism.

TABLE 4-2. The Decline in Murder and Total Violent Crimes in the United States and New York City, 1990–2000[a]

| | 1990 | | 2000 | | Change 1990 to 2000 | | | |
| | Number of | | Number of | | Absolute change | | Percent change | |
Jurisdiction	Murders	Violent crimes	Murders	Violent crimes	Murders	Violent crimes	Murders	Violent crimes
United States	23,438	1,820,127	15,586	1,425,486	–7,852	–394,641	–34	–22
New York City	2,245	174,542	673	75,692	–1,572	–98,850	–70	–57
Rest of U.S.	21,193	1,645,585	14,913	1,349,794	–6,280	–295,791	–30	–18

Source: FBI, Uniform Crime Reports, prepared by the National Archive of Criminal Justice Data (http://bjs.ojp.usdoj.gov/dataonline/).

a. Violent crimes include murder, rape and sexual assault, robbery, and assault.

Three researchers surveyed 231 analyses of rehabilitative strategies.[16] From this survey, Robert Martinson, one of the researchers, concluded: "With few and isolated exceptions, the rehabilitative efforts that have been reported so far have had no appreciable effect on recidivism." Thus, he asked: "Do all of these studies lead us irrevocably to the conclusion that nothing works?" His answer: "Our present strategies" for rehabilitating criminals "cannot overcome, or even appreciably reduce, the powerful tendency for offenders to continue in criminal behavior."[17] Sounds pretty conclusive.[18] The null hypothesis won. Again.

Thus, by the 1980s, reported James McGuire of the University of Liverpool and Phillip Priestly of Peace Close, this "nothing works view had become deeply embedded in the thinking of most levels of the criminal justice system."[19] Indeed, it had leaked from criminal justice to social policy generally and entered the broader policy culture.[20] The null hypothesis has become the universal presumption: Nothing works.[21] So while William Bratton and Jack Maple believed that the New York Police Department's (NYPD's) CompStat worked to reduce crime,[22] others started from precisely the opposite premise.

The Search for Cause-and-Effect Explanations

If you want to start a brawl at a convention of criminologists, simply proclaim that you—and you alone—*know* the answers to three questions: What caused the big crime drop in the 1990s? What caused the U.S. crime drop? What caused the New York City crime drop? In recent years, perhaps no cause-and-effect question in public policy has generated more alternative explanations, more books and articles, and more debate—not all of it genteel.

Indeed, there are at least ten different possible explanations (I apologize for leaving out your favorite), with some coming in multiple flavors and others having complex causal connections.[23] (See box 4-1.) Each explanation has its advocates and detractors. None could be the sole cause of any crime drop anywhere. Many made some contribution, if only a small one, and perhaps only in specific circumstances.

The first eight explanations are not police influences. They are societal influences (which are described in more detail in appendix A and summarized in box 4-1). Yes, the police were involved in putting more criminals in prison (Explanation 3; see table A-2 in appendix A). But primarily what put more criminals in prison were policy changes such as "three strikes and you're out" or "habitual offender" laws that half the states enacted. The police may have arrested more people for broken-windows offenses. But the 50 percent increase in people under correctional supervision during the 1990s is not primarily a result of changes in policing.

This chapter focuses on the potential contribution of the two explanations directly involving the police: Explanation 9: More Cops; and Explanation 10: Innovative Policing.

Explanation 9: More Cops

During his 1992 campaign for president, Bill Clinton pledged to put an additional 100,000 police officers on the streets. In 1994, Congress authorized $8.8 billion in federal grants to state and local governments to "increase police presence" and to encourage community policing.[24] (See Explanation 10B.) To manage these grants, the U.S. attorney general established the Office of Community Oriented Policing Services, known by its acronym: "COPS."

Thus, during the 1990s, the number of U.S. cops grew—but not by 100,000. In 2000, which the U.S. Government Accountability Office calls the "peak year" for these grants, COPS "contributed about 17,000 additional officers—or about 3 percent of the total number of sworn officers nationwide." From 1994 through 2001, GAO estimates, federal funding "paid for a total of about 88,000 additional officer-years."[25] Yet, as simple as it might seem, Edward Maguire of the University of Nebraska and his colleagues report that (at the national level) "counting cops is not easy."[26] Consequently, note Maguire and John Eck of the University of Cincinnati, "estimates of increases in police strength contain some (unknown) degree of measurement error."[27]

BOX 4-1. Ten (Plus) Possible Explanations for the Big Drop in Crime in the United States

1. Randomness (and regression toward the mean)
   Because crime is random, any unexplained jump in crime is apt to be followed by a drop in crime.

2. Demographic Shifts (specifically the consequences of *Roe* v. *Wade*)
   The legalization of abortion reduced the number of crime-age males two decades later, and because abortion was legalized in New York before it was legalized in the rest of the country, crime was apt to drop first in New York.

3. More Criminals in Prison
   With an increase in incarceration rates, fewer professional criminals were able to commit crimes, and potential criminals were deterred.

4. The Decline in the Use of Crack Cocaine
   Those in the crack cocaine business used guns to protect their product and turf, and thus the drop in crack use reduced the number of guns on the streets.

5. Economic Growth
   An improved economy generated alternative and attractive sources of income that were legitimate.

6. Social Services for the Victims of Domestic Violence
   As social-service agencies focused on domestic violence, they offered shelters and legal aid, and the number of intimate-partner homicides dropped.

7. Collective Efficacy
   Improved individual citizenship and effective community organizations increased some communities' collective efficacy and action at crime prevention.

8. The (Fall and) Rise of Institutional Legitimacy in Society
   Public investments in the institutions of criminal justice, economic support, and education helped to suppress criminal behavior.

9. More Cops
   With more police on the street, more criminals are arrested, and potential criminals deterred.

10. Innovative Policing
    The leaders of police departments experimented with a variety of policing strategies including:

    10A. Problem-Oriented Policing
    10B. Community Policing
    10C. Broken-Windows (Quality-of-Life) Policing
    10D. Aggressive Policing
    10E. Hot Spot Policing
    10F. CompStat

Although no accurate estimate is available, the number of cops on U.S. streets clearly increased during the 1990s.[28] Certainly, in New York City, the number of cops increased. In 1993, the year before Rudolph Giuliani became mayor, the city had 34,600 uniformed officers; in 2000, the number peaked at over 40,000. (During that time, federal funding helped the city hire 4,000 additional officers.)[29] Clearly, NYPD's 5,400 additional officers, a 16 percent increase, could have helped to reduce crime.

These additional cops could have caught more bad guys who were then locked up (see Explanation 3) and, by their mere presence, deterred others. Most of the scholars who have investigated this question have found little causal connection between the increase in the number of police on U.S. streets during the 1990s and the decrease in crime. "Overall," conclude Eck and Maguire, "hiring more police officers did not play an independent or consistent role in reducing violent crime in the United States."[30] Observing that "there is a modest inverse association between police levels and crime," John Worrall and Tomislav Kovandzic of the University of Texas at Dallas concluded: "COPS spending had little to no effect on crime."[31]

For the nation, Zimring agrees: "The quantitative increase in police may have played a small role in the national crime decline. But perhaps not."[32] Moreover, after the increase in the number of police officers in New York City during the 1990s, NYPD's force dropped during the following decade—from over 40,000 to less than 33,000. This drop of nearly 20 percent meant that NYPD's uniformed force was lower than when Bratton became commissioner in 1994.[33] Yet the city's crime continued to decline—and to decline more significantly than in the rest of the United States.

Crime Drops in the 1990s—and in the 2000s Too

In the 1990s, murders in New York City dropped by 70 percent. In the rest of the country, the decline was just 30 percent. For this decade, New York City accounted for 20 percent of the U.S. decline in murder (1,572 out of 7,852). From 2000 to 2010, the murders in New York City dropped again, though by "only" 20 percent. Yet that was bigger than the U.S. decline of 5 percent. During this decade, New York City accounted for 16 percent of the decline in U.S. murders (137 out of 841). (See table 4-3.)

The same applies to the drop in total violent crime. It was much bigger in New York City than in the rest of the country—in the 1990s *and* in the 2000s. In both decades, New York's percent drop in violent crime was triple that in the rest of the country. (See table 4-4.) Of the city's drop in crime over these two decades,

TABLE 4-3. The Decline in Murders in the United States and New York City, 1990, 2000, and 2010

Jurisdiction	Number of murders			Absolute change			Percent change		
	1900	2000	2010	1990–2000	2000–10	1990–2010	1990–2000	2000–10	1990–2010
United States	23,438	15,586	14,745	–7,852	–841	–8,693	–34	–5	–37
New York City	2,245	673	536	–1,572	–137	–1,709	–70	–20	–76
Rest of United States	21,193	14,913	14,209	–6,280	–704	–6,984	–30	–5	–33

Source: FBI, Uniform Crime Reports, prepared by the National Archive of Criminal Justice Data (http://bjs.ojp.usdoj.gov/dataonline/).

TABLE 4-4. The Decline in Violent Crime in the United States and New York City, 1990, 2000, and 2010[a]

Jurisdiction	Number of violent crimes			Absolute change			Percent change		
	1990	2000	2010	1990–2000	2000–10	1990–2010	1990–2000	2000–10	1990–2010
United States	1,820,127	1,425,486	1,246,248	–394,641	–179,238	–573,879	–22	–13	–32
New York City	174,542	75,692	48,430	–98,850	–27,262	–126,112	–57	–36	–72
Rest of United States	1,645,585	1,349,794	1,197,818	–295,791	–151,976	–447,767	–18	–11	–27

Source: FBI, Uniform Crime Reports, prepared by the National Archive of Criminal Justice Data (http://bjs.ojp.usdoj.gov/dataonline/).
a. Violent crimes include murder, rape and sexual assault, robbery, and assault.

Zimring wrote: "The size and the length of the decline are without precedent in the recorded history of American urban crime."[34]

Moreover, while the number of NYPD's sworn officers declined after 2000, the number increased in the rest of the country. In 2000, local police departments had 441,000 sworn officers. By 2007, the number had grown to 463,000.[35] It is difficult to attribute New York's drop in crime during the 2000s (see tables 4-3 and 4-4), to any increase in NYPD's force.

Explanation 10: Innovative Policing Strategies

Actually, the debate over the cause(s) of the crime drop in New York City and the United States focuses on what the police did. Did they simply work harder? Or did they work smarter, employing new, innovative strategies? If so, did this working harder or working smarter have a causal impact on crime?

Certainly those who created new policing strategies believe so. Bratton and Dennis Smith of New York University emphasized that: "the managers of urban police forces have in fact reinvented American police administration, and in doing so have contributed to dramatic reductions in crime all across the nation."[36] Bratton made the same point about New York in a book chapter titled "Crime Is Down in New York City: Blame the Police."[37]

What, exactly, were these new policing strategies? Six innovations compete for credit for reducing crime: (10A) problem-oriented policing; (10B) community policing; (10C) broken-windows or quality-of-life policing; (10D) aggressive policing; (10E) hot-spot policing, and (10F) CompStat.

To a police chief, these innovations look like a Chinese menu. Column A contains several versions of problem-oriented policing, while Column F has several different types of CompStats. A police chief can select an item from Column A, ignore Column B, focus on some but not all quality-of-life concerns in Column C, choose from different levels of aggressiveness in Column D, decide on how many hot spots are worth attention in Column E, and create its own version of CompStat from variations in Column F. In New York City, for example, Bratton's two predecessors as commissioner—Benjamin Ward and Lee Brown—had been major advocates of community policing. Bratton, however, was not a fan of traditional community policing and essentially disbanded it, moving authority and responsibility up to the precinct commanders.[38] Nevertheless, he employed in interconnecting ways aspects of the other strategies.

Explanation 10A: Problem-Oriented Policing[39] was developed by Herman Goldstein of the University of Wisconsin. "The police have been particularly susceptible to the 'means over ends' syndrome," he argued. They should focus, he continued, "on the results of policing—on the effect that police efforts have on the problems that the police are expected to handle." The police, Goldstein continued, need to identify "these problems in more precise terms, researching each problem, documenting the nature of the current police response, assessing its adequacy and the adequacy of existing authority and resources, engaging in a broad exploration of alternatives to present responses, weighing the merits of these alternatives, and choosing from among them."[40]

Goldstein's problem-oriented approach is challenging. Each police precinct has to learn how to identify its own particular problems (its performance deficits), analyze their unique features, and respond with its available resources. Problem-oriented policing requires an analytical mindset. There is no formula to copy, no model to drop neatly into the organization. One precinct's problems may look similar to another's, yet they are not identical. Neither are the circumstances or resources. Thus, rather than mimic another's approach, each police department has to develop its own capacity to analyze its unique problems.[41]

Explanation 10B: Community Policing[42] is based on Goldstein's problem-oriented policing. "Community policing consists of two complementary core components, community partnership and problem solving," explained the Bureau of Justice Assistance in the U.S. Department of Justice. Think of community policing as problem-oriented policing at the beat-cop level. "The 'community' for which a patrol officer is given responsibility should be a small, well-defined geographical area," argued the bureau. Because individual patrol officers "have the most extensive contact with community members," the bureau continued, "they will provide the bulk of the daily policing needs of the community."[43]

"The concept of community policing," wrote Malcolm Sparrow of Harvard's Kennedy School, emphasizes "the community as an agent and partner in promoting security rather than as a passive audience."[44] Thus, community policing could help to create a community's "collective efficacy." (See Explanation 7.)

Bratton dissented from the idea that the 7,000 new cops hired in 1990 by Lee Brown (his predecessor as NYPD's commissioner) and Mayor David Dinkins (Giuliani's predecessor) to do community policing could have had much of an impact:

The average kid joining NYPD at that time was a 22-year-old, with only a high-school (12 years) education:
—Many of the new hires had never held a job until they applied to NYPD.
—Many had never even driven a car.
—Many lived outside the city and had never interacted with a minority person.
—Many were under 21 and not even old enough to legally drink.

And these were the 7,000 young police officers who were supposed to solve the problems of New York City, one of the most complex cities in the world, after only six months of police academy training. They were simply not equipped to deal with the city's problems of race, crime, and disorder.[45]

Explanation 10C: Broken-Windows (or Quality-of-Life) Policing was defined by James Q. Wilson and George Kelling, then both at Harvard, in an influential 1992 article in the *Atlantic Monthly* titled "Broken Windows":

> Social psychologists and police officers tend to agree that if a window in a building is broken and is left unrepaired, all the rest of the windows will soon be broken. . . . one unrepaired broken window is *a signal that no one cares,* and so breaking more windows costs nothing [emphasis added].[46]

"Broken windows" is a metaphor dramatizing a bigger problem. After all, a window that is already broken isn't hurting anyone. A broken window is, however, "a signal" that "no one cares" and, thus, that a neighborhood might be dangerous. Wilson and Kelling listed other signals: "panhandlers, drunks, addicts, rowdy teenagers, prostitutes, loiterers, the mentally disturbed."

These are "not violent people, nor, necessarily, criminals, but disreputable or obstreperous or unpredictable people."[47] Yet, Wilson and Kelling continued, "the prospect of a confrontation with an obstreperous teenager or a drunken panhandler can be as fear-inducing for defenseless persons as the prospect of meeting an actual robber; indeed, to a defenseless person, the two kinds of confrontation are often indistinguishable." Moreover, these "broken windows" invite the real criminals. "Serious street crime flourishes in areas in which disorderly behavior goes unchecked," they argued. "The unchecked panhandler is, in effect, the first broken window."[48]

Thus, Wilson and Kelling wrote, the police have a responsibility to prevent all of these metaphorical windows from being broken and, when they are, to fix them quickly. "The police ought to protect communities as well as individuals," they wrote.[49] Their strategy is often called "broken-window" policing or "quality-of-life" policing.[50] If the police can help improve the quality of life of a neighborhood, they will reduce citizens' fear of crime, and people will then return to the streets, thus restraining the behavior of potential criminals.[51]

In 1984, David Gunn, president of the New York City Transit Authority, set out to eliminate the graffiti from the subway cars.[52] Graffiti has never attacked a single human. It has never been arrested. Still, in 1979, over a decade before the broken-windows article was published, Nathan Glazer argued that the city's subway riders were "assaulted" daily by graffiti that contributed to a "sense of a menacing and uncontrollable city" that was "incapable of humane management."[53] In five years, Gunn eliminated graffiti from every subway car.[54]

Then, when Bratton became head of the transit police in New York in 1990, he made a major effort to deal with "the quality of life violations" in the city's subways: aggressive panhandling; turnstile jumpers, and "people living in the subway stations and tunnels." He sought to eliminate the "broken windows" that signaled "no one cared." One captain in the transit police created "Operation Glazier"—because a "glazier" is someone who fixes broken windows.[55]

By 1997, Glazer appreciated that he was no longer "assaulted" by graffiti on the subway cars. Indeed, he observed a variety of other improvements in New York City. Although he suggested that changes in the behavior of individuals were certainly a contributor, he also wrote: "We have become more skeptical about what government can do, but these positive changes, at least in crime, suggest that we have become too skeptical."[56]

Explanation 10D: Aggressive Policing is possible because police exercise a lot of discretion. As Michael Lipsky of Demos wrote in his classic book, *Street-Level Bureaucracy,* "policemen decide who to arrest and whose behavior to overlook." Because there are so many laws and thus so many opportunities for citizens to violate one, Lipsky continued, "policemen are expected to invoke the law selectively."[57] To Zimring such discretion included "the very aggressive use of stops by the police, stop and frisk procedures, and arrests of suspicious persons for minor crimes to remove them from being an immediate threat and to identify persons with outstanding warrants."[58] During the 1990s and the 2000s, NYPD officers were often more aggressive.

This might look like just another version of quality-of-life or broken-windows policing—or what others have called "zero-tolerance policing." Bratton, however, argued that this is not what he did: "Zero tolerance is neither a phrase that I use nor one that captures the meaning of what happened in New York City."[59] Zimring concluded that even when NYPD officers were making what looked like quality-of-life arrests, they did so in search of those who were wanted for much more serious offenses.[60]

Explanation 10E: Hot-Spot Policing is more than Maple's "Cops on the Dots," but not that much more. Two criminologists, Anthony Braga of Rutgers University and David Weisburd of George Mason University, define it as "the application of police interventions at very small geographic units of analysis."[61] The police identify specific localities—the "hot spot" on a street corner, at a building, in a neighborhood with a criminal history—and then employ problem-oriented policing (Explanation 10A) to strategically focus resources on eliminating the crime. These strategies include aggressive policing (stop-and-frisk tactics), arresting individuals for "broken-windows" behavior, and arresting individuals for serious crimes. They also include eradicating the "broken windows": demolishing vacant buildings that are serving as drug dens, installing high-luminous street lights, conducting strict building-code enforcement. They include strategies for engaging and mobilizing the community. Think of it as "Cops plus a lot of other regulators and resources on the really nasty Dots."

Explanation 10F: CompStat[62] gets credit (from some but not everyone) for reducing crime in New York City. In 2001, Bratton and Smith argued:

> Since the introduction of Compstat in 1994 through fiscal 1999, major declines were reported in all categories of crime in New York City and *in all 76 precincts*. In fact, New York City outperformed the nation in all categories, often by a wide margin, and was an early and leading contributor in the crime reductions reported nationally. . . . evidence is overwhelming that since Compstat's inauguration, the pace of crime reduction dramatically increased [emphasis in the original].[63]

CompStat gets credit elsewhere too. In Australia, where the states are responsible for policing and where every state has adopted some version of CompStat, both the police and independent researchers report that the leadership strategy has had an impact.

Lorraine Mazerolle of Queensland University, and her colleagues, Sacha Rombouts, and James McBroom, described the impact of Queensland's version of CompStat (called Operation Performance Reviews or OPRs): "COMPSTAT generally—and Queensland's OPRs in particular—can be an effective police management mechanism, which results in observable reductions in reported crime." Queensland inaugurated its OPRs in 2001, and from data covering 1995 through 2004, Mazerolle and her colleagues concluded that "the introduction of OPRs contributed to a statistically significant reduction in total reported offences." Specifically, they wrote, it "prevented around 972 crimes" and saved the state approximately A$2.7 million.[64]

In January 1998, the New South Wales (NSW) Police Service created its own strategy: "Operation and Crime Review." Marilyn Chilvers and Don Weatherburn of the New South Wales Bureau of Crime Statistics and Research concluded that, over the next two-plus years, the NSW "police were responsible for the fall in crime which occurred after the introduction of the OCR process." They were, however, cautious, noting that "the results presented here cannot be regarded as providing definitive evidence that the OCR process did reduce crime."[65]

Separating the Competing Explanations

For the 1990s decline in crime—in New York City and the United States—no explanation (except for the *Freakonomics* focus on abortion) has generated as much debate and dissent as these innovative strategies in policing. "Criminologists gave police and other public officials something of a free ride as they claimed credit for the 1990s crime drop," wrote Richard Rosenfeld, Robert Fornango, and Eric Baumer of the University of Missouri.[66] "It's like trying to take credit for an eclipse," said Raymond Kelly, Bratton's predecessor as NYPD's commissioner.[67] Still, in 2002, when Kelly returned to NYPD as commissioner, he did not terminate CompStat but continued it.

Innovative policing is not one explanation but at least six.[68] Thus, any effort to attribute any part of any decline in crime to specific policing strategies requires a careful clarification of which specific versions of which specific strategies were employed by which specific jurisdictions.

Unfortunately, no one conducted an experiment to sort out these six different approaches. The director of the Federal Bureau of Investigation (FBI) never assigned 10 police departments to employ community policing (but not CompStat), while telling another 10 to implement CompStat (but not community policing).[69] Indeed, no one—not the director of the FBI, not the attorney general—could have convinced even a few of the nation's 20,000-plus police agencies[70] to engage in such an experiment. In the United States, policing is very decentralized—with individual jurisdictions vigilantly guarding their authority and prerogatives. Thus, each police department employed its own variants of these strategies.

Moreover, these presumably distinct strategies may somewhat depend on and reinforce each other. Braga and Weisburd wrote that "dealing with crime hot spots has been a key component of many recent police innovations such as Compstat, community policing, and problem oriented policing." Indeed, they observed, CompStat "could be instrumental in implementing and managing a robust hot spots policing program."[71] Whether a police chief chooses to emphasize problem-oriented policing, or broken-windows policing, or hot-spot policing, or any other innovataive strategy, he or she may also employ a CompStat leadership strategy to keep everyone focused on implementation.

Zimring observed that "only the brave would try to allocate causal credit when a kitchen sink full of changes happened together." Yet he opted to be brave—or, at least, prudently brave. First, he offered two big conclusions:

> The two important tactical measures that almost certainly reduced crime in New York City were (1) the emphasis on hot spots for enforcement,

aggressive street intervention, and sustained monitoring; and (2) the priority targeting of public drug markets for arrest, surveillance, and sustained attack.

Then he observed: "Compstat probably made a measurable contribution, but this is not a certainty."[72]

Actually, CompStat is qualitatively different from the other five innovative policing strategies. It isn't a front-line tactic designed to alter significantly the interactions of the police (and other municipal resources) with citizens and the community. It is a leadership strategy designed to affect the behavior of the entire organization. It doesn't happen at the point that a patrol officer comes in contact with a citizen or someone who might have committed a crime. Instead, CompStat is a strategy that a police department's leadership team uses to ensure that beat officers do, indeed, engage in problem-oriented, or broken-windows, or hot-spot policing—whatever front-line tactics the leadership team seeks to implement. CompStat can help a commissioner keep the department focused on employing its crime-reduction strategy (or strategies), to motivate individuals, teams, and precincts to pursue this crime-reduction approach with intelligence and energy, to learn what is working (and not working), and to help everyone in the department improve. For any CompStat to be effective, however, a police department needs to also be developing (or improving) its set of crime-reduction strategies.[73]

The Futile Search for a Single Explanation (Let Alone a Panacea)

"The research community has reached a consensus on the basic contours of the 1990s crime decline—the who, what, when and where," wrote Rosenfeld. Yet, he continued, this research community "still argues about the why."[74] This debate may be unfortunate but inevitable. As Warren Friedman of the Chicago Alliance for Neighborhood Safety observed, the "data are subject to varying interpretations, causation is hard to identify with certainty and the debate is complicated by a significant amount of individual and institutional self-interest."[75]

As Rosenfeld noted, "major social phenomena, such as serious crime, are rarely driven by a single factor."[76] Jeremy Travis, now the president of John Jay College of Criminal Justice, echoed this point: "There is no single cause or explanation for the recent decline in crime"; after all, "the nature of crime and the factors that contribute to it are complex and tightly interwoven."[77] Indeed, any effort to separate the impact of external forces from the impact of leadership and management in *any* policy area in *any* jurisdiction confronts similar perils. Any effort by any public agency to achieve any particular result using a single tactic is doomed.

No wonder that, from all this discussion and debate, Michael Jacobson, president of the Vera Institute of Justice, concluded: "The precise causes of New York's crime decline will be debated by social scientists until the Sun hits the Earth."[78]

"Policing strategies may have some importance in reducing crime," acknowledged Andrew Gimber of the Institute of Economic Affairs in London, "but they are not a panacea."[79] Mark Kleiman reiterated the point: "CompStat is no panacea."[80] But who said it was? Certainly not Bratton. Nor Maple. None of the advocates for problem-oriented policing, or quality-of-life policing, or CompStat have ever (as far as I can discover) asserted that their approach is "a panacea."

Does CompStat Work?

This, of course, is the question for which everyone would like *the* answer. Kleiman, however, resisted: "The question 'Does CompStat work?' makes about as much sense as the question, 'Does surgery work?'" Instead, Kleiman argued, it all depends:

> The efficacy of the CompStat management model depends on several factors, including the skill and ruthlessness of the command staff implementing it, the existence of a repertoire of crime-reducing tactics for local commanders to implement, and basic competence at the patrol-officer and sergeant level. Compstat is part of a management approach, not a substitute for a strategy.[81]

Sometimes surgery works. Sometimes it doesn't. Surgery never works all of the time. Some surgical procedures work more frequently than others. And the overall success rate will depend on the problem that the surgeon is trying to fix. Moreover, the success of a specific surgical operation performed by a specific surgeon on a specific patient depends on a large number of factors: the seriousness of the problem, the surgical procedure chosen, the skill of the surgeon (for this particular procedure), the nature of any unexpected complications, and, inevitably, luck.

Similarly, CompStat doesn't automatically work or not work. It doesn't "work" in policing any more than a sacrifice bunt "works" in baseball. Whether a sacrifice bunt "works" or not depends on a variety of factors. Here are two:

1. Purpose combined with context: Does there exist a purpose to be achieved to which the sacrifice bunt might make a significant contribution? If it is the bottom of the ninth with no outs and the game is tied, a sacrifice bunt might make a lot of sense. If it is the bottom of the eighth, and the team is behind by seven runs, a sacrifice bunt is silly.
2. Skill: Does the batter have the ability to execute an effective sacrifice bunt?

CompStat "is just a tool," argued Maple. "In the hands of the mediocre, it's useless. In the hands of a great leader, it can be Excalibur."[82]

5

Committing to a Purpose

What specific purpose will the leaders of a public agency or government jurisdiction commit to achieving?

Forgetting our objectives is the most frequent act of stupidity.
FRIEDRICH NIETZSCHE, philosopher[1]

The only point at which very much leverage can be gained on the [bureaucracy] problem is when we decide what it is we are trying to accomplish.
JAMES Q. WILSON, political scientist[2]

In 1994, when William Bratton first became New York's police commissioner, he pledged to reduce the city's crime by 40 percent in three years.[3] This was a specific purpose—a significant commitment. When *Governing* magazine gave Bratton one of its "Public Officials of the Year" awards, it noted. "Most criminologists considered it a crazy idea—undoable, career suicide."[4]

"I've never seen anything like it," observed criminologist Lawrence Sherman. Sherman, who began his career as an NYPD analyst and who had studied 30 police departments over the previous 25 years, noted:

> Police chiefs routinely say, "Don't expect us to bring down crime, because we don't control its causes." But Bratton says just the opposite. It's the most focused crime-reduction effort I've seen. It will take time before we can say how much effect it has had, but this clearly is new. When I sat in at Compstat, I thought, "Bratton is using crime data for management by objective—a basic idea that's never been tried before."[5]

CompStat, wrote Phyllis McDonald of Johns Hopkins University, "rests on five basic principles." Why *five?* Because to Jack Maple's list, McDonald added a fifth, which she placed first. This additional principle is: "Specific Objectives."[6]

Acknowledging Responsibility

"Wait a second," you might say. "Aren't public executives supposed to have specific objectives?" "Aren't the police supposed to be responsible for controlling crime? Why does William Bratton get so much credit simply for doing what police were supposed to do? Isn't he just like the little boy declaring that the king has no clothes? Why should he win so many awards simply for being the first police executive to declare that the clothes were missing from his own department?"

Yes . . . Then again, he actually did something about it. Bratton was not just a sidewalk observer who blurted out the obvious truth as the naked police chief marched by. He was in the parade. He was leading the parade. Bratton did not just recognize the reality. He publicly acknowledged his organization's responsibility to improve performance and then committed himself to make it happen. Starting in 1994, the New York police commissioner—and thus the New York Police Department—would commit to lowering the level of crime in the city.

NYPD's CompStat strategy was an innovation in leadership and management that was based on two core ideas—one philosophical, the other operational. CompStat is most famous for the operational idea: the collection of CompStat's functional components, many of which can be physically and personally observed by attending one of the meetings. Without the first philosophical idea, however, the operational idea lacks a practical focus. To produce meaningful results, operations needs the chief executive to make a personal (as well as the organizational) commitment to achieve a specific public purpose.

Some public executives are quite willing to create an operational Performance-Stat: data, maps, meetings, . . . the observable stuff. They miss, however, the underlying philosophy. Or they understand it but ignore it—seeking to earn credit for being innovative by mimicking the visible, eye-catching features. Significantly, however, they fail to commit to achieving a specific public purpose.

Single-handedly, William Bratton changed the philosophical perspective of policing. After his 27 months as NYPD's commissioner, noted *Governing,* "American police chiefs were judged by one thing: Is crime up or down?" That is the way Bratton thinks *he* should be judged. That is the way he thinks *his colleagues* should be judged. As Bratton was wont to tell mayors: "If you have a police chief that can't get crime down, get yourself a new police chief."[7]

Bratton was not about to let himself or his own police department off the hook. First in New York (1994–96), then in Los Angeles (2002–09), and again in New York (2014–), the police would operationally accept and publicly declare that they were responsible for the level of crime. Bratton committed himself and his organization to a specific public purpose: reducing crime.

The Cops Are Irrelevant

To many criminologists, Bratton's willingness to establish the specific objective of reducing crime was shocking because they all "knew," cops have little impact on crime. Society had come to view crime as pathological yet predictable human behavior that was driven by social, economic, and psychological factors that the police could not influence. Yes, whenever a crime was committed, the police could respond—preferably quickly and professionally, rather than torpidly and incompetently. Then, *if* the police were conscientious—and *if* a citizen knew what had happened and was willing to tell the cops—the bad guys would get caught, convicted, and sent away. Sometimes this happened; sometimes it didn't. If it didn't, it wasn't the cops' fault.

In 1994, the same year that Bratton took over NYPD, David Bayley of the State University of New York, published his book on *Police for the Future.* Bayley opened chapter 1, "The Myth of the Police," with a simple, declarative statement:

> The police do not prevent crime. This is one of the best kept secrets of modern life. Experts know it, the police know it, but the public does not know it.

Moreover, Bayley provided some "evidence for this heretical and disturbing assertion." First, he noted, "repeated analysis has consistently failed to find any connection between the number of police officers and crime rates." Indeed, Bayley continued, "the primary strategies adopted by modern police have been shown to have little or no effect on crime."[8]

But if all of the experts and the police knew this, why did Bratton not know this too? Wasn't he supposed to be an intellectual cop—a well-read cop? Wasn't he aware of this evidence?

He must have been. After all, decades before, James Q. Wilson, the nation's senior scholar on policing, had laid out the same argument in his classic book, *Varieties of Police Behavior.* If "the police administrator," wrote Wilson, "knew how to prevent crime, of course he would." Unfortunately, continued Wilson, the top cop "is in the unhappy position of being responsible for an organization that lacks a proven technology for achieving its purpose."[9]

If Bratton lacked a proven technology to pull it off, wasn't he crazy to commit to a specific public purpose—with its specific performance target?

Crime Is No Longer a "Social Disease"

The conventional, professional, and scholarly wisdoms were all lined up against Bratton. Crime, everyone knew, was a social disease. For the cops, this is convenient: They are off the hook.

The idea that crime is a "social disease" is found in a variety of intellectual traditions. "Doctors view human beings as societal organisms," wrote one member of the medical profession; thus, "doctors may see 'crime' as a social disease needing treatment."[10] A University of California sociologist wrote that "we simply do not understand the etiology of crime as a social disease."[11] And the social-disease perspective is not merely a product of 1960s' thinking. Nearly a century ago, George Elliott Howard, the president of the American Sociological Society, argued that "the criminal is the creature of environment, of wrong social conditions which may be remedied."[12]

Thinking of crime as a social disease has not been limited to social scientists and bleeding hearts. William Rutledge, the police chief of Detroit from 1926 to 1930, was an early advocate for creating the FBI's "uniform crime reports." Why? Because, he argued, police are "in the absurd position of endeavoring to diagnose and cure a social disease with little knowledge of its causes, its nature and its prevalence."[13] In the 1980s, Benjamin Bowling observed, "The view that 'blaming the police for a rise in crime is like blaming doctors for an increase in disease' had become something of an orthodoxy."[14]

Still, nothing captured the conventional wisdom about the causes of crime better than *West Side Story*—set, coincidentally, on the West Side of Manhattan. A-Rab, a member of the Jets pretending to be a judge, declares: "Juvenile delinquency is purely a social disease." Indeed, this theme is reiterated by Stephen Sondheim's lyrics in "Gee, Officer Krupke," with the Jets explaining that, because they were raised by parents who were drug addicts and alcoholics, "natcherly we're punks!" Riff, the leader of the Jets, ends the song by observing, "no one wants a fella with a social disease."

This social-disease precept had not escaped Bratton. The police were told, he observed, "that the causes of crime were economic and social and that we could have no impact on these so-called causes." Social scientists, he continued, "speak of crime as a sort of disease that criminals are at risk of catching, through no culpability of their own, and for which the police have no responsibility or ability to prevent." Bratton, however, dissented: "I believe strongly that the single most important cause of crime is human behavior, not social, economic, demographic, or ethnographic factors." Moreover, he wrote, the police "can control behavior to such a degree that we can change behavior."[15]

Cops Count

Thus, while sociologists and criminologists were searching for the social-disease etiology of crime, Bratton decided to do something about it. His cure? Cops!

Bratton is fond of saying: "cops count."[16] In 2007, on being reappointed as LAPD's chief of police, he observed that "crime does not go up and down by itself." Rather, he continued, "The most significant factor is cops. Cops count. I am proud to be a cop."[17] Later, he expanded on the point:

> Quite simply, cops count. We are one of the most essential initiators and catalysts in the criminal justice equation. Crime may go up or down to some degree when influenced by many of the old so-called causes—which I prefer to describe as influences—but the quickest way to impact crime is with a well-led, managed, and appropriately resourced police force.

Such leadership and management included, he continued, "accountability-focused COMPSTAT management principles."[18]

Cops don't automatically count. They can only count when their department has inspiring and committed, creative and intelligent leadership.

The Tyranny of the Rules

In the world of policing, Bratton was a subversive. First, he was willing to acknowledge his and his department's responsibility for crime. Second, he acted on this acknowledgment's logical implication and set a concrete target for the level of crime. With this insurgency, Bratton forced a philosophical shift in policing. Indeed, he also forced (or, at least, nudged) a philosophical shift in public management. For if police executives are willing to publicly acknowledge their responsibility for crime—for results—should not other public executives acknowledge that they have a similar responsibility? If police executives are willing to publicly commit to targets for their results on reducing crime, should not the executives of other public agencies establish their own targets for producing specific results?

Not that Bratton was the first public executive since Moses to accept personal responsibility for achieving a specific public purpose. Many others have done so. But Bratton, Maple, and their NYPD colleagues did so despite their ability to get off the hook with the social-disease excuse. Moreover, they also created a set of core leadership principles and key operational components to achieve their purpose. They matched their leadership principles and operational components to their philosophical commitment to a specific purpose and a concrete target.

Still, these concepts and components are irrelevant without the philosophical commitment to a concrete target. Without a target, there can be no performance strategy, for there is nothing for the strategy to achieve. Without a target, there is nothing on which to follow up. Without a target, the meetings are just bull sessions and the data are mere numbers. Until the chief executive publicly commits to achieving a specific public purpose—and an associated performance target—the operational units have nothing to accomplish.

Throughout the twentieth century, government operations were driven not by specific public purposes, let alone concrete targets. In the United States, the political corruption of the late nineteenth century begot the progressive movement, which sought to create a rational government—one that was not responsive to the whims of public officials but that obeyed well-specified formalities. The consequence was bureaucracy—with its often-underappreciated pluses and its well-known minuses.

In a bureaucracy, operations are driven by rules.[19] When confronted with a problem, civil servants can do a quick search through their operations manual. From its collection of rules, they can select and deploy the one that (most closely, though rarely exactly) matches the immediate situation. All wonderfully, perfectly rational.

If they search correctly, civil servants will identify the rule designed to govern their situation. Unfortunately, in any unique situation, following the officially established rule may not be useful or appropriate. Indeed, for any situation, the relevant rule may not be obvious. Or there may appear to be several relevant rules, with some contradictions among them. But, if a civil servant can find a (nearly) appropriate rule in the operations manual, only to later discover that it doesn't work, he or she is not at fault. Whoever created the rule is.

Nothing quite captures the power of the operations manual and its rules as the exchange during the Cuban Missile Crisis between Defense Secretary Robert McNamara and Admiral George Anderson, chief of naval operations. For the U.S. blockade of Cuba, McNamara had a specific and important purpose—to send a political message to Soviet Premier Nikita Khrushchev—and he wanted to be sure that the Navy's actions would support (not undermine) this purpose—that the U.S. Navy would not do something stupid that would trigger a nuclear war. Thus if the U.S. Navy were to intercept a Soviet ship bound for Cuba, McNamara asked, what would the Navy do? Anderson picked up the Manual of Naval Regulations, waved it in McNamara's face, and exclaimed: "It's all in there." Predictably, McNamara was not satisfied: "I don't give a damn what John Paul Jones would have done. I want to know what you are going to do, now."

In this debate between purpose and rules, McNamara did not win. Anderson got the last word: "Now, Mr. Secretary, if you and your deputy will go back to your offices, the Navy will run the blockade."[20]

From Rules to Results

The power of the rules certainly applies to police. When a 911 operator receives a call from a citizen or when a police officer arrives at the scene of a crime, he or she will follow one (or more) well-established rules—all very routine. Indeed, for an officer (or any other bureaucrat) the definition of a good job is following the rules. If you follow all of the rules, if you abide by the official routines, you are—by definition—doing a good job. In accordance with Frederick Winslow Taylor's principles of scientific management, someone else—someone much smarter than you—has thought carefully about what front-line workers should do. Front-line workers are not supposed to think; they are supposed to follow the rules.[21]

For a bureaucracy—and bureaucrats—the supremacy of the rules is comforting. If you master the rules and follow them, you have satisfied the conditions of your employment. It isn't your job to figure out what the organization is supposed to accomplish. That is captured by the various rules that someone else created and that you are obligated to follow. Indeed, if you assiduously follow the rules, you can't get into trouble. What a deal!

Bratton, however, repealed this deal. If a police department is to reduce crime, it can't rely on the rules. If the cops are to reduce crime, they have to think. If cops are to count, they have to figure out how to eliminate particular crimes by eliminating particular criminals—criminal, by criminal, by criminal. Bratton's commitment to the specific purpose of reducing crime cannot be achieved within the framework of bureaucratic rules. Achieving any public purpose requires active leadership throughout the organization.

The philosophical idea underlying CompStat—the focus on achieving specific results—is its biggest innovation. This leadership commitment to a specific purpose, not the operational components, is CompStat's most significant contribution to principles and practices of performance leadership.

Jack Maple Comes to Baltimore

In 2000, when Martin O'Malley became mayor of Baltimore, the city had multiple problems. One was crime. Baltimore's violent-crime rate per 100,000 people was, 2,458—higher than for any of the 34 U.S. cities with a population over 500,000. Of these large cities, Baltimore's murder rate of 40 per 100,000 was lower than only two: Washington, D.C. and Detroit, both of which were often called the nation's "murder capital."[22]

In the fall of 1999, after O'Malley won the Democratic Party's nomination for mayor, he began to focus on how to govern the city. After all, a Republican last served as mayor in 1967. Thus, while O'Malley campaigned for mayor, he also asked Jack Maple to help him create CompStat.

Maple, however, had always thought that the CompStat strategy should be adopted by schools and hospitals, park and fire departments. He hoped for a future in which every agency providing "vital services has identified its primary objective and has established a way to measure progress toward that goal, . . . and a regular forum at which the agency's leaders question their subordinates in excruciating detail about their intelligence-gathering systems, their deployment, their tactics, and their follow-up."[23] After he and Bratton left NYPD in 1996, Maple consulted with a variety of police departments. Now, however, his client would be a mayor. This was Maple's chance.

So, as he drove around Baltimore with O'Malley, Maple pestered his client. Couldn't he use CompStat for housing? For parks? For streets? O'Malley wasn't so sure. Maple was, as always, persistent. As O'Malley recalled:

> Jack Maple insisted that everything could be 'Stat'ed' and everything could be measured. And we used to play this game where I would throw things at him and then he'd reel back and rattle off 14 performance measures for whether or not we're reaching at-risk children.[24]

In June 2000, within six months of taking office, Mayor O'Malley launched Citi-Stat—an effort to apply the CompStat leadership strategy to an entire government.

Purpose in Baltimore: Service Delivery

Bratton pledged to achieve a specific public service: to reduce crime. O'Malley also pledged to achieve a specific public purpose: to improve city services. O'Malley's purpose was not quite as focused as Bratton's. In any jurisdiction, the chief elected official has more problems and broader responsibilities than any agency director. Nevertheless, as O'Malley launched CitiStat his purpose was clear. He wanted to improve the lives of Baltimore's citizens, which meant—he decided—improving service delivery. This became the specific purpose of CitiStat.

In Baltimore in 2000, improving city services meant improving operations. Most city departments are what Wilson called "production organizations"; both their operations and outputs are observable.[25] And, in Baltimore, both its core operations and its basic outputs were inadequate. Poor services were not the sole source of the city's problems, but they certainly contributed. Moreover, operations were something that a new mayor might be able to affect directly.

Still, in focusing on outputs over outcomes, in emphasizing mundane service delivery rather than visionary public value, O'Malley was making a leadership choice. A different mayor might have chosen a different purpose (or none at all). He or she could have selected a more aspirational policy purpose such as improving the lives of citizens or making Baltimore a world-class city. But none of these people were elected. O'Malley was. Thus, in a democracy, the mayor was *authorized*—indeed, I would argue, *obligated*—to select a purpose for his administration to achieve. O'Malley chose to focus on getting city employees to do existing tasks more effectively, efficiently, and punctually, often saying that he wanted to move Baltimore "from spoils-based patronage politics to results-based performance politics."[26] O'Malley's choice of purpose is quite defensible.

As the mayor's team   particularly Michael Enright, first deputy mayor, and Matthew Gallagher, director of CitiStat—began to examine the workings of city government, they realized that many city services were plagued by serious operational problems. They didn't learn this from numbers or spreadsheets. Rather, O'Malley, Enright, and Gallagher learned this as they drove and walked around the city. Work wasn't getting done. And when it was done, it was done poorly. The data points were visual. O'Malley's leadership team could *see* them.

Indeed, as part of their preparation for the next agency biweekly session, the CitiStat staff would take pictures. Then, during the session, they would project onto the wall these "data"—these very current "data." An agency head couldn't get away with saying: "Oh, we fixed that problem last week."

Targets and Data: From 911 to 311

To achieve his purpose, O'Malley set a specific performance target for each service request. If a citizen complained about a dirty alley, it would be cleaned in 21 days. A rat-rubout request would receive a response within five days. Sewer water in a basement would get action in one day. To do this, however, Baltimore needed to track its data.

When Bratton set a specific target of cutting crime by 40 percent in three years, he already had a source of data. In 1968, New York had created the first 911 phone number for emergency calls, establishing a procedure for collecting data on reported crimes. And because NYPD had been reporting its crime data to the FBI every year, NYPD had the baseline data necessary to determine its progress.

Moreover, 911 comes with a big advantage: It is simple to remember. Everyone knows it. A little child knows it. When there is an emergency, people know exactly what to do: Call 911! Every year, some young child rescues a family member by calling 911.[27] Great.

But 911 also comes with a big disadvantage: it is a simple to remember. Everyone, even a little child, knows it. Consequently, when people want to talk with a city agency, they also call 911—even for a nonemergency. Why not? Everyone, even a little child, knows that 911 connects them to someone who can help.[28] Too many calls, however, tie up the 911 operators. Not great.

Thus, in 1996, the Baltimore Police Department established a 311 number for nonemergency calls to the police.[29] Then, in 1999, Chicago created the first 311 line for all city agencies. Since then, numerous cities have created 311 phone lines, which they advertise as "one call to city hall."[30] Call 311, and you can ask a question, request a service, or (if necessary) get connected to the right person in the right department. In 2001, when Michael Bloomberg campaigned for mayor of New York City, he complained that the phone book's blue-page listings of city-agency phone numbers ran on for 14 pages.[31] Once a city establishes its 311 line, explained David Eichenthal, who served as director of Chattanooga's Office of Performance Review, citizens no longer have to play the game of "blue-pages roulette."[32]

In Baltimore, when a citizen calls 311 with a problem—abandoned vehicle, rodent infestation, low water pressure—the operator enters the relevant information on a computer screen's template designed to contain all the data needed for that service.[33] Then the operator gives the citizen two pieces of information: (1) a service request number, so the citizen can log into the city's web site and check on the progress; and (2) a target date for completing the service. For some services, this "target resolution time" might be one or two days. For others it might be several weeks. For example, in 2013, the Bureau of Water and Wastewater told citizens that a request to repair a sewer overflow would be completed in one day, while a request to repair a surface (such as a sidewalk) would take 30 days.[34]

311 + CitiTrack = Commitment

The 311 operator sends each citizen's "service request"—an "SR" in CitiStat lingo—to Baltimore's CitiTrack database and to the relevant agency. An SR to fill a pothole goes to the city's Transportation Department; an SR to clear a downed tree goes to the Department of Recreation and Parks. And when the department has completed the SR—when it has filled the pothole or cleared the tree—it enters that into the CitiTrack database.

CitiTrack creates a record of when each such request is made and when the responsible city agency fulfills it. The combination of 311 plus CitiTrack provided data about the results that O'Malley (and subsequent mayors) sought to achieve. CitiTrack data reveal how well each city agency is doing in responding to citizens' 311 service requests compared with its target resolution times.

Moreover, citizens are able to check how well the city is doing against the mayor's commitments. A citizen can check to see how well the city is doing on the service requests he or she has made. And aggregate data are available on the Open Baltimore website.[35]

With 311, CitiTrack, and CitiStat, O'Malley was making a performance commitment—a specific, public, and quite visible service-delivery commitment: Baltimore would complete each SR by a specified time. (Elliot Schlanger, the city's chief information officer from 1999 through 2006, explained that if an agency meets its service-delivery target 80 percent of the time, this result was considered a success.)[36]

Because Baltimore is a typical frost-belt city, its streets have potholes—lots of potholes. Thus, the iconic example of O'Malley's service-delivery commitment became the 48-hour pothole guarantee. If a citizen calls 311 to request that a pothole be filled, the 311 operator (after entering the relevant information) tells the citizen that the pothole would be filled within 48 hours.[37] That's commitment!

With CitiTrack data, a mayor can determine if an agency is fulfilling its service-delivery commitments. Is the city making good on its 48-hour pothole guarantee and other target resolution times? "We can make that claim because we have the data to back it up," said Schlanger. "It's not acceptable for a constituent to call and ask when a pothole will be fixed and we say, 'When we get to it.'"[38]

Indeed, once the mayor made his commitment public (after, of course, consulting with the head of transportation), it became a significant commitment. The mayor had announced his commitment—his personal commitment. He was stuck. So were his successors. What would you do if you were the next mayor? Announce your 72-hour pothole guarantee?

In January 2007, when Sheila Dixon was inaugurated as O'Malley's successor, she declared, "I will tackle the smallest pothole."[39] In 2010, when a plague of potholes hit the streets of Baltimore, Richard Hooper, the chief of the city's transportation maintenance division, urged citizens to call 311 to report potholes. Hooper, known as the city's "King of Potholes," made it clear that he and his pothole crews intended to fulfill the 48-hour "guarantee."[40]

The War on Potholes

"Top city gripes: Potholes, dirty streets and noise." That's how the *New York Post* announced a 2005 survey of neighborhood and community leaders conducted by

"Citizens for NYC," a nonprofit that supports neighborhood efforts to improve the city's quality of life. In Queens and Staten Island, the top complaint was potholes; in Brooklyn, potholes ranked second. Citywide, the top problem was potholes. "Violent crime barely caused a ripple," reported the *Post*. "It ranked 20th overall on the list of the worst problems."[41] In 2006, violent crime dropped to 24th, behind lack of parking (4th) and noisy neighbors (12th). Somewhere, Jack Maple was smiling.

Yet some people have complained: Why is Baltimore fixated on fixing potholes? Why is a mayor devoting so much time and money to potholes? Filling a pothole is simply an input to a city's transportation services. The number of potholes repaired within 48 hours, they argue, is a silly measure. It contains no information about the quality of the streets or transportation services provided for those without a car.

Mayors, these people argue, should focus on improving the city's entire transportation system. And, if streets are an essential component of that system, a mayor should concentrate on measuring and improving traffic flow. At least, a mayor ought to measure the smoothness of the streets not the number of potholes filled. In fact, why doesn't some innovative mayor figure out how to construct streets so that they never have potholes? Or, if potholes are a problem, why doesn't a mayor develop a better way to fill potholes?[42]

Unfortunately, since the invention of asphalt, potholes have plagued humanity. We humans can land on the moon and clone sheep. Every winter, however, potholes defeat us. These urban terrorists hide under the street. We know they are somewhere. But where? And when will they attack?

In 2009, from March 11 through April 11, Washington, D.C., held its first "Potholepalooza" during which it filled 6,084. In 2010, from March 5 through April 5, the District's Potholepalooza filled 7,609 potholes.

Every year, Honolulu patches over 60,000 potholes. "I am pleased to report that after less than three months in office," announced Mayor Mufi Hannemann in March, 2005, "we are making significant progress in our war on potholes."[43] A war on potholes? In Honolulu? How often does it freeze there?

Until science figures out a way to eliminate potholes, mayors will have to deal with them. After all, citizens—a.k.a. voters—care about potholes. Citizens want potholes fixed—and fast. Actually, in Baltimore, when citizens called in an SR for a pothole, they sometimes expected more. CitiStat's Gallagher reported:

> In some instances, these follow-ups have identified customer expectations that exceed the City's service capabilities. For example, follow-up

on pothole complaints has often found that, although the Department of Transportation crews filled the potholes, some customers surveyed wanted entire streets resurfaced.[44]

What's a mayor to do?

The Basic-Services Imperative

City government is in the service-delivery business. It provides police, fire, library, education, transportation, and trash-collection services. Citizens judge a mayor not by parsing policy-initiative nuances, but observing whether or not these basic services get delivered. When Senator Barack Obama ran for president, he noted:

> The mayors have some of the toughest jobs in the country, because that's where the rubber hits the road. We yak in the Senate. They actually have to fill potholes and trim trees and make sure the garbage is taken away.[45]

Citizens may not be able to judge the president's macroeconomic policy, but they can certainly tell whether their mayor is filling the potholes, trimming the trees, and trucking off the garbage.

And plowing the snow. The failure to clear the streets after a snow storm can lead to early retirement.[46] Just ask Chicago's ex-mayor Michael A. Bilandic, Madison's ex-mayor Joe Sensenbrenner, or Seattle's ex-mayor Greg Nickels. Even if you are a governor, don't take a vacation during a snow storm; just ask Connecticut's ex-governor Thomas Meskill. Few incumbents can get away with the line attributed to Jasper McLevy: "God put the snow there; let him take it away." Actually, McLevy never said it, which may help explain why this socialist served as mayor of Bridgeport, Connecticut from 1933 to 1957—12 terms.

"You can see snow." Boston's mayor Thomas Menino offered a theory about snow: "It's not like an issue of substance," he said. "Snow is visible." Moreover, the mayor noted, "you can see when a car can't get up the street."[47]

The same goes for potholes not filled, trees not trimmed, and garbage not taken away. A mayor's failures are very visible. Takoma Park, Maryland and Santa Cruz, California have declared that they are "nuclear free zones." But if a mayor can't fill the potholes, trim the trees, and truck off the garbage, his or her nuclear-weapons policy will be irrelevant at the polls.

Mayors deliver dozens of services.[48] If citizens become sufficiently unhappy with these services, some—perhaps many—will vote with their feet. Thus, to improve life in Baltimore, O'Malley concluded, he had to improve service delivery.

About which specific services do citizens really care? This is another advantage of 311 plus CitiTrack. Citizen calls to 311 reveal which problems most trouble them. If they call, they care. If they don't call, they don't care (at least, not as much). And, if citizens believe that their service request will be acted on, they are even more likely to call it in. Using 311 plus CitiTrack, a mayor can learn what services the city needs to deliver.

Indeed, providing core services is a public executive's first test. When confronted with Hurricane Katrina, the U.S. Federal Emergency Management Agency failed to demonstrate managerial competence. And its attempts to cope with the aftermath weren't much better. Both during and after Katrina, FEMA could not fulfill its basic-service imperative. That's one reason why, in 2010, FEMA's new leadership team launched FEMAStat.

Graffiti Removal in Baltimore

Graffiti is the scourge of cities. To some it is "art"; to others, however, it is vandalism. Except for the "artists," most citizens—particularly those on whose buildings and neighborhoods this "art" is inflicted—hate graffiti. Citizens associate graffiti with gangs and gang violence;[49] graffiti conveys the impression that no one cares about the community's safety.[50]

Thus, mayors also hate graffiti. This includes not just O'Malley but also his two successors: Dixon and Stephanie Rawlings-Blake, who followed her. Along with potholes and snow removal, graffiti is one of the most visible symbols of a city's competence. A mayor's inability to fill potholes, plow snow, and remove graffiti suggests to voters and visitors that the mayor cannot get the basics right. And if the mayor can't produce these technically straightforward outputs, how can he or she foster more complicated social outcomes?

Moreover, the challenge isn't just getting rid of the graffiti. It's getting rid of the graffiti *fast*. "Removing graffiti rapidly," argued a U.S. Justice Department report, reduces the "time graffiti is visible, thus thwarting offenders' objective of having graffiti be widely seen."[51]

In Baltimore, when a citizen calls 311 to request that some graffiti be removed, he or she is told that it will be "abated" within three days. This, however, did not always happen. In 2008, the city's Department of Public Works was closing only two-thirds of these SRs within three days and, on average, was taking nearly three-and-a-half days.

In January 2009, Steve Sharkey moved four miles east from Baltimore's City Hall, where he was a CitiStat analyst, to Public Works's Kane Street Yard to become chief of its Special Services Division. Sharkey's daily commute changed, and the nature of his job changed even more. He was no longer the analyst seeking to identify performance deficits and suggest ways to eliminate or mitigate them. Now, he had both the *analytical task* of identifying his division's performance deficits and developing the effective operational responses, and the *operational task* of making those strategies work.

The Special Services Division provided city residents and visitors with over a dozen different services. It cleaned dirty alleys and dirty streets, plus Baltimore's Inner Harbor. Sharkey's division also "abated" the city's graffiti.

Public Works had a Collections Division, which picked up the city's trash. Then, six months after Sharkey moved to Special Services, responsibility for recycling shifted from his division to Collections. Still, these two divisions shared staff—workers who, after a little training, could perform another of Public Works's many tasks. Indeed, the Department had given most of these workers enough cross-training so that they could do many of its tasks. For example, after a one-day training session, a worker would know how to clean dirty alleys; and there wasn't much ambiguity about when the alley had been cleaned.

Graffiti abatement, however, was more complicated. It wasn't enough to obliterate the graffiti. The crew had to convert the public eyesore into something presentable. This required discretion: If the graffiti were painted on brick, the crew needed to sandblast it off. Yes, most of the department's workers could obliterate the graffiti (and thus the graffiti "artist's" tag); but citizens might think what remained was just as annoying. One worker simply painted over all cases of graffiti in red.

Sharkey concluded that he needed continuity. He needed crews who would exercise some intelligent judgment each time they cleaned up a different case of graffiti. He needed crews that would choose the most effective "abatement" approach—sandblasting the brick; painting over concrete with the closest matching color, using chemicals to remove paint from many types of metals. He needed crews who (without spending days returning a wall to its pristine, pre-graffiti condition) would leave it looking significantly better. Yet, with budget cuts, the workers scheduled for graffiti duty were frequently shifted to recycling.

So Sharkey set out to create dedicated graffiti-abatement crews with the skills and outlook to produce the desired results. This required him to learn who performed well and who didn't. He tracked the crews' performance—using data as well as his own observations. "Every two weeks I was looking at the data to guide me," he recalled. He also had to learn the operations side, so that he could "look deeper into the numbers."

As a result, Sharkey made a number of operational changes. He reduced the number of two-person graffiti crews from eight to four, selecting the four that had proven capable of doing the work. He also ensured that all four crews dedicated to graffiti had pressure washers; thus when they discovered a case of graffiti that required pressure washing, they didn't have to pick up a pressure washer the next morning and return to finish the prior day's job. Using CitiTrack data, Sharkey focused each crew's daily assignments on a smaller area so it didn't have to travel as far between tasks. Most importantly, he identified the workers he could "trust" to do the job intelligently and assigned them to a graffiti crew full time. This approach created stability, ensuring that these workers always knew what their job would be. "Crew morale went up," noted Sharkey, and "crew quality went up."

Indeed, by the second half of 2009, crew performance was clearly up. Table 5-1 compares performance during a two-year-plus period before mid-summer 2009 with performance during another two-year-plus period afterward:[52]

Period 1: 31 months, January 2007 through July 2009
Period 2: 33 months, August 2009 through April 2012

During the first, 31-month period, the Graffiti-Abatement Teams were missing their targets:

1. The average time to close 311 SRs was well over three days;
2. In only five months (of the 31) did they close 80 percent or more of the 311 SRs within three days;
3. In a total of nine months, they closed 60 percent or less of the 311 SRs within three days; and
4. There were 18 months (or more than half of the 31 months) during which the average time to close the 311 SRs was greater than three days.

During the second, 33-month period, the Graffiti-Abatement Teams improved significantly:

1. The average time to close 311 SRs was consistently below two-and-a-half days;
2. In 12 months (of the 33), they closed 80 percent or more of the 311 SRs within three days;
3. In only three months did they close 60 percent or less of the 311 SRs within three days; and
4. There was only one month during which the average time to close the 311 SRs was greater than three days.

TABLE 5-1. Performance on Abating Graffiti 311 Service Requests, 2007 to Early 2012

			Number of months during which the ...		
			percent of 311 SRs closed within 3 days was greater than 80	*percent of 311 SRs closed within 3 days was less than 60*	*average time to close 311 SRs was greater than 3 days*
Year	*Total 311 SRs*	*Average days to close 311 SRs*	*For these months performance is good*	*For these months performance is not so good*	
2007	6,446	3.2	5	2	6
2008	6,647	3.4	0	3	6
2009 (Jan–Jul)	3,924	3.8	0	4	6
2009 (Aug–Dec)	1,764	2.3	2	0	0
2010	4,166	2.1	5	1	0
2011	8,601	2.3	4	2	1
2012 (Jan–Apr)	2,066	2.1	1	0	0

Source: Baltimore CitiStat Office.

In any organization, improving performance requires two organizational competences: the *analytical capacity* to identify performance deficits and to suggest how these performance deficits can be eliminated or mitigated, and the *operational capacity* to make it happen—both to figure out how to make it happen and to motivate the people who will make it happen. Putting these two essential competences together in the same organization—and also in each of its subunits—is a leadership challenge.

Martin O'Malley Had It Easy

Cities are operational governments. They deliver direct services to citizens, who can easily observe these services, determine whether they have been delivered (or not), and thus evaluate performance. Every day, citizens get "data" on crime, potholes, and graffiti. They do not use a spread sheet. They use their eyes.

Not only are most city agencies what Wilson called "production organizations," they also carry out what Christopher Pollitt of Katholieke Universiteit

Leuven in Belgium called "production" tasks. Wilson focused on types of *organizations*.[53] Pollitt distinguished two types of *tasks*: "a 'production' task such as the issuing of driving licenses is standardizable, predictable, and measurable in ways that a 'coping' task such as mental health counseling is not."[54]

For a production organization that produces visible outputs, both executives and citizens have an easier time evaluating performance. In addition to measuring outputs, the agency's leadership team can observe the organization's operations. Thus the leadership team can more easily identify its performance deficits. Anthony Downs of the Brookings Institution wrote: "The easier it is to define a bureau's social functions clearly or to perceive its degree of success, the more the bureau is likely to receive fast feedback pressures to conform to specific conceptions of 'desired' performance."[55] Once the leadership team has identified a performance deficit in production, it can focus on eliminating (or mitigating) it.

To this natural advantage that production organizations have for improving their results, O'Malley added one more: 311 and CitiTrack, which converted the natural visibility and observability of city services into very explicit and very current data that provided unambiguous measures of performance.

Thus, like Bratton, O'Malley also had it easy. As a mayor, he was in charge of a production government with the responsibility for a variety of production tasks for which the desired performance was not open to much ideological debate. Moreover, the resulting outputs were visible and observable, making it easy to collect relevant and current data.

Yes, O'Malley never had it "*easy*." But, compared with the challenge of creating a PerformanceStat strategy for an organization with coping tasks, he certainly had it "*easier*." Compared with other public executives, he was lucky. Unlike many other public executives, however, he both recognized and exploited this luck.

Luck is recognizing it. Every police commissioner is lucky in some way. So is every mayor. So is every public executive. But do they recognize their luck—and then act on it?

Thinking Seriously about Purpose and Performance Deficits

Compared with CitiStat, creating a results-producing FEMAStat was more challenging. "FEMA's mission is to support our citizens and first responders to ensure that as a nation we work together to build, sustain, and improve our capability to prepare for, protect against, respond to, recover from, and mitigate all hazards."[56] After a disaster, many emergency services are provided by state and local governments and nonprofit organizations. FEMA directly provides some, but certainly not all.

FEMA has both production responsibilities and coping responsibilities, including coping with the inadequacies of state, local, nonprofit, and volunteer organizations. It can only *help* these first, second, and third responders. It can't easily convert its mission into daily production tasks for which it can collect operational data.

Still, FEMA has an important purpose. And, like any organization, it has performance deficits to identify and fix. FEMA's leadership team may have to think harder than Bratton's or O'Malley's. Still, every leadership team that launches its own PerformanceStat has to think carefully and analytically about its specific purpose. Only then can the team identify the performance deficits that it needs to eliminate to help achieve that purpose.

To realize the potential of PerformanceStat, a leadership team needs to start with purpose, which it can then use to identify performance deficits and set targets.

6

Establishing Responsibilities
Plus Discretion

What organizational subunits led by what individuals should be delegated the responsibility and discretion for accomplishing what results by when?

Leadership is irresponsible when it fails to set goals and therefore lets the institution drift.
PHILIP SELZNICK, organizational theorist[1]

Discretion vitalizes agencies, infusing them with energy, direction,
mobility, and the capacity for change.
PETER SCHUCK, Yale Law School[2]

In 2007, Lisa Nuñez retired as the chief deputy director of the Los Angeles County Department of Public Social Services, and Sheryl Spiller succeeded her. Inevitably, a major change within a leadership team brings other changes. And Spiller made one consequential change: who was primarily responsible for the department's performance.

For the Bureau of Workforce Services, Nuñez had placed the operational responsibility with its four division directors. Each director oversaw the work of five to ten local offices that provided temporary financial assistance and employment services. Thus, at the DPSSTATS meeting, the four division directors did the reporting. Nuñez wanted each division director to know what was going on in all of his or her division's offices and to be able to answer questions about what was happening in each of them.

The directors of the local offices were also at the meeting and able to answer in more detail. Nevertheless, through her conduct of the DPSSTATS meetings, Nuñez made it clear who was responsible for operational results: the division directors.[3]

When Spiller replaced Nuñez, she made a conscious decision: She moved responsibility down to the local offices. Now the director of each local office would be responsible for answering questions about his or her performance. The four division directors would still be in the DPSSTATS room, but a question would be directed to one of them only if it concerned an issue common to two or more of the division's offices.

Obviously, under Nuñez, the director of each local office had still been responsible for the results produced by his or her office. Similarly, under Spiller, each division director was still responsible for the results produced by his or her division. But the primary locus of responsibility was different. Under Spiller, a local office director would feel more personally responsible; he or she would have to come to the DPSSTATS meetings prepared to answer a wide variety of questions. After all, a local office director would expect that Spiller would be much more likely than Nuñez had been to ask him or her a direct question. And thus a local office director would have a better chance of being able to shine by providing a cogent explanation about what the local office was doing to fix a performance deficit. Conversely, a local office director would also have a better chance of being embarrassed by having no idea that the office had a problem let alone what to do about it.

Choosing Who Will Be Responsible

Who is responsible—and for *what?* The locus of primary responsibility can be set at different levels. In the New York City Police Department, the responsible levels were the boroughs and their precincts. Thus, the responsible persons were the borough and precinct commanders.

In an organization with geographic subunits—boroughs and precincts; divisions and offices—it may be obvious who is responsible for what. Still, as an organization seeks to improve performance, it may not necessarily be at all obvious *who* should be responsible for *what.* Thus, when an organization creates its own PerformanceStat, one of the key choices is: Who will get the initial questions? Who will stand at the podium first? In making this decision, the leadership team decides (if only implicitly) who is responsible for what results.

No one in the PerformanceStat room is off the hook. The members of the leadership team can ask anyone a question. They can invite anyone to the podium. Still, by selecting who will be asked the first question, the leadership team has dramatized who has the primary responsibility.

At what level of the organization should the primary locus of responsibility—and thus discretion—be placed? There is no universally correct answer. Every choice has its pluses and its minuses. The answer depends on a leadership judgment: Who needs to focus *most* on improving its performance? If the divisions are taking their responsibility for performance seriously, but they can't get office directors to pay attention to performance—to make operational improvements that produce better results—it may make sense to move the locus of responsibility down to the office level. Conversely, if the division directors (and their small staffs) are disengaged from the task of producing results—if all they ever say is: "If you gave me better local-office directors, my division would perform better"— then it may make sense to move the responsibility up to the division level.

Like many PerformanceStat design decisions, where to locate primary responsibility is a judgment call. It all depends on a variety of factors—from the availability of effective managers at different levels, to the nature and location of the key performance deficits that need to be fixed. Different people—drawing on their professional experiences—will make these judgments differently

Thus, Nuñez and Spiller could *both* have made very intelligent decisions. Nuñez could have decided to focus first on the division directors because (perhaps) she could not obtain the cooperation of the office directors until their direct supervisors were fully engaged. Then, when Nuñez retired, Spiller could have discovered (perhaps) that the division directors were indeed actively and creatively engaged; thus she could have decided that it was time to move the level of responsibility to the local offices. Indeed, if Nuñez had remained as chief deputy director, she might have decided to do exactly what Spiller did. Conversely, if Spiller had been the chief deputy director at the beginning of DPSSTATS, she might have made the same decision that Nuñez did.

Bureaucracy, Bureaucracy

In attempting to improve performance, the leadership team of a public agency or government jurisdiction faces a variety of obstacles. Many can be summarized in a single word: "bureaucracy."[4]

On this planet, the government of every jurisdiction is a prototypical bureaucracy. Almost everyone employed in government is a "bureaucrat."[5] Public agencies possess all the characteristics that have been ascribed to bureaucracies by the savants: Max Weber, the German sociologist; Anthony Downs; and James Q. Wilson:[6] They have a fixed jurisdiction of responsibility, carry out specific tasks as prescribed by rules and procedures, are divided and subdivided into distinct units that are assigned one or more of these tasks, are staffed by permanent employees who are specialized experts in particular tasks (and/or in the rules that govern these tasks), are hierarchically controlled,[7] and create and rely on voluminous paper trails. Weber argued that a "bureaucratic organization" possesses a "technical superiority" that came from its "precision, speed,[8] unambiguity, knowledge of the files, continuity, discretion, unity, strict subordination, reduction of friction and of material and personal costs."[9] As Weber explained it, "Bureaucracy is like a modern judge who is a vending machine into which the pleadings are inserted together with the fee and which then disgorges the judgement together with its reasons mechanically derived from the code."[10] All very impersonal.

Indeed, public bureaucracies are (or are supposed to be) impersonal. "In an ideal-type bureaucracy," observed Johan Olsen of the University of Oslo, "bureaucrats are responsible for following the rules."[11] Thus, we all get our trash picked up in the precisely the same way; no one gets any favoritism. It makes no difference which crew is picking up our trash; if it is a different crew this week, it will still follow the same standard operating procedures.

This is the bureaucratic ideal. Eliminate discretion. Figure out "the one best way," and then have everyone implement it.[12] The one best way is designed for the average situation, and, unfortunately, the actual situation is rarely identical to the average situation. Reality intervenes. If anything real is to be accomplished, discretion is inevitable. There never is—never was, and never can be—a universal, "one best way." Still, government's bureaucracies seek to squelch discretion.

To an elected chief executive who seeks to accomplish specific purposes, the bureaucracy's impersonal rules can be a royal pain. They diffuse responsibility. Bureaucracies are not only impersonal in how they follow the rules. They are also impersonal in how they assign responsibility. If everyone follows the rules, no human is responsible. The rules are.

Theoretically, the purpose of the bureaucratic hierarchy is to establish clear lines of responsibility. But the operational consequences are quite different. Sure, a front-line worker was the person who actually took the action. But this individual was only following the explicit or implicit orders of a front-line supervisor, who was only implementing the explicit or implicit rules promulgated by the staff of an oversight agency, who were only fulfilling the provisions of an explicit or ambiguous law enacted by legislators, who were responding to often-conflicting demands from stakeholders. Who is responsible, indeed?

Establishing Responsibility

For any public executive, an inability to establish responsibility for any specific performance deficit is frustrating. Urban citizens have a large number of prosaic expectations: They want recreation buildings heated in the winter and cooled in the summer. They want street drains unclogged and overflow water out of their basement. They expect that city government can perform these routine tasks with Weber's "speed" and "precision." And when government does not, citizens do not reflect on the social-psychological complexities of organizational behavior, on the rules imposed by oversight bureaucrats, or on the political intrigues behind the compromises that allocated the city's limited budget.

A mayor also has expectations. A mayor expects that city employees will read the water meters accurately and send out the proper bills to the proper addresses promptly. A mayor expects that city employees will do these tasks with speed and precision. When city government fails to do a task either with speed or with precision, a mayor will try to determine *who* did not do *what*.

Unfortunately, a mayor will discover that, in the city's bureaucracy, no individual is responsible for any specific result. The organization itself is supposed to be responsible, but not any individual. But given that an organization can't take responsibility—only people can—the concept of "organizational responsibility" is ludicrous and, for a mayor, not useful. Yet, compared with other public executives, mayors (and police commissioners) have it "*easier.*"

To an elected chief executive, the challenge of establishing responsibility becomes more complicated when the output to be produced or the outcome to be achieved does not fit into an existing bureaucratic slot—when it cannot be addressed by existing or new rules or by tasks assigned to a distinct subunit. When Martin O'Malley became mayor of Baltimore, childhood lead poisoning was one such problem. Reported the *Washington Post:* "He gets mad: 'It's a sin how many little children in this city have lead poisoning,' he says furiously. 'And can you believe that the health commissioner and the housing inspector weren't even sharing information on this?'"[13] When a problem can only be addressed when two bureaucratic units cooperate and coordinate, who is responsible?

If the members of the leadership team of any organization want to establish responsibility for particular results, they need to find a way to establish *personal* responsibility. They need to get specific individuals to accept responsibility for specific results.

Focusing Responsibility

Social psychologists—particularly Bibb Latané of the University of North Carolina and John Darley of Princeton University—have concluded that a "diffusion of responsibility" can permit (even encourage) people to avoid taking action to resolve a problem. If an individual believes that many others are available to help, he or she is less likely to bother.[14] Indeed, observed Latané and two of his colleagues, "when many hands are available, people actually work less hard than they ought to."[15]

In a large public agency, responsibility is very diffused. For most results to be produced, no one individual does all the work. Each result is produced by a variety of individuals, each of whom makes a small but necessary contribution. Thus, the agency's leadership team cannot easily separate out the value of each individual's contribution to determine who is contributing and who is not.[16]

Furthermore, these individuals may not understand the value or necessity of their contribution. Consequently, to create responsibility, the leadership team needs to establish the importance of each contribution and to assign that contribution to a specific individual or to a specific team.

Moreover, large organizations provide any individual with an always-relevant excuse: "I couldn't do what I was assigned to do, because [someone: you fill in a name] failed to do [something: you fill in a task]." Large organizations provide multiple opportunities for individuals to shed responsibility by pointing a finger at someone else.

It might help to point a finger at a specific person who failed to do a specific, requisite task. But often that isn't necessary. The excuse-maker may simply have to observe that he or she lacked some particular resource that, as everyone recognizes, is required to complete the task. In fact, an all-purpose, all-circumstance bureaucratic excuse is: "If I had the resources, I would get it done."

Taking responsibility is not a natural act. And taking responsibility in a public forum is perverse. One governor told his department heads: "Never put a number and a date in the same sentence."[17] Moreover, organizational norms send signals: Taking responsibility is a bad idea for you individually—and a bad idea for all of us collectively. In many organizations, the social cues that people receive suggest that taking responsibility is antisocial.

In Baltimore, O'Malley wanted city agencies and employees to deliver basic services with speed and precision—and with a concern for the individual citizen's needs. Thus, he needed a way to focus responsibility for each service on the appropriate agency, on the manager and managerial team of that agency, and on the agency's employees. But can a chief executive do this in a large, public, bureaucratic organization?

PerformanceStat—with its targets, its data, its meetings, and its follow-up—is one way to focus responsibility.

Bureaucratic Continuity

Still, establishing responsibility in a bureaucracy is inherently difficult. As Weber also observed, "once it is fully established, bureaucracy is among those social structures which are the hardest to destroy."[18] One of Downs's principles of bureaucracy is "The Law of Diminishing Control: The larger any organization becomes, the weaker is the control over its actions exercised by those at the top."[19]

The bureaucrats use several euphemisms to distinguish their own permanence from the transience of political officials. Every "We-Be" understands both the political truth and the operational implications of those four letters: "*We be* here before you're here. *We be* here after you're here."[20] Others use the words "residents" and "tourists." The bureaucrats are "residents"; the elected officials and their political appointees are "tourists." The tourists need to be tolerated but not taken seriously.

The plethora of formal rules reinforce this continuity. They ensure that no matter who is making a decision or implementing a procedure, it is done the same way. The bureaucratic residents are (so scientific management would have you believe) all interchangeable parts. They will all follow the same rules (in presumably the same way). Sociologist Robert Merton called this the "norm of impersonality."[21]

This rule-driven "continuity" of an impersonal bureaucracy has some obvious advantages. If obeyed, it ensures that all citizens are treated the same. When you enter a government office, it doesn't make any difference what line you get in or, when you get to the front of the line, who provides the service you request. This bureaucrat will apply the appropriate rule. It's simple fairness. When the bureaucrats follow the rules, they ensure that government is treating all citizens consistently and thus (by definition) fairly.[22]

Indeed, following the rules—faithfully and impersonally—is itself a value. In the absence of an external market for government's services, the rules define what it means to do a good job.[23] The degree to which these rules are followed is the measure of both value and success.[24] Results are irrelevant. Outputs or outcomes are disconnected from the work. In a bureaucracy, an appropriately applied rule *is* the desired result.

Thus, public executives need to convince those who manage and work in their bureaucracies that results—outputs (if not outcomes)—are more important that the rules.

Bureaucratic Cultures and Clans

Bureaucracy is not the only barrier to improving performance. Every public agency also has its own organizational culture: a set of fundamental, shared assumptions that—people have learned through experience—help solve their individual and collective problems.[25] These assumptions are taught to new employees so they will know how to think and act in future situations.[26] Anne Khademian of Virginia Tech describes culture as "the informal, the symbolic, the subtle yet nevertheless critical factors that drive the way the job gets done"[27]— and, I might add, what jobs get done and what ones don't.

In government, different units will have confronted and solved different problems and thus will have evolved different cultures. Consequently, the leadership team of an organization, as well as the managers of any subunit, will find that the directives and incentives they employ to affect behavior must compete for influence with the shared assumptions of the subunit's culture.

William Ouchi of the University of California at Los Angeles labeled an organization with a culture strong enough to have a direct impact on the thinking of its members—and thus an indirect impact on their behavior—a "clan."[28] Many large public bureaucracies develop a very strong culture—with their own internal (and competing) control mechanisms—and thus become such a clan. A social service agency can become its own clan. A fire department can become its own clan.[29] Each clan has its own culture with its own shared assumptions and implicit norms about the kinds of behaviors that are acceptable or not.

A "clan" can exercise remarkable control over the behavior of its members. A clan develops a "social agreement on a broad range of values and beliefs" and "relies heavily on ritualized, ceremonial forms of control," observed Ouchi, "which by their nature are subtle and are ordinarily not visible to the inexperienced eye."[30] Yet these methods of control reflect, he continued, "a relatively complete socialization process which effectively eliminates goal incongruence between individuals."[31] Among individual members of the clan, that is. There can still remain significant incompatibility between the goals of an organization's leadership team and the goals of the members of a subunit clan.

Changing the Psychological Contract

In any organization, wrote Denise Rousseau of Carnegie Mellon University, the employees can perceive that they have a "psychological contract" with their employer.[32] Rousseau defines such a "contract" as the "beliefs individuals hold about the exchange relationship between themselves and an employer, in essence, what people understand the employment relationship to mean."[33] Thus, rewriting the psychological contract can be perceived by employees as altering or even violating what Alvin Gouldner of Washington University labeled the "norm of reciprocity."[34] Indeed, Rousseau observed, once a psychological contract is established, it can "resist revision except when circumstances signal the need to revise an old schema or create a new one."[35] Still, people may not agree that current "circum-stances" are producing an unambiguous "signal" that warns of an obvious "need" for change. With differing interpretations of the circumstances, some may accept the need to revise the psychological contract, while others may aggressively resist.

Ouchi notes that "in a bureaucratic control system, the norm of reciprocity is reflected in the notion of 'an honest day's work for an honest day's pay,' and it particularly contains the idea that in exchange for pay, an employee gives up autonomy in certain areas."[36] Of Baltimore, Michael Enright made a similar observation: "This is a very-blue-collar, an-honest-day's-work-for-an-honest-day's-pay type of administration."

Yet, as these descriptions of the employer-employee contract suggest, a num-ber of issues remain open to differing interpretations: What is "an honest day's pay"? What is "an honest day's work"? The employee and the employer may have quite different views about how much "honesty" in a day's work is required by what level of "honesty" in the day's pay. Moreover, how much autonomy needs to be surrendered for that pay? Under some circumstances—particularly when the outputs of the job are well specified and can be easily observed and evaluated—the employer may not ask the employee to surrender much autonomy in *how* the job is done. Nevertheless, the employer will expect that the employee will have very little autonomy to devote time to non-job-related activities.

Focusing Responsibility (continued)

When William Bratton and Jack Maple created CompStat, they focused respon-sibility on NYPD's geographic subunits. The department is divided into eight "patrol boroughs," which are further subdivided into a total of 76 precincts. Polit-ically, New York City has five boroughs: Manhattan, Brooklyn (Kings), Queens, the Bronx, and Staten Island (Richmond). But the Police Department (like many other city departments) has organized itself into eight patrol boroughs by divid-ing the three biggest boroughs (Manhattan, Brooklyn, and Queens) into two "patrol boroughs" each (for example, Queens North and Queens South). A bor-ough commander was responsible for his or her borough. A precinct commander was responsible for his or her precinct. Bratton "decided to focus accountability and authority at the precinct commander level." NYPD "pushed responsibility and accountability down," he wrote, "to the precinct commander level, so that we really had 76 miniature police departments."[37]

Even with these geographic subdivisions, establishing responsibility was not easy. It required bringing the previously independent units within each precinct under the precinct commander's authority. In addition to geographic patrol units, to which patrol officers were assigned, NYPD had a variety of functional units: Detectives, Narcotics, Robbery, Warrant. Officers from each of these units worked out of a precinct; they did not, however, report to the precinct commander. They operated independently.[38] As Maple was wont to say:

> The biggest lie in law enforcement is: "We work very closely together." And of course it's never a fainthearted lie. It's never just "We work closely together." It's always "We work very closely together—very closely."[39]

You and I both suspect that this lie does not apply solely to law enforcement.

Bratton eliminated these bureaucratic fiefdoms. No longer would a precinct's narcotics squad or warrant squad operate independently from the precinct commander. Naturally, these squads found this change annoying. Not only had they lost their independence; they also were now part of a larger responsibility framework. No longer were they left alone to follow their own routines and priorities; now they had to work cooperatively with the rest of the precinct to help achieve its new performance targets. Bummer!

Responsibility for What?

"I set the macro-level goal of crime reduction and enhancing quality of life, but then let precinct commanding officers manage at the precinct or micro-level by determining how best to do this," explained Bratton. Thus, "precinct commanders could decide how many and how best to use beat officers. They were charged with developing problem-solving initiatives because precinct commanding officers had the experience and knowledge to solve complex crime issues."[40]

By setting the purpose of reducing crime, but not each precinct's strategy or tactics for doing so, Bratton created 76 crime-fighting experiments. Each precinct commander was responsible for solving "complex crime issues," by "developing problem-solving initiatives." Thus, Bratton reported, they "developed problem-solving tactics and deployed officers according to a strategy they developed specifically to work on problems in their precinct."[41]

For subunit managers to achieve any prescribed purpose, to produce a particular result, to attain a specific target, they need authority and resources. Thus, by focusing not on the rules but on the results, Bratton gave his precinct commanders not only the responsibility for achieving that purpose but also the necessary authority:

> I ensured that commanding officers were put in charge of their personnel and their assignments. They were given the authority to put together a co-ordinated and focused plan to attack crime in their precinct. They were

able to identify crime "hot spots" and assign necessary patrol officers, detectives, undercover and narcotics officers to these problems. I gave precinct commanding officers the authority and made them accountable.[42]

Maple, however, emphasized that a precinct commander was not responsible for the precinct's "crime." Rather, the precinct commander was responsible (a) for understanding the characteristics and patterns of the precinct's crime and (b) for having a strategy for dealing with that crime. "Nobody ever got in trouble because crime numbers on their watch went up," asserted Maple. "Trouble arose only if the commanders didn't know why the numbers were up or didn't have a plan to address the problems."[43]

In some ways, the approach taken by Bratton and Maple puts *more* responsibility on the precinct commander. Now, this manager is responsible:

—for understanding the data;
—for knowing what is causing changes in the data;
—for understanding the subunit's own unique problems (what its own, specific performance deficits are);
—for developing a strategy to deal with the problems and to eliminate or mitigate the performance deficits;
—for knowing whether this strategy is working; and
—for explaining all this to subordinates, peers, superiors, and the public.

Subunit managers may not be able to fully control their outcomes—for example, their levels of crime. But they can control their own analytic and strategic work.

It is silly to hold people responsible for things they cannot control. Many public managers cannot control their organization's outputs, let alone its outcomes. If, however, they have the necessary authority, discretion, and resources, they are capable of doing quite a lot. They can control the analytical task of identifying and understanding their performance deficits. They can control the problem-solving task of designing a strategy for eliminating or mitigating this performance deficit. And, they can implement this strategy and learn from it.

Any public manager who has the necessary discretion can be held responsible for intelligent analysis, problem solving, implementation, and learning.

Discretion, Experimentation, and Protection

For an organization to produce results, it needs discretion. When faced with a new feud between two gangs, a precinct commander needs discretion to prevent an outbreak of violence.[44] When confronted with an outbreak of potholes, a maintenance bureau director needs discretion to allocate maintenance crews to pothole duty while still covering other core tasks. *If public executives are unwilling to delegate discretion, they cannot hold subunits and their managers responsible for producing specific results.* Such discretion includes both the freedom and the authority to allocate resources—people, equipment, dollars—as well as the freedom and authority to experiment with new strategies.

To produce results in a new situation, the responsible manager may need only to reallocate some resources to match the particulars of the situation. Although these particulars may be different, the nature of the situation is recognizable. The organization can deal with it effectively, if—though this might be a big *if*—it has the freedom and authority to reassign people, reprogram equipment, and rebudget dollars. In such a situation, all this discretion is designed to permit the responsible manager to deploy established tactics in different (but recognizable) ways so as to achieve the leadership team's purpose.

In other situations, however, the particulars may be anomalous. Individually, the particulars might be quite familiar. Collectively, however, they have coalesced into something weird—into a situation no one has seen before. Thus, no one can produce the desired result simply by reallocating existing resources to implement established tactics. The novelty of the particulars demands a novel strategy. But what novel strategy? This is not obvious. The managers need discretion to experiment.

Experimentation is, however, dangerous. The first experiment might fizzle out. The second might also collapse. Such failures put the organization and its managers in jeopardy. If the experiments don't work, the desired results will not be achieved. This might merely inconvenience citizens. Or the harm might be serious. In addition, the reputation of the experimenting unit (and, perhaps, the entire organization) could be dimished. This can hinder its ability to attract resources—adequate funding, quality people, continued discretion—and thus its ability to produce future results. A screwed-up experiment can hurt long-run performance in many ways.

Still, if the subunit relies on established rules that were not designed for the novel situation, it faces the same danger. If it follows the official prescriptions, citizens could be inconvenienced or harmed. The reputation of the organization could be just as hurt. Failing to exercise discretion—thus being labeled as a stupid or incompetent bureaucracy—can be just as dangerous as exercising the discretion necessary to experiment with a strategy that might or might not produce the desired results.

Of course, the manager and the entire organization could rely on a Nuremberg Defense, asserting that they were merely following the rules officially established by superiors. This might work legally; after all, nobody did anything illegal or immoral. But, it is less likely to work politically. A public agency that screws up publicly ends up with public blame.

Consequently, the mangers of a subunit charged with producing specific results need more than *discretion*. They also need *protection*—assurance that their intelligent and justifiable exercise of discretion will be supported publicly by superiors regardless of whether their judgment produced the intended results.

A true grant of discretion cannot be informal or secret. It has to be official and public. It has to come with the acknowledgment that the exercise of discretion is just that—the use of judgment in circumstances for which the best strategy is not obvious. This acknowledgment has to come with the expectation that, when the subunit manager chooses an approach that some vocal stakeholders claim has failed, superiors will provide explicit support: "The manager made a judgment call that didn't work out as planned, but there was never a guarantee that any strategy would work, and the manager's choice was creative, intelligent, and quite reasonable."

If this expectation of support does not exist, subunit managers will simply follow the most defensible rule. For these managers will have concluded they have no true discretion. And a manager with no discretion is a manager who can escape responsibility.

"The Fear of Discretion"

As Steven Kelman of Harvard's Kennedy School observed, the plethora of rules, procedures, and regulations in government "reflects a fear of granting discretion to public officials." The rules, he noted, are driven by "the fear of allowing public officials to use good sense and good judgment." Indeed, notes Kelman, "we fear discretion because we do not trust officials to live up to high standards of probity unless we keep a close eye on them."[45] In the United States, wrote Peter Schuck, "this fear is so chronic and pervasive that it constitutes a defining element of our political and legal cultures, accounting for much that is admirable—and much that is pathological—about American government."[46]

Kelman focused his analysis of "the fear of discretion" on the rules that constrain the decisions of procurement officials. Yet, this fear is common throughout government.[47] "In the modern era, we have grown suspicious of discretion," observed Kate Stith of Yale Law School in her analysis of federal judges' sentencing discretion. Indeed, she continued, "a central campaign of the modern age—extending far beyond sentencing and the criminal justice system—has been to reduce the discretion of government officials."[48]

"The federal Sentencing Guidelines," wrote Stith and José Cabranes, a circuit judge on the U.S. Court of Appeals, are an "attempt to repress the exercise of informed discretion by judges." Behind these "guidelines" (which are more than mere suggestions) is the presumption, they continued, that "the judge is supposed to perform an automaton's function by mechanically applying stark formulae set by a distant administrator."[49] Max Weber would have loved it.

In fact, concluded Stith and Cabranes, "the federal sentencing reforms of the 1980s sought to relocate authority from individual sentencing judges to a distant administrative tribunal of experts not influenced by the particulars of each case at hand."[50] Yet when sentencing criminals or improving performance, the particulars are important. Weber's computerized judge would need to know the particulars—all of the particulars.

These particulars make discretion inevitable. A set of rules do not—indeed, cannot—match each unique set of particulars to a single, unique rule. There cannot be a rule for every distinct combination of particulars (unless the number of rules is infinite). Yet, if no rule precisely matches a set of particulars, there will be several potential but not-quite-right rules from which to choose. None will be perfectly pertinent; each will be close yet somewhat off. Even in a world in which everyone agrees to base every decision on one set of rules, everyone will often have to exercise discretion in deciding which rule to employ.

To permit public executives to exercise discretion, however, a government has to solve the corruption problem. For, as Schuck observes, "discretion has its decidedly dark side." Although, he continues, "it is not the only form of bureaucratic power, it is surely the most troubling."[51] Yes, no government can ever eliminate corruption. Just look at today's headlines. Still, if government fails to create auditing systems to uncover, punish, and deter corruption, it can't allocate discretion. If it does, it has empowered the corrupt and tempted the corruptible.

In the United States, over roughly three decades (1890 through 1920), the progressive movement sought, among other objectives, to eliminate corruption. Reforms in civil service, procurement, and budgeting constrained the discretion that elected officials and their cronies used to hire relatives, give contracts to friends, and spend public funds for personal gain. The resulting growth of government rules was also intended to eliminate government waste and improve its efficiency.

Today, however, the situation is reversed. The rules restrain not just corruption but also efficiency and effectiveness. To many, the rules have become a source of waste and a cause of inefficiency. If we want results—if we want government to improve performance—we need to give public executives the ability to exercise intelligent, performance-enhancing discretion. To improve the performance of any public agency or governmental jurisdiction, the leadership team has to figure out how to control serious corruption while promoting performance-focused discretion.

The Performance Tradeoff:
Specific Results for Operational Discretion

The rules don't just prevent corruption. They also tell people what to do when. If a leadership team de-emphasizes the rules, isn't it giving up control?

Not if the leadership team gives each unit something very explicit to accomplish. Not if it establishes specific performance targets. Actually, without specific targets, the leadership cannot claim to have *produced* any results. Without first establishing targets, it is simply declaring that every random, apparently positive event is a victory.

At NYPD, found Barry Sugarman of the University of Massachusetts, this is what happened:

> For the new accountability [for results] that they [NYPD's senior executives] imposed on their middle managers to succeed, they had to give up much of their traditional overcentralized, ineffective attempts to micromanage the 76 precincts of NYC. They had to learn new roles, how to be demanding but helpful supervisors to the newly empowered middle managers (COs [precinct commanding officers]). But note that top executives created these new roles *for themselves* during the early phase of reform.[52]

Neil Carter, of the University of York, made the general point: "Performance indicators are an instrument for exercising central control over services while pursuing a policy of decentralization."[53]

Government agencies need "clear objectives and goals," argued Peter Drucker. Then, he continued, they "have to think through priorities of concentration which enable them to select targets; to set standards of accomplishment and performance . . . to set deadlines; to go to work on results; and to make someone accountable for results."[54] Concluded Drucker, "To have a chance at performance, a [government] program needs clear targets, the attainment of which can be measured, appraised, or at least judged."[55] As Philip Selznick wrote, "Leadership is irresponsible when it fails to set goals and therefore lets the institution drift."[56]

To decentralize authority, argued Dean Esserman, "we need to find leaders." Esserman has served as police chief for Stamford, Connecticut, and Providence, Rhode Island, and most recently for New Haven, Connecticut. Like many other police executives, he was influenced by Bratton, serving as general counsel for the New York Transit Police when Bratton was its chief.

Unfortunately, Esserman's effort to "find leaders" creates a chicken-and-egg dilemma: How can you identify the leaders to whom it makes sense to delegate discretion until they have demonstrated their ability to use their discretion wisely? Still, in Stamford, Esserman let the lieutenants take charge. After all, they were already in charge, but not in charge of accomplishing anything. Yet Esserman was also clear: "I'm going to be after you, if you ever forget that what you're doing is about results." Observed Esserman, "If you give them responsibility and authority, more often than not they will rise to the occasion."[57]

"You have to redesign the roles of the real leaders if you want to be a good leader yourself," noted Esserman.[58] And a significant part of that redesign is figuring out how to decentralize authority in return for improved results. To do that, however, the leadership team first has to decide what—specifically—it wants to accomplish.

Responsibility for Results

What subunits, led by what individuals or teams, should be responsible for improving what aspects of performance? To this question, there is no right answer. There exists no model that provides a universally applicable resolution to this leadership question. It is silly to slavishly imitate the approach employed by Nuñez or Spiller, by Bratton or Esserman, or by O'Malley.

There is, however, an important principle underlying any effort to improve performance:

> It is *essential* to employ some organizational framework for establishing precisely what subunits led by what individuals or teams should be *responsible* for achieving what specific *results.*

An organization will not miraculously produce improved results until it has established who is responsible for producing those results. And because every organizational situation is different—just as every social service agency and every police department and every city is different—the choices made by every leadership team will, inevitably, be different. It would be tempting to copy another organization's model—NYPD's prototype, DPSS's template, Baltimore's system.

Unfortunately, every leadership team has to think. It has to base its choices on its own performance deficits, the operational capacities of its subunits, and the leadership skills of its people.

Conscious Leadership Choices

Who should have the authority to exercise discretion to accomplish what? This is a leadership decision—a strategic choice. To achieve any public purpose, a leadership team has to decide what subunits, led by what individuals, should be delegated what responsibility and what discretion for accomplishing what purposes—for producing what results.

As is so often true in the exercise of performance leadership, the precise choice is less important than actually making one: a clear, explicit, visible choice. This need to choose the subunits to which to delegate responsibility is similar to the need to choose the performance deficit on which the organization will next focus. Every alternative has both pluses and minuses. Thus choice of the level of the organization on which to focus primary responsibility for results—and thus the level to which to delegate discretion—is less important than the decision to choose. The leadership team needs to make an analytical, conscious, explicit, and visible choice.

These decisions are not technical tasks. They are leadership responsibilities.

7

Distinguishing PerformanceStat's Effects

What kind of results—what kind of improvements in performance—can be attributed to various PerformanceStats?

"Nothing new works and, if it works somewhere else, it must be because they are weird."
TONY BOVAIRD and ELKE LÖFFLER [quoting others], Governance International[1]

We can never do merely one thing.
GARRETT HARDIN, ecologist[2]

On May 3, 2010, Mitch Landrieu became mayor of New Orleans. Unfortunately, concluded David Osborne (of *Reinventing Government* fame), Landrieu "inherited the least competent city government I'd ever seen in this country and the most corrupt."[3] On his second day in office, the mayor appointed Andy Kopplin to be his first deputy mayor. Kopplin quickly hired Oliver Wise to be policy director and Jeffrey Hebert to be director of blight policy. Within a year, Wise was the director of the city's new Office of Performance and Accountability. By then, however, Kopplin, Wise, and Hebert had already held four BlightSTAT sessions.[4]

Even before August 2005, when Hurricane Katrina devastated the city, stated Forward New Orleans, a coalition of business and community organizations, the city's blight "far exceeded reasonable tolerance."[5] The Greater New Orleans Community Data Center reported that in March 2010 over a quarter of the city's residential addresses (57,000 of 216,000) were unoccupied, reflecting either blighted buildings, empty lots, or vacant but habitable homes. Indeed, New Orlean's 27 percent was higher than Detroit's 20 percent, though it was down from its own 34 percent of two years earlier.[6]

95

Thus, in March 2010, when mayor-elect Landrieu created 17 transition task forces, one focused on blight. When this task force released its report in April, it recommended 15 "action items" for the first 100 days plus another seven for the first six months. These recommendations included such innovative ideas as: "review and evaluate demolition procedures," and "devise a plan and a timetable for the removal of FEMA trailers."[7] Wonderfully vague.

In September 2010, however, when Mayor Landrieu announced his "Blight Strategy," he was specific. He set a target for the FEMA trailers: They would be gone by January 1, 2011.

Not quite. At the end of 2010—five-plus years after Katrina—the city still had families living in more than 250 of these trailers, and they fought to remain in their "homes." The U.S. government was naturally reluctant to throw them out. Still, after one year of Landrieu's Blight Strategy, only seven trailers remained, with the last family holding on for four more months.

BlightSTAT in New Orleans

Eliminating the FEMA trailers was not the major focus of Landrieu's blight strategy. His September 2010 announcement included a bigger, more significant target: "to eliminate up to 10,000 blighted and/or vacant properties over the next three years."[8] Moreover, Landrieu identified a list of the "problems with the city's current approach to blight":

—No single definition of blight and blight eradication
—No overall goal for blight reduction
—No one accountable for meeting goals
—Very few, if any, performance measures
—Blight eradication operations are fractured and uncoordinated
—Little prioritization of limited resources for fighting blight
—No comprehensive set of data to guide decision making
—Low morale in key departments"[9]

Looks like a standard list of the problems that prevent all kinds of public organizations from producing any kind of result.

Landrieu also announced that he would create a "CitiStat process for managing blight eradication." The BlightSTAT sessions, he explained, would "monitor progress on meeting citywide blight goals" and "help identify what works, what doesn't, and what needs to change in order for the City to meet its goals."[10] Just 35 days later, New Orleans held its first BlightSTAT meeting.

Of course, eliminating blight in New Orleans—or any city—is not one task. It requires the coordination of multiple tasks by multiple people in multiple organizations. Indeed, the city's Blight Strategy noted that "to eradicate blight, the government must be able to:

—Take control of problem properties, through code lien foreclosures, tax lien sales, or expropriation;

—Ensure that problem properties are properly maintained or demolished once they are controlled by the government; and

—Redevelop [these properties by the private sector] into a productive use."

Unfortunately, Landrieu's team "found that nearly all elements of this process were dysfunctional,"[11] Thus, the Blight Strategy announced in September contained over a dozen specific elements (see table 7-1).

In addition to the macro outcome target—reduce blighted properties by 10,000 by January 1, 2014—New Orleans established numerous output targets:

—demolish at least 100 highly visible, blighted structures per month;

—cut the grass on 1,500 vacant lots by the end of 2011;

—inspect 400 properties per week (1,600 per month) with each of eight inspectors doing 12 per day;

—hold approximately 270 code-enforcement and environmental-health hearings per week, 1,090 per month, and 13,080 per year;

—complete 50 Sheriff's code-lien foreclosure sales by the end of 2010; increasing the capacity of the Sheriff's office to 1,000 in 2011 (with a pilot sale of 15 to 20 properties in January and five a week afterwards).[12]

The list of outputs targets was long and specific.

Even achieving any individual output target was not always an individual task for an individual governmental unit. For example, explained Wise:

For code lien foreclosures to work, you need the entire "blight conveyor belt" working like clockwork. Because if one piece of the process goes awry, you can't take action on nuisance properties by foreclosing on them or knocking them down. The ability to monitor the whole conveyor belt (not just one piece of it) is what makes BlightSTAT so valuable.[13]

And the number of inspections did go up. The city's code enforcement director, Pura Bascos, created 13 inspection districts, each with its own inspector, and with six case managers handling two (or three) districts. The performance purpose was clear: to create in each inspector a sense of personal responsibility

TABLE 7-1. The New Orleans "Blight Strategy" From Strategy to Action: The Big Picture

Data-driven decisionmaking	Blight tool alignment and improvement	Organizational architecture and processes	Strategic deployment of resources	Place-based revitalization
Coordinate all blight-tracking information systems.	Prioritize code enforcement and sheriff's sales as the primary tool for acquiring blighted properties.	Consolidate Departments of Code Enforcement and Environmental Health to streamline inspections.	Create CitiStat process for managing blight eradication program.	Coordinate property disposition strategy with place-based community development strategy.
Create GIS blight map.	Demolish, deconstruct, and maintain blighted properties and lots.	Streamline and scale up administrative hearings.	Use placed-based principles in the deployment of resources.	Facilitate ability of adjacent property owners to acquire blighted properties.
Integrate neighborhood data into city's blight-tracking system.		Building capacity to execute sheriff's sales.		Utilize NORA's ability to land-bank properties for strategy redevelopment.[a]
		Adapt NORA to be an effective sustainable land-banking organization.		

Source: Blight Strategy: City of New Orleans, September 30, 2010.
a. NORA is the New Orleans Redevelopment Authority.

for the outputs—the inspections in his or her district—and to do the same for each case manager.

Initially, however, not all inspections were quality inspections. When presented at an administrative hearing, they proved inadequate. Moreover, the improved capacity to inspect properties was not matched by an improved capacity to conduct hearings. Thus, New Orleans accumulated a growing backlog of inspected properties that needed a hearing before they could be seized.

Also, analysis of the data suggested several changes. Initially, the city's priority was on inspections near schools and playgrounds. But to seize more buildings

TABLE 7-2. Age of Scheduled but Uncompleted Inspections,
City of New Orleans, February and October 2011

Date	≤ 30 days	> 30 but ≤ 60 days	> 60 but ≤ 90 days	> 90 but ≤ 180 days	> 180 days	Average age (days)
February 4	0	137	83	223	459	179
October 14	140	36	14	5	0	30

Source: New Orleans Office of Performance and Accountability.

quickly, it changed its emphasis. When a property owner claimed to have fixed the problems identified during the original inspection, the city quickly did a reinspection so that the case could proceed to a hearing. The city also ratcheted up its capacity to hold these hearings by contracting out more work to administrative hearing officers and making the effort a higher priority.

New Orleans also concluded that it was both more efficient and more effective not to seize blighted properties for the owner's failure to pay property taxes but instead to use code lien foreclosures to take control of them. If the administrative-hearing process finds that property is, indeed, blighted (and the owner did nothing to fix it) the city can demolish the building or sell it at an auction.[14]

In just a year-and-a-half, the BlightSTAT strategy had some significant accomplishments:

—The number of monthly inspections rose from 628 in October 2010 to 1,480 in March 2012—not quite up to the monthly target of 1,600, but more than double.

—The average age of scheduled inspections decreased by 83 percent—from 179 days in February 2011 to 30 days in October 2011 (see table 7-2).

—In 2009, the Law Department had filed nine writs of seizure against the owners of blighted properties, a step required before they could be sold at auction. In 2010, the number of filed writs increased to 68, and in 2011 it jumped to 1,003.

—The average time to complete an inspection was reduced by 40 percent from 36 days in the first quarter of 2011 to 21 days in the first quarter of 2012.

—The capacity of the Hearings Bureau grew steadily (see figure 7-1), though it never hit the target of 1,090 hearings per month.

—Within a month of Landrieu's Blight Strategy announcement at the end of September 2010, demolitions jumped to over 100. In 2011, demolitions exceeded the target of 100 per month in all but four months, and the average for the year was 170 demolitions per month. In the first eight months of 2012,

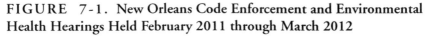

FIGURE 7-1. New Orleans Code Enforcement and Environmental Health Hearings Held February 2011 through March 2012

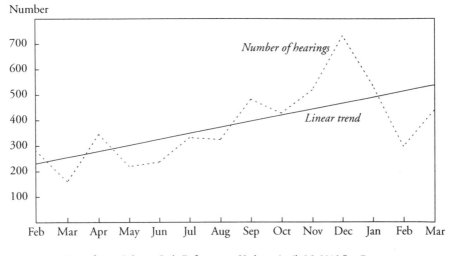

Source: "City of New Orleans, Code Enforcement Update: April, 26, 2012," p. 7.

demolitions again averaged over 100, though dropping off during the summer (see table 7-3).

PerformanceStat and Public Trust

In New Orleans as elsewhere, citizens have grown cynical about government's ability to accomplish anything. Consequently, data about demolitions (for example) are not apt to have much of an impact if the blighted buildings on *your* street are still standing, especially after multiple phone calls to city hall. Yet at least one citizen of New Orleans—Charlie London, an activist with the Faubourg St. John Neighborhood Association—has been impressed. For over two-and-a-half years, London attended every BlightSTAT session (all are open to the public) and after the one on April 12, 2012, he reported: "I can tell you without a shadow of a doubt that the people at the table in these BlightSTAT meetings are passionate and purposeful in their desire to have New Orleans continue to grow, prosper and be blight-free." Indeed, comparing his city with Chicago and Philadelphia, London concluded: "The City of New Orleans' perspicacity and initiatives has positioned our city as the clear leader in the fight against blight."

TABLE 7-3. Demolitions of Blighted Buildings in New Orleans, October 2010 through August 2012

Year	Month	Demolitions	Annual total and monthly average
2010	October	99	Σ = 427
	November	146	Ave = 142
	December	182	
2011	January	72	Σ = 2034
	February	97	Ave = 170
	March	292	
	April	301	
	May	284	
	June	180	
	July	174	
	August	131	
	September	68	
	October	185	
	November	93	
	December	157	
2012	January	277	Σ = 1010
	February	103	Ave = 126
	March	144	
	April	129	
	May	134	
	June	114	
	July	63	
	August	46	

Source: New Orleans Office of Performance and Accountability, "City of New Orleans: BlightSTAT, Reporting Period, June–July 2012" (August 8, 2012), and "City of New Orleans: BlightSTAT, Reporting Period, August 2012" (September 12, 2012).

London recognized that citizens still had a right to be frustrated with how many blighted properties remained. Nevertheless, he noted, the city had only "two highly competent, motivated and passionate lawyers" who are "working on filing writs for [the] code lien foreclosure process" and that they "get 65 cases completely researched and ready for adjudication each month." Concluded London, "I dare say a highly staffed private firm would have trouble doing the same considering the amount of research and fact checking that is required to produce a writ."[15]

In July, 2012—by which time New Orleans had held 35 BlightSTAT meetings—Landrieu announced that the city had reduced blight by 4,500 units.[16] A month later, Greater New Orleans Community Data Center released a different number: blighted homes and empty lots, which had totaled 43,755 in September 2010, when Landrieu announced his big target, were down to an estimated 35,700 in March 2012—a drop of 8,000.[17]

Obviously, which properties to label as "blighted" is a judgment call—not for those that are pristine or dilapidated, but for those at the margin. Still, regardless of whose data you use,[18] the trend in New Orleans over the first two years of BlightSTAT was significant. People noticed—not because they looked at the data, but because they looked at their neighborhood.

Of those governmental jurisdictions and public agencies that seek to employ a PerformanceStat leadership strategy, municipal governments and their agencies often have a distinct advantage. The things they do—making New York's streets safe or eradicating New Orleans's blight—are visible to citizens.

By first making an explicit and public commitment to eradicate 10,000 blighted properties, and then making significant and visible progress toward that goal, Mayor Landrieu's BlightSTAT also contributed, in Oliver Wise's words, to "building public trust."

The Challenge of Verifying Impact

Identifying the results produced by most PerformanceStats is more challenging than identifying the results produced by a CompStat. Indeed, thinking analytically about the results produced by almost any PerformanceStats (other than the CompStats) is much more challenging.

Why? Because police agencies have baseline data. For decades, they have been collecting data related to performance: output data, such as arrests; and outcome data, such as crimes.

In contrast, most other public agencies have lacked the capacity to collect performance data. Sure, they collected financial data and personnel data (because they are legally obligated to do so). Some even collected activity data such as the number of bureaucratic hoops jumped through. Aside from police departments, only a few have collected data that could reveal whether performance was up or down. Most lacked a performance baseline from which to measure progress.[19]

In 1999, when Martin O'Malley became mayor of Baltimore, as he later reported, "City managers did not know how many vehicles were in our public works fleet."[20] If a government doesn't have data on the number of trucks and cars it has, it is unlikely to have data on the results they produce.

In an ideal *scientific* world—not an ideal *citizen-service* world—government would complete the baseline, data-collection phase before launching the performance-improvement phase. But citizens are unlikely to reelect a mayor whose campaign slogan is: "We've devoted our first four years to constructing our data-collection system and establishing baseline performance metrics; now all you have to do is give us another four years to implement the performance-improvement phase." Real catchy, huh? Bet *your* mayor didn't try it.

Creating an Effective MentalHealthStat

In May 2007, the Los Angeles County Department of Mental Health (DMH) launched STATS: "Strategies for Total Accountability and Total Success." DMH is a complex organization with a complex mission. With an annual budget at that time of roughly $1.5 billion and approximately 3,600 employees, it provided services to over 200,000 individuals every year. DMH directly operated programs at 75 locations and co-located some of its operations at another 100 sites. It also contracted for services with a thousand different nongovernmental organizations and individual practitioners.

Where should it start? How should it start? As others have done, DMH started with basic, yet important, administrative and process measures. After all, social service agencies are required, by other governmental units, to collect lots of data. Moreover, improving administrative processes can help reduce costs, and increase revenues, thus freeing up resources to improve services. Every year, DMH had millions of dollars in unrealized revenue because it was not completely, quickly, and accurately submitting claims to Medi-Cal (California's Medicaid program) for services eligible for reimbursement. Thus, when Paul Arns, the department's chief of clinical informatics, and Robin Kay, its chief deputy director, launched STATS, they focused on "three core operational process metrics":[21]

1. "Direct services": the percent of nonsupervisory staff time spent on reimbursable services.[22] DMH wanted to make sure that clinical staff were documenting and submitting the forms for all reimbursable work. Like all humans, these mental health clinicians hate "wasting" time filling out forms, when they could be doing something useful.

2. "Benefit establishment": the percent of clients with Medi-Cal benefits. Whenever it delivered services to an individual who was eligible for Medi-Cal, DMH wanted to make sure that it would, indeed, be reimbursed.

3. "Claim processing lag time": the time it took to process a claim.[23] DMH
   wanted to make sure that reimbursement forms were submitted promptly.

DMH chose to fix these three performance deficits first.

For claim processing, DMH set a target: 70 percent of claims submitted within
14 calendar days. Over the 11 months before May 2007, when DMH launched
STATS, the percentage submitted within 14 days had never been above this
threshold. (See table 7-4A.) In early 2006, it had risen above 70 percent for three
brief months but then had dropped even below 60 percent on two occasions.

Then, having set its 70 percent target, DMH held its first STATS meeting in
May 2007. The percentage of reimbursement requests that were submitted within
14 days quickly jumped above the target. And it stayed there. Consequently, for
the first full year of STATS—May 2007 through April 2008—75 percent of the
claims were submitted within 14 days. (See table 7-4B.) Indeed, the improvement in performance was sufficient to drive the percentage for the entire calendar
2007 above 70 percent.

Finally, the performance stayed above the targeted level. (See table 7-4B.)
After DMH introduced STATS in May 2007, performance stayed above the target through calendar year 2009. In fact, in calendar year 2009 it never dropped
below 75 percent. (See table 7-4A.)

As a result of its focus on these three performance deficits, DMH's annual
reimbursement jumped by $5.2 million from $40.8 million in FY 2006–07 to
$46.0 million in FY 2006–07.[24] Obviously, it is impossible to separate out how
much of the $5.2 million can be attributed to the focus on each metric. Indeed,
some of the success could be because STATS made accurate, quick, and full reimbursement a significant and visible priority. Moreover, these three initiatives were
based on a common purpose—ensuring DMH is fully reimbursed for the eligible
services that it delivers—thus reinforcing each other and further complicating
any effort to separate out each individual metric's cause and its monetary effect.

Like the New York Police Department (NYPD), DMH has its own four
"core tenets":

—Accurate and timely data shared by everyone at the same time
—Training and technical assistance for managers and supervisors
—Continual follow-up and assessment
—Adoption of a problem-solving model that fits the culture and work of the
organization.

Familiar. But not identical.

TABLE 7-4A. Reimbursement Requests Submitted within the 14-Day Target, 2006–09, Los Angeles County Department of Mental Health

| | | | Claims submitted on target | | |
| | | | Number | Percent | |
Year	Month	Total claims	for month	for month	Percent for year
2006	Jan	61,181	38,302	63	63
	Feb	56,300	32,666	58	
	Mar	66,902	47,808	71	
	Apr	55,497	40,947	74	
	May	61,877	45,379	73	
	Jun	60,599	39,462	65	
	Jul	53,540	30,097	56	
	Aug	60,600	35,704	59	
	Sep	50,450	31,445	62	
	Oct	55,522	33,405	60	
	Nov	50,529	27,253	54	
	Dec	45,294	27,395	60	
2007	Jan	56,558	35,957	64	72
	Feb	51,187	34,333	67	
	Mar	56,757	38,660	68	
	Apr	54,075	37,015	68	
	May*	57,366	42,372	74	
	Jun	54,064	40,346	75	
	Jul	53,241	40,478	76	
	Aug	58,171	43,238	74	
	Sep	49,839	38,091	76	
	Oct	58,820	44,235	75	
	Nov	51,581	38,409	74	
	Dec	45,561	34,225	75	
2008	Jan	56,823	42,750	75	74
	Feb	53,732	39,741	74	
	Mar	56,321	42,710	76	
	Apr	60,424	44,551	74	
	May	55,305	39,754	72	
	Jun	55,169	40,272	73	
	Jul	58,590	44,245	76	
	Aug	53,072	41,153	78	
	Sep	55,051	41,520	75	
	Oct	61,183	45,494	74	
	Nov	48,923	35,161	72	
	Dec	56,790	42,776	75	

(continued)

TABLE 7-4A. (*continued*)

Year	Month	Total claims	Claims submitted on target		Percent for year
			Number for month	Percent for month	
2009	Jan	58,653	44,624	76	78
	Feb	56,488	42,443	75	
	Mar	64,826	50,588	78	
	Apr	64,192	49,755	78	
	May	58,745	45,395	77	
	Jun	63,665	49,744	78	
	Jul	66,361	53,264	80	
	Aug	61,569	47,329	77	
	Sep	63,728	47,926	75	
	Oct	62,471	48,187	77	
	Nov	54,000	42,727	79	
	Dec	61,881	49,107	79	

Source: Los Angeles County Department of Mental Health.
*DMH started STATS in May 2007.

TABLE 7-4B. Reimbursement Requests Submitted within 14-Day Target, for Five Different 12-Month Periods, Los Angeles County Department of Mental Health

12-month period	Total claims	Claims submitted on target	
		Number for period	Percent for period
Calendar Year 2006	678,291	429,863	63
May 2006 April 2007*	656,988	416,105	63
Calendar Year 2007	647,220	467,359	72
May 2007 April 2008**	655,943	491,146	75
Calendar Year 2008	671,383	500,127	74

Source: Los Angeles County Department of Mental Health.
*The 12 months before DMH started STATS.
**The 12 months after DMH started STATS.

For example, the first tenet comes with six more words: "shared by everyone at the same time." And DMH's third tenet—"Continual follow-up and assessment"—is not identical to Maple's fourth. DMH's follow-up is not "relentless" as its own fourth tenet reveals: "Adoption of a problem-solving model that fits the culture and work of the organization."[25]

AT DMH, front-line employees and front-line supervisors aren't cops. They are social workers. The aggressive, in-your-face style for which Maple and NYPD's CompStat became infamous is unlikely to work in any mental health agency. Thus, DMH's leadership team needed to adapt the core principles and key components of CompStat, CitiStat, and other PerformanceStats to mesh with its own purposes and particular organizational ethos.

Closing Washington, D.C.'s Used Car Lots

As mayor of Washington, D.C., Adrian Fenty could get annoyed. Many of the District's citizens detested the unsightly (and often rat-infested) used car lots that populated their neighborhoods. So, their mayor detested them too. To see what could be done about them, Fenty started using CapStat—his version of PerformanceStat.

Unlike the CitiStats in Baltimore and elsewhere, Fenty's CapStat focused not on ongoing operations but on specific problems. He would get obsessed with a problem and decide to do something about it. "He doesn't think about agencies; he thinks about issues," explained Victor Prince, a former CapStat director. Thus, CapStat meetings were not organized around a formal schedule of regular (for example, monthly or quarterly) meetings with each focused on an individual city agency. Instead, once Fenty focused on a problem, he might hold a CapStat meeting about it on Monday. Then maybe another on the following Monday. And perhaps another on Thursday, just three days later. In addition to the "action items" memos that CapStat staff produced after each meeting, the frequency of the meetings provided lots of follow-up and feedback. Fenty "wants the sessions organized as citizens think of the issue," explained Kevin Donahue, the first CapStat director. "CapStat sessions examine a single issue that cuts across agency boundaries," continued Donahue. "The question of who's around the [CapStat] table is who does this person [the head of the lead agency] need to get the job done."

This was Fenty's approach to the offensive used car lots. Did they have all the necessary permits? Many didn't. Where they violating any laws? Many were. Indeed, many were engaged in illegal activities. Some were not actually selling cars, but illegally storing them to be sold in Maryland or elsewhere. Others were chop shops for stolen cars. Over seven months (from October 31, 2008 to May 11, 2009) Fenty held seven CapStat sessions on "Code Enforcement Issues With Used Card Lots," bringing together every city manager with responsibility for the enforcement of civil regulations or criminal laws for used car lots.

Soon, the city started enforcing its existing regulations. This approach, Fenty's team concluded, was easier and quicker than launching a criminal investigation. The city also created new regulations, for example limiting the number of cars that could be displayed on the front of a lot to four.

By January 2009, the city had closed about a hundred illegally operating, used car dealerships. Naturally not all of their owners thought this was fair. Indeed, in response to complaints, when the Department of Consumer and Regulatory Affairs issued its final regulations, it relaxed the size of the bond that an outdoor lot required. Still, some fought back, suing the city but unsuccessfully.

Moving Homeless Individuals into Supportive Housing

On January 11, 2007, nine days after taking office, Mayor Fenty announced his "action plan" for the District that included:

> Launch CapStat, a program that fosters accountability and efficiency in government (1 week).
>
> Working with a private non-profit, initiate an effort to explore a Housing First policy to address homelessnes (90 days).[26]

This "housing first" policy sought to move homeless individuals directly into permanent, subsidized housing. (This approach is in contrast to the traditional one of providing individuals with space in a homeless shelter while also providing support services, for example, to treat their addictions and find them employment so they will become "housing ready.")

The District, however, had a large number of homeless shelters. With so many beds available, the "housing ready" approach would be the default. Consequently, on April 2, 2008, Fenty announced that, by October 1, he would close the Franklin Shelter, a 300-bed facility for homeless men in the old Franklin School downtown. To close the shelter, the city needed to find subsidized housing for the men it would displace.

Finding supportive housing had been the subject of a CapStat session two months before. The target was to find permanent housing for 400 individuals by October 1. A week following the public announcement, Fenty and City Administrator Dan Tangherlini held another CapStat meeting on this target. But nothing much happened. They held a third meeting in July and another in

FIGURE 7-2. Number of Homeless Individuals Placed in Supportive Housing, Washington, D.C., October 2007 through November 2008[a]

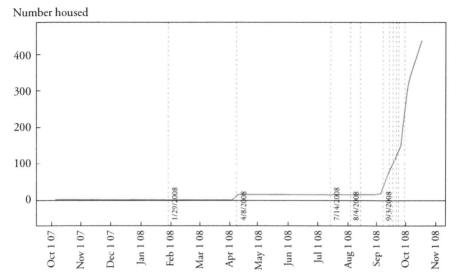

Source: CapStat, Washington, D.C.
a. Dashed lines refer to dates of CapStat sessions on the topic.

August. Still, by early September only 17 individuals had been moved into supportive housing. That's when the schedule changed. In three weeks in September, Fenty and Tangherlini held five CapStat sessions on the placement of homeless individuals in supportive housing.

The District did not, however, control the housing vouchers that gave the homeless access to permanent housing. These were distributed by the District of Columbia Housing Authority (DCHA), which reported not to the mayor but to an independent board. Moreover, the funds for these vouchers came not from the mayor's budget, but from the U.S. Department of Housing and Urban Development. Nevertheless, Fenty got DCHA's director to attend these CapStat meetings—indeed, to sit directly across the table from him. This engendered cooperation—the speedy approval of housing vouchers for homeless men.

Results jumped. By the end of September, Fenty's persistent focus had moved nearly 300 individuals into supportive housing. By mid-October the total reached 440.

Figure 7-2 illustrates the relationship between the CapStat sessions (designated by vertical, dashed lines) and the results of homeless individuals placed in supportive housing. As Tangherlini has remarked, deadlines can be an "unremarkable but incredibly effective" management tactic. "There's a great deal of discipline about deadlines," he noted.[27] "To make sure you're getting something done, it's a Management 101 tool to use a deadline. Oddly enough, it hasn't been applied as aggressively throughout this organization, frankly many organizations."[28]

The impact of the CapStat sessions on the number of homeless people placed, as illustrated by figure 7-2, was dramatic. When Shaun Donovan, the U.S. secretary of Housing and Urban Development, launched HUDStat in 2011, he used this hockey-stick curve it to illustrate the influence that an effective PerformanceStat can have.

Politically, However, Performance Is Not Enough

In July 2010, *Kiplinger's Personal Finance* ranked Washington, D.C., third on its list of the nation's "best cities," calling it "chock-full of job prospects, entertainment venues and great neighborhoods."[29] Two months later, Mayor Adrian Fenty lost his bid for a second term. Unfortunately for Fenty, competent management can rarely be the sole basis for a reelection campaign. Personal style is also influential—often determining.

When Fenty took office in January 2007, he promised to run the city "like a business."[30] This perspective may have affected not only his internal strategy for managing the city but also to his external approach for connecting with citizens. To many of the District's voters, Fenty was aloof and inaccessible, brash and arrogant. His leadership style was frequently described as uncompromising, dismissive, offensive, imperial. His zealous effort to eliminate the blighting used car lots—many considered it overzealous—alienated people who thought he was also picking on legitimate small business owners. Peter Harkness, the founding publisher of *Governing* magazine, described him as "a young, energetic, impatient and abrasive reformer with the political skills of a drill sergeant."[31] One political advisor noted that "Adrian believes consensus building is overrated."[32]

A week before the election, the *Washington City Paper* endorsed the incumbent, noting that on "public policy matters . . . it's hard not to love Fenty." Still, the editorial highlighted his "gratuitous dissing of D.C. employees" and noted that "Fenty has bungled the job of making poorer residents feel a part of the new D.C." Still the paper concluded: "Vote Adrian Fenty. He's a jerk, but he's your jerk."[33]

Despite his accomplishments—indeed, through his aggressive approach to achieving many of them—Fenty alienated the District's African American population. In his reelection campaign against the chairman of the city council, another African American, Fenty won 53 of the city's 58 majority-white census tracts, but only 10 of the 118 that were majority-black.

When Fenty ran for mayor in 2006, he talked about efficiency and competence.[34] After his election, Fenty posted on the District's website both an annual "Performance Plan" and an annual "Performance Accountability Report" for each of 78 city agencies, boards, commissions, departments, and offices.[35] While mayor, Fenty commented: "I have a thesis that people judge a mayor on how government works."[36]

After his defeat, Fenty argued that "you can criticize me on many things. But you can't criticize me on results."[37] Indeed, the president of the Greater Washington Board of Trade had noted that Fenty "gets results."[38] A year later, however, Fenty did observe that his reelection campaign "was not, at the end, a discussion that was about performance and results."[39]

Fixing the Collection, Analysis, and Reporting of DNA Samples

When Baltimore's Mayor Martin O'Malley ran for governor of Maryland, he pledged to create StateStat. In January 2007, when Matt Gallagher moved from director of Baltimore's CitiStat to director of Maryland's StateStat, he found numerous "opportunities" to improve the performance of state agencies.[40] To identify what these opportunities might be, Gallagher asked each agency for its last four years of reports from the legislative auditor. Given that the job of any auditor is to identify problems, these reports offered a multitude of such "opportunities."

The next month, the auditor released a report on the Department of State Police (DSP) cataloging problems in the "collection, analysis, and recording of DNA samples that could negatively impact the timely identification of individuals who have committed crimes." The audit found:

—Approximately 25,100 DNA samples collected from individuals convicted of qualifying crimes and imprisoned were not analyzed and/or entered into the statewide DNA database.
—DSP did not collect DNA samples from certain individuals as required and could not account for certain samples that had been collected.[41]

Gallagher saw these failures "as an enormous opportunity." After all, "in this CSI-sensitized world," he said, "people have a reasonable expectation that DNA evidence is a tool of law enforcement" and that Maryland would be "leveraging this kind of technology" to protect the public.

Here was a performance deficit that could mobilize people and not just the state police. For not all of these operational failures were its responsibility. The department had been the subject of the audit. Yet, while its DNA lab was responsible for analyzing the samples, the responsibility for collecting them was "diffused over a number of state agencies."

Gallagher quickly realized that Maryland's StateStat would, in several important ways, have to be qualitatively different from Baltimore's CitiStat. In the city, he recalled, "our greatest successes were focused in on individual agency efforts." The state, however, was organizationally "more complex" with "continuums of state agencies that touch these types of issues." Thus, he and his staff spent "a much greater part of our StateStat time trying to integrate a lot of processes"—"to break down silos."

Still, the first and most obvious challenge was to fix the backlog at the State Police Forensic Science Laboratory. At the end of 2006, the lab had 24,300 samples sitting on its shelves that had been processed but not uploaded into CODIS, the FBI's "Combined DNA Index System." Because no one had made it a priority, the lab had become a bottleneck. It didn't make sense to collect more samples if the major consequence would be purchasing more shelves.

When Gallagher began to push, the State Police lab pushed back. It didn't have enough staff and couldn't fill positions because of low salaries. The staff were dedicated but, because of their job classifications, were prohibited from earning overtime. For existing staff, "there were no activity standards," and the lab wasn't tracking its progress. When Gallagher asked why not, he was told, "We really don't want to waste time tracking what we do. We're busy doing other things."

To Gallagher, this was "really not acceptable"—particularly given that the lab was doing "an absolutely horrendous job."

With any PerformanceStat, "an absolutely horrendous job" is a good place to start. It provides a big opportunity for improvement. And once the organization commits to fixing "an absolutely horrendous job," it can't merely move it up one notch to "an ordinarily horrendous job," or even "a not-so-bad job." It needs to improve from "absolutely horrendous" to very good. When the performance deficit is a backlog, the only meaningful definition of "very good" is zero backlog.

Gallagher started conducting weekly DNAStat meetings. He told the lab's managers, "As uncomfortable as this may be for you, you are going to have start telling us everything you are doing every single week." Also, he emphasized that, for the state police, this was just a beginning:

We're going to bring Maryland State Police into the [StateStat] process. But for the first couple of months, we're going to live, breathe, sleep DNA.

That's all we're doing. There are other things screwed up at the State Police, but this is the only thing we are going to focus on. So we gave them a single-page [data] template.

This one page, which the StateStat staff reviewed weekly, contained data on how many DNA samples the lab had received, how many it had shipped to a vendor to be processed, how many it had received back from the vendor, and how many results it had reviewed and uploaded into CODIS. The template also contained personnel data, including the hours worked by the scientists, nonscientists, and interns. This one page permitted the StateStat staff to track both the lab's output of samples tested and its inputs of staff work.

Still, improving the performance of existing personnel was not enough. The lab could not clear the backlog with its current staff, and yet it had personnel vacancies because of low salaries for forensic scientists and its lackadaisical approach to recruiting. When the lab did recruit, hire, and train new staff, some would leave for higher-paying jobs. The lab did need some help; as with any PerformanceStat, accountability goes both ways. Thus, while Gallagher and his staff pushed for more productivity from the current staff, they also worked to fix the low salaries and overtime restrictions.

Although the legislative auditor had focused on the state police, this department was only part of the problem. It had responsibility for processing the samples and for collecting them when its officers investigated a crime. Yet other state agencies were also "required" to collect DNA samples. The Department of Correction was responsible for collecting samples from every person it incarcerated; the Division of Parole and Probation had the same responsibility for the people it supervised; the Department of Juvenile Justice was also supposed to collect samples from its juvenile offenders. Yet these agencies often failed to do so. "They didn't view it as their responsibility," recalled Gallagher. "They viewed this as a mandate. They viewed it as something that had been imposed by the legislature" for which they had been given no budget. In each agency, the top managers had other priorities.

The task of collecting DNA samples is not technically complex: Just swab the inside of a person's mouth to collect a few cheek cells. Thus, the StateStat staff began to collect data on how the responsible agencies were doing, thus making these performance deficits visible. "Week in, week out," Gallagher would ask: "How many did you collect this week? How many are you going to collect next week?" As a result, the Division of Parole and Probation trained over 600 employees to take samples. And the Division's "supervisees" from whom DNA samples were collected in 2007 jumped from 129 in April to 13,329 by December (see table 7-5).

TABLE 7-5. The First-Year Results of DNAStat, DNA Samples
Collected by the Maryland Division of Parole and Probation, 2007

Month	Apr	May	Jun	Jul	Aug	Sep	Oct	Nov	Dec
Samples collected	129	235	1,653	4,024	6,326	8,776	11,296	12,385	13,329

Source: StateStat, Maryland.

Moreover, by the end of 2007, the state police had uploaded all of the 24,000 samples in the original January backlog (see table 7-6). Over the four previous years (2003 through 2006), Maryland had uploaded 14,341 samples into the CODIS database; in 2007 and 2008 the state uploaded 45,380 samples—three times as many in half the time.[42] As a result, the number of DNA profiles that Maryland had entered into the FBI's CODIS database jumped from 28,155 in January 2007, to 53,078 in December 2007, and then to 75,574 in December 2008.[43] In just two years, Maryland nearly tripled the number of DNA samples it sent annually to CODIS.

Of course, unlike your average PerformanceStat analyst, the public is not mesmerized by data. What gets citizen attention is an outcome—a specific outcome. And Maryland soon had a story to tell about an outcome from its DNAStat.

On August 13, 2007, Alphonso Hill, who had been incarcerated since 2002 for rape, finally had a DNA sample taken. Nine days later, CODIS matched his DNA to six other unsolved rapes. Just 15 days after obtaining Hill's DNA sample, Maryland charged him with all six. In November 2008, after being linked to four more rapes, Hill was sentenced to eight more 60-year prison terms.

Baltimore's 48-Hour Pothole Guarantee

When Mayor O'Malley launched CitiStat, his most visible target was the "48-hour pothole guarantee." In March 2001, he observed: "fixing a pothole isn't complicated," and "this certainly is a measurable outcome." Then, repeating what became one of his major management themes, he noted: "We need to watch it more. Things that get watched get done." Finally, just to be sure that his announcement was quotable, O'Malley was both specific and clever: "No ifs, ands, or bumps! Repairs will be made within 48 hours. Guaranteed."[44]

Water has a peculiar characteristic: like most substances, water contracts as it gets colder—until the temperature drops to 39° Fahrenheit. Then, water starts expanding. When water freezes at 32°, it expands dramatically. Then, of course, when the temperature rises, water contracts until at 39° it starts expanding.

TABLE 7-6. The First-Year Results of DNAStat, DNA Samples Tested by the Maryland Department of State Police, 2003–07

Outputs	Calendar year					Percent change 2006–07
	2003	2004	2005	2006	2007	
DNA samples uploaded to the CODIS[a] database	3,757	2,913	2,708	4,963	24,932	400
Matches[b] to uploaded samples in database	38	139	166	220	287	30

Source: StateStat, Maryland.

a. The FBI's Combined DNA Index System.

b. A "match," "hit," or "positive comparison" occurs when the DNA profile from a crime scene sample matches a DNA profile in a database of convicted offenders, in a database of individuals arrested for specific crimes, or in a database of other crime scenes.

On any road, water seeps into any crack. Whenever the temperature drops to freezing, the water expands, making the crack slightly bigger. When the temperature increases, the ice melts, and more water seeps in. When the temperature drops again and the water freezes, the crack grows again. After multiple freezing and thawing cycles, the crack graduates to be a pothole.

As a result, in frost-belt cities, where on any winter day, temperatures can oscillate between, say, 25° and 45°, potholes flourish. Citizens find these potholes annoying—and a symbol of local government's incompetence: "If they can't even fix the potholes. . . ."

In fiscal year 2002, Baltimore began tracking the number of service requests (SRs) received through its 311 system, as well as how long it took to fulfill them. Table 7-7 provides the data on pothole filling that were available for that year aggregated into two-week intervals.[45] Not all of the data that the mayor would have liked to watch were available. Nevertheless, data collection has to start with what is available. So this is how Baltimore started. As with any initial effort to collect data about anything, it was hardly complete.

Four years later, however, data collection had improved significantly. (See table 7-8.) Now the city not only knew how many new potholes citizens reported to 311 and the average number of days that it took to fill them. It also knew the percentage of these service requests that were fulfilled within 48 hours plus the number not filled by that target. For FY 2006, these data reveal, potholes reported to 311 were, on average, filled within one day. Moreover, in only four of that year's 26 two-week periods, did the city fail to fill more than 90 percent of them within 48 hours. Not perfect. But not bad.[46]

TABLE 7-7. Baltimore Department of Transportation, Performance in Fulfilling Pothole Service Requests, FY 2002 (July 1, 2001, to June 30, 2002)

Two weeks ending	Jul 6	Jul 20	Aug 3	Aug 17	Aug 31	Sep 14	Sep 28	Oct 12	Oct 26	Nov 9	Nov 23	Dec 7	Dec 21	Jan 4	Jan 27	Feb 1	Feb 15	Mar 1	Mar 15	Mar 29	Apr 12	Apr 26	May 10	May 24	Jun 7	Jun 21
Number of new potholes reported													40	30	48	73	74	48	54	101	138	123	153	183	165	1
Average days to fill													0.6	7.4	1.0	1.1	0.8	2.0	0.4	0.9	0.7	0.7	0.7	0.4	0.4	16.4
Percent filled on time																									95.8	0
Number not filled on time																									7	3

Sources: Fourteen CitiTrack statistical reports, created for the Department of Transportation from December 12, 2001, to June 22, 2002.

TABLE 7-8. Baltimore Department of Transportation, Performance in Fulfilling Pothole Service Requests, FY 2006 (July 1, 2005, to June 30, 2006)

Two weeks ending	Jul 15	Jul 29	Aug 12	Aug 26	Sep 9	Sep 23	Oct 7	Oct 21	Nov 4	Nov 18	Dec 2	Dec 16	Dec 30	Jan 13	Jan 27	Feb 10	Feb 24	Mar 10	Mar 24	Apr 7	Apr 21	May 5	May 19	Jun 2	Jun 16	Jun 30
Number of new potholes reported	312	288	289	261	234	252	212	246	286	268	268	223	315	510	514	519	588	454	486	449	596	553	519	408	649	416
Average days to fill	0.7	1.2	0.4	0.5	0.9	0.5	0.5	0.9	0.5	0.4	0.4	0.9	0.5	0.5	0.6	0.9	0.8	0.5	0.5	0.4	0.7	0.5	0.8	0.6	0.9	0.9
Percent filled on time	92.2	90.1	95.5	96.2	96.4	98.1	94.1	98.6	95.2	98.2	85.5	99.1	99.0	96.5	97.5	92.0	98.7	98.6	99.8	93.6	97.0	89.6	96.5	85.6	87.1	
Number not filled on time	25	28	12	12	9	9	4	15	4	13	5	32	3	5	18	13	47	6	7	1	39	17	54	15	93	54

Sources: Twenty-six CitiTrack statistical reports, created for the Department of Transportation from July 16, 2005, to July 1, 2006.

These data reveal something else. Over four years, the number of pothole SRs jumped significantly. In FY 2002, the *biggest* number potholes reported to 311 for any two-week period was 183; in FY 2006, the *smallest* number reported was 212. From FY 2002 to FY 2006, the number of SRs that the city received for filling potholes more than doubled. In the two-week period ending on March 15, 2002, 54 citizens called in an SR for potholes; in the two-week period ending on March 10, 2006, 454 citizens made that SR.

For this jump in SRs, there are (as always) many alternative explanations.

1. Weather became significantly worse, causing more thawing and freezing.
2. Streets deteriorated.
3. The city started using deficient asphalt to fill the potholes.
4. Pothole crews started filling them badly.
5. Citizens discovered that they could call 311 and take out their frustrations with city government with a real city employee.
6. Citizens learned that, if they called 311 to report a pothole, it would actually get filled.
7. Baltimore's citizens learned that, if they called 311 to report a pothole, it would actually get filled *within 48 hours.*
8. [Insert your own favorite explanation.]

It isn't possible to separate out how much of these different explanations contributed to the increase in SRs. Still, like others outside of Baltimore to whom I have shown these data, I have concluded that explanations 6 and 7 had something to do with it.

Everything Is Connected to Everything Else

These examples illustrate the challenge of determining whether any leadership strategy has an impact. Public executives work within a bureaucratic and governance system in which everything is connected to everything else.[47] They recognize that anything they do will never have one, isolated impact. Rather, any action will ripple through a large, complex, and adaptive system[48] of interconnected people and organizations. Some of these adaptations may improve performance. Some may not. Thus, the leadership team needs to anticipate negative adaptations and devise tactics to neutralize them.

Effective public executives recognize Garrett Hardin's wisdom: "We can never do merely one thing." In these seven words, Hardin describes reality. We may think in doing only *one* thing we are producing only *one* desired effect. But, because the one thing we do acts on a complex adaptive system, it will have multiple effects. Thus, Hardin extrapolates from his *description* of reality to a *prescription* for dealing with this adaptive world: "We can never do merely one thing, *therefore we must do several* in order that we may bring into being a new stable system."[49]

Public executives employ a PerformanceStat leadership strategy to create a new, higher performing organization. They recognize that, to do so, they will have to do many things. They recognize that the actions they take will not have independent effects. Indeed, they seek to design a *series* of actions that will interact to create a greater impact than would result from adding up their individual influences. Initially, they may simply seek to ratchet up performance one notch. But in doing so, ambitious executives hope to learn what works and what doesn't, and to use this learning to do several more things so they can ratchet performance yet another notch or three.

Initially, they aren't sure what will work. They have hunches—theories derived from their own experiences and from the experiences of others. They are, however, pretty sure that they can't do merely one thing. They can't merely articulate their purpose or collect data. They can't merely hold meetings or provide feedback. To have a significant impact on performance, public executives have to do a variety of different things that they combine to form a coherent, macro strategy.

But what things? What combinations of things? How do public executives put together a coherent combination of things? They don't know. They have to guess. The combination that they meld into their leadership strategy is always a guess.

Then, as they get feedback, they learn. They may learn (or think they learn) that some of the things they are doing are having the intended impact, while others aren't. They may also learn that some of these things are having a synergistic impact. And, in the process, they evolve and modify their own cause-and-effect theories—and thus their macro strategy.

Still, this learning is strictly a guess. Public executives can never be sure. Because their strategy has so many moving parts, they can never separate out which things are having how much of an individual impact. And they certainly cannot separate out which things are having how much of a synergistic impact.

Consequently, regardless of what leadership strategy they have chosen, effective executives are consciously (and unconsciously) mixing, combining, and adapting a variety of leadership behaviors (see chapter 15). They are trying to figure out what works, and in this search they are quite ecumenical, willing to borrow and adapt promising ideas from anyone, anywhere.

Public executives are under significant pressure to produce results. They have, at most, four years to accomplish something significant. Their direct boss, plus the legislature, stakeholder groups, journalists, and citizens, expect that they will produce real results—and do it quickly. They do not have the luxury to engage in a careful experiment to test one specific version of one small component of one leadership strategy. Effective executives are constantly tweaking their approach, looking at the data, experimenting with the theories they have acquired from years of trials and errors, observations, meetings, readings, seminars, and conversations.[50]

Such executives don't just collect performance data. They don't just conduct performance meetings. They don't just ask follow-up questions and circulate follow-up memos. These activities are not another set of bureaucratic requirements. Effective executives collect data to learn what is working and what isn't. They conduct performance meetings to learn what changes might create what improvements. They engage in follow-up discussions to motivate people and units to experiment with new approaches.

These executives tend, however, to be less interested in how much of any performance improvement can be attributed to the data vs. how much to the meetings. They make little effort to separate out such influences. They accept that any improvement in performance will require multiple actions by multiple people. They strive to foster adaptive feedback loops among actions, people, and units. They expect that multiple actions by multiple people will function not independently but synergistically.

Effective public executives do not rely on a neat, linear logic model of industrial production: inputs providing resources for a manufacturing facility to produce outputs, which customers turn into outcomes. Instead the operational logic model of effective executives contains multiple feedback loops—feedback loops that already exist in their world, plus those they create. Unfortunately, the complexity of these feedback loops makes performance difficult to predict.[51]

This is the value of "management by groping along."[52] Effective executives know what they want to accomplish; they just don't know how to do it. If the causal connection of executive action to results is strictly linear—without synergies or feedback—it is comparatively easy to predict in what ways (if not how much) the results will move in response to specific, individual actions. If, however, there exist some feedback loops (and the executives have created some more), the causal interactions will be difficult to predict. After all, these interactions involve not mechanical or electronic systems, but capricious humans.

To achieve their purposes in such a world, effective executives grope along, testing strategies and gauging their impact, trying different combinations of the ones that appear most effective. Then, once they "learn" that a series of actions (through the synergy of various feedback loops) appears to have some positive impact on results, they keep employing them. They tweak them. They try to learn from them. They want to know what works and why.

Or Was It Pure Luck? How Would We Know?

Did any of these PerformanceStats really "work"? Can we attribute any improved results to any PerformanceStat? Is it possible to produce a plausible explanation based on changes in the data, on testimony from participants and observers, on our knowledge of organizational behavior of *how* a PerformanceStat might have contributed to better results?

But is any such "plausible explanation" anything more than a self-serving justification? In New York, crime was already going down before William Bratton became police commissioner. What did CompStat contribute?

In Baltimore, it could be that changes in the performance of city agencies that occurred at the beginning of this century would have happened regardless of who was elected mayor in 1999 and regardless of what strategy this mayor employed. Still, our familiarity with the "lethargy" of large organizations suggests this is unlikely.[53] It could be that something else (something that neither participants, nor observers, nor theory have suggested) somehow produced improved results. For example, regression toward the mean (see chapter 4) is one possible explanation. At the end of the twentieth century, Baltimore was in bad shape. After years of deterioration, it had nowhere to go but up. Or, it could have continued to go down.

Still, if any reasonable mayor in Baltimore, or New Orleans, or Washington had done a few reasonable things, perhaps beleaguered city employees, desperate for leadership, would have responded with creativity and enthusiasm. A new mayor could simply have hired competent agency heads, promoted middle managers with potential, and encouraged them to make things better. Maybe city employees would have responded without data, analysis, and meetings—without follow-up or persistence. Maybe all these mayors really did was identify, recruit, and promote good people and inspire them a little. Sure, O'Malley, Landrieu, and Fenty did more. But maybe better people were all that really counted. This is a plausible explanation.

But not the only one. When Tony Bovaird and Elke Löffler tried to convince public executives in the United Kingdom to employ strategies that worked in continental Europe, they were told: "Nothing new works and, if it works somewhere else, it must be because they are weird."[54] Maybe these public executives were able to make some improvements in performance only because they were certifiably weird.

The number of possible plausible explanations is large. Without rerunning history thousands of times, there is no way to decide which explanations are more plausible than others.[55]

The Futile Search for Proof

No one will ever *prove* that citizen confidence in Baltimore's ability to fill potholes *caused* the increase in 311 calls. Similarly, no one will ever *prove* that BlightStat caused the reduction in blight in New Orleans—or even that BlightStat caused a quarter of blight reduction.

Yet, we do know something that permits us to believe that *some* of the things these mayors did had an impact on the behavior of *some* of the people working in city government: Most large organizations—whether they are in the public, for-profit, or nonprofit sectors—do not spontaneously improve their performance. In a million reruns of history, such spontaneity might happen. It is not impossible. It is, however, highly improbable.

Thanks to the experiments conducted in 1859 by chemist and microbiologist Louis Pasteur, we no longer believe in the "spontaneous generation" of life. Unfortunately, there are no experiments to test the theory of the spontaneous generation of organizational results. Still, I suspect that few scholars or managers believe that anything so inordinately rare is a serious explanation for the performance improvements under O'Malley, Landrieu, Fenty, or other public executives who used something like a PerformanceStat leadership strategy.

Our understanding of how and why any PerformanceStat leadership strategy in any governmental jurisdiction or any public agency might produce better results must rest both on the empirical specifics of what the leadership team did and on the theoretical concepts that describe what happens within organizations when leaders do these things.

This examination of cause and effect continues in chapter 14 and in chapter 15. But first, a few more chapters on PerformanceStat's core leadership principles and key operational components.

8

Collecting the Data

*What kind of data can help determine the current level of performance, reveal
key performance deficits, and suggest opportunities for the next improvements?*

The only man I know who behaves sensibly is my tailor;
he takes my measurements anew each time he sees me.
The rest go on with their old measurements and expect me to fit them.
GEORGE BERNARD SHAW, Nobel Prize–winning playwright[1]

Unless a team has data about how it is doing, however, there is no way
it can learn. And unless a team learns, there is no way it can improve.
J. RICHARD HACKMAN, Harvard University[2]

As mayor of New York City, Ed Koch asked friends, as well as citizens on the
streets, "How'm I doing?"[3] Koch was looking for data— data to assess his
performance as mayor, to reveal where his performance deficits might be, and to
suggest opportunities for improvement. Unfortunately, he didn't have any obvious source of data to help answer these questions. As mayor, he got real data on
only one day out of 1,461—every four years on election day. But such data were
not timely enough to be used to make strategic changes.

Ed Koch was a politician. So what kind of performance data did he want? He
didn't ask, "How's the city doing?" He didn't ask: "How's the police department
doing." Koch asked, "How'm *I* doing?" He wanted data on the performance
of Ed Koch.

Koch could have taken a poll with open-ended questions: "How is the mayor
doing?" But coding the responses to provide informative feedback could be difficult. So Koch, who wanted timely data on how *he* was performing, went around
asking people, "How'm I doing." This wasn't scientific, but for what it lacked
in statistical validity, it offered immediacy and intensity. Many people, Koch
learned, were quite willing to give him a real earful.

The Data Imperative

Suppose you decided that you wanted to lose weight. (Not you personally; your weight is perfect.) So put yourself in the shoes of someone else who wanted to lose weight. What would you need? Two things: a strategy and data.

First, you would need a weight-loss strategy. You could choose from the "wellness" shelves of any bookstore or library. You could choose nutritional supplements advertised in a magazine. You could find something on the web. You could invent your own strategy. (Only drink beer. Never eat on Tuesdays.) People invent all kinds of weight-loss strategies. In 1998, the entire town of Dyersville, Iowa created its own weight-loss strategy.[4]

Second, you would need data. You would need a scale to generate the data on your progress. Each morning, you would collect data and post them on the refrigerator. You might annotate the data with what you ate the previous day to reveal how well you followed your strategy.

What would happen if you were instructed to lose weight but denied access to a scale? Without these data, how could you learn whether you were making progress? How would you determine whether your strategy was working?

If you wanted to lose weight, and you couldn't get a scale, you would look for other forms of data. You might get a tape measure. With it, you could measure your girth. Then, if your waistline decreased, you could conclude that you were losing weight. This would not be the best measure of progress. It would not tell you how many pounds you had lost.

Still, you would be employing a theory—a cause-and-effect theory. If my weight-loss strategy is working, two things will happen: (1) I will actually lose weight, and, (2) because of my loss of weight, my waistline will shrink. This is strictly a theory. It might be true. It might not. If your waistline decreased by two inches, you could not tell how much weight you lost. (You could do some research, but the results would apply to the average person in some study—not precisely to you.)

If you want to produce a result—whether it is weight lost or blight removed—you need data to help measure progress. Unfortunately, public executives often lack a simple, reliable, widely accepted mechanism for collecting data on the results they want to produce. They can't get data that directly reveal how much progress they are making. Lacking a scale, they go looking for a tape measure. They recognize that their tape measure isn't perfect. As others deplore its obvious flaws, they accept that their tape measure may be the best available.

This measurement problem could be even more complicated. Suppose you were trying to lose weight but neither the scale nor the tape measure had been invented. Suppose no one (including you) had even conceived of either measuring device. What would you do?

You would have to go looking for data that might somehow be connected to weight loss. Maybe you would keep a record of how many spoonfuls you ate each day. This might be useful. It does reflect a theory. If you eat less, you will weigh less. But you could never be sure whether or not the things that you are eating will add pounds to your body. A spoonful of some foods might be easily burned off; a spoonful of something else might quickly expand your girth. If you had a validated theory, one that told you which foods to eat and which to avoid, this might work. Or not. Weight is also influenced by exercise.

Indeed, this cause-and-effect theory would be quite unreliable. Without some data on your weight, you would have absolutely no idea how much progress you were making. In this case, you might have to rely on asking your family and friends: "How'm I doing?"

The Search for Data

Any effort to improve performance requires some kind of data that are somehow related to the desired results—data that can help the organization understand whether or not its performance is improving. It needs data to tell it how well it has done in the past, how well it is doing now, and how well it is doing next month, or next year, or. . . . "Implicitly," notes Dennis Smith, "pressure to achieve results implies the ability to measure results."[5]

But what data? What data might be useful? Where might a PerformanceStat team find useful data? How would the members of this team know what data to look for? How would they know when they had found some data that might be useful? All this is rarely obvious.

Still, a leadership team that wants to improve performance has to start somewhere. To do so, it might begin with five simple but potentially helpful questions:

What data do we collect now?
What data could we collect easily?
What data should we collect?
How might we collect these data?
What data would we really like to have but can't (at least at the moment) collect?

This search for the data is driven by two needs— analytical and motivational:

What kind of data do we need to *analyze* our current level of performance and to determine our current performance deficits?

What kind of data do we need to *motivate* people to make the operational improvements necessary to eliminate (or mitigate) our key performance deficits?

As Alice Rivlin of the Brookings Institution observed in her classic book, *Systematic Thinking for Social Action*, "Performance measures for social service are not, of course, ends in themselves. They are prerequisites to attempts both to find more effective methods of delivering social services and to construct incentives that will encourage their use."[6] Data have both analytical and motivational value.

"Accurate and Timely Intelligence"

When it comes to collecting data, some public agencies have it easier than others. Police departments are those rare public agencies that *automatically* collect data they can use to analyze and improve their performance. Every day, every police department collects data on its arrests—a key output—and on (reported) crimes—a key outcome. Moreover, these data are more than aggregate counts. A police department collects a lot of data about every crime report and every arrest made: who, where, for what crime(s), with what witnesses. This simply happens. No police chief has to invent a data-collecting mechanism.[7]

A police department is not required, however, to do anything with these data. In the United States, it can voluntarily forward these data monthly to the FBI, which compiles them into its Uniform Crime Reports.[8] Nevertheless, just because a police department collects detailed crime and arrest data is no guarantee that it uses them. No one may ever even look at these data. Still, every police department possesses some potentially useful data. But where? In the early 1990s, the New York Police Department's (NYPD's) data were in the precincts.

Jack Maple was obsessed with data—"accurate and timely" data. Again, the inspiration came to him while sitting in Elaine's. On this night, Maple observed Elaine Kaufman, who was certainly a hands-on manager, checking the restaurant's tape that tallied the evening's receipts. "She knew at all times," recalled Maple, "exactly how well the night was going." And, "If the receipts were down, she'd look for her waiters: Were they loitering near the coffee service area or were they out on the floor, anticipating and attending to the customers' every need?"[9]

Then Maple made an analytical comparison: "How different business was in the NYPD, I thought. We didn't check our crime numbers hourly, daily, or even weekly. Headquarters gathered the numbers every six months." Moreover, what did the precinct commanders do with their data? "I couldn't imagine that many of our precinct commanders checked the tape on their crime numbers every day." And if they did, Maple wondered, how did they use their data: "If the numbers were going the wrong way, would any of them be out on field inspections to determine what was going wrong?"[10]

To Maple, the contrast between Elaine's and NYPD's use of data was glaring. From the comparison, Maple developed some insights about data and strategy. NYPD—the precincts and headquarters—needed current data. Both needed to analyze these data to identify performance deficits and to develop new tactics or strategies: "We're not interested in looking at six-month-old data the way the FBI would; we need the crime numbers at least weekly. At the precinct level, we'll look at it every day, just like checking in on the Dow Jones Industrial Average."[11]

For headquarters, Maple wanted timely data. Operationally, this meant weekly data. So he required each precinct to deliver its data to One Police Plaza every Friday afternoon where they could be entered into a common format permitting analysis. Then, Maple created an electronic template and required the precincts to deliver a disk to headquarters every Friday. This solved the data-entry problem and facilitated analyses. Today, the precincts simply enter their data onto NYPD's servers, to which the analysts at headquarters have instant access.

"Bring Us Whatever Data You Have"

With the request, "Bring us whatever data you have," Mayor Martin O'Malley launched his effort to employ data to improve service delivery in Baltimore. O'Malley had a purpose. Unlike a police chief, however, he didn't have any data related to his purpose. In 2000, Baltimore's agencies did not collect any data that had anything to do with the results they were supposed to produce.

All organizations, however, do need to keep two kinds of data for two operational purposes: to carry out internal administrative functions; and to satisfy requirements for external reporting. Thus, like all public, private, and nonprofit organizations, every city agency had financial data. And like any organization larger than a family, every city agency had personnel data. So that's what Baltimore's agencies brought to CitiStat: data on finances and personnel.

Thus, CitiStat initially focused on an easily identifiable performance deficit: excessive overtime. Was overtime one of the city's biggest performance deficits? From a purely abstract perspective, O'Malley considered it unacceptably large. Certainly, without careful and consistent controls, overtime in any organization can creep higher. And, from existing data, the CitiStat staff could easily produce some useful first-order analysis revealing what agencies, what subunits within what agencies, indeed what supervisors of what subunits, were the biggest users (or abusers) of overtime.[12]

In FY 2001, the first full year of CitiStat's operation, Baltimore claims to have saved $6 million by reducing overtime and another $1.2 million by reducing absenteeism.[13] Over seven years (FY 2001 through FY 2007), Baltimore reported an accumulated savings from reduced overtime of $30.9 million over the FY 2000 baseline.[14] O'Malley's overarching purpose had nothing to do with overtime. By reducing overtime, however, he generated the budgetary equivalent of a revenue increase.

O'Malley's purpose was to improve basic service delivery.[15] And once Baltimore had its 311 phone number and its CitiTrack database up and running, his leadership team began to get data directly related to the results he wanted to produce: How well was the city responding to citizen concerns? Were city agencies meeting their service-delivery targets? If not, which ones were they missing? Who was missing them? Why? Given that these data were very current, the analyses and the performance deficits were also very current. Indeed, each CitiStat meeting could focus on data from the previous two weeks—or on a specific datum as an example of a larger problem.

What data to collect? This is rarely obvious. Sometimes the choice will be strictly opportunistic: What data do we have? Eventually, however, a Performance-Stat team will need data that reveal how well it is doing in achieving its public purpose. Unfortunately, the easily available data may be only loosely connected to that purpose. And the data that are most directly connected to that purpose can be hard (perhaps impossible) to identify, let alone collect.

What Data Will Help How?

Compared with a public agency, a business firm has a narrower, well-defined purpose. Moreover, there exist well established measures for determining how well a firm is achieving its purpose. Yet within a firm, reported Marshall Meyer of the Wharton School and Vipin Gupta of Simmons College, "the most commonly used performance measures tend to be uncorrelated with one another," which (they argued) explains why business has created so many different ones.[16]

To many, market share is a useful, leading indicator of financial success: If a firm can increase its market share, goes the logic, it will improve its long-run profitability. As Bryan Sharp and his colleagues at the University of South Australia wrote: "It has been known for many years that there is a positive relationship between market share and profitability."[17]

Not so fast, dissented Denise Rousseau: "Organizational success in obtaining market share often bears little relationship to other performance indicators."[18] Stuart Jackson of L.E.K Consulting even argued that expanding market share can *hurt* a firm's long-term financial prospects: "Market share, as most companies use it, is a misleading and dangers measure," wrote Jackson. "Higher market share often means lower profits and lower return."[19]

Baseball managers face the same problem of finding useful data. In my youth, baseball had a few simple measures of a player's performance. For batters: batting average, runs batted in, and home runs. For pitchers: won-loss record and earned run average. It was a simpler era.

Then along came the analytic wonks from SABR, the Society for American Baseball Research. These "sabermetricians" invented a galaxy of new performance measures: SLG for slugging percentage; OBP for on-base percentage; and OPS for on-base plus slugging. Why? Because none of the old measures perfectly captured all aspects of a hitter's performance. Different measures capture different types of outputs. None fully captures a player's contribution to the team's purpose: To win baseball games.[20]

Yet these efforts to develop performance measures are done for an undertaking with two important and simplifying characteristics: (1) The purpose is clear: to win games, and (2) The rules are very specific, well enforced, and not subject to much change.

Neither of these characteristics apply to government.

Public executives should not expect to easily uncover performance data that completely capture how well their organization is doing in producing results for citizens. Indeed, if executives in business and baseball have a difficult time identifying useful performance data, public-sector executives will find this even more challenging. The task is to identify data that are (1) correlated with the organization's purpose, and (2) relatively easy to obtain. Finding data with both characteristics is rarely easy. Reported Pamela Cardillo, the director of Providence's ProvStat, "the most difficult part of my job is crafting a meaningful metric."[21]

Data and Performance Deficits

The purpose of the U.S. Federal Aviation Administration (FAA) is "to provide the safest, most efficient aerospace system in the world."[22] Straightforward enough. Yet, this mission provides no hint about *how* to improve performance. The FAA needs to identify key performance deficits. Yet, what kind of data could the FAA use to determine when it had eliminated or mitigated some of them?

How about deaths from airplane accidents? Transporting passengers safely is the ultimate outcome. Every death is a clear performance failure. Fortunately, deaths from airplane accidents are rare. It is difficult for the FAA to use these few data points to improve performance. Nor do these data really help citizens evaluate the FAA. Given the random nature of airline accidents, even if the FAA improved many aspects of airline safety, this year's fatalities could still go up.

To improve performance, the FAA needs data. It needs data that capture some of its most significant problems—performance deficits that could contribute to fatalities. How about near misses? If the FAA can drive down the number of near misses, it will also drive down the potential for deaths. Yes: The relationship between near misses and deaths is probabilistic. The number of near misses could go down, and deaths could go up. Conversely, the number of near misses could go up, but deaths still go down. Regardless, the FAA might decide that one significant performance deficit is too many near misses and carefully collect data on their number and characteristics. In fact, the FAA does collect such data through the Aviation Safety Reporting System.[23]

What to do with such near-miss data?[24] Some simple analysis might reveal a large number of near misses in a particular category: near misses at specific airports or in specific regions; near misses during specific times of the day, days of the week, or seasons of the year; near misses involving specific aircraft or specific airlines. The analysts don't know where to look; they have to guess at potentially relevant categories. Still, only once it collects and analyses its data does the FAA have a basis for deciding which performance deficit(s) to fix next.

Every organization has multiple performance deficits. Thus, the leadership team needs to focus. This choice is a judgment. It is also a leadership responsibility. It reflects the leadership team's analysis about which of its many performance deficits to tackle next. The FAA in the United States and the Civil Aviation Authority (CAA) in the United Kingdom have the same responsibilities. Yet in any given year, the specific problems facing these two agencies may be quite different. Thus, the leaders of the FAA and the CAA—in their respective efforts to improve airline safety—might focus on different performance deficits. Nevertheless, the leadership teams at the FAA and the CAA cannot decide which performance deficits to attack until they collect (and analyze) data related to their purpose.

No Perfect Performance Measure

Unfortunately, there exists *no perfect performance measure*.[25] Some measures capture certain components of performance while missing others. Some measures suggest that results are improving while masking a significant deterioration in other aspects of performance. Some measures capture aspects of past performance but ignore important contributors to future performance.

Moreover, all measures create incentives. A publicized measure will encourage people to improve their score. Unfortunately, while seeking to improve this publicized measure, people and organizations may do little to achieve the organization's purpose. Indeed, in their zeal to improve their formal score, people may undermine the organization's efforts to achieve its real purposes. Any performance measure comes with unintended (and sometimes perverse) incentives and consequences.[26]

From a leadership perspective, the search is never for the [nonexistent] perfect measure. Rather, the PerformanceStat staff needs to look for the measure(s) that can best help everyone in the organization understand how well it is performing and what it should do next.

Of all the output measures in government with which I am familiar, the best is the childhood vaccination rate for measles. If this measure goes up, the world is a better place. Why? Because this vaccine produces the very outcome society wants. If you give a child the vaccine as the U.S. Centers for Disease Control recommends (two doses, with the first given after the child is one year old), the probability that the child is immune to measles is 99 percent.[27] This result is impressive. For most organizations, no output produces anything close to a 99-percent success rate for outcomes.

An additional plus comes from the "herd effect."[28] If you give the vaccine to every child in a neighborhood, even those few children for whom it does not create immunity will be better off. Even these vaccinated but unimmunized children will be much less likely to come into contact with a child who has the measles and, thus, are less likely to get it.

Of course, to motivate the people responsible for vaccinating children—and thus for producing the desired outcome of immunized, healthier children—a public agency cannot use the *immunization rate*. The immunization rate is an easily understood outcome measure. If you mastered long division, you get it. But public health agencies don't produce the outcome of *immunized* children. They produce the output of *vaccinated* children. The vaccine output produces—very directly—the immunization outcome.

For a government jurisdiction to get its immunization rate up, it will need to set a service-delivery (or output) target for the number of vaccinated children that the public health department produces. Then, the department will need to break that overall target down into targets for subregions, and then into targets for teams within those subregions.

For measles, the output-to-outcome theory is direct. The scientific evidence is clear. If every team makes its production target for vaccinations, so will all of the subregions and thus the entire jurisdiction. And, if every jurisdiction makes its production target, it will improve its immunization rate to the desired level.

What is the consequence of assigning performance targets to subregions and teams? One purpose is to motivate them. Indeed, once one of the subregions hits its target, the motivational pressure is on. Excuses (presented as explanations) are no longer convincing. One subregion has done it. Why can't the others? "Aren't you as good as they are?" "How come you can't do it?" (See appendix C, "The Motivational Consequences of Feedback and Rewards.")

Campbell's Law

How will subunits respond to this pressure? Will they do *whatever is necessary* to achieve their target?

Whatever is necessary? What might this include? Those who set the target presumably thought it meant first working harder and then working smarter.

Suppose, however, that the team is really feeling the pressure. Suppose it is already working harder. Suppose it can't figure out how to work any smarter. What other alternatives does it have? Harder and smarter are not the only options. A desperate team might invent another one.

Donald Campbell, the social scientist who focused much of his work on the evaluation of public policies, suggested another possibility: "The more any quantitative social indicator is used for social decision-making, the more subject it will be to corruption pressures and the more apt it will be to distort and corrupt the social processes it is intended to monitor."

"Crime rates are in general very corruptible indicators," concluded Campbell, as are achievement tests in education.[29]

Pressures to reduce crime and improve test scores have produced such distortions and corruptions. In 2011, a special investigation of the Atlanta Public Schools found that "cheating occurred throughout the school district" on Georgia's 2009 Criterion-Referenced Competency Test. It involved 178 educators, including 38 principals.[30] It may have been the biggest U.S. cheating scandal on standardized tests, but certainly not the only one.

In New York City, retired police officers reported that precinct commanders had been under pressure to downgrade felonies to misdemeanors, or simply not report a crime at all. This misreporting, the study's authors concluded, caused reported felonies to be at least 13 percent lower than they would have been otherwise.[31]

Data distortions and corruptions are not unique to the United States. Neither of these two examples destroyed as many lives as China's Great Leap Forward, which killed 36 million during the "Great Famine" of 1958 to 1962. Chairman Mao Zedong pressured the leaders of the people's communes to establish unrealistically high production quotas for grain and to report success in achieving these impossible results. Then, when faced with severe punishment for not meeting their quotas, reported Yang Jisheng of *Yanhuang Chunqiu,* the communes produced "exaggerated crop-yield claims."[32] Indeed, writes Frank Dikötter of the University of Hong Kong, "the distortion was at its greatest at the very top, as false reporting and inflated [production] claims accumulated on their way up the party hierarchy."[33]

The distortion and corruption about which Campbell worries comes in two forms. That great American philosopher (and head of Tammany Hall) George Washington Plunckett distinguished between "dishonest graft" and "honest graft": "Dishonest graft was illegal, and you could go to jail for it. Honest graft was perfectly legal, but everyone knew it was graft.[34] Similarly, I distinguish between "dishonest cheating" and "honest cheating." Dishonest cheating is illegal; you can go to jail for it. Honest cheating is perfectly legal, but everyone thinks it is cheating.

In educational testing, there exist numerous forms of "dishonest cheating": teachers giving students the problems and answers before the test; teachers telling the students the answers during the test; teachers erasing wrong answers and replacing them with correct ones. The list of possibilities is long, and some educators have gone to jail for dishonest cheating.

Honest cheating is called "teaching to the test." It is not illegal. No one goes to jail for it. Nevertheless, it illustrates how putting pressure on people (teachers) and teams (schools) to improve on a specific performance measure can produce the distortion about which Campbell worries. After all, achievement tests do not—indeed, cannot—capture *all* of the theoretical concepts, cognitive capabilities, and analytical skills citizens want students to learn. Some concepts, capabilities, and skills will be easier to test objectively than others; those will be on the exam. And, teachers—being human—will teach to this test.

Thus, educators are wont to observe that the challenge in educational testing is designing "a test worth teaching to."[35] Yet, research has shown, reported Daniel Koretz of Harvard University, that even tests "designed to be 'worth teaching to' can generate distorted incentives and inflated test scores."[36]

So get over it. Don't seek the perfect performance measure. It doesn't exist. Don't waste countless meetings debating whose measure is without defects. All measures have them. Don't hire consultants to create the ultimate measure.

Instead, start with a good measure (or three). Not great. Not perfect. Just good. But from the beginning, try to identify its inadequacies. Recognize what problems the measure might create; then, as you implement your performance strategy, be alert for the emergence of such flaws.

Next: Can you live with these flaws? Or must you make some adjustments? Perhaps some minor adjustments? Or maybe some major changes? Implement these improvements. Still, don't believe that this round of improvements—or the tenth round—will eliminate all of the flaws. They won't. Get over it.

Also check other measures. What other indicators could suggest that a team is distorting the data? Organizations that use one measure as a target to drive performance need to check a variety of other measures: Given a team's progress against its target, are other measures behaving in consistent ways? Or is there something "funny" about the data? If so, what does this "funniness" suggest about possible "funniness" in the team's behavior? (More on this in chapter 9.)

Data as an Early Warning

On any given day, the New York City Department of Correction (DOC) is responsible for the safekeeping of between 13,000 and 18,000 inmates—detainees who have been accused of a crime and are awaiting trial, or individuals who have been convicted of a crime and sentenced to less than a year in jail. Despite its name, the department is not in the "correction" business; inmates are not detained long enough for the department to improve their behavior when they reenter society. Rather, the department is in the housing business.

When Martin Horn became DOC commissioner in 2003, he decided that one of his department's primary responsibilities was to keep its inmates, its staff, and the city's citizens safe from violence. Indeed, on its website, the department lists (after its head-count data on inmate population, admissions, and average length of stay) data on incidents of stabbings and slashings.[37] Thus, DOC has some advantages similar to those of the police department. Everyone—particularly everyone who works in the prisons—agrees on which way these data should go. Moreover, during the normal course of doing its business, the department collects data on stabbings and slashings plus other inmate-on-inmate, inmate-on-staff, and staff-on-inmate violence.

DOC calls its version of PerformanceStat TEAMS, for "Total Efficiency Accountability Management System." Think of it as CorrectionStat. And in the department's "primary indicator report," which is prepared just before the monthly TEAMS meeting, the first several pages of data focus on security—everything from stabbings and slashings, to weapons recovered (including shanks, shivs, and razors), to visitor arrests.

These are after-the-fact data. They reveal how dangerous the department's facilities were last month. Aggregate data about the past may, however, have little predictive power. Still they do provide the basis for further, more detailed analysis. If analysts can disaggregate the data—breaking them down to focus on particular inmates, or wards, or shifts, or even particular guards, weapons, or assaults—they may discover some micropatterns that suggest some small tactical modifications or major strategic shifts that will reduce some specific types of violence.[38]

As for predicting the future, DOC identified an easily available and quite predictive indicator of potentially dangerous events: data on commissary sales to inmates. A slashing injures only one inmate (or maybe a few). A riot can injure many more. And who would know when some inmates are planning a riot? Other inmates. What might these inmates do? Inmates know that after the riot, they will be locked in their cells. They won't be able to go to the prison's commissary. Not a happy time. Thus, when the prison grapevine reports that a riot is imminent, inmates stock up on whatever they would like to have in their cells during the post-riot lockdown.

For anyone managing a prison, a very useful indicator of a potential performance deficit—a hint that some inmates may be planning a riot—is a spike in commissary sales. They may suggest something, but what exactly? What actions should who take based on these data? A spike in commissary sales may suggest that a group of inmates is planning a riot. It does not, however, suggest who is in the group, when the riot might occur, or how to prevent it.

Dials, Tin Openers, and Alarm Bells

A spike in commissary sales is what Neil Carter of the University of York called a "tin opener" or maybe an "alarm bell." Carter and his colleagues divided performance measures into three categories: dials, tin openers, and alarm bells.

—Dials are *prescriptive* performance measures. They provide "a precise measure of inputs, outputs, and outcomes based on a clear understanding of what good and bad performance entails." Dials are directly "linked to objectives or targets."

—Tin openers are *descriptive* performance measures. "By opening up a 'can of worms' they do not give answers but prompt interrogation and inquiry." Tin openers "by themselves provide an incomplete and inaccurate picture" of performance.

—Alarm bells are *proscriptive* performance measures. They warn that "things are happening which should not be tolerated in a well-run organization."[39]

Carter admitted there may be some overlap.[40] In DOC headquarters, a spike in commissary sales rings an alarm bell. But it also opens a can of worms, raising a variety of questions: Why are inmates considering a riot? Who should do what to prevent or control the riot? What can be done to eliminate or mitigate the causes and thus prevent future riots?

As a performance measure, the measles vaccination rate is a dial. It reveals directly how well a health department is preventing measles. As Carter noted, "implicit in the use of PIs [performance indicators] as dials is the assumption that standards of performance are unambiguous."[41] In such a case, he continued, "'performance' can be read off the dials: that is, there is a set of norms or standards against which achievement can be assessed."

In government, however, most performance measures are tin openers. They suggest the need for some analysis. They "trigger questions," wrote Carter. Thus, "it is less important," he continued, that these measures "should be totally accurate than that they point managers towards problems that require remedial action."[42]

Tin opener measures can suggest that a performance deficit exists. Unfortunately, they do not necessarily reveal its nature, let alone who should do what. And in some ways, alarm bells are simply noisier versions of tin openers— but only if the organization is listening. A performance measure works as an alarm bell only if it rings at a frequency to which the organization has already tuned its ears.

Inputs, Outputs, and Outcomes

Performance measurement has its own mantra: "Don't measure inputs. Don't measure process. Don't measure activities. Don't measure outputs. Only measure outcomes." Theoretically, this makes a lot of sense. Outcomes are the objective. And the causal connection between inputs and outcomes is, at best, uncertain. More inputs do not guarantee better outcomes. More cops (input) do not guarantee less crime (outcome).

The same applies to processes and activities (mental-health therapy sessions), and to outputs (potholes filled)—though as you move along the value chain from inputs, to processes and activities, to outputs, the connection to the outcomes becomes closer. Still, even improved outputs do not guarantee improved outcomes. The police can increase their inputs: more cop cars. They can increase their activities: more cops patrolling the streets. They can increase their outputs: more people arrested. Yet, all that may not reduce crime (let alone improve citizens' sense of safety).

Unfortunately, outcomes are difficult to measure. Moreover, even when public executives have outcome data, they still confront two problems: the timeliness problem and the attribution problem.

Timeliness: Maple wanted timely data. Delays reduce the value of the data. Yet, sometimes the real outcomes don't happen until years or decades later. Executives might be able to use outcome data to learn what strategies *had* worked and what ones had *not*. They might not, however, be able to do that until much later. And how could they use such delayed evidence to improve current performance? The use of outcome data can create an unacceptably long delay in the feedback loop designed to improve current performance.

Attribution: An outcome is the result of a complex interaction between the outputs of government and the actions of society. If outcomes improve, how much of that improvement can be attributed to the actions of government and how much to societal factors? (The controversy about CompStat's impact illustrates the attribution problem.)

Both the timeliness and attribution problems confound any effort to determine the effectiveness of elementary and secondary education. The real, ultimate outcome that citizens seek from our public schools, I have argued, is children who grow up to become productive employees and responsible citizens.[43] Unfortunately, it is quite difficult to determine whether a school district is producing this outcome. There is the problem of deciding how to measure whether an adult is a "productive employee" let alone a "responsible citizen." But even if someone solves this measurement problem and creates some easily collectable and widely accepted measures of these two outcomes, there remain the timeliness and attribution problems. These outcome data are not available for years, indeed decades, after the (now former) children have left school. If a student had grown up to be a notably productive employee and an especially responsible citizen, how much of this economic and civic contribution can be attributed to his or her schools, family, community, church, or influential mentor?

To avoid the measurement, timeliness, and attribution problems, we don't even try to obtain any real *outcome* data on schools. Instead, we create and collect output data: standardized test scores. Such output data have some obvious advantages: They cover some necessary (though not sufficient) skills for success in life. Students will not grow up to be productive employees or responsible citizens if they can't read and do long division. Such output data also have some obvious deficiencies: The causal connection between these measured outputs and the desired outcomes is neither direct, obvious, or proven. A child who scores well on such tests could grow up to be a very clever con artist.

Performance Data in Public Welfare

In 1998, Jason Turner, commissioner of the New York City Human Resources Administration (HRA), created JobStat, a PerformanceStat strategy for its welfare-to-work effort. Similarly, in 2005 (without any interaction), Bryce Yokomizo, director of the Los Angeles County (LAC) Department of Public Social Services (DPSS), created DPSSTATS (for "DPSS Total Accountability, Total Success").[44]

Both agencies have a public purpose: To help families move from dependence on welfare to economic and psychological independence. HRA emphasizes its "commitment to move cash assistance recipients to employment," observing that it "provides temporary help to individuals and families with social service and economic needs to assist them in reaching self-sufficiency."[45] DPSS states that it "serves an ethnically and culturally diverse community through programs designed to both alleviate hardship and promote health, personal responsibility, and economic independence."[46]

What to measure? How could either agency collect data revealing whether its performance was excellent or poor, improving or deteriorating? What kind of data could it either use to determine its current level of performance, to ascertain what approaches (if any) are working, to diagnose its key performance deficits, to reveal opportunities for improvement, and to suggest strategies to be pursued?

It is not obvious. Any kind of outcome data would present the agency with both the timeliness and attribution problems. Consequently, both HRA and DPSS rely on data other than outcomes.

Moreover, from the perspective of citizens and voters, there is a big difference between a police department and a social service department. All citizens care about crime. They are personally concerned about *when what* crimes are committed *where* (and newspapers report such data), and about *how many* people are arrested for these crimes. For a police department, citizens pay personal attention to both the outputs (arrests) and the outcomes (crimes). For a social service agency, however, there exist no simple, obvious, and useful data on outcomes (how many people's lives are improved by how much?). And the output data— how many people received how many services of what kind—do not affect the average citizen directly or daily. Nor do the newspapers report these data.

To help just one family become self-sufficient and economically independent, both HRA and DPSS have to get a sequence of tasks right. If either agency does not properly do a task in this sequence, it creates a significant performance error. And if either agency is making the same mistake multiple times, it has a significant performance deficit. Consequently, both JobStat and DPSSTATS collect data on how each office handles each task.

These organizations also set performance targets for these tasks—targets for inputs or processes or even outputs, but hardly outcomes. For example, when HRA launched JobStat, it set a process target for its first year: 100 percent of its recipients would be "engaged" (in a work experience program, or education, or job training). For the second year, HRA set an output target: 100,000 job placements.[47]

On May 31, 2012, a DPSSTATS meeting examined a variety of different measures. One set of data focused on the welfare-to-work participation rate (LAC's equivalent of NYC's "engagement" rate) for which the target was 50 percent. DPSS was above 40 percent in all five months of the reporting period, but never hit the 50-percent target. Moreover, one of the seven regions had not hit the 50-percent target once during that period, and its director was asked what actions would be taken to achieve the target. Indeed, Phil Ansell, DPSS's chief deputy and a key architect of DPSSTATS, who was running the meeting, kept raising operational questions: Does X happen? Can we find out if Y is true? What can we learn from these data about Z?

Reporting on Inputs, Activities, Processes, and Outputs

Both HRA and DPSS administer programs established by the U.S. government, which provides a significant proportion of the funding. Thus local agencies are required to report to the feds a variety of very specific input, activity, process, and output data. Moreover, if some of these data are deficient—if they are outside the permissible range—the U.S. government can penalize the agency financially by reducing payments. Consequently, both NYC's HRA and LAC's DPSS are quite focused on satisfying all federally prescribed criteria for inputs, activities, processes, and outputs. They carefully track such data.

"In the majority of what we do, there is no distinction between means and ends," emphasized Ansell. One of the department's core tasks is to determine eligibility for different government services. For Medi-Cal (Calfornia's Medicaid program), DPSS only determines eligibility; it has no role in the delivery of Medi-Cal services. DPSS doesn't even know whether the people it certifies as eligible bother to obtain any services. And for this responsibility, Ansell argued, the process is the output and the outcome. "As far as our role is concerned, the delivery of the right amount [of financial support and other services] at the right time is the outcome."[48]

Therefore, Ansell continued, the various *process* measures that DPSS uses—and that are the basis for many DPSSTATS discussions—are also *outcome* measures. These are the measures for which the state and the feds hold the agency accountable. These are the measures about which citizens (through their elected officials) care. Citizens want people to *get* the money and services for which they are eligible in a timely manner; and they want people *not* to get any services for which they are not eligible. Through the democratic process, higher levels of government decide who is eligible for what support and services.[49] DPSS's role, concluded Ansell, is to faithfully administer these policies.

Data for JobStat

In 2013, HRA's JobStat sessions covered 25 different measures for each Job Center. On its monthly "JobStat Report," HRA listed these measures in five categories: qualified placements and participation; engagement process; application process; fraud prevention; and case management process. The first measure on the list was "Qualified Reported Placements" of public assistance beneficiaries into employment. This is JobStat's primary output measure. For job placements, each Job Center has an annual target, which depends on its caseload size. A center's JobStat Report lists this target, year-to-date placements, the percentage of its target that it has achieved, and its rank compared with the other Job Centers.

For example, for 2013, HRA had a citywide target of 88,000 job placements, of which the Dekalb Job Center in Brooklyn was assigned 4,647 placements. On Dekalb's March report, the year-to-date placements totaled 848 or 18 percent of its annual target.[50] HRA also reported that, citywide through March, job placements had totaled 15,974, also 18 percent of its annual target of 88,000.[51]

HRA wants those receiving assistance to also be engaged in a "work-related activity." Thus, on a center's JobStat Report, its first "Engagement Process" measure is the "employment plan initiation rate." Other data on the JobStat Report include several processing rates such as the "OCSE [Office of Child Support Enforcement] Referral Rate," and the "SNAP [Supplemental Nutrition Assistance Program, a.k.a. Food Stamps] Application Timeliness Rate." Each has a target rate, as well as a minimally acceptable rate; for example, for OCSE referral rate, the target is 95 percent and the minimally acceptable rate is 80 percent.[52] On the JobStat Report, all the data—other than jobs placements—are activity, process, or administrative measures.

Data for DPSSTATS

In Los Angeles County, DPSS collects and publicizes a variety of data. Its quarterly "Caseload Characteristics Report" runs over 450 pages and describes those receiving assistance by age (under 1, 1-2, 3-5 . . . over 65), primary language

(Armenian, Cambodian, . . . Tagalog, Vietnamese), gender, citizenship status, and ethnic origin. DPSS reports such data for the county and for different geographic subdivisions (including departmental district, service planning area, and Congressional district).[53] DPSS also publishes a monthly "Statistical Report" that includes the same countywide caseload information, plus data on application processing and terminations. This report includes multiple graphs showing ten-year trends in monthly data for total caseload as well as "persons aided" by different programs (CalWORKS, General Relief, . . . In-Home Supportive Services) and the county's monthly unemployment rate.[54] Finally, "DPSSTATS maintains an inventory of more than 200 different performance measures."[55]

Every measure has a constituency. This constituency could be a well-organized stakeholder or advocacy group. It could be a constituency of one—an influential member of the Los Angeles County Board of Supervisors or the California legislature. Once a public agency starts collecting data, limiting the number of measures is difficult.

With 200 performance measures, DPSS has lots of data to collect, analyze, digest, and discuss. Obviously, it does not discuss all 200 at every DPSSTATS meeting. Any organization that has so much data so easily available—has to figure out how to focus. What is important? What is irrelevant? What data, while very important, are not quite as important as the core data that provide real information about how well the organization is doing, that reveal its performance deficits and that suggest what it could do differently? DPSS addresses this difficulty in two ways.

First, to ensure that local offices concentrate on core activities, DPSS collects data on eight activity measures. These cover customer service ("seen in 20 minutes" plus "participant satisfaction"), application progressing (for CalWORKS, General Relief, Food Stamps, and Medi-Cal), Medi-Cal redetermination processing, and the Food Stamp error rate. If an office earns a satisfactory score on all of its measures, it earns a "star" that is prominently displayed on its director's name plaque at the next DPSSTATS meeting.[56]

One of these eight measures is "food stamp applications processed timely." The target is 90 percent processed within 30 days. To dramatize how well the department, its four divisions, and its 26 offices are doing, the DPSSTATS staff creates a variety of bar charts. Each division has a bar chart showing for each of its offices the number of applications pending for 31-to-45 days, 46-to-90 days, 91-to-180 days, and 181+ days.

Second, two months before each DPSSTATS meeting, its director, first Karen Kent, succeeded by Gabriela Herrera, and the DPSSTATS staff get together with

Ansell. The purpose is to decide—from the list of 200 different types of data that it tracks—the measures on which to focus. Essentially, the staff is selecting the "performance deficits" [my words, not theirs] on which DPSS, its divisions, and local offices need to concentrate: From all of the many different ways to think about (and collect data on) the department's performance, what does it need to fix next?[57]

Kent noted that every time DPSS focuses on a new measure, it raises a variety of policy, procedural, and practical issues.[58] "The new measures generate (a) the best discussion and (b) the most uneasiness in people," observed Kent. Why? They generate the best discussion because people are trying to figure out what the measures mean. What do they mean analytically; what behavior are the measures capturing? What do they mean operationally; how will who have to change what behavior to look good on the new measures? They generate uneasiness because the new measures may make people look bad. They may require people to change significantly how they do their work, the priorities that they have set, or the information that they have to collect. The new measures will be on top of the existing measures, inevitably making life more uncomfortable.

For many public agencies, the data that are available in a timely manner are often limited to input, activity, process, and output data. Unfortunately, the causal connection between such operational data and the outcomes that the agency is attempting to produce is rarely direct, obvious, or proven.

Identifying Useful Mental Health Data

In 2007, the Los Angeles County Department of Mental Health (DMH) observed that "the metrics used to evaluate and monitor department operations were often inconsistently reliable, insufficiently available, or inadequate to the task. This, along with the inevitable 'crisis of the week,' also led to a lack of clarity regarding departmental priorities."[59]

So how should a department of mental health measure its performance? How can it identify data that are both available and reliable? How can it identify—and use—measures that keep everyone focused on the agency's priorities? How, exactly, should it measure its performance?

DMH concluded that its "ultimate test is whether the lives of people with psychiatric disorders improve."[60] Still, how would it measure any such improvement? DMH can measure inputs, activities, and processes. How, however, might it measure outcomes or even outputs?

In looking for useful performance indicators, DMH's leadership team wanted to answer three performance questions:

1. "Are we delivering good clinical services?"
2. "Are we doing so in a way that represents good business practices?"
3. "Do administrative processes support the service programs in these efforts?"[61]

Nevertheless, when it came to selecting their measures, the department was consciously practical. It went looking for data that were:

1. Important and meaningful. Are these data relevant to the department's core purposes and operations?
2. Readily available. Can these data be obtained from existing data sources?
3. Easily interpretable. Would a change in these numbers clearly reveal whether things are getting better or worse?
4. Operationally moveable. Is this a measure that program managers can directly affect?[62]

If a metric did not satisfy any one of these four criteria, the department could not use it to improve performance. (For police, the answers to these four questions are clearly all "yes." For most public agencies, however, the answers will rarely be an unambiguous "yes." If anything, they are more apt to be a clear "no.") Thus, what measures might DMH have or find that satisfy all four criteria? Would data that satisfied these four criteria be outcome measures? Or even output measures? What data could possibly reveal whether the department was achieving its purposes? How could it determine whether the lives of people with psychiatric disorders were improving?

DMH chose to focus on two outcome measures and one output measure: (1) homelessness; (2) drug and alcohol abuse; and (3) after a period of inpatient, psychiatric care, quick access to outpatient services.[63] If DMH could drive down homelessness and or substance abuse among its client population, it would certainly be serving them well—and society too. And if the department could drive down the time it took to move those recently released from an inpatient psychiatric facility into outpatient care, it would also be serving them and society well.

A decrease in these three measures for the department's client population clearly suggests—but does not prove—that the department is improving the lives of people with psychiatric disorders. Consequently, if the department can obtain accurate data on these three output measures for its service population, it can determine whether or not it is making a difference.

Performance Measurement Is Not Performance Management

A visitor from Mars might conclude—from listening to all of the performance rhetoric on Earth—that "performance measurement" is the same thing as "performance management." Many people use the phrases interchangeably, somehow assuming that they are the same. This assumption is strictly implicit, of course. I know of no one who has said or written "performance measurement = performance management." Nevertheless, scholars, managers, and journalists frequently use the phrase "performance management" when all they are really discussing is "performance measurement." It's as if to *measure* performance is to *manage* performance.

Many public agencies collect lots of performance data. Not all of them analyze their data to identify performance deficits or to decide what to do next. Some agencies analyze their data. Yet not all of them act on the implications of their analyses.[64] Some agencies publish performance data. Yet, inserting data into an annual report or posting data on a website dashboard is not the same as analyzing the data. Nor does it automatically motivate organizations to change their behavior or mobilize people to produce better results. To be effective, a PerformanceStat leadership strategy requires more than the collection, analysis, and publication of data.

To improve performance, data are necessary. But they are hardly sufficient. By themselves, data accomplish very little. They will not—magically and without any human intervention—produce improved results. Improving results requires both an analytical wizard, who can discern what the data reveal about what the organization should do next, and a motivational maestro, who can get people to do it. Or, maybe all it requires is a single leader—a human who is both smart enough to remember and use long division and brave enough to set specific targets.

Performance measures have a multitude of purposes. They can be used to evaluate, control, budget, motivate, promote, celebrate, learn, and improve.[65] Indeed, in any effort to *improve* performance, public executives will certainly have to use their performance measures to *evaluate*, to *motivate,* and to *learn.*

Performance *measurement,* however, is not performance *management.* It is certainly not performance *leadership.*[66]

9

Analyzing and Learning from the Data

How can the data be analyzed to diagnose performance deficits, to nominate opportunities for improvement, to identify what approaches (if any) are working and why, and to suggest new strategies?

"God has chosen to give the easy problems to the physicists."
CHARLES LAVE, University of California, and JAMES MARCH, Stanford University[1]

"Discovery consists of seeing what everybody has seen
and thinking what nobody has thought."
ALBERT SZENT-GYÖRGYI, 1937 Nobel Prize winner in medicine[2]

Robert Dunford, superintendent in chief of the Boston Police Department, opened the department's biweekly CompStat session with a question: "What's going on on the street?" Shootings in Boston were off, and Dunford wanted to learn why. As he told the department's 50 top managers, "If we can identify what we are doing, we can replicate it."

Dunford's question provoked a variety of answers: "Maybe the drug units" were having an impact, noted one officer. "There's hardly anyone at the usual spots," observed another. One district commander suggested that it might be "aggressive patrol." "Quicker indictments" proposed another, explaining that the grand jury was working better so that someone arrested on Friday night would be indicted on Tuesday, not six months later.

Indeed, Dunford's question—and his search for learning—generated numerous explanations that could be organized into three broad categories:

1. It was the weather. During the previous weeks, Boston had experienced a lot of rain.

2. It was the police—particularly aggressive patrol and quicker indictments that were getting the "high-impact players" off the street.
3. It was purely random. Noted one officer: "Crime goes up. Crime goes down."

As he had done before, Dunford was trying to get his department's leadership team to think analytically—to learn from the available data. Not everyone, however, was prepared to do so.

The Data Never Speak for Themselves

These multiple explanations for this drop in shootings debunk the seductive cliché: "The data speak for themselves." For data can "speak" only through a framework, a theory, a cause-and-effect concept, a perception of the world and how it works. All frameworks provide a way of thinking, and the world is full of them. When we analyze problems, we use a framework—usually implicitly and unconsciously—to organize and structure our thinking.

Long division is such a framework that is useful in a variety of circumstances. For this framework can, by creating a comparison, help us decide whether a number is big or small.

Economics provides another framework. So does psychology. Both help us think about how people behave. Yet our conclusions about any specific observation or prediction of human behavior may depend on which framework we choose.

Analytical frameworks can be powerful. "Practical men, who believe themselves to be quite exempt from any intellectual influences," wrote John Maynard Keynes, "are usually the slaves of some defunct economist."[3] "The thinker," observed Oliver Wendell Holmes, Jr., knows that "after he is dead and forgotten, men who never heard of him will be moving to the measure of his thought."[4] People may believe that they are analyzing their data from their own unique perspective. But they would be wrong.

Data are collections of abstract digits: 7, 9, 4, 6 . . . (or, inside a computer, ones and zeros). To interpret the data, we need a framework—a lens through which to observe the data and extract from the otherwise incomprehensible gibberish some knowledge: a coherent pattern, a valuable lesson, a revealing cause-and-effect relationship, an implication for action.

For decades, astute observers have railed against this data-speak-for-themselves nonsense. In 1932, Carl Becker, then president of the American Historical Association, observed that "to suppose that the facts, once established in all their fullness, will 'speak for themselves' is an illusion."[5] "Be aware of the intellectual traditions and choices out of which the 'data' emerge," cautioned Gary Marx, professor emeritus at MIT. "The facts do not speak for themselves. Look for the ventriloquists in the wings."[6] When James Heckman accepted the Nobel Prize in economics, he was unequivocal: "The data do not speak for themselves."[7]

Yet, the cliché lives.

The choice of a framework is a subjective judgment. When analysts choose a framework, they draw on past successes and failures to find patterns in similar data. Still, the conclusions drawn from the data depend more on the analytical framework chosen than on the data themselves. And given the diversity of frameworks available to analyze any collection of data, multiple interpretations are possible. If different people—sincere, honest people—observe identical data from different frameworks, they can reach different, even contradictory, conclusions. (Remember the blind men and the elephant?)

Those who claim that "the data speak for themselves," are saying nothing more than: "If you look at the data using *my* framework, you will see precisely what *I* see." Moreover, these people are implicitly saying, "You should *only* use *my* favorite framework [for if you do, you will reproduce my analytical conclusions and agree precisely with my policy prescriptions]." Those who assert that the data speak for themselves reject the possibility that using different frameworks might reveal useful insights. They are unwilling to accept that there might be alternative interpretations and thus different possible policy implications.

Peter Blau, in his classic book, *The Dynamics of Bureaucracy*, wrote: "Data do not speak for themselves but only answer questions the investigator puts to them."[8] In choosing a framework with which to examine data, the analyst is choosing to ask some questions—and *not* to ask a large number of others.[9]

The data do not speak independently of the analyst. The data do not speak independently of the framework. The data do not speak independently of the questions. The data only speak when an analyst, using a specific framework, asks a specific question. If the answers are useless, it may be because the questions were nonsensical. A civil servant in Sweden observed: "Perhaps we ask the wrong questions, because although we get lots of answers we do not get the answers we need—the answers that tell us about the results."[10] The data cannot answer any question until someone establishes a framework—an economics framework, a psychology framework, a baseball framework—with which to analyze the question and evolve the answer.

The data never talk back to the analyst: They don't say: "Hey, dumb analyst, you are using the wrong framework." The data don't say: "Please, analyst, if you would ask a different question, I could give you a more helpful answer." Reported Milford Wolpoff of the University of Michigan: "I have been in rooms with data and listened very carefully. They never said a word."[11]

Learning by Asking What Questions?

If the data only answer questions put to them, what questions does an agency's leadership team want its analytic staff to ask? Here are six questions whose answers might reveal how well the organization is doing in achieving its purpose, and what it might do to improve.

Three questions about strategic effectiveness:

1. How well are the organization and its subunits currently doing?
2. What performance approaches are (or have been) working?
3. Why are the successful approaches working, and why are the unsuccessful ones not?

Three questions about performance deficits:

1. What performance deficits are inhibiting the organization's ability to achieve its purposes?
2. What opportunities for improvements should the organization tackle first?
3. What new innovative strategies might the organization pursue?

Analysts can answer these questions only if the organization has collected data—relevant data.

Still, how can analysts ask these questions? How should they interrogate the data? Exactly what do they want to learn from the data? What kind of analysis of what kind of data would provide the leadership team some useful insights?

The Analyst's Search for Insight, Evidence, and Strategy

In response to any of these six questions, the available data will rarely generate a single, declarative answer. The data are unlikely to reveal that one successful approach is working because of one solitary cause, or to isolate the one pivotal performance deficit to be fixed next. Clever analysts, however, may be able to exploit the data to generate some significant insights, to suggest some possibly effective strategies. To employ a PerformanceStat strategy, the leadership team needs people throughout the organization with the analytical mindset that is constantly looking for such insights and strategies.

They need analytical skills to quiz the data for evidence about what is and what isn't working. They need the imagination, creativity, and flexibility necessary to generate insights about *why* a subunit is performing better or worse. And, from that insight, they need an understanding of human and organizational behavior to craft some new tactics and strategies that might motivate significant performance improvements.

Any PerformanceStat strategy requires analysts who will interrogate the data. Ideally, this thinking would be done both by the PerformanceStat staff and by subunit managers (or, though this is often a luxury, by a subunit analyst). Regardless of where an analyst sits, however, he or she will be looking for several things:

1. To distinguish between (a) singular problems that can be directly eliminated by unique actions, and (b) patterns of problems that require systemic remedies.
2. To describe the patterns and to suggest possible remedies that could be applied organizationwide.
3. To compare the operational effectiveness of different subunits at eliminating or mitigating the systemic problems, to identify the tactics and strategies that appear to be working, and thus to help every unit to learn and improve.

For this kind of analytic thinking, there exists no formula. It requires creative people who are willing to muck around in the data, rummaging for patterns that others don't see, foraging for insights, dissecting apparent coincidences for something more than pure randomness.

This is not data "mining." That metaphor suggests both that there exists a very specific mine in which the analyst is looking for a very specific ore. It isn't even data "prospecting," with the analyst looking for a specific ore but not knowing where a mine might be. In Robert Parker's *Cold Service*, Hawk explains to Spenser, "We are looking for somebody we may not recognize when we find him."[12]

The analyst is looking for something—but doesn't know what it looks like, let alone where to find it. The analyst might have a theory—perhaps drawn from experience with apparently similar data, or perhaps a guess about what might be important. Yet, while pursuing this theory, the analyst is alert for other possibilities: blips in the data; things that don't add up (mathematically or metaphorically); something that doesn't quite look right. As Albert Szent-Györgyi put it: "Discovery consists of seeing what everybody has seen and thinking what nobody has thought."[13]

Unfortunately, people with this imaginative, innovative, and ingenious mindset are rare. They are often viewed by their more serious, sober, and staid colleagues as certifiably weird. Yet, such analysts—the Hawks and Spensers of the real world—can rummage through the data for insights that their more decorous colleagues will miss.

Providence's ProvStat

In January 2003, David Cicilline was inaugurated as the new mayor of Providence, Rhode Island and announced "the creation of ProvStat . . . to show, at any given moment, exactly how we are doing in fighting crime, educating our children, and managing our finances."[14] In March, Cicilline, his department heads, and the new ProvStat director, Pamela Cardillo, traveled to Baltimore to observe CitiStat. In June, they held their first ProvStat meeting.

Starting with three pilots, Cicilline and Cardillo went looking for agencies with data. There were few. "Everyone talked in anecdotes," recalled Cardillo. "No one could quantify anything."[15] Still the fire department and the tax collector's office had some data, both historical and current. Yet, neither had analyzed their data. "Nothing had ever been counted," noted Cardillo. "Nothing had ever been tracked."[16]

For the pilot, Cicilline and Cardillo also wanted a service-delivery department. They chose the Parks Department, which had almost no data and no capacity for analysis. "The entire Parks Department was paper driven," recalled Cardillo, though it did collect data on employee attendance.[17]

Fixing Park Maintenance

Parks had two divisions: Forestry handled the city's 20,000 trees,[18] and Grounds Maintenance took care of the parks: the city's crown jewel, the 435-acre Roger Williams Park (with a zoo, a carousel, and a greenhouse), plus 110 other parks. Yet, park maintenance was strictly ad hoc. Crews of three to six men were supposed to mow and clean each park at least once a month; but it wasn't obvious what was happening. After a crew serviced a park, it filled out a form recording the weather for the day, the work done, and the number of people in the crew. This form disappeared into a file folder in a filing cabinet, never to be seen again.[19] Like other city departments, noted Cardillo, Parks was hurt by its "lack of adequate technology and infrastructure."[20] "Nothing was collected electronically" in the service-delivery departments, she recalled. "It took nearly two years building the tools to collect the data."[21]

In Parks, a key performance deficit was the absence of appropriate workplace behavior. When one member of a maintenance crew was late for work, the others waited at the garage; the crew started its work only after the last member showed up. There were no formal or informal sanctions for tardiness—or absenteeism, or the overuse of sick time, or taking vacation during the summer months (even

FIGURE 9-1. Incidents of Maintenance Employees Arriving Late or Leaving Early, Providence Department of Parks, July 2004–May 2006

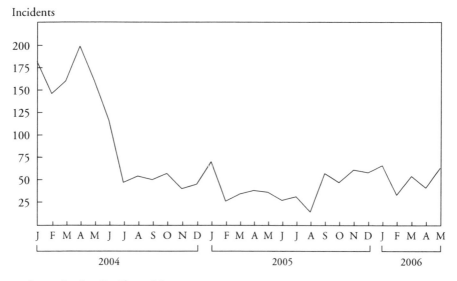

Source: ProvStat, Providence, R.I.

though the crews were told to take vacation before July 1 or after Labor Day). Furthermore, city employees were not required to work outside if the temperature rose above 90° (which happened 17 times in 2004), and rain affected the work schedule. Finally, special events at individual parks (plus squeaky-wheel demands to fix something *now*) disrupted the schedule. The crews appeared to rotate through the parks at random.

One ProvStat meeting revealed that the Department of Public Works had a policy for dealing with tardiness: first offense, a verbal warning; second offense, a written warning; third offense, suspension from work. In August 2004, Parks adopted this policy. Yet before it was formally implemented, maintenance managers began clamping down, sending a signal that arriving late or leaving early was no longer acceptable. Thus, in the spring of 2004, such behavior became less frequent. (See figure 9-1.)

Inappropriate employee behavior included the abuse of sick time. ProvStat's data revealed that some employees were frequently out sick on—surprise?—Mondays and Fridays. After these data were discussed at a ProvStat session, the Parks' superintendent and the city's Human Resources Department created a

TABLE 9-1. Sick Days Taken, Maintenance Staff, Providence
Department of Parks, 2004 and 2005

Month	Full days		Partial days		Total days[a]		
	2004	2005	2004	2005	2004	2005	Percent change
January	138	164	64	68	170.0	198.0	14
February	137	92	68	65	171.0	124.5	– 37
March	187	136	87	65	230.5	168.5	–37
April	132	89	87	55	175.5	116.5	–51
May	129	101	80	77	169.0	139.5	–21
June	141	121	87	76	184.5	159.0	–16
July	164	115	67	68	197.5	149.0	–33
August	173	100	60	51	203.0	125.5	–62
September	145	122	67	83	178.5	163.5	–9
October	146	134	63	70	177.5	169.0	–5
November	143	105	71	64	178.5	137.0	–30
December	159	78	100	53	209.0	104.5	–100
Total	1,794	1,357	901	795	2,244.5	1,754.5	–28

Source: ProvStat, City of Providence, Rhode Island.
a. Total days = (full days) + ½ (partial days).

new, sick-day policy (similar to the tardiness policy with verbal and written warnings followed by suspension), which was implemented in January 2005. During
the next year, sick days taken by maintenance employees dropped by 28 percent.
(See table 9-1.)

Merely getting employees to work their required hours was not enough to significantly improve park maintenance. Thus, in June 2004, to try to understand
maintenance, the ProvStat staff built a database to track who was doing what,
where, and when. Next, using the paper records, the staff filled in the database
back to January 2004. Then over the winter of 2004–05, they analyzed the data,
concluding that maintenance needed to deploy the existing staff and equipment
more efficiently. Maintenance in large parks was different from maintenance in
small parks. Large parks required lawn tractors; for small parks, however, the
most appropriate equipment might be a weed whacker.

Thus, in early 2005, Providence reorganized the work of its Grounds Maintenance division based on the size of the parks, not their location. Roger Williams Park got its own, dedicated maintenance staff. The large parks were still

organized into two divisions: South Neighborhoods and North Neighborhoods. The big change was the creation of one two-person crew to handle all of the city's 17 small parks. Cardillo reported that Alix Ogden, then parks superintendent, "credits data with being instrumental in reorganizing the parks—and how she reorganized it."[22]

The small-parks crew had a fixed weekly schedule: On Monday, the crew picked up the weekend's trash from all 17 parks. On Tuesday, Wednesday, and Thursday, it visited each park on a regular schedule, mowing and providing other routine maintenance. (If a park was scheduled for Wednesday maintenance and rain or some hitch prevented the crew from doing that week's work, the schedule did not slide. All of the parks that were on Thursday's schedule got their regular maintenance, and those that were missed waited until the next week.) On Friday, the crew again picked up the trash at every park.

Table 9-2 illustrates how small-park maintenance changed from a 23-week, mid-spring-to-early-fall period in 2004 to the same period in 2005. For these 23 weeks in 2004, a crew did maintenance work at the Alphonso Street Playground six times in five different weeks; a crew visited this park twice in June, once in August, twice in September (both times in the same week), and once in October. For a seven-week period in July and early August, no crew did any maintenance work at the Alphonso Street Playground.

For the first three weeks of August, 2004, no crew visited 10 of the 17 small parks. For 16 straight weeks from mid-June through early October, the Jennifer Rivera Park got no maintenance. Zero. And from late May through early October—the time when citizens most use their parks—maintenance crews did not visit the Pleasant Street Park for 19 straight weeks.

By 2005, however, the crew dedicated to small parks had significantly improved the consistency of its maintenance schedule. Over the same 23-week period, the number of times these 17 parks received regular maintenance more than doubled from 106 in 2004 to 250 in 2005. And during the eight high-use weeks of July and August, the number of times these parks received regular maintenance nearly tripled—from 32 in 2004 to 91 in 2005 (not including the missing data for the first full week of August).

Maintenance coverage wasn't perfect. During the last week of July and the first week of August, the crew made only six visits to the 17 parks—missing two-thirds of them. Still, for most of 2005, for most of the parks, the time between maintenance-crew visits was rarely over two weeks. Indeed, excluding the week for which no data are available (August 7-12, 2005), 13 of the 17 small parks never went more than two weeks without a maintenance visit.

TABLE 9-2. Frequency of Small-Park Maintenance Visits, Providence Department of Public Works, May to Early October, 2004 and 2005

Park name	Total weeks visited (May–Oct.)	May 2004 2[a,b]	9	16	23	30	June 2004 6	13	20	27	July 2004 4	11	18	25	Aug 2004 1	8	15	22	29	Sep 2004 5	12	19	26	Oct 3
Alphonso St. Playground	5							1	1									1			2			1
Baxter St. Playground	8			1				1		1		1		1				1		1				1
Brassil Memorial Park	10			1		2			1	1	1			1		1		1			1			1
Columbus Square	7					1		1		1			1				1				1			1
Diamond St. Playground	6			1				1		1								1			1			1
East St. Park	7				1				1	1		1		1				1			1			
Fox Point Memorial	8			1	1	1				1	1			1		1								1
Jennifer Rivera Park	2					2			1															
Mattie Smith Playground	7				1					1				1	1			1			2			1
Morris Ave. Playground	4								1				1				1				1			
Ninth St. Park	9			1	1			1	1		1							1			1	1		1
Pearl St. Park	4					2			1									1						1
Pleasant St. Park	1				1																			
Preston & Ives Playground	7				1			1		1	1	1				1								1
Salisbury St. Playground	6				1			1		1								1			1			1
Summit Avenue Park	9				1			1	1				1			1		1			1	1		1
Waldo St. Tot Lot	6					1		1						1				1			2			1
23-week total	106	0	0	5	7	12	0	9	7	8	4	3	3	5	1	4	2	10	0	1	15	3	0	13

Park name	Total weeks visited May–Oct.[a]	May 2005					June 2005				July 2005					August 2005					September 2005				Oct
		1	8	15	22	29	5	12	19	26	3	10	17	24	31	7	14	21	28	4	11	18	25	2
Alphonso St. Playground	16	1	1		1	1		1	1		1	1	2			n.a.	1	1	1	1	1		2	1
Baxter St. Playground	17	1	1	1	1	1	1	1	1	1	1	1	1			n.a.	1	1				1	1	1
Brassil Memorial Park	14	1	2	1		1	1		1		1			1		n.a.	1			2			1	1
Columbus Square	16	1	1	1	1		1			1		1			1	n.a.	1	1	1		2		1	1
Diamond St. Playground	17	1	1	1	3	1	1	1		1	1	2			2	n.a.	1	1	1	1	1	1	1	1
East St. Park	10	1	1	1		1				1			1			n.a.	1	1						1
Fox Point Memorial	12	1	1	1	1	1		1		1		1	2			n.a.						1	1	1
Jennifer Rivera Park	16	1	1	1	1		1		1		1	1	2			n.a.	1	2			1		2	1
Mattie Smith Playground	15	1	1	1	1		1	1	1		1	1	3			n.a.	1	1				1		1
Morris Ave. Playground	13	1	1	1			1	1		1		1		1		n.a.	1			1			1	1
Ninth St. Park	15	1	1	1	2		1	1	1	1	1	1			1	n.a.	1			1	1	1	1	1
Pearl St. Park	15	1	1		2		1	1		1	1	1	2			n.a.	1	1		1			2	1
Pleasant St. Park	14	1	1	1			1	1	1		1	1		1		n.a.	1	1		1		1		1
Preston & Ives Playground	14	1	1	1		2	1	1						1		n.a.	1			1		1		1
Salisbury St. Playground	16	1	1	1	1	1	1	1		1	1	1	1		1	n.a.	1	1		2			2	1
Summit Avenue Park	12	1	1	1			2		1		1	1				n.a.	1					1	1	1
Waldo St. Tot Lot	18	1	1	1	1	1	1	1	1	1	1	1		1	1	n.a.	1	1		1		1	2	1
23-week total	250	16	17	12	15	10	13	9	12	11	11	16	15	6	6	0	14	13	7	12	14	7	21	17

Source: ProvStat, Providence, R.I.

a. The dates are for the Monday of the five-day work week.

b. The number in each cell indicates the number of times each park received maintenance that week. Cells with no numbers indicate the park received no maintenance.

n.a. Not available.

For these 17 parks in 2004, however, this was *never* the case. During these 23 weeks of 2004, only one small park, Brassil Memorial Park, received 10 maintenance visits. During the same period for 2005, no park received less than 10 visits.

Prior to 2003, city government wasn't measuring its performance against objectives, Cardillo observed. Why? Because there were no *real* objectives—nothing to which city managers paid any attention. ProvStat, however, forced department directors "to identify outcomes." Through ProvStat, the city's managers "learned that using data to manage is invaluable," she continued. "They are looking at things through a totally different prism." Indeed, "ProvStat's real impact was introducing data-driven decisionmaking throughout the city." ProvStat, Cardillo concluded, "drove the modernization of the city of Providence."[23]

In 2010, David Cicilline was elected to Congress, and Angel Taveras was elected mayor. To Cicilline, ProvStat has been "an incredibly important tool" and "a huge success." Indeed, he concluded that without it, he would not have produced the results he did.[24] For a year-and-a-half, Taveras continued to employ the strategy. By July 1, 2012, however, ProvStat was gone.

The Need for Causal, Output-to-Outcome Theory

Childhood vaccination for measles is an output that is very connected to the desired outcome. Vaccinate the child properly, and the probability is 99 percent that the child is immunized. Impressive. If a public health agency sets a performance target to vaccinate 98 percent of the children in its jurisdiction, and if it achieves its target, it has had a significant impact on their health.

Public health agencies benefit from the work of public health researchers. For some interventions, such as vaccination against disease, these researchers generate data connecting government's operational output (vaccination) to society's desired outcome (immunization).

Most public agencies are not so fortunate. Government's outputs are not the only factors affecting the outcomes. Indeed, it can be quite difficult to determine how much—if any—of a societal outcome was caused by government's output. Providence can reorganize its maintenance crews, it can ensure that they work a full shift. It can measure the cleanliness of its parks, and how much citizens enjoyed them. Still, even if citizen enjoyment goes up, the city cannot conclude that ProvStat or Parks *caused* the improvement.

When a public agency can measure only its outputs but not its outcomes, it needs a cause-and-effect theory—a causal explanation about why its outputs are producing, or contributing to, the desired outcomes. In Providence, this causal explanation is straightforward: People are more likely to enjoy and use clean parks.

And if there was no other major change at the parks—no new soccer pitches and baseball diamonds—reasonable people could attribute increased citizen enjoyment to the increased cleanliness. But a reasonable conclusion is not proof.

In public health, it is possible to test such cause-and-effect relationships rigorously, creating accurate and useful theories with well-documented probabilities. For most public agencies, however, the theory will remain just that: a theory. It may be possible to collect data suggesting that the theory has some validity. But it will rarely be possible to prove the theory. Still, the data can be analyzed to evaluate the evidence behind the theory.

Compared with What?

Any analysis involves a comparison: Is this number big or small? That depends on the number with which it is compared. Is this change significant or irrelevant? It too depends on a comparison. How big compared with the baseline? How big compared with similar changes?

What, however, should be compared with *what?* The choice of what data to collect may depend as much on the opportunities for meaningful comparisons as for the ability of the data to directly answer specific questions. In fact, data can help answer any question only if they can be compared with other similar data.

For a basis of comparison, there are numerous possibilities. Three traditional ones are:

1. The organization's own historical performance. These data could reveal whether or not the organization is improving. For example, the job-placement data for the most recent quarter could be compared with the job-placement data for the previous quarter or the same quarter last year.
2. The performance of similar organizations. These data could reveal if the organization is doing better or worse than the rest of the world. For example, a local office's job-placement data for the most recent quarter could be compared with the job-placement data for other local offices for the same quarter.
3. A pre-established performance target. These data could reveal if the organization is living up to its commitments. For example, job-placement data for a local office could be compared with its job-placement target.

What to choose? It isn't obvious. Sometimes there are data problems, sometimes there are comparison problems, and sometimes there are both. If an organization never collected data on past performance, there is no way to compare current performance with historical performance. Undoubtedly there exist similar organizations (and similar subunits), yet none of them have precisely the same circumstances (problems, resources); any differences in the data could be attributed to such circumstances. An organization may have set some specific performance targets; still any difference may depend less on the results the organization produced and more on the targets it created. For any differences among the data, there always exist multiple, alternative, and competing interpretations.

Moreover, once a PerformanceStat staff concludes that its analytical comparison has produced a meaningful differential, it still faces a second analytical question about cause: What *caused* this differential? *Why* was this year's performance better than last year's? *Why* was one organization's performance better than another's? *Why* was performance better than the target?

Specifying the Counterfactual

Any evaluation also requires a comparison. To decide whether something is super, acceptable, or lousy, the question remains: "Compared with what?" The scientific, gold-standard answer is "the counterfactual"—*what would have happened* without the intervention of the program or policy or strategy? Rarely, however, can we determine *what would have happened.*

For example, what is the counterfactual for the NYPD's CompStat? That is, what would have happened to crime in New York City if, in 1994, William Bratton and Jack Maple had not created CompStat? We'll never know. We can't know. Throughout the 1990s, crime was declining everywhere in the United States; but in New York City, it dropped more rapidly. That's not proof. Maybe NYC's drop in crime was actually caused by the aliens who landed in Roswell, New Mexico in the summer of 1947. We cannot eliminate all of the other multitudinous explanations.

The evaluator's search for a comparison requires data—data that reveal what happened with the program plus data that somehow reveal *what would have happened* without the program.

The Gold Standard of Comparison

Riding to the rescue is the gold standard for comparisons: the double-blind, randomized, placebo-controlled experiment. Done properly, this experiment can eliminate all but *one* of the variables that could potentially influence the result, and thus eliminate all but one explanation.

The classic example is the 1954 experiment to determine whether the polio vaccine developed by Jonas Salk was effective. Some children were given the vaccine (and only the vaccine); others were given an identical looking placebo. Who received the vaccine and who did not was determined randomly; no human could influence (even unconsciously or indirectly) each decision. Moreover, neither the children, their parents, the individuals who administered the vaccine, nor the doctors who examined the children for polio knew whether the child received the vaccine or the placebo.

"The vaccine was a success," reported Paul Meier of the University of Chicago. Roughly 200,000 children received the vaccine, and another 200,000 got the placebo. Of those who received the Salk vaccine, 57 got polio; for those who received the placebo, the number was 142—nearly three times as many.[25] Observed the *American Journal of Public Health,* the experiment demonstrated that the "vaccine was notably harmless and the benefit undoubtedly significant, especially against the paralytic form of the disease."[26]

The randomized, placebo-control design, which required elaborate record keeping to track which children got the vaccine and which got the placebo, ruled out alternative explanations. Who got the vaccine and who got the placebo was decided randomly; no human bias—subtle or subconscious—could influence who got the vaccine and who did not.[27] Also, the control group was strictly denied the vaccine. No one else had access to the vaccine. Parents fearing that their child had received the placebo could not secretly obtain the vaccine. Moreover, no one knew who got which; this eliminated the possibility that children or parents or medical professionals who knew who did and did not receive the vaccine could, though some subtle, psychological influences, stimulate physiological reactions in the children or prejudice a physician's diagnosis. Finally, each child in the experiment received either the vaccine or the placebo, but no other intervention; this approach isolated the vaccine as the only treatment and permitted a comparison between just two, very well defined alternatives.

If the experiment discovered that those who received the vaccine and those who got the placebo had different incidences of polio that was statistically significant, there could be *only one* possible explanation: the Salk vaccine. This double-blind, placebo-controlled experiment—which eliminated all other possible causes for any difference in the outcomes for the treatment and control groups—is the "gold standard" that every policy researcher would love to employ to determine whether a policy intervention really works.

The Advantage of AgencyStat (compared with JurisdictionStat)

Comparing performance can be easier for a public agency than for a government jurisdiction. An agency may have several (or many) subunits all of which have the same public purpose and collect the same data. In this situation, there exists an obvious answer to the "Compared with what?" question. An agency's leadership team possesses a built-in basis for comparing, analyzing, appraising, and diagnosing the performance of its subunits. (Plus, these subunits can learn from each other.)

In a governmental jurisdiction, however, each subunit is different. Each has its own mission and produces different results. Thus, each has a different basis for analyzing, appraising, and diagnosing its performance. The jurisdiction's leadership team cannot compare the fire department's results with those of the parks department.

Because JurisdictionStat lacks an obvious internal basis of comparison, it needs performance targets for each agency. At the citywide, countywide, and statewide level, the elected chief executive needs a basis for comparison for each department. In large jurisdictions, departments may have subunits, but many JurisdictionStats focus on jurisdiction-wide results. To assess jurisdiction-wide performance, to answer the "compared with what?" question, the elected chief executive needs some kind of performance targets.

Even large agencies cannot create an obvious basis of comparison for all their subunits. The agency has only one budget office, one personnel office, one legislative-liaison office. For these staff units, there is no obvious basis of comparison. At an AgencyStat session, a staff unit can tell appealing stories about what it did and what it accomplished. But unless the staff unit has a target, there is no obvious basis of comparison. The director of the Baltimore Public Works Department cannot compare the performance of the department's human resources office with the performance of the human resources offices in the Boston or Boise Public Works Departments.

At the Los Angeles County Department of Public Social Services, the DPSSTATS staff collects a wide variety of data concerning the performance of different units, and the department's leadership conducts monthly meetings for both line units and staff units. Reported Karen Kent, then the director of DPSSTATS, her department's PerformanceStat works much better for line units than staff units, precisely because the staff units have no obvious basis of comparison.

Learning from the Positive Deviants

A PerformanceStat can be construed as a strict, holding-people-accountable system with an emphasis on punishing the poorest performers. That is how Comp-Stat was portrayed in HBO's "The Wire." A PerformanceStat can, however, be designed to foster learning—with an emphasis on understanding what the top performers are doing, on helping the poorest performers improve, and on ensuring that the meetings provide everyone with the opportunity to learn what appears to be working elsewhere in the organization.

Indeed, to be truly effective, to help *all* subunits improve their results, a PerformanceStat has to be more about learning than about accountability. Rather than berating managers whose results are lagging, the leadership team needs to help them learn *how* to improve. For an agency with multiple subunits with similar responsibilities, fostering this learning is easier.

With 76 different precincts, the New York Police Department has, potentially, 76 different laboratories for crime-fighting experiments—and thus for learning. Some precincts may be consistently producing better results than similar precincts. Over the previous six months, the 116th precinct in Queens might have produced significant reductions in burglaries—reductions that did not occur in other similar precincts: the 74th and 82nd precincts in Brooklyn, the 51st precinct in the Bronx, and the 2nd and 27th precincts in Manhattan.[28]

In such a situation, the commander of the 116th could be asked to explain what the precinct is doing and how he or she thinks it works.[29] Moreover, if the performance of the 82nd has repeatedly been below other precincts, NYPD's chief of patrol could suggest that the commander of the 82nd ask the commander of the 116th for advice and assistance. (If the formal and informal rewards are not limited to just a single winner (or two), the high-performing directors have no reason to withhold their knowledge. See appendix C.)

How do agencies and jurisdictions improve their performance? How can they learn how to improve? If subunit managers have been delegated responsibility plus discretion—which means they have the authority to experiment—they have an opportunity to learn. They may not experiment consciously; they may merely stumble into something new that produces (or appears to produce) better results. They may not even know that their results are better. Still, the comparative data will reveal that some units are performing better.

These are the "positive deviants."[30]

Positive deviants are doing something differently. They may not know what they are doing differently. Even if they know what they are doing differently, they may not understand the cause-and-effect relationship: *How* is what they are doing differently contributing to their superior results? Still they are doing something new, different, better. The analytical challenge is to figure out what that new, different, better something is—and *how* it works.

Any analytical effort to improve performance requires fostering, identifying, and then learning from the positive deviants. This is the critical "*How?*" question.

Identifying Performance Deficits

Every organization can improve its performance. But before an organization can decide how to produce better results, it needs to identify its performance deficits—those places along its value chain where it is doing an inadequate job. This analytical effort to discover potential (and meaningful) performance deficits is a search for patterns. Unfortunately, there exists no universally useful, analytical, pattern-identifying technique. Sometimes, however, experience suggests what patterns to go looking for.

When Tom and Ray Magliozzi (the brothers of Car Talk fame[31]) seek to identify an automobile's performance deficit—the cause behind a malfunctioning car described in a phone conversation—they draw on years of diagnostic work. The brothers have examined thousands of cars with thousands of problems, and they appear to have remembered every one. Thus, when a caller to their radio show gives them a few clues about a car's problems, the brothers can—without looking under the hood—compare the details in the caller's description with previous patterns that they have seen, identify a similarity, and diagnose the vehicle's performance deficit.

Public executives, however, face a more complex challenge. After all, Tom and Ray know they will be asked only about a car or a truck—a piece of equipment with a well-known, interacting collection of mechanical and electronic parts. They know they will *not* be asked about how to improve park maintenance or mental health services.

Executives and analysts in public agencies who seek to uncover their most operationally significant (or easily fixable) performance deficits have to look for patterns. Where do they go looking for patterns? What makes a seemingly random collection of data coalesce into a pattern? How do they discover a pattern they weren't looking for? Indeed, what is a pattern? What kinds of patterns can reveal (or, at least, suggest) a performance deficit?

In Providence, analysts discovered a number of patterns: maintenance employees taking sick days on Fridays and Mondays; maintenance employees arriving late for work; parks receiving no maintenance for weeks or even months. With the relevant data organized in a useful way, these patterns were easy to detect. Without the relevant data, however, there is nothing to detect. Without a useful way to organize the relevant data, patterns remain obscured.

Maps, Dots, and Cops—and Analysis

Among the reasons why police departments would have been more likely than other public agencies to invent a PerformanceStat-like strategy was the availability of a simple, first-order analytical tool: On a map, put a dot for each crime and then look for patterns.

"Let's say we're having a problem with Laundromat robberies in Brooklyn," explained Sergeant John Yohe, who was one of NYPD's first CompStat analysts.[32] "I can pull from the CD all the listed Laundromats in Brooklyn, map them, shade in color the ones that are already robbed and see if we can spot a pattern. There's a lot of possibilities."[33]

Putting dots on a map and looking for patterns is not, however, a revolutionary analytical framework. Putting dots on a map wasn't even invented by the police. It started in public health. John Snow is famous for his 1854 mapping of the location of cholera deaths in London, and using the concentration of deaths on a map to demonstrate the local source of the disease: the Broad Street water pump.[34]

Even within policing, putting dots of crimes on maps did not originate with NYPD's CompStat. When Bratton was a young police lieutenant in Boston, he had "requisitioned gigantic maps" of his district, "papered all four walls with them," and then "put up dots: red dots for burglaries, blue dots for robberies"— earning him the nickname "Lord Dots."[35]

The beauty of a crime map is that you don't need a degree in econometrics to identify where the dots—and thus the crimes—are clustered. You simply "see" the pattern. The immediate tactical response is summarized by Maple's mantra: "Map the crime and put the cops where the dots are." Or more succinctly: "Put cops on dots."[36]

Today the maps and the dots are computerized. In the Los Angeles Police Department, these maps are quite sophisticated. LAPD doesn't just use circular dots. The department displays triangles for robbery, squares for aggravated assault, circles for burglary, stars for auto theft, and diamonds for theft from a motor vehicle. A small circle with a smaller diamond inside indicates that a shot was fired, and a gang crime gets a six-pointed star. Finally, each "dot" is colored-coded by watch: red for midnight to 6:00 a.m.; orange for 6:00 a.m. to noon; green for noon to 6:00 p.m., and blue for 6:00 p.m. to midnight.[37]

Still, the key analytical and strategic insight remains the same: Put cops on dots.

Putting cops on the dots does not, however, work for every crime. Mapping white-collar crime would be of little use. If NYPD mapped securities fraud and discovered that most was located near Wall Street in lower Manhattan, what would it do? Have a corps of cops collect in front of the New York Stock Exchange? That would neither deter nor catch many security-fraud criminals.

Yet, when other public officials created their own JurisdictionStats and AgencyStats, they often mindlessly mimicked CompStat's maps. Even if the performance deficits they were trying to identify would not be revealed by any collection of dots, they still created maps. Many governments possess the technological capacity to create their own maps (and any who don't have vendors knocking on their door).

The maps look nice. They wow people impressed by high-tech gadgetry. But will they actually help? The maps are a valuable framework only to the extent that they (1) help reveal patterns and (2) suggest new or better strategies.

Disaggregating the Data

"We are disaggregating those two spikes in crime," said Boston's Police Commissioner Edward Davis. For most of the first nine months of 2010, homicides had been down in the city—except for two spikes: one in May and the other in late August and early September. So Davis had his department's analysts examining the data. "If we study it closely enough, we might have some answers."[38]

Analysis requires a disaggregation of the data.[39] By separating the data into their relevant components, the analyst can compare them, looking for patterns and insights: Which components are big; which are small? Which are increasing; which decreasing? Which are *too* big—bigger than expected? Which are changing too fast—faster than expected? In the search for insights, these comparisons can be among different but similar components. Or these comparisons can be with what should have happened "normally"—professional expectations based on years of experience. It is impossible to learn anything from a single data point; its significance can be gauged only by comparing it with another.

A city's total crime for a month—a single, aggregate number—reveals nothing. It cannot suggest who should do what. If, however, this total is compared with last month's or last year's aggregated number, a trend might appear. But until these totals are disaggregated (by crimes, geography, and time), the patterns—and the relevant performance deficits—remain hidden. Only by disaggregating the data can the analyst make the comparisons necessary to identify patterns, and perhaps their causes, and thus maybe strategies for dealing with the causes.

Again, the police have an advantage. Even a new recruit can "see" the value of disaggregating the data by crime, location, and time. If, on Saturday nights, citywide homicides are down but auto theft is up in two zones, the police get a clue about how to allocate their resources.

Even for the police—and certainly for other public agencies—a map is not the only analytic tool.[40] An initial disaggregation of the data will rarely suggest a quick, simple, and effective strategy for dealing with a problem, or even suggest what the underlying performance deficit really is. More often, it will only suggest a more detailed, analytic approach—a further disaggregation that might provide more insight.

Along what dimensions should the data be disaggregated? It is rarely obvious. Indeed, any disaggregation—any search for comparisons, patterns, and insights—will involve a lot of guesses, a lot of trial and error. Veteran analysts, those who have already made a career's worth of guesses and errors, will have learned from their experiences. Still, they have to guess. Their guesses, however, may be better. They may need fewer guesses and disaggregations to learn something worthwhile, to identify and understand specific performance deficits, and then to suggest specific strategies for eliminating or mitigating them.

The Search for Useful Analytic Frameworks

How might a PerformanceStat's staff conduct its analysis? What analytical framework should it use?

These questions have no answers. There is no officially certified Performance-Stat analytic methodology, nor should there be.[41] There exists no computational routine, no mathematical tool, no statistical template that will reveal every organization's every performance deficit and simultaneously suggest the perfect strategy for eliminating each. Even within a specific policy area, there exists no one best analytic practice. Not for policing. Not for park maintenance.

In any situation, some analytical frameworks will be more useful than others. What are they? For this question, the most honest response is the ubiquitous: It all depends. Unfortunately, it is never obvious on what exactly it does or might depend.

An analytical framework might appear to illuminate patterns and still provide no clue about the underlying cause of the patterns, little information about the real performance deficit(s), and absolutely no hint about what to do. Some education in analytical techniques might prove useful by suggesting what disaggregations might offer some insight. Some formal analytical techniques might produce numerous numbers but not reveal what performance deficits might exist. Every analytic technique is designed to understand (and, perhaps, help solve) specific problems. But if the nature of the problem is unknown—indeed, if it is not even known if a problem exists—it is difficult to know what kind of analysis to employ.

Fortunately, there is one analytical technique that every analyst knows and that can prove useful in a wide variety of circumstances. This technique is so elementary that every public manager knows it too. It is so elementary that every analyst and every manager learned it in elementary school. It is: Long Division.

Long division compares two numbers: outputs with inputs. Outputs in May with outputs in March. The outputs of maintenance crew A with the outputs of crew B. Long division creates ratios that can be undeniably revealing or insipidly uninteresting. Long division might produce a number that is astonishingly big or startlingly small. Or it might produce a number that everyone expected. Unfortunately, before you actually do the arithmetic, you don't know which. If you did, you wouldn't have to bother.

What to divide by what? Again: It all depends. But it is rarely obvious. Any organization whose performance is worth analyzing comes with an array of data—data that it routinely collects, data that exist but that no one has thought to collect, plus data that could be collected if someone made an effort. The analyst or manager can divide any of these numbers by any other number. So what? What might the resulting ratio reveal?

Often, experience suggests what might be usefully compared with what. Analysts who have worked for years in one policy world have accumulated insights, intuitions, and instincts that help them guess intelligently about what to look for and how to find it. Experience helps an analyst search for insights into the nature of the organization's performance deficit with both knowledge about how the organization behaves as well as hunches about where to look for new insights about what is happening. Skilled professionals have accumulated a catalogue of patterns and can quickly identify each one.

Experience also creates blinders. Thus naïveté may help too. The innocent neophyte will ask questions that the experienced professional "knows" aren't worth asking. The neophyte might create ratios that the pros assume will never be informative. Naïveté ensures the analyst approaches the search for insights with both a lack of subconscious prejudices about how the organization and its people are behaving as well as few preconceptions about where to look. Sometimes naïveté helps the neophyte to see things that the pros miss.

Whoever is doing the analysis—be it the experienced professional or the naïve neophyte—needs to possess what Malcolm Sparrow calls the "habits of mind" and "patterns of thought" that lead them to "slice and dice" the data, "molding and testing different problem-definitions and specifications."[42] They have to be prepared to immerse themselves in the data—to look at them from a variety of perspectives using a variety of frameworks and to go searching for other data that might (but only might) reveal something interesting.

Not only is it not obvious what to divide by what. It is also not obvious to whom to give this long-division assignment. Ideally, a PerformanceStat staff would have at least two people: the experienced professional who knows exactly where to go looking for useful ratios, and the innocent neophyte who applies long division to numerous numbers with no preconception about what the resulting ratio might reveal.

Sparrow is fond of saying: "Pick important problems and fix them."[43] The operational challenge is to get the organization to fix the identified problems. But first comes the analytical challenge: to identify important problems. And the task of identifying problems may come with fewer suggestions for analytical strategies than the task of fixing them comes with suggestions for operational strategies. In a large, complex organization, identifying and understanding truly important problems—problems that are worth fixing—may be similar to looking for a needle in a haystack.

The Beguiling Metaphor about Connecting the Dots

To read the newspapers, many people have in their formal job description the task of "connecting the dots." Yet, they can't even do this simple task. And when they don't, others will excoriate them for "failing to connect the dots." Many in the U.S. intelligence community have been criticized for their failure to "connect the dots." Yet, is this analytical work of connecting-the-dots as simple as the metaphor suggests?

In any field, analysts face the challenge of finding patterns in a mélange of data. Often, they don't even know what they are looking for. In such cases, the connect-the-dots metaphor is simplistic and misleading. It suggests that there exists something called dots, that these dots come in a simple, standardized, visible form, that they are displayed in a conspicuous format, that to each dot is attached a specific and visible number, and that any fool can connect them.

Indeed, this metaphor is derived from the connect-the-dots puzzle that five-year-olds solve easily. How come these idiots can't connect their dots?

Metaphors are essential for communication. They quickly convey an idea. Yet, metaphors are essentially simplistic. They lack nuance. Sometimes (to use a metaphor), they miss the target. Or hit the wrong target. Or hit nothing and sail off toward Alpha Centauri.

Unfortunately, the dots we want the intelligence community to connect are not laid out on a single piece of paper. They are not numbered sequentially: 1, 2, 3, . . . up to, say, 15.

Actually, there exist a gazillion dots. One or two of the connectable dots may be on one piece of paper (or in one database). But the other dots are spread all over in various databases, file folders, desks, emails, pockets, floors, and multiple people's brains. Someone has to recognize numerous, nonobvious connections. Computers can do some of this work, but only if a human asks them the right questions.

Moreover, the dots are not numbered sequentially. They aren't even all "dots." What one person perceives as a superfluous pile of fluff, another deciphers as a relevant and revealing dot.

It is much more complicated than looking for a needle in a haystack—for this metaphor also fails to capture the complexity of the task. Looking for a needle in a haystack comes with three big advantages. You know exactly what you are looking for. You know what it looks like. And you know where to look. Yet when PerformanceStat analysts go looking for the proverbial (not physical) needle, they don't know what they are looking for. Will the relevant "needle" be a virus, a groundhog, or an asteroid? And what does this virus, this groundhog, or this asteroid look like? If you stumbled across one, how would you recognize it? A relevant needle is rarely a gun with smoke drifting up from the barrel. And if the analysts don't know what they are looking for, they are unlikely to know where to start looking for it. What might be a relevant haystack, and what does it look like? (Is it disguised as a baseball park?) And where does anyone find one of these haystacks?

A PerformanceStat analyst who is looking to identify a performance deficit faces a much bigger analytical challenge. In fact, it isn't even obvious what the challenge is.

After the United States made two counterterrorism mistakes, *Washington Post* columnist David Ignatius wrote about "clues that were lost in a blizzard of information" in the intelligence community's much-too-big database.[44] But no single database contains all of the clues. Moreover, a "clue" doesn't come with a red label on its big toe reading, "Clue: Pay Attention." And answers won't come from a small, previously established, well-defined list of alternatives (for example, Col. Mustard with the Candlestick in the Billiard Room).

Clues lost in a blizzard of information: This metaphor suggests that there exists a blizzard through which smart people should know how to search for obvious clues. But analysts looking for the patterns can't just look in one blizzard of information. They also have to look in disparate "galaxies of facts," in multiple "oceans of data," and in myriad "nebulae of rumors." Oh yes: They should remember to check under the rug.

PerformanceStat analysts are looking for a pattern—a pattern in the data that gives them some insight into their organization's performance deficit(s) and suggests a strategy for eliminating or mitigating this deficit. But what pattern? What is a pattern? What pattern might be relevant? How would PerformanceStat analysts recognize a relevant pattern when they see one? Finally, from this pattern, how do they learn something useful?

Sometimes a pattern is just one data point—one, very weird data point. When compared with all the other data points that analysts (or ordinary humans) have accumulated throughout their lives, this data point is so weird that it is easily distinguishable from every other data point. Such a data point might be people taking flying lessons but with no interest in learning how to land. "That's funny. I thought landing was the most important part of flying."

Still, is this weirdness important? Does this weird data point reveal anything? A weird data point may not reveal anything useful. It may, however, suggest that, perhaps, there is some underlying phenomenon—something that can only be uncovered through additional investigation and analysis. Or the data point could simply be wrong. Most databases are full of inaccurate data points.

A pattern might be multiple people trying to blow up airplanes. So we concentrate our energies on preventing people from blowing up airplanes. Prefer to travel on a train?

Analysis as a Search for Patterns and Strategies

One analytical choice concerns how finely to disaggregate the data. Should the analyst look at comprehensive macro-data for the entire jurisdiction? Or should the analyst disaggregate the data into its most individualistic nano-components? Again, the answer is rarely obvious. Sparrow writes about "the art of picking the right levels of aggregation" and suggests that this should be somewhere in between "broad, general phenomena" and the "minutiae" of individual events.[45]

At the end of the year, an analyst in a public works department could examine the pothole-filling data: Was the total number of potholes filled up or down (from previous years)? From such summary data, the analyst could discern little about the nature of the pothole problem(s). A macro-level aggregation of data rarely provides even a hint about a department's performance let alone how to improve it.

Alternatively, the analysts could disaggregate the data at a very fine level in both geography and time. For example, the analyst could break the potholes-filled data down by every street address and by every day of the year. But this nano-level analysis would contain almost exclusively zeros (no potholes filled at this address on this day). This, too, would be uninformative—revealing nothing about the city's pothole patterns. Neither examining a jurisdiction's data from 35,000 feet with the naked eye, nor examining it at the street level with a microscope, is apt to be particularly revealing. Neither exposes the nature of the performance deficit or suggests what potholes would be susceptible to what pothole-filling strategies. And neither would suggest whether repaving entire streets, or using different pothole-filling material, or . . . would produce better transportation results.

An informative level of analysis lies somewhere in between the completely comprehensive macro and the finely differentiated nano. Unfortunately, the appropriate level of disaggregation will rarely be obvious. Someone has to guess. The experienced pro and the naive neophyte may make different initial guesses. Both guesses could prove valuable. It is not preordained that one single level of disaggregation will provide all the insights. Every level of disaggregation *could* produce a useful understanding of one of the organization's performance deficits. No one will know until someone looks at the data and thinks what nobody has thought.

The Luck of "That's Funny"

In the summer of 2009, a Boston CompStat analyst noticed that over a two-month period four different cases of seafood—valued from $400 for five boxes of shrimp, to $2,300 for eight cases of lobster and 90 lbs. of shrimp—had been stolen from delivery trucks near Fanueil Hall. No analyst had programmed a computer to check for stolen seafood. Indeed, no Boston cop was worried about lobster larceny. Gang violence, not disappearing shrimp, were on that summer's CompStat agenda. Still, when any analyst saw a *second* case of missing seafood, the logical reaction would have been: "That's funny." Then, the analyst would go looking for a pattern.

Isaac Asimov, the biochemist, popular science writer, and author of numerous books of science fiction, wasn't interested in helping public executives recognize patterns. He was interested in how scientists made new discoveries. Asimov's insight into the process of discovery in science is captured in his oft-quoted saying: "The most exciting phrase to hear in science, the one that heralds the new discoveries, is not 'Eureka!' (I found it!) but 'That's funny. . . . '"[46] Asimov didn't mean "that's funny, ha-ha." He meant, "that's funny, weird"—weird enough to warrant further investigation. And when someone with Sparrow's "habits of mind" and "patterns of thought" comes across two cases of seafood stolen from trucks in the same location, he is apt to say to himself, "that's funny" . . . and then go looking to see whether it was a coincidence or reveals a significant underlying pattern.

Boston's CompStat analyst may have been lucky, simply stumbling across some data that looked funny. Yet, this analyst didn't just mumble "that's funny" and turn to other work. This analyst was prepared to recognize his luck and to follow up on his newly acquired data. In an 1854 lecture at the University of Lille, Louis Pasteur remarked: "dans les champs de l'observation le hasard ne favorise que les ésprits préparés."[47] Or, in one of the many translations: "In the field of observation, chance only favors the prepared mind."

Psychologist Gary Klein called this "intuition: recognizing things without knowing how we do the recognizing." Klein's intuition is not ESP. From his research, he concluded that "intuition grows out of experience"; it draws on "expertise that the person clearly has but cannot describe." From experience, Klein concludes, experts recognize familiar patterns as well as "notice anomalies." Yet, he writes "because patterns can be subtle, people often cannot describe what they noticed, or how they judged a situation as typical or atypical."[48] Chance favors the mind that has been prepared by experience to recognize both common patterns and weird aberrations.

The search for patterns and for the underlying performance deficits that a pattern may reveal, often begins with the simple exclamation: "That's funny!"

10

Conducting the Meetings

*How can the regular, frequent, and integrated PerformanceStat meetings
be conducted to ensure that they both reveal opportunities to enhance
performance and drive such improvements?*

Most people in the world learn things faster when they know they're going to be tested on them.
JACK MAPLE, Deputy Police Commissioner, New York City Police Department[1]

> When they [Prime Minister Tony Blair's key advisors] spoke to me about
> education policy, it was usually to press me for new and bolder ideas.
> No harm in that, of course, but I used to say to them, "Why don't you
> also ask me whether we have implemented existing policy effectively
> and whether it is making a real difference on the ground?"
> SIR MICHAEL BARBER, Head of Prime Minister Blair's Delivery Unit[2]

"Attention on deck!" a man in uniform bellows. Everyone stands. In from the back room, strides the New York City commissioner of correction. It is 8:00 on a Thursday morning in a double-wide trailer on Rikers Island—the beginning of the monthly meeting of "CorrectionStat."

Actually, no one calls it "CorrectionStat." The official name is TEAMS, for "Total Efficiency Accountability Management System." Still, think of it as CorrectionStat. For it is the Correction Department's adaptation of CompStat.

In lower Manhattan, it is a Friday morning, a little before 9:00. People are gathering for the monthly meeting of "ProbationStat." The commissioner of probation mingles with the department's staff and visitors, asking questions about both their professional and personal lives.

Again, no one calls it "ProbationStat." The official name is STARS, for "Statistical Tracking, Analysis, and Reporting System." Still, think of it as ProbationStat. It, too, is an adaptation of CompStat.

At the meeting on Rikers Island (in the middle of the East River, between the Bronx and Queens), over half the people are in uniform. Two stars on their shoulder. Or three stars. The chief of the department wears four stars. The wardens of the city's 14 facilities wear one star.[3] It is a military-style organization with a daily head count of approximately 13,000 inmates and annual admissions of roughly 100,000 individuals. The department has nearly 11,000 employees of which approximately 9,500 are uniformed correctional officers.[4]

The city's Department of Probation is, however, quite different, for it is staffed primarily by social workers.[5] The department's staff of approximately 1,200 work out of 17 offices (four each in Manhattan, Brooklyn, and the Bronx, three in Queens, and two on Staten Island).[6] They supervise 85,000 probationers, 60,000 adults and 25,000 juveniles.

Between 2003 and 2009, when someone bellowed "Attention on deck!" the commissioner of correction who emerged from the back room to chair the monthly TEAMS meeting was Martin Horn. Over these same years, the commissioner of probation who conducted the monthly STARS meetings and mingled with the staff beforehand was Martin Horn.

For six years, Horn was the top executive of both departments, chairing both versions of PerformanceStat. Both TEAMS and STARS are direct descendants of the New York Police Department's (NYPD's) CompStat. Nevertheless, Horn understood that his two organizations were very different. The quasi-military nature of the Department of Correction required, he recognized, not only a very formal meeting, but also a very formal executive. In contrast, yelling "Attention on deck!" at social workers would have subjected a probation commissioner to derision and disdain. Horn could not run ProbationStat the way he ran CorrectionStat. He could not run either of his PerformanceStats the way NYPD ran CompStat or the way the Human Resources Administration (HRA) ran JobStat. Each department is part of the same government; yet they are different. Thus Horn needed to adapt the PerformanceStat leadership strategy to the culture of each.

Meetings and Purpose

Collecting, organizing, analyzing, and distributing performance data—none of this is enough. People will ignore the data, particularly data they don't understand, data they can rationalize as biased against them, data they feel unable to influence. The director and managers of any subunit may find the data embarrassing; these data may subtly suggest or explicitly reveal that the subunit is performing poorly. Moreover, these data do not tell them *how* to improve. Indeed, it is rarely obvious who should do what. A variety of outside influences affect these data. Without some help, poorly performing subunits will continue doing what they have always done: perform poorly.

The meetings can, however, contribute significantly to a PerformanceStat's potential, if an agency or jurisdiction can use them to:

Focus everyone on the chief executive's purpose: What are we trying to accomplish?

Establish responsibility: Who should do what by when?

Provide operational updates: What are different subunits doing and accomplishing?

Follow up on prior commitments: Were the previously agreed-upon actions taken?

Identify performance deficits: What isn't working?

Diagnose causes: Why isn't it working?

Develop strategies: How can we eliminate this performance deficit?

Establish performance targets: Who should achieve what result by when?

Invest resources: What resources do we need to implement these strategies?

Identify positive deviants: What do the comparative data reveal about who is succeeding?

Help everyone learn: How can others adapt what is working?

Recognize accomplishment: Who deserves thanks for significant improvements?

Reprove the recalcitrant: Whom should we reproach for indifference, incompetence, or insubordination?

Tell stories: What examples of performance-improving initiatives can we use to foster a results-focused culture?

Despite this long list of possible operational reasons for conducting regular PerformanceStat meetings, they are widely perceived to be strictly an accountability-holding forum[7]—like the old Roman Forum, though without the carnivorous lions.

What's Going On?

First-time visitors to any PerformanceStat meeting won't have the foggiest idea what is going on. Everyone is talking in code—in the universal code of the policy field, as well as its local dialect. And the acronyms are flying. These visitors can get a gist of whether things are going well from the questions and answers, the tone of the discussion, the body language. They will not, however, be able to follow the specifics. People appear to be jumping from issue to issue, from problem to problem. The participants could, however, be examining one big problem with lots of issues, lots of complications.

First-time visitors cannot tell. They have no idea what was discussed at last month's meeting or last year's. They have no idea whether this subunit has been doing particularly well over the last several meetings, or particularly poorly. They can figure out whether the subunit's managers are cooperative or clueless, engaged or evasive, but they will lack the historical perspective to figure out why. They will completely miss the follow-up.

It's as if they had been given a novel to read, but told that they had to start on page 95. Then, after they got to page 115, they were stopped and asked: Who was who? What was going on? They would not even have comprehended the basics of the plot.

The same is true of people who first watched a PerformanceStat's 30th session without having seen the first 29. They would have no idea what went before. Thus, they would misinterpret words, questions, and answers. They'll pick up the praise; such words need little context. But what they might think is a subtle suggestion, everyone else in the room would recognize as a clear directive. What new visitors might think is an innocuous question, everyone else would recognize as a clear rebuke.

Even after observing their fourth meeting, these visitors may not understand the entire plot. For over the past weeks or months, everyone else in the room will have been living the issues raised at the last session. Even if the visitors have gone to four meetings in a row, they will miss days of personal interactions. They won't have followed the experiments with new ideas, let alone their successes and failures. They won't have examined the latest data (unless someone gives it to them the day before the meeting). And they won't have observed the two preparatory meetings that were held a day or two before: the meeting that the organization's leadership team held to go over the key issues to be covered; and the meeting the subunit's director and managers held to go over the questions they think will be asked.

Still, an observer's second meeting could be very instructive. If, that is, the agenda for this second meeting focuses on the same subunit and the same set of issues as the first. Then, if the visitors are observing an effective PerformanceStat session, they will see the continuity. They will realize that these meetings are not a random collection of disjunctive exchanges but an ongoing deliberation about how to make specific improvements in specific aspects of the subunit's performance. They will begin to appreciate the follow-up.

In October 2003, I visited Baltimore's CitiStat for the first time, observing the sessions for the Bureau of Water and Wastewater and the Department of Recreation and Parks. In January 2004, I returned for my second visit. I was lucky. In January, I saw the same two agencies that I had observed in October. "I get it," I said to myself. The basic issues raised in October were also on the January agenda. I did not comprehend the details, yet the continuity was obvious.

As the definition of PerformanceStat in chapter 3 emphasized, this leadership strategy is complex and subtle. It is not merely—as it is so often portrayed—a series of accountability-holding confrontations. What happens at the meetings is important, indeed, essential. Still it is only the most visible aspect of the strategy. Consequently, if all visitors do is sit in on a meeting or two, they may fail to observe, let alone appreciate, the strategy's subtlety.

Sure, these visitors can return and review their notes carefully. They might even be able to review what happened by watching a video of the session they attended (and maybe even some other sessions for the same subunit). Still, they won't be fully up on the issues, completely aware of the subtleties of the conversation, or alert to nuances in ordinary words.

Besides, they won't have internalized the acronyms.

Who's Running the Show?

Still, a few things may be clear—for example, who is conducting the meeting. After all, someone launches the meeting, introduces any visitors, runs through any housekeeping tasks, and begins the questioning. But it might not be obvious who's actually in charge.

On November 5, 2008, at the Los Angeles Police Department's CompStat, the meeting was conducted from beginning to end by Charlie Beck, then chief of detectives. LAPD divides the city into 21 areas (its equivalent of precincts), and (as usual) the performance of three areas was examined that morning. At the beginning of the session for each area, Beck introduced Jeff Godown, the head of the CompStat unit, to go over the basic data for the area. When Godown had finished his review, Beck began the questioning.

After a while, Police Chief William Bratton walked quietly into the room. He sat down next to Godown, looked through some of the materials in the day's binder, and listened to the discussion. After a while, he left. Bratton never asked a question. He never said a word. Visitors who were concentrating on the discussion could have missed his coming and going.[8] Yet everyone in the room knew it was Bratton's meeting, and that he had fully delegated the responsibility for running the meeting to Beck. (In October 2009, it became Beck's department and meeting, when he succeeded Bratton as LAPD's police chief.)

In other circumstances, however, it may not be obvious to outsiders who is running the meeting let alone how much authority this individual has. The person chairing the meeting may be doing nothing more than that, moderating a discussion. Someone with significant authority might be in the room, but he or she might have done absolutely no preparation. He or she might not have read the briefing memo that summarized the possible issues to be examined (if there was such a memo), attended the preparatory session for deciding which key issues to focus on (if there was such a session), or thought about what aspects of the subunit's performance warranted review.

Some meetings are run by no one—unless you count the subunit director who is putting on his or her own slide show. But such a show-and-tell presentation that covers only topics raised by the subunit's slides is *not* a PerformanceStat meeting. It is little more than rambling chat about unrelated issues. It is not about identifying performance deficits and fixing them. To be worth the valuable time of the people attending a PerformanceStat meeting, a designated individual needs to focus the discussion on those aspects of the subunit's performance that are improving and those that need to improve.

The chief executive does not have to run the meeting. At both NYPD and LAPD, Bratton did not run the meetings. Often, he did not attend. Nevertheless, it was Bratton's meeting: He wanted it to happen, he wanted it to happen the way it happened, and he wanted the people who ran the meeting to be in charge.

The same can be true for every *real* PerformanceStat. The chief executive does not have to conduct the meetings personally. He or she does, however, need to make it unambiguously clear that PerformanceStat is important, that it is central to the management of the organization, and that the meetings are an integral part of his or her leadership strategy.

In the first few years after Martin O'Malley created CitiStat, he attended many of its meetings. By the third year, however, he had delegated responsibility for running the CitiStat meetings—indeed, for running the city—to Michael Enright, his first deputy mayor. Yet Enright did not do this flamboyantly. Meeting after meeting, he primarily asked questions, more questions, and still more questions. To understand what wasn't working and why, he drilled down into the operations of each department, asking specific managers to step to the podium to answer questions about their responsibilities. And, at the conclusion of each conversation, Enright would state—or perhaps appear to merely suggest—what needed to be done by the next meeting.

Visitors could easily have underestimated Enright's authority. "Copying Citi-Stat should be easy," they could have told each other. "The mayor doesn't even have to run the meeting. Anyone can run the meeting." Yet everyone who worked for the city knew that Enright was in charge.[9] In city government in Baltimore, no one with any sense would have tried to make an end run around Enright to get to O'Malley. That would have been professional suicide.[10]

Over time, Matthew Gallagher, director of CitiStat (and even younger members of the CitiStat staff), operated with the same level of mayoral authority. When Enright was absent, Gallagher ran the meetings. When the discussion focused on an issue for which a young staffer had done the work, he or she could ask questions that everyone else in the room accepted as authoritative (even if they resented being quizzed by someone so professionally and chronologically their junior).

For a PerformanceStat strategy to be effective, those who conduct the meetings need the chief executive's explicit authority. As Joseph Curtatone, mayor of Somerville, has often said in a public setting, "My director of SomerStat speaks for me."

The Brutal

NYPD holds its CompStat meetings at One Police Plaza in lower Manhattan, with a hundred of the city's finest watching. In its 1996 cover story on the drop in crime in the city, *Time* magazine succinctly characterized these sessions: "Effective precinct commanders," observed *Time,* "merely get grilled to a medium rare." In contrast, "those who show up unprepared, without coherent strategies to reduce crime, are fried crisp."[11]

Indeed, the manner in which Jack Maple and Louis Anemone, the chief of patrol, conducted NYPD's CompStat meetings can be described as brutal. Here's one journalist's description:

> A more stressful employee review would be hard to imagine on Wall Street. Anemone and Maple tossed no softballs, tolerated no excuses, and cut no breaks. When they found a befuddled or complacent commander, they tore him apart. One CO [commanding officer] was thrashed so badly he broke into tears. . . . Some [COs] tried to doublespeak their way off the hot seat. . . . Others tried to cook the books, but the eagle-eyed Anemone was hard to fool. According to a former high-ranking police source, at least one [precinct commander] was dumped for underreporting crime.[12]

Another journalist reported: "Maple presided over Compstat with humor, swagger, praise, or insult, depending on what was necessary."[13]

Maple is gone, but that reputation continues. More than a decade after the story in *Time,* the *New York Times* reported NYPD Commissioner Raymond W. Kelly had "barred spectators from CompStat meetings in light of complaints from some commanders that they had been ridiculed in the forum in front of outsiders." Roy T. Richter, president of the Captains Endowment Association, which represents NYPD's retired officers, expressed his concern that if CompStat is "used as a sword to subject a commander to humiliation before his peers, I don't think it's an effective management tool."[14]

Nothing has quite symbolized the take-no-prisoners style of NYPD's Comp-Stat sessions as much as the 1995 confrontation that Maple and Anemone had with Tosano (Tony) Simonetti, the commander of Brooklyn South. As Simonetti (according to one version of the story) "seemed to be fudging his way through a report" of his statistics and crime-fighting strategies,[15] there appeared on the big video screen behind him "a computerized drawing of Pinocchio with his nose growing."[16]

In its 1996 cover story, *Time* did allow that CompStat is more "than terror-izing captains at early-morning meetings."[17] Still, the reputation endures. To many in New York and elsewhere, the meetings of NYPD's CompStat—indeed, of other CompStats and many PerformanceStats too—are inherently confronta-tional, humiliating, and brutal.

This is "accountability." To many, CompStat is all about accountability. The theory is clear. If top managers don't hold their subordinates accountable, who knows what will or won't happen. From this doctrine of organizational life—that people need to be "held accountable"—is derived a more mundane imperative: People who screw up need to be punished.

This concept of "accountability"[18] can be used both to explain what any PerformanceStat is and to justify confrontational meetings. Little wonder that so many people—particularly those who have never been to a single Performance-Stat meeting; especially those who learned about CompStat by watching HBO's series "The Wire"[19]—think that the primary purpose of these meetings is to hold lazy and incompetent managers accountable.

Certainly the subunit managers who must report at such meetings may con-clude that they are only about accountability. When Michelle Rhee was chancel-lor of the District of Columbia Public Schools, she created SchoolStat. Some called it "TortureStat."[20]

Yet, at the many PerformanceStat sessions that I attended (I never observed NYPD's CompStat or Rhee's SchoolStat), I have seen very little of the humilia-tion for which the strategy is so infamous.[21] Certainly at the Los Angeles County

Departments of Mental Health and Public Social Services, Pinocchio is not apt to improve performance.

The Gotcha-Game Debate

Like NYPD's CompStat, Baltimore's CitiStat developed a reputation for brutal questioning. This is hardly surprising. Maple helped O'Malley create CitiStat. And like Bratton, Maple, and Anemone at NYPD, O'Malley, Enright, and Gallagher were impatient. *Governing* magazine described the mayor as "restless for results."[22] O'Malley and his leadership team were unwilling to tolerate agency managers who were complacent about the city's need to improve performance. They pushed hard, and when they discovered a manager who failed to appreciate their performance imperative or who refused to cooperate, they found a replacement.

Moreover, for years, the presentation that Baltimore developed to explain CitiStat emphasized the toughness of their approach. One slide was titled, "Surprise visit to municipal facilities highlights the need for improved supervision." Yet, it had little to do with CitiStat. Rather, the slide featured a visit that Enright had made in 2000 to a Department of Public Works facility where he asked a simple question: "What's that?" It was an elaborate, private, for-profit barbeque pit that a city employee was running on city property on city time. As would happen in any organization, this individual quickly became an ex-employee. Yet, the barbeque operation was not discovered at a CitiStat meeting. It was simply a result of Enright's propensity for walking around. It made a great story. So did "Mollie the Fire Dog"—a personal pet that a firefighter convinced the city to support, costing the city, from 1998 to 2001, $112,360.[23] Baltimore used both stories to illustrate how they cracked down on errant employees. In the process, they fed CitiStat's reputation as brutal.

In September 2008, at the Maryland Stat Summit hosted by Baltimore's Mayor Sheila Dixon, one attendee raised the issue. This conference included people from Baltimore city government and Maryland state government, plus others from around the state and country including Somerville's Curtatone. Whenever any large group discusses anything about any PerformanceStat, people are bound to ask: "Isn't this just a gotcha game?"

This time, the question concerned who gets to see what *before* Baltimore's biweekly CitiStat meetings. The day before each meeting, a CitiStat analyst prepares, for the city's leadership team, a memo identifying key issues to be discussed, follow-up topics from previous meetings, including data and often photos. This memo is not, however, distributed to the agency. Thus the question:

Why doesn't the agency that is appearing before the mayor's leadership team get to see the questions that it will be asked? If the agency knew the questions it will be asked, it can prepare itself better. Doesn't this prove that the mayor's office is playing gotcha?

Some people in the room shared this concern. Others suggested that the approach taken by Baltimore and some jurisdictions and agencies had a few advantages.

First, noted several people, the data used by CitiStat analysts were not secret. Every agency had its own data too. Often, the data used by PerformanceStat analysts come from the agency itself. In a police department, the CompStat staff gets its data from the department's districts, which obviously have their data before the CompStat staff does.

Others noted a second advantage: If, before a PerformanceStat meeting, a subunit is told the questions it will be asked, it will prepare to respond to *only* those issues—ignoring the others.

Maybe, however, the PerformanceStat staff is focusing on trivial problems or asking the wrong questions. Maybe the line agency understands its own problems better than an analyst working in a far-off location. Maybe the agency, from its own analyses of its own data, will identify the key performance deficit on which it should focus next.

Thus, the "secrecy" of the memo prepared by PerformaceStat staff has a third advantage: It encourages each subunit to continuously analyze its own data—*all* of its data. It motivates a second set of analytical eyes that can identify problems and suggest potential solutions.

Subunit managers who are really focused on results create their own agendas, complete with performance deficits they have identified plus the help they need to eliminate or mitigate them. In the room during a well-structured Performance-Stat meeting are representatives from all the support agencies—budget, personnel, legal, procurement, IT—whose help is needed for any initiative. Once a decision is made, the room contains the people whose cooperation is necessary to make it happen.

Contenders and Pretenders

At the Maryland Stat Summit, Gallagher offered a fourth advantage: The meetings help separate "the contenders from the pretenders." Frequent Performance-Stat meetings provide the chief executive with information about the leadership skills of people several layers down in the agency—helping to identify those who should be given additional responsibility. In 1991, Valentina Ukwuoma,

an immigrant from Nigeria, started work at Baltimore's Department of Public
Works as a recycling program inspector. A decade and a half later, she was the first
woman to be appointed director of the Bureau of Solid Waste.

How did this happen? Naturally, Ukwuoma's career path took several turns.
But one thing that kept her path going up was the city's constant focus—meeting
after meeting—on results. When managers are asked questions at a Performance
Stat meeting, some complain or mumble. Others, however, are prepared with an
answer or a proposal. Or they reply: "I don't know today. But, in two weeks, I
will." After watching a PerformanceStat session or two, even an outsider (who
isn't sure what the problems are or what the solutions might be) can, by listening
to the answers and scrutinizing the body language, separate the pretenders from
the contenders.

At the summit, Anthony Barksdale,[24] the city's deputy police commissioner
for operations who ran the city's CompStat meetings, offered another example.
The department had a suspect in a rape case, but lacked enough evidence to arrest
him. But Barksdale's staff discovered that the suspect had an outstanding warrant
for his arrest on another crime. Asked Barksdale: How come "the colonel, major,
lieutenant, sergeant, and detective" in the district couldn't find this warrant but
Barksdale's staff could? Doesn't this suggest a management shortcoming?

In New York, one precinct commander reported: "When I go to one of those
[CompStat] meetings they have the stats on my precinct. But I have to know it
better than they do. I have to be able to describe what's happening, where, and
what I'm doing about it. And the same thing goes for my sergeants."[25]

When creating their PerformanceStat, some jurisdictions and agencies have
consciously tried to avoid playing gotcha. Before each meeting, they circulate all
the data, analyses, and questions to every subunit.

Providing these data, analyses, and questions has an obvious benefit. It reduces
the anxiety of subunit managers. After all, a manager who must answer pointed
questions about his or her unit's performance in front of superiors, peers, and
subordinates can find the experience intimidating. Making the questions public
can reduce this anxiety.

Providing these data, analyses, and questions also has some disadvantages. It
does not motivate subunits to conduct their own analyses of their data. And it
limits a chief executive's ability to evaluate individual managers.

PerformanceStat doesn't have to be a gotcha game. It can be a leadership strategy for producing results. Each agency or jurisdiction that seeks to employ the
strategy needs to think carefully about how to adapt the core leadership principles
and key operational components to best improve its performance. Sometimes an

insubordinate or incompetent manager may well deserve rigorous questioning. At NYPD, in Baltimore, and elsewhere, such questioning has encouraged some managers to retire. In most circumstances, however, the questioning merely needs to be persistent.

Once subunit managers recognize that the meetings will happen (and happen and happen) and that the questions will be persistent (and persistent and persistent), they will realize that PerformanceStat is just one more part of the organizational landscape, one more activity in which they must participate. Some will even learn how to use data, analysis, and the meetings to accomplish their purposes for their subunit.

Making the Minutiae Meaningful

On Friday, February 9, 2001, at Boston Police headquarters, I attended my first CompStat meeting (then called a "Crime Analysis Meeting"). In this, my first exposure to the PerformanceStat strategy, I was struck by the retail nature of the discussion—the focus not on the macro but on the micro. At this meeting, Boston's police were not scrutinizing macro trends or analyzing disaggregated data. Yes, they did have some data. B&Es (breaking and entering) were up 20 percent citywide but down 9 percent in the police district under discussion. The real focus, however, was on specific "impact players." Indeed, the officers talked about them by name; everyone in the room seemed to know them. They also discussed specific problems. At one high school with a significant gun problem, the principal had failed to do very much; the district commander had finally convinced the principal to fix the side doors and to set up metal detectors (though they weren't working yet).[26]

This meeting was hardly unique. At most of the PerformanceStat meetings I have observed, the discussion has been very retail, focused on a series of particular, micro problems. Each problem was identified either through analysis of data or from personal observation. For each problem, the discussion has focused on what the line manager had done, will do, or should do. At these meetings, the manager of the reporting unit needs to be able to explain what the unit is doing about its specific, micro problems.

The organization's leadership team does not, however, see these problems as isolated incidents. They have chosen to focus on each micro problem precisely because it illustrates a macro, organizationwide failing—a performance deficit that they want everyone to recognize and that they would like their entire organization to tackle.

The managers of the subunits may dread appearing at PerformanceStat. They may view their next session to be yet another trial by fire. To survive this trial, they need to be able to provide satisfactory answers to every question they are asked. And they are rarely asked open-ended analytical questions: "Could you tell us what kind of data you've been analyzing recently and what you have learned from your analysis?" Rather, they are asked specific questions about particular operational problems: "Could you tell us what you are doing about your inability to hit your quarterly target for placing welfare recipients in jobs?" Thus, as they prepare for their next session, subunit managers need to anticipate each question and prepare very responsive answers.

The questions at a PerformanceStat meeting can easily reinforce the propensity of the operational units to focus on a series of small (and apparently unconnected) problems. As a manager from a central staff agency at one PerformanceStat session told me, "To them, it's always granular." Thus, the leadership team has to explain and dramatize how the individual granules are connected to each other and to the organization's purposes.

An Embarrassment of Questions

Whenever anyone directly quizzes people about their performance problems, data, deficits, and strategies, the questions have the potential to be humiliating. In a PerformanceStat session, if the subordinate managers have failed to identify their problems, compile and analyze their own data, diagnose their own performance deficits, think through their strategic responses to these deficits, or act on the commitments that they made during the last session, they can easily humiliate themselves. Whenever a question is asked about some aspect of performance, the subunit manager will certainly be embarrassed if the only response is: "I don't know." ("I don't know" is a much better answer than inventing some data on the spot.)

Still, why do so many managers—even experienced managers—dread PerformanceStat meetings? Why do they fear that they will be humiliated by questions about things that they should know better than anyone else in the room? I think the answer can be found in the traditional way that most organizations conduct business: They rarely ask subunit managers explicit questions about specific aspects of their subunit's performance. And if they do, they do not ask these questions in a room full of people. In some organizations, such questions may be considered impolite, even disrespectful. An effective PerformanceStat session—and the questioning inherent in it—disrupts a comfortable, contented, complacent culture. It is designed to do so.

The meetings and the questions are essential for an effective PerformanceStat. Through these meetings, the leadership team learns what is going on in the field, what is working, what is not working, what needs to be improved. The leadership team uses these meetings to motivate those with the most knowledge to analyze their performance deficits and develop strategies to eliminate them. It uses these meetings to follow up on the implementation of these strategies. PerformanceStat is more than a database. Improving performance requires individuals to examine their data and to develop and experiment with new ways to produce better results. About Washington's PerformanceStat—what the state called Government Management, Accountability and Performance, or "GMAP"—Governor Christine Gregoire emphasized, "No one gets in trouble at GMAP for bringing forth data that show we're not achieving our goals." But, she continued, "You get in trouble if you don't have an action plan for what you're going to do about it."[27]

To anyone not accustomed to standing in a room surrounded by superiors, peers, and subordinates looking at you—focusing on you—a PerformanceStat meeting can be intimidating. Moreover, questions about you and your unit's performance—not generic, hypothetical questions, but specific questions based on your unit's data—can feel disrespectful, perhaps even personally threatening. In fact, each question does, by definition, *question* you and your subunit's performance. Underlying the question—indeed, the need for asking the question—is the concern that you and your unit might not be performing as well as you claim, as well as you could, as well as you should. At a PerformanceStat meeting, the implicit reason for asking you any question is the assumption that you (might) need to improve. Most of us think we are doing quite well, thank you.

Most managers have advanced through their organization without ever being questioned about their performance. Thus, such questions, even when posed gently, can feel threatening. And the quasi-public nature of the questioning contributes to the manager's dread. It is one thing to be questioned by your boss in private. It is a very different thing to be questioned in front of your peers and subordinates.[28] To be effective, a manager needs respect from peers and deference from subordinates. A poor showing at PerformanceStat can destroy both. Maybe you can do better the next time. Still, everyone will remember when you didn't know what your own organization was doing.[29]

A leadership team that seeks to truly improve its performance will have to ask subunit managers explicit questions about specific aspects of their unit's performance. If these questions focus on what needs to be done to produce better results, some will inevitably be embarrassing. But the inevitability of these questions can also motivate managers to identify their own performance deficits and develop strategies to attack them.[30]

The Persistent and the Relentless

If Jack Maple was nothing else, he was "relentless." He advocated "relentless follow up." He believed in being "relentless." Jack Maple believed that all cops should also be "relentless."[31]

The word "relentless" comes, however, with some awkward connotations. For "relentless," the *Dictionary of Synonyms* lists "unrelenting, merciless, implacable, grim" and notes that relentless implies "an absence of pity or of any feeling that would cause one to relent and to restrain through compassion the fury or violence of one's rage, hatred, hostility, or vengeance."[32] Certainly, Jack Maple's relentlessness is consistent with some of these connotations.

Still, at any PerformanceStat meeting, the questions need not express rage, hatred, hostility, or vengeance. They need not be "relentless." They need only be "persistent."

At the Los Angeles County Department of Public Social Services (DPSS), Directors Philip L. Browning and Sheryl L. Spiller have certainly been persistent. At every bimonthly meeting of DPSSTATS (for "DPSS Total Accountability, Total Success"), they distributed data on eight services—from the "Food Stamp Error Rate" to "Participant Satisfaction"—for each of the 28 districts in the Bureau of Workforce Services.

These comparative data are displayed graphically. One piece of paper charts with green-yellow-red ratings each district's performance for each service. If a district earns a green for all of its services, it gets a star added to its director's name card at the next meeting. Indeed, this page also includes a star for each district that earned one. A second piece of paper displays for every district the periods for which it won a star, plus the total won by each district. While some districts struggle, others consistently win stars.

No one has to say anything. Neither Browning nor Spiller read the names of the winners, or mention the chart. Everyone sees it. Everyone gets it. And because there are 28 districts, no district director can complain that his or her poor performance is caused by the district's singular (and uniquely unfortunate) circumstances. After all, if the district located in the heart of South Central Los Angeles can consistently win stars, it is difficult for other district directors to claim that their circumstances account for their fewer wins. As a result, many of the district directors see themselves in competition with their colleagues— though, because every district can win if it hits its targets, this competition is not cutthroat. (See appendix C, "The Motivational Consequences of Feedback and Rewards.")

Every director obviously prefers to have his or her district rated all green. No director wants too many yellows. No director wants a single red. Every director wants to win a star every month. Each director's ego—and professional reputation within DPSS—is caught up in these ratings. No rebuke is required. Sheryl Spiller can lead the applause for particular accomplishments, while letting ego-driven motivation drive the rest.

DPSS's charts separate the contenders from the pretenders. They reveal the pretenders—those whose record is plagued by yellows or reds. They identify the contenders—the directors whose districts are consistently winning stars—and suggest who might help their colleagues or warrant promotion.

These charts are inescapable. Yet, the charts themselves exhibit no rage, no hatred, no hostility, no vengeance. This is Los Angeles. As LAPD's Sergeant Joe Friday would have said: They are "just the facts." No one is publicly criticized. There is lots of applause. But those with the yellows and the reds—those without the stars—get the message.

Those who chair PerformanceStat meetings need not be brutal or relentless. They do, however, need to be persistent. As the organization improves, the leadership team may choose to focus the meetings on different performance deficits. Still, the core definition of what constitutes good performance—the purpose plus the results needed to achieve that purpose—must remain relatively stable. Sub-unit managers and directors need to know what is expected of them. They need consistency in the results they are supposed to produce. They need to know that the charts will remain the same, meeting after meeting (until a new performance deficit is identified). Then they can focus their energy on improving performance against the established standards.

Persistence combined with stability—not relentless rage—are key to effective PerformanceStat meetings.

The Overreaction to the Brutal and the Relentless

Some who sought to create their own PerformanceStat did get Maple's message about follow-up. Primarily, however, they got Maple's message that this follow-up was *required* to be "relentless." They may never have visited NYPD's CompStat. Still, they absorbed the meaning of "relentless" from the popular media, which vividly conveyed the tone of these meetings (see chapter 2). They did not believe, however, that they should publicly embarrass anyone—ever.

The obvious way to eliminate any humiliation is to eliminate any follow-up. Or to make all follow-up questions innocuous. The easiest way to ensure that no one is publicly embarrassed is to eliminate all criticisms, even those implicit in comparative data.

This effort to avoid all criticism is one of the major errors that agencies and jurisdictions make when they seek to create something they would like to believe can have the impact of a real PerformanceStat.[33] A PerformanceStat imitation with zero or sterile follow-up might be worse than no PerformanceStat at all. If the data that document any subunit's performance are to have any meaning, they need to be compared with something. Is performance good, adequate, or poor? This question can only be answered by comparing current data with some standard—a standard established by past performance, by the performance of similar units, or by a performance target. Following up by making such a comparison need not be "relentless." It need not be brutal.

It just needs to be persistent.

Of course, persistent follow-up—the ongoing, repetitive questioning about a subunit's chronic performance deficits—may annoy its director and managers. They may complain that they cannot reasonably be expected to even mitigate this performance deficit. If, however, the performance standard is a reasonable one and the subunit has adequate resources, or if similar subunits are achieving this standard, persistent attention to a chronic performance deficit hardly seems irrational, let alone malicious.

Still, some public officials, offended by the brutal, have opted for the bland.[34]

The Bland

Sometimes, the reaction to PerformanceStat's reputation for brutal questioning has been an overreaction. Some public officials have concluded that any PerformanceStat must, by definition, humiliate subordinates. As a result, some decided not even to experiment with the strategy. Others sought to create their own kinder, gentler version. In doing so, they may install an insipid imitation. Call it "PerformanceStat Lite." Rather than committing themselves to creating a strategy that will help them to achieve their agency's or jurisdiction's specific purposes, they begin with a quite different commitment: No one should ever be humiliated. With personnel comfort and organizational tranquility dominating purpose and results, they promise a congenial process that will dishonor no one.

Superficially, their process looks like a PerformanceStat. It may have data, fancy technology, and meetings. But it lacks a persistent focus on a specific purpose—on producing real results.

Creating PerformanceStat Lite is easy: Just invite subunits to come in for show-and-tell. This lightens the workload for the leadership team. No one needs to create, let alone manage, a staff of analysts. No one needs to collect (or even look at) any data. No one needs to prepare for each meeting. No one has to do any follow-up. Someone creates a schedule of meetings. The chief executive's staff just shows up. These staffers are all smart enough to ask an appropriate question or two. Then, after an hour, everyone leaves with a warm feeling as if they have accomplished something. After all, they too, like all *au courant* public executives, have created their own, nifty version of this PerformanceStat thingee.

Of course, the directors and managers of the subunits quickly catch on:

> This is a waste of time, but at least we don't get embarrassed or abused. Yeah, we have to prepare. A pain in the butt. Fortunately, the boss doesn't prepare. No one will have looked at any data, so no one will know enough to ask a penetrating question. Besides, they will be worrying about the next crisis (or checking their BlackBerrys). And, if they do stumble onto one of our vulnerabilities, we can just promise to get back to them with an answer. But no one takes notes, so they'll forget about it.

Clever subunit managers would, for each meeting, deliver a presentation that is completely disconnected from all previous ones, ensuring that the leadership team can never do any follow-up.

Still, PerformanceStat Lite is not completely without merit. Each subunit's manager and key staff do have to prepare. They want to look good. They want to demonstrate that they and their subunit are competent. They want to convince their superiors that they are accomplishing something. Thus, they might try to think through what they should be doing. They might consider what aspects of their work their superiors consider important. And they might imagine the questions that their superiors might ask and develop their best response to each.

They cannot be too cavalier about the meeting, too careless in their presentation. Still, if they do design their slides diligently, they will not be seriously challenged (let alone embarrassed).

Unfortunately, visitors to a meeting of PerformanceStat Lite cannot see the unrealized potential. They may conclude, "we were just lucky to observe a meeting with a wonderfully effective subunit."

The visitors could, however, ask some penetrating questions of their own: "What results are you trying to produce? What performance deficits are you trying to eliminate? What are your performance targets? What has your strategy actually accomplished?" If these visitors found the answers unfulfilling, they might figure out that they were watching a pseudomorph—a MimicStat that completely lacked the PerformanceStat potential.

The Balanced

PerformanceStat meetings need be neither brutal nor bland. Between Pinocchio's brutality and show-and-tell's blandness lies a balanced approach. It is quite possible to create meetings that are analytical without being embarrassing, that are motivational without being adulatory.

Such meetings are driven by purpose. They focus on what the organization needs to do next to achieve its purpose. They analyze the latest data, examine the performance deficits that each subunit needs to attack next, explore alternatives for eliminating or mitigating these deficits, learn from what has worked so far, consider strategies for future improvement, and recognize managers and subunits that are making progress. All the while, those who conduct the meetings keep everyone focused on creating meaningful yet realistic results.

There is no formula for conducting such meetings—no protocol that, if faithfully followed, ensures that everyone is committed to achieving the organization's performance targets. Indeed, the individual who chairs the meeting, along with the rest of the leadership team, needs to be constantly adjusting his or her analytical perspective and motivational style. Who needs to do what next? Do we intensify or relax the pressure? Should we set another incremental target, or is it time for a stretch target? And how do we motivate not only the people in the room but the rest of those who work in the agency and actually produce the results? (Appendix B gives some tips on how to set up and run a regular PerformanceStat meeting.)

Does the Los Angeles County Department of Public Social Services get perfect balance? There is no "perfect" balance. In DPSS, some district directors might find their repeatedly revealed deficiencies—too many yellows and reds, and too few stars—to be humiliating. Others might think that with over half the districts earning stars that the reward isn't all that meaningful. Even in an organization with as many districts as DPSS, some managers still might claim that their district is so unusual that they cannot do what their peers have achieved. For DPSSTATS, however, the balance is probably pretty good.

Accountability without the Brutality

Kimberly Flowers joined Baltimore's CitiStat staff in 2002 and two years later became Mayor O'Malley's director of the Department of Recreation and Parks. She experienced the CitiStat process from both sides of the podium and understood the impact that the meetings have on the behavior of the city's line managers. "Every two weeks you have to go in and explain and defend" what you are doing, observed Flowers. "The benefit" of the meetings, she argued, is that managers "have to speak to the data" because "someone is watching your data at all times." Baltimore's managers "are accountable for their data," she said, and "that's new." With CitiStat, emphasized Flowers, "it's a different level of accountability."[35]

Baltimore created this new level of accountability without any of the legendary brutality.

Jeff Godown also emphasized the importance of the meetings for accountability: "Bringing people together on a regular basis and holding them accountable for what they are paid for is what has made a difference." Of course, Godown's use of the phrase "holding them accountable" makes the meeting sound brutal. In fact, he made this comment after a CompStat session that was anything but.[36]

Charlie Beck had conducted this meeting. He was polite and civil in his questioning, often introducing a new topic with a compliment. Neither Beck nor his colleagues uttered a cross word or a derogatory adjective. Still, he was direct in his questioning. But even the most pointed question—even a question that suggested that a problem existed—was asked politely. Did area commanders and their subordinates feel that they were being "held accountable"? Certainly.

LAPD divides the city into "areas," not precincts, and, that morning, three areas were up for review. Each review took about an hour, with a short break in between. At the break after the second review, Beck had an email on his BlackBerry from the commander of the area reviewed first apologizing for inadequate performance. Beck had never been the least bit brutal; throughout the morning his demeanor was calm and composed—invariably polite.

Yet everyone knew. This area commander knew. Beck knew. Everyone else in the room knew. Even I knew. The area commander—and the area—had not performed well.

Still, at CompStat meetings in Los Angeles, as at CitiStat meetings in Baltimore, no one was being abused.

Analysis, Problem Solving, and Learning

Effective PerformanceStat meetings achieve a variety of purposes. They provide operational updates, reveal deficiencies, and create accountability. They remind everyone of the chief executive's purposes. Still, these sessions often appear to focus on who will be responsible to do what by when, and even more particularly, on who failed to do what by when.

Yet, an effective PerformanceStat session involves more than revealing deficiencies and demanding improvements. To be effective, it needs to be a problem-solving meeting. It needs to identify specific problems and analyze ways to fix them. What are the causes? What are the alternatives? What could we learn from others—either within our organization or elsewhere—who have tackled similar problems and attained some success? What do we have the operational capacity to do? What are the resource requirements? Once the problems have been identified, those in the room need to think through who might do what next. Then, at the next meeting, people can report back on what they have done, what has happened, and what they have learned.

The thinking that drives an effective PerformanceStat meeting is not the exclusive responsibility of a group of analytic wonks working in the basement of some headquarters annex. Much of the analytical and strategic thinking has to be done collectively through discussion and debate among the chief executive's leadership team, the managers of the relevant subunits, and the managers of the support agencies. Otherwise, the analysis is little more than a technical exercise that fails to have operational impact.

The discussion during the regular PerformanceStat meetings converts what might be an exclusive wonkdom of obscure data and nerdy analysts into an opportunity to make significant improvements in performance—to realize the PerformanceStat potential.

11

Carrying Out the
Feedback and Follow-Up

How can who organize the follow-up to the meetings' discussions to ensure that the problems identified, the solutions proposed, the decisions taken, and the commitments made are, indeed, acted on?

Conscience is the inner voice which warns us that someone may be looking.
H. L. MENCKEN, the "Sage of Baltimore"[1]

A system without feedback is a system out of control.
DENNIS SMITH, New York University[2]

As part of JobStat, the New York City Human Resources Administration (HRA) requires its 29 Job Centers to conduct their own, monthly CenterStat—their own mini-JobStat. At one CenterStat, there were 11 people in the room. Two were representatives from a vendor that found jobs for welfare recipients; eight were public managers from HRA, mostly white and middle-aged; one was a very young African American. He was probably 20-plus years old, but the kid looked 16.

This CenterStat session began with a presentation from the vendor, accompanied by some questions from the center's director. At one point, early in this discussion, the kid interrupted an answer from the vendor: "That's what you said last month."

I said to myself: "Promote the kid."

Clearly, the youngest person in the room got it. He understood that CenterStat was more than a series of *pro forma* meetings. He understood the meeting's purpose. He recognized the necessity of follow-up. And although he was the person in the room with the least status (I found out later that he was the notetaker), the kid was willing to interrupt to make an essential point: The vendors could not simply return each month with the same explanation—the same excuse. If CenterStats are going to improve performance, each discussion has to be more than a repeat of the previous month's.

To be effective, any PerformanceStat strategy requires follow-up. Jack Maple certainly thought follow-up was essential. It was one of his four—very visible, very publicized—principles. Yet many agencies and jurisdictions that have created something that they call ***Stat completely miss the value and necessity of the follow-up.

Such follow-up provides the all-important feedback that reveals how well an organization is doing. Bureaucratic "rigidity" and "ossification," argued Anthony Downs, are "most likely to occur in bureaus that are insulated from feedbacks," from "loud" complaints "from clients, suppliers, regulatees, rivals and allies." Conversely, he wrote "the rigidity cycle is least likely to occur in bureaus that are under strong and constant pressure from such feedbacks."[3] With frequent feedback, a PerformanceStat leadership strategy can disrupt the ossification.

The Focus on Follow-Up

Follow-up consists of the questions asked during one meeting about the problems examined, the data analyzed, the strategies debated, and the commitments made at previous meetings. With this verbal, personal, and quasi-public follow-up, other forms of follow-up cannot be easily ignored. If a subunit's director and managers know that they will be questioned personally at the next PerformanceStat session about these problems, data, strategies, and commitments, they will pay attention.

Somerville's SomerStat has its own version of follow-up, which it calls the "task list." This list, stored on a spreadsheet, specifies the task to be completed, the name of the individual with primary responsibility for the task, and the names of others who need to contribute to its completion.

Somerville begins every SomerStat session for every city department with a discussion of its task list. After every meeting, the SomerStat staff updates the task list. Then, every Friday, the SomerStat staff creates a set of personalized task lists and sends every agency head his or her own. "We are definitely relentless about follow-up," reported Stephanie Hirsch, the former director of SomerStat. As a result, the task list "has definitely become part of the culture."

Baltimore's CitiStat has the follow-up memo. Each of the half-dozen CitiStat analysts has primary responsibility for three to five city agencies. During a

**BOX 11-1. Format of a Typical Follow-Up Memo
for Baltimore's CitiStat**

To: Bureau Chief of Agency X

From: CitiStat Team

Subject: CitiStat Meeting—Follow-Up

As a result of our recent meeting, please act on the following by the next meeting scheduled for [the same time on the same day two weeks in the future]. Please provide a brief written response to the items listed below, and submit all information to the CitiStat Office by Friday [of the week before the next meeting].

1. Provide . . .
2. Review . . .
3. Explain . . .
4. Investigate . . .
5. Ensure . . .
6. Determine . . .
7. Adjust . . .
8. Explore . . .

CitiStat session, the agency's analyst takes notes and then, by 5:00 p.m. writes a one- or two-page follow-up memo to the agency outlining actions to be taken before the next meeting in two weeks. (See box 11-1.)

Baltimore's memo drives the follow-up. It reminds the agency of the key assignments made during the meeting. It reminds the agency that the members of the mayor's leadership team are unlikely to forget the issues. The problems, data, actions, and commitments have been written down and distributed.

Over the next two weeks, Baltimore's CitiStat analyst follows the agency's progress and examines its data. Then, by 5:00 p.m. on the day before the agency's next CitiStat session, the analyst prepares a memorandum running a dozen pages or more outlining an agenda for the next day's meeting, with suggestions for how much time should be devoted to each topic. Finally, 10 minutes before the meeting, the analyst and the director of CitiStat go over the agenda.

For follow-up questions to be fair, they need to be based on some kind of follow-up document: Somerville's electronic task list or Baltimore's memo. After every PerformanceStat meeting, a specific individual has to prepare a specific follow-up document.

Follow-Up as Reminder

Why is this follow-up important? What does it accomplish? Why does an effective PerformanceStat need real, meaningful follow-up?

The first answer to the "Why follow-up?" question is very basic. The follow-up *reminds* each subunit's management team of what they are supposed to accomplish by when. Without such an explicit and visible reminder about their responsibilities for long-term results, these managers are apt to focus their attention and effort on more visible, more immediately urgent problems. Public managers have lots of responsibilities—more than they can accomplish in any one day. They have to triage. Inevitably, they will pay attention to those responsibilities for which they are being most directly and frequently harassed.

Every human—and certainly everyone working in government—is constantly bombarded with requests (or demands) to do particular things. Every public manager receives requests from supervisors, legislators, stakeholders, journalists, subordinates, colleagues within government, . . . friends from outside. These requests do not come with equal salience, but they do come in large numbers—and often with a claim of extreme urgency. (How many emails with the "urgent" symbol populate your inbox?) Indeed, by the time agency directors make it back to their office from a PerformanceStat meeting, they will have confronted several people who asked them to do something. And, upon arriving in the office, they will find a pile of phone calls to return and emails to answer.

On several occasions, Nobel Laureate Herbert Simon emphasized the mismatch between the glut of information we humans receive and our mental capacity to pay attention to this information:

> In a world where attention is a major scarce resource, information may be an expensive luxury, for it may turn our attention from what is important to what is unimportant. We cannot afford to attend to information simply because it is there.[4]
>
> What information consumes is rather obvious: it consumes the attention of its recipients. Hence a wealth of information creates a poverty of attention, and a need to allocate that attention efficiently among the overabundance of information sources that might consume it.[5]

For every public manager, indeed for every modern human, attention is a scarce resource. The follow-up is designed to focus everyone's individual and collective attention on the next tasks—to remind everyone that the problems examined and commitments made at the last PerformanceStat meeting are important, very important.

Follow-Up in Medicine

In medicine, follow-up has a long and distinguished pedigree. Why does your physician's office call you 48 hours before your appointment? Because too many people forget. (Not you, of course; you have never forgotten an appointment.) A simple phone call reduces the number of no-shows.[6]

This tendency to forget—to fail to do what we know we should do for our own personal health—applies not just to physicians' appointments. We also fail to follow their advice. We fail to abide by their explicit directives. For everything from diet and exercise to taking our medications, we humans are hardly diligent at following the suggestions and instructions of our physicians. Physicians are constantly frustrated by our chronic failure to pay attention to their guidance.

Patient compliance with physicians' general recommendations and explicit instructions has been found in numerous studies across a variety of diseases and therapies to often be very low. Marshall Becker and Lois Maiman of Johns Hopkins School of Medicine report from their survey of the medical literature "disturbingly low rates of cooperation or 'compliance' with prescribed medical regimens in both preventive and curative situations" noting, for example, that "at least a third of the patient populations in most studies fail to follow physicians' recommendations."[7] For prescription medications, one study found compliance with instructions averaging about 50 percent and ranging from zero to *over* 100 percent.[8] No wonder our physicians call with reminders?

Whether a physician is treating a chronic cough, Hodgkin's disease, or an inflammatory pseudotumor, the research suggests that "persistent follow-up" is required.[9] One Australian study of patients who had surgery for colorectal cancer found "evidence of improved survival of patients undergoing more intense follow-up compared with those having minimal surveillance, with an estimated overall 5-year gain of up to 10%."[10]

To "enhance patient compliance," one practicing physician "drew lessons from the sales profession," and urged his colleagues to "always follow up."[11] Indeed, the study of consumer behavior and its implications for marketing suggests the underlying reason for the need for follow-up: We humans just don't pay attention.

Actually, as Simon emphasized we can't pay attention. Our cognitive capacity to pay attention is limited.[12] Every day, we are bombarded with too many suggestions and pressures, too many requests and demands, too many messages and stimuli. We can't comply with them all. We can't acknowledge them all. We can't even recognize them all. We listen to a few and ignore the rest. What else can we humans do?

How can a chief executive's leadership team keep every subunit director focused on the tasks discussed during its PerformanceStat? The answer is: Follow-up, Follow-Up, and then more *Follow-Up*. To ensure that (from PerformanceStat meeting to office) people do not forget the commitments they have made, an essential component of any effective PerformanceStat strategy is the follow-up— follow-up that is very explicit, very visible, and very persistent.

Follow-Up as Informative Feedback

That's all? Follow-up is just a reminder? Do public executives, after regular, frequent meetings, really have to send out a blizzard of memos just to remind people about what they are supposed to do? Isn't it their job? What's the connection between follow-up and performance? Does follow-up serve another significant leadership and managerial purpose?

Yes: The follow-up also provides specific feedback on performance. Public service institutions "need to define measurements of performance," argued Peter Drucker, and then "they need to use these measurements to '*feed back*' on their efforts—that is, they must build self-control from results into their system."[13]

This feedback happens during an effective PerformanceStat meeting: The follow-up questions are designed to compare a subunit's actual performance with its targeted performance. Then, after the meeting, the follow-up memo not only reiterates some of these comparisons but also specifies the performance that is targeted for the future and thus establishes the basis for future comparisons.

Dennis Smith argues that "a system without feedback is a system out of control." In fact, the concept of "feedback" arises from control theory,[14] where the feedback is designed to compare the current circumstances with the targeted outcome. Using this feedback, it is possible to create a "closed-loop control system" that continuously loops back the latest data to compare with the target. Then the challenge is to design a strategy that will minimize the difference between the two (subject to a variety of constraints, such as cost).

A simple example is a thermostat. This little electromechanical device on your wall constantly compares two important pieces of information: (1) the target temperature (as specified by your setting) and (2) the actual temperature (the feedback provided by its thermometer). The difference between the target and the actual tells your heating, ventilation, and air conditioning (HVAC) system how to adjust its performance: If the actual temperature is too much below the target, turn on the furnace. If the actual temperature is too much above the target, turn on the air conditioner. If the actual temperature is close enough to the target, do nothing. (Should we call it "ThermoStat"?)

In contrast, an "open-loop control system" (one that lacks any such comparative feedback) must essentially operate by dead reckoning—without any way to compare current circumstances with the desired outcome. How could you decide whether to turn on the furnace or the air conditioning if your only information was what the temperature had been a week or a month ago? To be useful, a HVAC system needs very current data.

The value of feedback applies not only to producing the desired temperature in a room but also to producing the desired performance in an organization.[15] Improving performance also requires two important pieces of information: (1) the targeted level of performance, and (2) the current level of performance. Without both, you can't decide what to do next. To design an improvement strategy, you need the ability to compare where you are with where you want to be. A GPS gizmo can tell you the coordinates of exactly where you are, but if you haven't specified the coordinates of where you are trying to go, you don't know what to do. Conversely, if you know exactly where you are trying to go but have no idea where you are, you also don't know what to do. Without a target for the level of future performance, and without data on the level of current performance, a public executive cannot design a strategy for improvement.

An effective PerformanceStat creates a variety of feedback mechanisms. The frequent meetings—persistent examinations of performance deficits; serious efforts to learn from the positive deviants— may be the most effective. But innovative executives can find other ways.

Each week, for example, Baltimore surveyed a sample of citizens whose service requests had been closed to determine if they were satisfied with what the city had done. From the results, the city learned a lot. For example, satisfaction was higher if the service produced a visible output—such as a pothole filled or a tree trimmed. But some requests for city services—such as complaints about rats—left nothing visible behind; if no one was home when the city's rat rubout crews put poison into the rats' burrows, citizens think the city did nothing. So, the city learned to leave tags on doors, announcing the service that had been provided.

Moreover, reported Matthew Gallagher, "CitiStat regularly distributes to department heads a list of closed service requests that customers, through the surveys, reported not being done."[16] This feedback not only tells department heads about the effectiveness of their work. It also tells them that the mayor's leadership team knows too.

Feedback with Comparative Data

For an AgencyStat with multiple subunits with similar responsibilities, one way to provide informative feedback is with data that compare the results produced by similar subunits. Moreover, the leadership team can display such comparative data in two compelling ways:

—**The Bar Chart** is very simple. It displays accomplishment data for each unit and may include a horizontal line that defines the target for all units. Regardless of whether there is a target line, everyone immediately focuses on the tallest bar (why is this unit doing so well?) and on the shortest bar (why is this unit doing so badly?).

—**The List** is even simpler. On one piece of paper, there are two columns. Column A contains the names of the units that made their target for the previous period (year, quarter, or month). Column B contains the names of the units that did not make their targets. When "The List" is distributed at a meeting of sub-unit directors, their behavior is predictable. First, they look for their own unit's name; then they look for the names of their colleagues' units.[17]

These two quite ordinary ways for providing comparative feedback about results can quickly grab managers' attention.

Moreover, both these feedback strategies can motivate people provided they have agreed on:

1. the purpose they are pursuing;
2. the targets to be achieved by when and by whom; and
3. the indicators used to compare the results produced by subunits.

And, if the incentives are aligned with the purposes, targets, and indicators (always a big *if*), they can also foster learning from the "positive deviants."

Three Critical Pieces of Information

The Bar Chart and The List provide everyone with three critical pieces of information:

1. This feedback tells everyone—every manager and every employee—how well his or her unit is doing.
2. This feedback tells everyone how everyone else's unit is doing.
3. This feedback tells everyone that everyone else knows how well his or her unit is doing.

To be motivational, this information must be public—or, at least, quasi-public. This performance feedback must be distributed to everyone who has a role in achieving the overall target as well as achieving his or her individual unit's targets. It doesn't work if people are only told the height of their own subunit's bar. It doesn't work if people are only told if their unit is in Column A or in Column B. It only works to motivate improvement and foster learning if everyone gets all three pieces of comparative information. The Bar Chart and The List can motivate people because they provide a basis for social comparison. (See appendix C.)

Such displays of comparative information also help to explain why PerformanceStat sessions are so frequently described as brutal. They may be brutal because of the language used to express displeasure with the gap between a subunit's performance and its target. But even if the language is innocuous, the feedback may still feel brutal. The subunit's director and managers are having their performance explicitly compared against a previously established and previously accepted standard. And they are found wanting in front of peers and subordinates. They are receiving this feedback not one-on-one in a private closed-door discussion but in front of numerous others; and most people (even if they disdain or even despise those with whom they work) care about their professional reputation. In such circumstances, the kindest words can only soften but not eliminate that very public sting.

Feedback as Motivation

The feedback provided by these three critical pieces of information can be motivational. It gives direction to every manager's ambition, initiative, and energy. If an individual's "ego ideal"—the kind of person the manager thinks he or she should be[18]—includes these substantive accomplishments, feedback can motivate the manager to strive to achieve them.

After all, there will be another opportunity to produce improved results. The next PerformanceStat meeting is already scheduled. And the follow-up memo specifies the improvements to be made by then. The director and managers of a subunit do not have to guess; the follow-up memo specifies the standard by which they will be judged at the next meeting.

Consequently, although today's meeting may have felt brutal, the next one provides an opportunity for redemption. Indeed, the explicitness of the follow-up memo is both a minus and a plus. It is a minus because it clarifies how much work must be done to achieve the standard. It is a plus for precisely the same reason. The follow-up memo specifies the future basis for earning either a reprimand or praise. William Bratton emphasized that it was possible to earn either.

It wasn't all calling people on the carpet. When someone did particularly well we told them, "You did an excellent job here." We made a point of sharing their good ideas with the rest of the commanders, first to spread good police technique, and second to encourage and motivate good workers.[19]

From 2003 to 2011, as the police chief of Providence, Rhode Island, Dean Esserman took a similar approach.

Bill Bratton taught me something which I never forgot. He said: "Go out there, as chief, and try to find somebody doing something right instead of wrong. Go catch him doing something right." I spent every day running around trying to catch people doing something right.[20]

PerformanceStat meetings provide the leadership team with an opportunity to recognize people for an "excellent job," for "doing something right." They provide subunit directors and managers with the opportunity to earn esteem—both self-esteem and the esteem of others. PerformanceStat provides people with an "esteem opportunity."[21]

This opportunity—not merely to avoid embarrassment but to actually shine—is the upside of the quasi-public nature of the PerformanceStat meeting. It may be a strictly internal management meeting. Citizens, legislators, stakeholders, and journalists may never be invited; they might not even know about the meeting. The room does, however, contain the manager's peers, superiors, and often subordinates. Although managers may not care about what journalists or legislators or stakeholders or citizens think, they care a lot about what the people with whom they work every day think. Most of them would prefer not to be embarrassed in front of these colleagues. Most of them would prefer to earn some esteem.

Both The Bar Chart and The List reward—with recognition and prestige— the high-performing units and their managers. Both reprove—with peer embarrassment—the low-performing units and their managers. Both of these simple feedback processes have the potential to motivate the behavior of those who value peer esteem to focus on the results that the organization seeks to produce.

Motivation for Cooperation or for Competition

PerformanceStat's quasi-public nature has the potential to motivate individuals and teams to try to get better. It also has the potential to motivate them *to learn* how to get better. It provides them with the opportunity to analyze what others in the room are doing and thus to learn.

Initially, this learning will focus on how to answer the leadership team's questions. What kind of answers do the members of the leadership team prize? What kind of answers do they disdain? By sitting in the room, watching the members of the leadership team analyze the performance of colleagues, observing their questions and noticing how they respond to different answers, subunit directors and managers gain some preliminary knowledge about how to cope.

Next, this learning will involve the specifics of their own subunit's performance. What kind of questions will *we* be asked at our next PerformanceStat meeting? What kind of answers can *we* give? What kind of answers should *we* give? A subunit's management group often decides to conduct its own meeting a day or two before it will appear at PerformanceStat.

These internal sessions will begin as DebatePreparationStat. They are designed to ensure that the subunit's director and managers know what questions they might be asked and to develop the best answers they can provide. But if the members of a subunit's management team are doing any real learning, they will figure out that their own sessions (originally designed to select the best words for answering tomorrow's PerformanceStat questions) can be also employed to think through what they and their subunit need to do to be able to answer the questions that (they anticipate) they will be asked in six months. Eventually, they will figure out that they can use these meeting to manage their subunit. This is when DebatePreparationStat morphs into a real AgencyStat.

Moreover, at some point along the way, the director and managers of a subunit will ask their colleagues from other subunits for advice: "The leadership team likes what you're doing. What can we do to earn the same esteem?"

How will these colleagues respond? Will they provide any useful information or assistance? As always, it all depends. In this case, it depends on whether PerformanceStat has been designed as a zero-sum game pitting different subunits against each other or whether every subunit has an opportunity to win.

If only one Job Center (or a very few) can win the HRA commissioner's gold star, Job Centers that are doing well have little reason to share their secrets with their colleagues. Actually, they have every incentive to *not* share their secrets. But if every Job Center can win—if every Job Center can earn a gold star by achieving its *own* performance target—then the directors of the high-performing Job Centers have no disincentive to withhold their secrets. Moreover, if HRA's leadership team asks the heads of a few successful Job Centers to explain how they did it to their colleagues, they are both rewarding these successful Job Centers and promoting learning.

Competition comes in two forms.

1. Competition against each other—in which there is one winner and a whole lot of losers—can easily become "cutthroat competition."
2. Competition against a target—in which every team can win by achieving its own target—is much more likely to be "friendly competition."

Competition can encourage cooperation—but only if it is "friendly competition," only if it is competition against a goal that gives everyone an opportunity to win. In PerformanceStat, that should certainly be the purpose. The purpose is not just to have one subunit be successful; the purpose is to have every subunit be successful. (For more detail, see appendix C.)

Missing the Well-Advertised but Imperceptible Follow-Up

The value of follow-up—specifically of "relentless follow-up"—has been well advertised. It is not a stealth concept, something available only to the cognoscenti.[22] Yet, all too frequently, those claiming to be employing a PerformanceStat completely miss this operational component and its underlying principles. Why? It is (I think) because a visitor cannot "see" the follow-up. Yet the meeting is full of follow-up. It is in the data and in the questions. No one, however, announces: "Here comes the Follow-Up."

Indeed, a well-organized PerformanceStat session will consist primarily of follow-up. The members of the leadership team who conduct the meeting may raise one or two new issues. But most of the data they introduce, most of the questions they ask, and most of the discussion with the managers of a subunit will reflect what transpired at previous meetings, plus what happened since the last one. Anyone who attended the previous meeting will immediately recognize this follow-up. For the data and the questions will reflect the history of data, questions, and discussions. Each PerformanceStat meeting is just one more discussion in a very long, ongoing deliberation about how to improve performance.

Praise and the Competency Trap

Ed Koch isn't the only chief executive who ever wanted to know, "How'm I doing?" All mayors, all politicians, indeed all of us humans seek feedback—primarily positive feedback. As Somerset Maugham observed in *Of Human Bondage,* "people ask you for criticism, but they only want praise."[23]

For any PerformanceStat strategy, this human desire creates a dilemma. For to motivate both organizational learning and improved performance, the leadership team cannot offer only praise. Neither can it offer only criticism.[24] The challenge is to balance the two—to ensure that the follow-up is both fair and motivating. One way to ensure that this month's criticism is fair is to base it on last month's (and last year's) agreement about the performance targets that everyone accepts are achievable with the current resources.

Still if performance consistently falls short of expectations, and thus the feedback is consistently critical, those being criticized may become convinced that they can never do anything that might warrant even a reduction in the criticism, let alone some modest praise.

Conversely, if the feedback consists of only praise, it lures everyone into what Barbara Levitt and James March of Stanford University called the "competency trap,"[25] which can capture any organization. Through experimentation and experience, an organization learns something that works (or, at least, appears to work) and becomes satisfied with its own performance. Thus, it does not bother to attempt to experiment with other strategies that might produce even better performance. Instead, it creates procedures and routines that institutionalize what it has "learned." The organization is "trapped" by its own, learned but limited, competency.

In some ways, dealing with a continuous string of praiseworthy performances is relatively easy: just raise the expectations by establishing new, more demanding performance targets, while assuring everyone that the subunit's past performance demonstrates that it possesses the competence (and resources) necessary to ratchet itself up to the next level. And, if the new target is a "stretch target," the subunit will be forced to seriously experiment with new strategies.

I define a "stretch target" as one that the subunit cannot achieve simply by working a little harder or a little smarter. A stretch target is sufficiently demanding that it requires the organization to experiment with, develop, and learn some entirely new strategies.[26]

In contrast, dealing with a subunit that continually demonstrates its inability to make even modest progress requires more desperate measures. Expectations can be lowered, but this hardly seems fair to others who are meeting—or even exceeding—theirs. Giving the assignment to a different, already-high-performance subunit doesn't seem quite fair either. At the same time, if the horse is irredeemably dead, more beatings at future PerformanceStat sessions will accomplish little. Instead, a subunit's continual inability to achieve its targets—while others are doing so—suggests that it needs a new management team.

Sometimes the persistent follow-up provides the PerformanceStat's leadership team itself with some important feedback. Sometimes it reveals that it is necessary to either readjust performance expectations, to develop new strategies, or to give the responsibility for achieving them to a new team. The usual demand is for more resources. In fact, however, the organization's "binding constraint"[27] may not be money. Instead, performance may be constrained by the subunit's managers' inability to design strategies that make the best use of the existing resources.

Follow-Up as Conscience

PerformanceStat is designed to make people conscientious. As H. L. Mencken suggested, this leadership strategy makes people conscientious by "looking"—by looking obviously, repetitively, and frequently at the same important thing, and by promising not to stop looking and looking and looking at that very same thing.

PerformanceStat could be described as a leadership strategy for deciding what important things need to be looked at, and then doing that looking in such an explicit and prominent way as to ensure that no one in the organization needs Mencken's small inner voice of warning. Everyone in the agency or jurisdiction knows that the chief executive and the leadership team are looking. Everyone in the organization knows that they were not only looking at the last meeting but that they will follow up by looking at the same thing at the next meeting, and at the next. . . .

The PerformanceStat leadership strategy is the organizational substitute for conscience.

What Duke Ellington, the jazz composer, pianist, and band leader, said about music has some obvious implications for PerformanceStat: It don't mean a thing, if it ain't got that follow-up.[28] As with almost everything else about an effective PerformanceStat leadership strategy, the follow-up *requires* persistence.

12

Creating Organizational Competence and Commitment

What kinds of human competences—skills, talents, knowledge, habits of mind, and patterns of thought—do managers and their front-line employees need to pursue performance improvements with competence, creativity, and commitment?

Most organizations seem to be managed brilliantly
for preventing people from performing at high levels.
GEOFF COLVIN, Senior Editor, *Fortune*[1]

I have yet to see a quota that includes any trace
of a system by which to help anyone to do a better job.
W. EDWARDS DEMING, the Father of Total Quality Management[2]

With a CompStat meeting two days away, the zone commander and his three key deputies sat down to prepare: What questions would they be asked? And, what answers should they give?

They nailed the questions—every one of them. Two days later when they appeared before the top brass, they were not asked a single question that they had not anticipated.

The structured ritual of the PerformanceStat meeting—questions that require considered answers—*can* be very valuable. Knowing that he would be publicly quizzed about what problems he faced and what he was doing (or planning to do) about them, this zone commander was compelled to prepare. And in preparing for these questions, the commander and his key deputies were simultaneously planning their strategy and tactics. They couldn't intelligently respond to the questions that they would be asked unless they could, first, anticipate them, and, second, develop an effective response to each.

Yet, their preparation lacked something, actually two somethings: data and analysis. They did no analysis of any data—unless you count as data the questions that had been asked in previous CompStat sessions, or regard as analysis the ability of professionals to anticipate their superiors' concerns. During the preparation, no one examined any of the zone's data on crime. No one analyzed whether any new patterns of crime had recently emerged.

They knew their gross totals. But they did not seek to identify any patterns or trends lurking within those totals. Were specific crimes up or down? Were the locations of crimes shifting within the zone? Did the data suggest a need to shift their resources—either geographically or temporally? No one tried to figure out what they might learn from previous successes and failures that they might apply in the next weeks or months. No one personally queried the data (or asked someone else to do so). There were no data to query.

Like many of the meetings that subunits hold just before they appear at a PerformanceStat session, this was strictly DebatePreparationStat.

The Need for Additional Human Competences

The zone commander and his three deputies are cops—effective cops. In addition, they had proven themselves to be effective managers of cops. That's how they rose through the ranks.

They were not, however, analysts. They never trained to be analysts. Maybe, many years ago, one or two of them had taken a statistics course. But neither as street cops nor as managers of street cops did they ever need to calculate a mean let alone a variance—or even eyeball any data (even data in the form of dots on a map). Their formal job descriptions did not require the use of data. Neither did the implicit requirements.

Indeed, the formal requirements for many professional jobs—including many public-sector managerial jobs—do not even include basic numeracy. Sure, everyone must be able, when tested, to add, subtract, multiply, and divide. Every professional can perform such grade-school wizardry: But how often do they use these skills? How often do they ask themselves: "Is this number big (or small)?" "If it is big (or small), what can I learn from it?" How often do they use long division to produce an enlightening ratio? How often do they use arithmetic to help them identify and understand a performance deficit?[3]

This zone commander had no staff analyst: hardly unusual. The department's analytical competence exists solely at headquarters. If the zone commander had a question that required a little analysis to answer, he would have needed to ask for help. Yet, without an analytical mindset, a commander might not know how to frame a useful question.

To improve performance, any organization needs the capacity to collect data about its performance, *plus* the ability to analyze such data. It needs people who can examine the current level of performance, disaggregate data, detect trends, expose patterns, identify performance deficits, and uncover the positive deviants. It needs people who can test potential strategies for eliminating or mitigating a performance deficit—plus people to implement these strategies. And it needs people who can learn from the managerial and front-line behaviors that are contributing to its successes (as well as its failures)—plus people who can exploit operationally this knowledge. (For a discussion of why some public officials lack some of these competences, see appendix D, "Causal Contributors to the Missing Competences.")

One of these necessary competences is analytical thinking. There are many more.[4]

From Bureaucratic Conformance to Purposive Performance

An effective PerformanceStat leadership strategy inherently involves a decentralization of responsibility and discretion. Sometimes, headquarters can identify key performance deficits. Sometimes, headquarters can develop an effective strategy for eliminating or mitigating such deficits. But even when headquarters can define the performance deficit and develop an effective strategy, it still needs subunit leaders who can implement that strategy with competence, creativity, and commitment.

The traditional bureaucratic system that focuses on procedures and rules doesn't produce results. It produces compliance. If the rules are specific enough and consequences for violating them are significant enough, people will comply. Compliance requires little creativity. Yet those who seek to produce results often discover that they must violate one or more rules. As Marc Zegans, a consultant, observed: "Rule-obsessed organizations turn the timid into cowards and the bold into outlaws."[5]

Improving performance requires public employees to be bold. Timid cowards will not produce improved results. Obediently following the bureaucratic rules requires one set of competences. Producing results requires an entirely different set. Indeed, to move from bureaucratic conformance to purposive performance, both organizations and individuals need to shed many of their rule-complying habits and develop some new perspectives, mindsets, and skills. The organization, its employees, and its collaborators need to think differently about their responsibilities. They need a broader and deeper set of skills. They need the competence to pursue purposes with creativity and (despite mistakes and criticism) with commitment.

Such competences need to be distributed throughout the organization. If a leadership team delegates to subunit managers responsibility for achieving specific performance targets and discretion for how to achieve them, it needs to ensure that these units possess the requisite human and organizational competences.[6]

When launching a PerformanceStat initiative, the leadership team needs to ensure that the subunits do not assume that all responsibility—for analysis, for strategy, and for leadership—resides in headquarters. They need to prevent subunits from concluding that headquarters is imposing on them high expectations for results without providing them with the operational capacity they need to meet these new and higher expectations. Yet, few public-sector efforts to improve performance include an explicit, conscious attempt to improve the ability of subunits, their managers, and their employees to produce the targeted results.

One counter example is Maryland's effort to get every law enforcement agency in the state to create its own CompStat. To help make this happen, the Governor's Office of Crime Control and Prevention offers a variety of resources including technical assistance, up-to-date crime maps created by Washington College, and training conducted by the University of Maryland.[7]

Discretion and Leadership Competence

If the members of an organization's leadership team realize that different subunits face different circumstances and have different performance deficits, and if they recognize that most people will work harder to prove themselves right than to prove their boss right, they may decide not to impose a single method on all subunits. Rather, they may decide to give each subunit the discretion to create its own approach for achieving its targets. But the leadership team cannot delegate this discretion unless:

1. The organization has solved the corruption problem. Otherwise the subunit managers will simply use the discretion to advantage themselves and their friends.
2. The subunits have the leadership capacity to exercise this discretion in an intelligent, analytical, and motivational way. Otherwise, the discretion will produce, at best, well-meaning mistakes.

To delegate discretion, emphasized Dean Esserman, police commissioners and chiefs need to develop leadership capacity in their precincts, zones, or districts:

We [in policing] talk a lot about decentralization, and a lot of it is just talk. People say that we need to give more power to everybody, that we need to flatten the organizations, and we do need to do those things. But to do it, we need to find leaders. Officers look for leadership, and the chief can't do it alone.

Moreover, Esserman argued, "you have to redesign the roles of the real leaders [the lieutenants and the sergeants] if you want to be a good leader yourself."[8]

Esserman's insights apply not just to police departments. They apply to any public agency. To delegate discretion, any organization needs to develop leadership at all levels.

Focus on Professional Competences

In most organizations, most people get promoted up the hierarchy because of their professional accomplishments—not necessarily for their analytical abilities, managerial skills, or leadership talents. The best child-welfare worker is promoted to child-welfare supervisor. The best IT programmer is promoted to IT supervisor.

Accomplished professionals, given the many demands for their skills, have little time or reason to take on managerial assignments. Occasionally, they may be called upon to chair a committee or head a task force. But they see these assignments as diversions from their core, professional responsibilities. They give little thought to the different competences that (future) managerial responsibilities might demand. Only rarely are they given help or guidance.

If they do one of these small "m" tasks well, however, they might be asked to do another. This could be a blessing—or a curse. It might take them away from responsibilities they find more personally enjoyable and professionally rewarding. With their ego ideal grounded in their profession, a brief management gig can be annoying. It will require interactions with outsiders, some of whom could be best described as "characters"—others as clueless or incompetent.

Since 1977, Robert Samuelson has written a column on economic affairs for *The Washington Post*. Yet this award-winning journalist has made it quite clear that he has absolutely no desire to manage anything. He once wrote, it "baffles me why people want to be managers." Managers, observed Samuelson, are "supposed to get results—to maximize profits, improve test scores, or whatever. Everyone must 'perform' these days and be 'accountable' (which means being fired, demoted or chewed out if the desired results aren't forthcoming)." All that managers get, he wrote, is "resentment from below; pressure from above; loud criticism of failures; silence over successes."[9]

Eventually, however, the fire department's best firefighter gets promoted to fire chief. Then what? What does he or she do now?[10] How long does it take this individual—whom everyone knows is *the best* firefighter—to understand that he or she is no longer supposed to fight fires? Except perhaps in a small-town department with only a dozen employees, the new fire chief's new job is to make sure that everyone else in the department does an excellent job at fire fighting. If this fire chief is doing the job right, he or she should never even have to show up at a fire (except to provide authoritative quotes for journalists on deadline). If the fire chief is doing the job right, the department's management team—from deputy fire chief to company commanders—will have developed the operational capacity to do their tasks.

The fire department could have planned ahead. The previous fire chief (or perhaps the mayor, or city manager, or a more-previous chief) could have recognized the leadership potential of this future fire chief. Thus, thinking about the future, someone could have sent the budding talent off to the National Fire Academy in Emmitsburg, Maryland for a six-day course in "Management Strategies for Success," or a ten-day course in "Effective Leadership Skills for Fire and EMS Organizations."

Unfortunately, unlike the private sector, government is often reluctant to invest in the development of even its most potentially valuable talent. What elected official wants to be criticized by a political opponent or crusading journalist for sending a public employee off for a week-long vacation in Emmitsburg? (Ever "vacationed" in Emmitsburg?) In the United States, the major exceptions are the federal government's uniformed services: the military services, Park Service, Forest Service, Public Health Service.[11]

Public officials have a variety of options for developing their management skills. The U.S. government has the Federal Executive Institute,[12] and devotes significant resources to the education of those who seek to join the Senior Executive Service. Some governments do send up-and-coming and senior managers to executive-education programs at various universities.[13] Some agencies conduct in-house training.

Often, however, such training focuses on how to comply with new routines imposed from above. In the United States, when the national government changes the requirements for one of its welfare programs, front-line workers in state and local social-service agencies need to take a day or two to be trained in the new system. When a state government changes the requirements for how law enforcement should conduct a traffic stop, local officers need training. Such training is not, however, designed to improve individual leadership skills or collective organizational competences. Its sole purpose is to ensure that everyone will comply with the new rules.

Accountability Cannot Coerce Competence

Samuelson captures the primary approach to improving performance in government: accountability in the form of "loud criticisms of failures." If we just hold people accountable for their failures, we are bound to motivate them to improve.

In the British Royal Navy, such motivational accountability involved more than criticisms of failures. In 1756, when Admiral John Byng failed to prevent the French from capturing Port Mahon, he was court martialed and executed by firing squad. In *Candide*, Voltaire lampooned the Admiralty's approach to accountability and motivation: "In this country, it is wise to kill an admiral from time to time to encourage the others."[14]

Today, such motivational accountability is more civilized. Still, it is based on the same assumption: Government does not need to develop its employees' analytical, managerial, or leadership competences. All it takes is a little accountability. With this pressure, as Samuelson notes, managers are "supposed to get results"—for example, "to improve test scores."

Richard Elmore of Harvard's Graduate School of Education has been skeptical that such accountability pressure will—all by its magical self—improve test scores. He noted the common belief that "school performance will increase to the degree that schools and school systems 'implement' accountability policy"—that "delivering clear information to schools and their communities about their performance will have a galvanizing effect on the people who work in them, and will cause them to do something they would not otherwise have done to improve teaching and student performance."[15] How, Elmore wondered, is this supposed to happen?

Elmore offered this *Gedankenexperiment:*

> Imagine schools . . . in which teachers have systematically squirreled away in their classroom closets all their best and most powerful instructional ideas and practices, saving them for the day when the accountability system smacks them on the head. Then, magically, the good ideas come out of the closet, and school performance, just as magically, increases.

In reality, Elmore concluded, "people in schools are working pretty reliably at the limit of their existing knowledge and skill."[16]

Elmore's implication is obvious: To improve the learning that happens in our schools, we need to improve the teaching competence of the staff. Indeed, for any public agency, Elmore's implication is equally obvious: To produce better results, we need to improve the competence of the people charged with producing those results.

Mark Moore made a similar argument: "If managers have an attractive purpose broadly supported by the political environment but lack the operational capacity to achieve it, the strategic vision [behind that purpose] must fail."[17] Yet, this critical "operational capacity"—the actual ability to achieve important public purposes—is often ignored. W. Edwards Deming was the father of total quality management; after World War II, he taught the Japanese how to be Japanese. Yet, Deming observed, "I have yet to see a quota that includes any trace of a system by which to help anyone to do a better job."[18]

And Deming was talking not about government but about business.

Governmental jurisdictions that seek to produce results cannot simply use accountability to coerce competence. If they want better performance, they need to develop the capacity to produce it.

The Audit Explosion

"The politics of accountability," argued Elmore, "tend to lead to an underinvestment in knowledge and skill, and an overinvestment in testing and regulatory control."[19] Michael Power has called this the "audit explosion."[20]

"Audit has assumed the status of an all purpose solution to problems of administrative control," observed Power. Yet, this "explosion of audits," he continued, is neither free nor cheap. And the cost isn't merely the direct, financial cost of conducting these audits. It also includes the need of the "auditee"[21] "to invest in mechanisms of compliance" and to "engage in elaborate strategies to make themselves auditable." For example, "the construction of auditable environments has necessitated record-keeping demands which only serve the audit process"[22] and "generates elaborate and wasteful games of compliance."[23] Still, "the control lobby," as Alasdair Roberts of Suffolk University labeled it, has a vested interest in maintaining (indeed, intensifying) the existing systems of control.[24]

Despite what the auditors would have us believe, their audits are not neutral. Auditors do not merely observe and report what has happened. Rather, Power wrote, "audits do as much to construct definitions of quality and performance as to monitor it." After all, "verificatory activity always requires that there is something verifiable."[25] Consequently, whenever the auditors decide they want to verify something, the auditees have to create a system to verify it. Thus, *the auditors have the power to decide what "performance" is for an organization.* If the auditors decide that they want to measure something, the organization will need to create a system to collect the requisite data. And once that data system is in place, the auditees need to do their work so as to produce data that satisfy the auditors' definition of good performance. Thus, in deciding what they will audit, the auditors directly influence how the auditees behave—becoming "an explicit change agent, rather than a pure verifier." These auditors, wrote Power, "overstep their purely auditing jurisdiction to become *de facto* policymakers."[26]

Thus, Power concluded that the cost of the audit explosion goes deep: It "interferes with and distracts the audited organization and its service capability in catastrophic ways."[27] Indeed, he wrote, "power has shifted from social workers, doctors, and other public sector workers towards auditors and quality insurance inspectors because the latter increasingly control the terms of public discourse."[28] The rules still win. They are just a different species of rules.

Like Elmore, Power argued that we should "devote more resources to creating quality rather than just to policing it."[29] A similar view comes from Andrew Gray of the University of Nottingham, Jane Broadbent of Roehampton University, and Jean Hartley of Open University: "This intensifying emphasis on improving performance has brought a perverse effect: a fixation with checking rather than doing."[30]

In the United Kingdom, Hartley and John Benington, also of Open University, observed, "central government has invested much more heavily in audit and inspection than in learning and knowledge sharing." Hartley and Benington have focused on the development of organizational competence through the transfer of knowledge among local governments. Yet, they wrote, the U.K. central government's "emphasis in audit and inspection has primarily been on compliance to a national standard, rather than local learning, knowledge-sharing and innovation." Moreover, they continued, this approach "implies that what constitutes 'best practice' is already known."[31]

The Need to *Help* the Managers Manage

Donald Kettl of the University of Maryland has called the "New Public Management" a "global revolution in public management." When it emerged first in New Zealand in the 1980s, it was captured by the phrase: "Make the managers manage." There was, however, a second approach to the new public management: "Let the managers manage." The first approach was based on the assumption that, because government agencies are monopolies, their managers had "little incentive to manage better." Thus, only if public managers are assigned very explicit, very visible, and very auditable "goals and performance standards," would they employ their existing competences to produce significant improvements. The second approach was based on precisely the opposite assumption: that public managers were so constrained by rules and regulations that they were unable to employ their competences to produce improved results. Thus, only if public managers are given flexibility could they employ their existing competences to produce significant improvements in performance.[32]

Underlying both versions of the New Public Management, however, is one common assumption: Public managers *know* how to improve performance. The question is how to get them to convert this knowledge into action: Do we need to *make* them manage? Or do we simply need to *let* them manage?

But maybe—just maybe—public managers do not really *know* how to improve performance. Maybe, because they have neither been obligated to improve performance nor given the necessary flexibility, they have never developed any competence at leadership. Maybe they have been so preoccupied with following the standard operating procedures that they never had time to worry about producing results. Maybe no one ever asked them what better performance might look like, let alone how to produce it. Maybe neither giving them more flexibility nor requiring them to achieve specific targets will—without some improvement in their leadership abilities—accomplish very much.

Maybe it isn't these competent professionals' fault that they don't know how to exercise performance leadership. Maybe rather than auditing them, we ought to *help* them. Maybe we should "*help* the managers manage." Maybe if we want middle managers and front-line supervisors to assume new responsibilities for producing results, we need to *help* them acquire the necessary competences. Any effort to improve performance needs people and teams with the managerial talent, leadership capabilities, and organizational competences necessary to achieve its purposes.

This need for any organization to develop its people is why the Los Angeles County Department of Mental Health has replaced Jack Maple's second principle ("rapid deployment") with one that is more universally applicable: "Training and technical assistance for managers and supervisors." Moreover, the department has created its own training video, "STATS: Introduction and Overview."[33]

The Four Human Components of Organizational Competence

Unfortunately, to anyone seeking to employ a PerformanceStat leadership strategy, the need to improve competence and commitment is invisible. Visitors can't see it during a meeting. No one talks about it. No slide emphasizes improving managerial competence. The most visible form of competence is the hardware.

Still, the leadership team may need to *help* their managers develop the analytic and leadership skills necessary to produce results. After all, for any organization, the most valuable and most scarce resource is human competence. As James Q. Wilson argued: "Talent is Scarcer than Money."[34]

So what kind of "help" might Elmore, or Moore, or Deming, or Hartley and Benington think that a public agency would need to employ a Performance-Stat leadership strategy? To improve performance, a governmental jurisdiction or public agency needs four kinds of human competences: (1) a results-focused mindset, (2) an analytical-learning bent, (3) broad leadership experience, and (4) purpose-driven persistence.[35]

Organizational Competence 1: A Results-Focused Mindset

John Linder, a management consultant, explained that prior to CompStat, which he helped William Bratton and Jack Maple create, NYPD's "business was to stay out of trouble, not to police the city."[36] Linder spoke of "public agencies that exist to keep from getting yelled at."[37]

Indeed, a new, results-focused mindset may create much cognitive dissonance:

> Sure there exists some evidence that this new results-producing idea (What do they call it? StatSomething?) works in some places. But how did these guys get away with it? If we did the same thing, we'd clearly be in violation of Regulation XOS-4002.

Of course, the new idea might not be in violation of any regulation. Or it might only *appear to be* in violation of some rule. Or it might simply be "known" that any deviant idea inevitably violates some regulation. In a risk-averse world, this conclusion makes sense. Why risk a career-damaging reprimand for a small (and maybe fleeting) improvement in results?

Nobody is against improving performance. Everyone is in favor—in principle. Yet all improvements come with costs. There might be opportunity costs: things that don't get done. There might be personal costs: careers jeopardized. The costs might include stress: the neuron overload from trying to understand how to switch from a quite-precise, easy-to-interpret, rule-driven system to some form of rather-experimental, difficult-to-comprehend, and more ambiguous results-based thinking.

Everyone will admit that the rules were maddeningly simplistic, often frivolous, occasionally contradictory, and usually dysfunctional. Everyone complains about the dumb rules. Still, everyone has devoted years to learning how to play by these rules. Now, they must learn how to cope with a different species of rules—ones that are evolving in ways that are not yet clear. They worry that they won't be able to figure out how to understand and play by the new rules.

To implement a PerformanceStat strategy, the leadership team needs to develop a results-focused mindset throughout the organization. Acquiring this new mindset is particularly essential for the layers of middle management, where the rules are most insistently saluted and careers are made by internalizing psychologically and obeying faithfully the rule-based culture.

In such an environment, any effort to shift from an allegiance to the rules to a focus on results will create dissonance.

Organizational Competence 2: An Analytical-Learning Bent

Unfortunately, few large organizations (public, private, or nonprofit) are managed by people with the analytical, evidence-based "mind-set" that Stanford's Jeffrey Pfeffer and Robert Sutton value.[38] Few have created the "culture of evidence-based decision making and research participation" that Denise Rousseau prizes.[39]

Thus a leadership team may find it difficult to infuse analytical learning into the everyday behavior of any public agency. People may accept—intellectually if not psychologically—that producing results is more important than adhering to the rules. They may, however, simply lack the ability to examine and draw lessons from relevant data (or even to determine what data might be relevant).

Baltimore did have one approach for improving the analytical capacity of its bureaus and departments. It promoted several CitiStat analysts into line-management jobs. In Washington, D.C., central analytical staff often made similar moves from CapStat to line agencies. Once the mayor's leadership team concluded that a senior analyst was ready for additional and broader responsibilities, they moved him or her to a line-management job, thus adding some analytical capacity—and a results focus—to yet another agency. This kind of leadership thinking and behavior is unusual. Most government agencies—even some that claim to have created their own version of PerformanceStat—possess little analytic capacity at the operational level.[40]

To build this capacity, the U.S. Federal Emergency Management Agency created the FEMAStat Fellowship, which brings in civil servants (general service grades 9 through 14) for six-month rotations in the FEMAStat office. These fellows, said the recruitment flier, "take a high-level, but behind-the-scenes role on some of the most important issues facing FEMA." The fellowship is open to all permanent, full-time employees of FEMA and the entire Department of Homeland Security, plus Presidential Management Fellows throughout the U.S. government.

This fellowship provides the FEMAStat office with some extra staff. But it has a longer-term purpose: to help employees acquire the analytical skills and habits of mind that are necessary to ratchet up performance. Then, FEMAStat sends them back to help others develop the capacity to analyze and learn from data. Hardly an innovative idea. Yet a too rare and quite valuable one.

A Leadership Academy for Middle Managers

The 6,000 employees of the New York City Administration for Children's Services (ACS) are responsible for ensuring "the safety and well-being" of the city's 1.8 million children. Each month, ACS receives over 5,000 reports of child abuse or neglect, conducts roughly 5,000 consolidated investigations, and finds "credible evidence" of abuse or neglect in approximately 40 percent of these cases. That's 2,000 credible findings each month, or 24,000 in a year. Each month, ACS places over 400 children in foster care, and its foster-care caseload is over 13,000.[41] No wonder that being the public executive responsible for child protective services has been called one of the "impossible jobs in public management."[42]

In July 2004, John Mattingly left the Annie E. Casey Foundation, where he was director of Human Service Reforms, to become the ACS commissioner.[43] Within two years, he had weekly ChildStat meetings up and running. As with any PerformanceStat, the meeting looked at the macro data and their trends. But each ChildStat session also scrutinized two specific cases from one of ACS's 20 local zones; the objective was to diagnose what happened, whether the staff had followed the requisite child-welfare procedures, but also whether the child's problem was taken seriously. ("We've treated this girl as 'a case,'" objected Mattingly during one meeting. If this child were our niece, he continued, we would have behaved very differently.)[44] Mattingly focused on what could be learned from these cases and employed citywide.

Mattingly's executive team quickly figured out how to learn from the ChildStat sessions—both what was happening at the line-worker level and what needed to change. But many of ACS's deputy directors in the city's five boroughs did not figure this out, and neither did most of the child protective managers in the zones. Most of these middle managers began their careers as social workers. As they demonstrated professional competence, they were promoted to be supervisors and then managers. But an excellent child protection specialist does not automatically become an excellent child protection manager, let alone an excellent deputy director.

In conversations with the Annie E. Casey Foundation, Mattingly evolved an idea for a Leadership Academy for Child Safety (which the foundation funded).

ACS commissioned the Research Center for Leadership Action at New York University's Wagner Graduate School of Public Service to design and implement the curriculum, which covered a wide range of topics: systems thinking, strategic thinking, teams, organizational change, and the use of data. The program also emphasized the responsibility of ACS staff both to compliance (with all legal requirements) and to quality (with a commitment to the family).

Heather Weston, who led the project for the Wagner School, reported that the most significant session involved Mattingly and his executive team sitting in the middle of a room arranged in the round and explaining why they created Child-Stat. Then, the middle managers entered the discussion, raising multiple issues: their distrust of the data (because of errors in data entry and the IT system); how they would improve the ChildStat meetings; and, most importantly, how they could adapt the ChildStat approach to improve child-welfare practices in their own offices.[45]

The Academy's first class of 30 managers graduated in December 2007. Since then the Leadership Academy has developed the leadership capacity of 300 of ACS's middle managers.

Organizational Competence 3: A Diversity of Leadership Roles

To Henry Mintzberg of McGill University, a "manager" is not just the CEO of a large corporation; managers include "vice presidents, bishops, foremen, hockey coaches, and prime ministers." Indeed, to Mintzberg, a manager is a "person in charge of an organization or one of its subunits."[46] Using this definition, any public agency has a large number of managers—from the chief executive to front-line supervisors (government's foremen).

Moreover, Mintzberg concluded that the job of all of these managers involves 10 roles. All managers have three interpersonal roles: figurehead, leader, and liaison. They have three informational roles: monitor, disseminator, and spokesperson. And they have four decisional roles: entrepreneur, disturbance handler, resource allocator, and negotiator.

In developing his 10 "roles," Mintzberg was critiquing what he called "the classical view" of what managers do[47] as set down in 1916 by the French industrialist Henri Fayol: "To manage is to forecast and plan, to organize, to command, to co-ordinate, and to control."[48] Then in 1937, Luther Gulick, president of the Institute of Public Administration, asked: "What is the work of the chief executive? What does he do?" Expanding on Fayol, Gulick answered with POSDCORB, which stood for seven activities: Planning, Organizing, Staffing,

Directing, Coordinating, Reporting, and Budgeting.[49] Mintzberg, however, was more interested in the "activities" of managers than in their "roles," which he argued, "tell us little about what managers actually do."[50]

A baseball team needs front-office executives and field managers with both the interpersonal skills necessary to supervise much-higher-paid prima donnas and the analytical ability to extract from their abundance of data some real and significant implications for their team's strategy. Similarly, in results-focused government, public managers need a large diversity of competences. They need sophisticated interpersonal and communications skills and the ability to exercise them both internally and externally. They also need basic analytical skills—a fluency and comfort with numbers and the ability to extract information from data. Still, public managers who possess both interpersonal and analytical skills are rare.

Creating the Necessary Human Competences

Consequently, when a governmental leadership team decides to create its own PerformanceStat, it discovers that most of its middle managers are good at solving the traditional problems of their profession. They are good at following established procedures and getting others to do so too. Give them a class to teach or a fire to put out—they know what to do.

Yet, they may lack both a results-focused mindset and the necessary analytical, managerial, and leadership skills. They have not acquired Malcolm Sparrow's "habits of mind" and "patterns of thought."[51] They have not been expected to learn by analyzing data let alone to exercise performance leadership. They have little training in either.

Yes, they have been taught arithmetic. Yes, they can do arithmetic. Yet, few are numerate. They don't think using numbers. They don't analyze their operational problems using numbers. They don't explain what they are doing using numbers. Even if they do not have a chronic case of math anxiety, they may still lack the "habit of mind" to frequently compare two numbers using long division.

The absence of these competences creates a challenge for those seeking to employ a PerformanceStat strategy: How do they identify, within their (rather bureaucratic) organization, people who have the analytical bent, the managerial skills, and the leadership talent necessary to make a results-focused strategy work? How do they foster these human competences throughout their organization?

Each subunit that has been given responsibility and discretion for producing results could be permitted to hire its own analyst. But unless the unit's analyst is able to explain the operational implications of the data in a nontechnical and convincing way, and unless the management team is able to understand, appreciate, and accept both the analysis and its implications, and unless the management team is also willing and able to act strategically on these implications, a subunit analyst will be of little use.

Developing Leadership Competences

How does a public agency develop its future managers' ability to undertake Mintzberg's 10 roles—for example, to negotiate, handle disturbances, and to be an effective figurehead? It isn't obvious. Of course, the agency could simply not bother to develop an individual's managerial talents. Rather than "make," it could "buy." Buying might be fine if all that the agency needed was a resource allocator or a liaison. But if an agency needs managers who can handle many of Mintzberg's roles—perhaps all 10—how easy will it be to find and buy such talent?[52]

Formal training isn't the only way for an individual to develop competence for management or leadership. In any organization but the smallest, there are opportunities to watch others in action and learn from them. Indeed, the members of a leadership team can formally encourage mentoring.[53] They can identify people who appear to posses the potential to become effective leaders. They can pair these neophytes with senior, experienced professionals who make a personal commitment to help develop the next generation of managers and leaders.

Serving as an apprentice has an established pedigree for learning the tacit knowledge of artisans. Paul Revere was an apprentice silversmith. Benjamin Franklin was an apprentice printer. Both Leonardo da Vinci and Sandro Botticelli served as apprentices to Verrocchio (Andrea di Cione). Today, most trades have formal apprenticeship programs through which neophytes learn their skills from a master.

Such mentoring need not be formal. But it does require conscious thought: Who in the organization appears to have leadership potential? What do they need to learn? Who can best help them learn it? Developing leadership talent also requires persistence. A mentoring initiative that withers away after 12 months sends a bad message: We aren't really serious.

Indeed, formal training may not be the most effective way to develop talent for all 10 roles. After all, a leader's knowledge is primarily tacit. As Mintzberg wrote: "Leadership, like swimming, cannot be learned by reading about it." To learn to swim, he observed, "one must get into the water, splash around, and practice various techniques with advice from someone who knows what skills swimming requires." Then, "with sufficient feedback," the student will learn to swim.[54]

"The same holds true for many management skills," continued Mintzberg, who focused on "leadership skills, [which,] perhaps more than any others, require participative training." Concluded Mintzberg, "learning is most effective when the student actually performs the skill in as realistic a situation as possible and then analyzes his performance explicitly." Little wonder that Mintzberg is an advocate of "on-the-job learning."[55]

Unfortunately, most public agencies rarely create even the basics for developing their talent. They don't bother to identify their up-and-comers, let alone match them with creative mentors. They rarely send their up-and-comers off for executive education. They do little planning about managerial succession. They don't even think about running simple, low-cost, high-potential-payoff experiments such as giving new people new challenges that need to be accomplished anyway and learning who is developing what competences. An agency or jurisdiction that is seeking to improve performance needs to run (using targets plus discretion) a lot of these experiments.

The members of a leadership team that has chosen to create its own PerformanceStat could simply identify people who they guessed had the potential to take on more responsibilities, give them some new, modestly more challenging assignments, and then *help* them—not just *let* them or *make* them, but actually *help* them—succeed. The leadership team could quickly learn a lot about who has potential and what these up-and-comers need to learn next.

Fostering the Performance Commitment

Although PerformanceStat is designed to produce results, real results are never produced during a PerformanceStat meeting. The executives and managers in the room are rarely the people who actually produce the results. To have a significant impact, a PerformanceStat strategy has to be more than a series of discussions among the organization's leadership team and its subunit managers. Somehow the data analyzed, strategies developed, and commitments made have to affect the daily, operational behavior of front-line supervisors and front-line employees.

Yet, these civil servants are not likely to become quickly and enthusiastically committed to the new PerformanceStat's focus on results. They are much more likely to ignore, oppose, or even sabotage the effort. In Baltimore, Matthew Gallagher reported:

> CitiStat encountered persistent resistance from many of City government's departments and long-entrenched department heads, managers, and even front-line employees. Some of the most popular refrains ran along the following lines:

—If we were not so busy collecting data, we could be out doing our jobs.
—We are already doing that.
—We tried that before and it did not work.[56]

Experienced bureaucrats have endured a succession of avant-garde initiatives that were soon abandoned. Why should they think this one is different? At a minimum, they can engage in passive resistance, ignoring or delaying various tasks until they discover that the follow-up is serious. Or they can employ proven tactics of bureaucratic warfare: "feigned acquiescence"[57] or "malicious compliance."[58] To many employees, PerformanceStat means change—uncertainty, psychological discomfort, and more or different work.[59] Resistance is inevitable.

Yet, not only do public agencies devote little effort to developing their operational capacity; they also devote little effort to building a performance commitment throughout the organization. Too often, they assume that the subunit managers who participate in the PerformanceStat meetings will (somehow) pick up the competences and commitment necessary to improve their subunit's performance. They assume that the accountability and motivational impact of the meetings will (somehow) filter down the hierarchy to front-line employees.

As with other aspects of PerformanceStat, the police have an advantage. Policing's roll call is found in few other organizations. These sessions at the beginning of every shift give the leadership team an opportunity to deliver an organization-wide message to every front-line worker. To Maple, citywide CompStat meetings were not the only time that NYPD's crime-fighting performance and strategies were discussed. Rather, he wrote, these issues "must become the subject of regular crime meetings at four different levels—between the executive corps and field commanders; between field commanders and their lieutenants; between lieutenants and their sergeants; and, most significantly, between sergeants and their officers at roll call."[60]

When John Timoney became police commissioner in Philadelphia, he introduced a new policy concerning when and how a police officer was to use "physical force, especially deadly physical force." Then, he "went to numerous roll calls to explain the policy and accept any questions." And when he created a policy eliminating the use of blackjacks and replacing them with pepper spray, he "made it a point once more to go to roll calls to explain the rationale."[61]

Every public agency and government jurisdiction has a hierarchy that the leadership team can use to distribute messages to the front line. Often, however, such messages are distributed through frequent updates to the official procedures manual—updates that every employee dutifully stuffs in the front of his or her bulging procedures binder never to be read (or even filed at the proper tab). Today the procedures manual is online, making it even easier to ignore.

If subunit directors lack an analytical aptitude, they won't be able to use their own data to develop their own performance strategies. If they have not acquired any leadership skills, they won't be able to implement their own strategies. And if they aren't personally committed to producing results, they won't bother anyway. If managers throughout an organization—from subunit directors to frontline supervisors—are not given training, are not supported by wise mentors, and are not given the discretion to experiment with their own ideas, they'll never develop the leadership competences and personal commitment necessary for producing results.

Unfreezing and Then Refreezing

Some middle managers may respond quickly to this shift in the organization's aerovane and attempt to improve their analytical abilities, to enhance their leadership skills, and to sharpen their focus on results. Still, they will remain sensitive to future changes in both the direction and the intensity of the organization's currents. If the intensity lessens or the direction shifts—no matter how slightly—they will detect it and readjust their behavior.

Over half a century ago, the social psychologist Kurt Lewin observed that improving an organization's performance is difficult:

> A change toward a higher level of group performance is frequently short lived; after a 'shot in the arm,' group life soon returns to its previous level. This indicates that it does not suffice to define the objective of a planned change in group performance as the reaching of a different level. Permanency of the new level, or permanency for a desired period, should be included in the objective.

Thus, Lewin advocated a three-step process for improving performance: (1) "unfreeze" old patterns of behavior; (2) "move" the organization to new behaviors that produce improved performance, and (3) "freeze" the organization at this new level.[62]

To create a results-focused organization, the leadership team may need to first destroy the existing, rule-driven, compliance-obsessed behaviors. Then, after moving to new, analytic-based, learning-engaged, results-focused behaviors, they will need to refreeze the organization. This new organization is not, however, frozen into a single, one best way for producing results. Instead, this "freeze" must be a subtle and sophisticated commitment to a flexible strategy for continuously learning how to better achieve public purposes.

Organizational Competence 4: Purpose-Driven Persistence

This refreezing requires persistence. Indeed, any effective PerformanceStat requires persistence—purpose-driven persistence. The organization's leadership needs to demonstrate its commitment to achieving its purposes, to improving its performance, and to producing results.

If members of the leadership team are sporadic in their participation in their PerformanceStat meetings, everyone will notice. If these key leaders are unprepared to ask probing questions, everyone will notice. If the schedule of the meetings is erratic, everyone will notice. If the meetings are frequently postponed or canceled, everyone will notice. If there is no follow-up, everyone will notice. Moreover, everyone will correctly interpret such lapses as a lack commitment.

If the leadership team is not persistent about its focus on results, the residents can wait out the tourists. The guardians of the rules may have gone into hibernation; but they will be alert for any thaw—for the moment at which the attention of the leadership team is diverted by a crisis, by an election campaign, by anything else that diminishes the commitment to results.

In government, nothing requires more persistence than a focus on results. Follow-up and feedback create this focus. The feedback on performance—the comparison of a subunit's recent results with its trends, with its targets, and with other units—is a not-so-subtle reminder that the results are important. Through persistent follow-up and feedback, an organization's leadership team can demonstrate its commitment to purpose, performance, and results.

13

Learning to Make the Necessary Adaptations

How does an agency or jurisdiction think through the modifications that it needs to make to the specific operational components of different PerformanceStats to ensure that its own, unique adaptation of this leadership strategy fits its organization and environment and thus achieves its specific purposes?

Creativity results from using old ideas in new ways, places, or combinations.
ROBERT SUTTON, Stanford University[1]

An individual understands a concept, skill, theory, or domain of knowledge to the extent that he or she can apply it appropriately in a new situation.
HOWARD GARDNER, Harvard University[2]

"Slumerville." That's what people called Massachusetts's densest city, known for its rundown housing, abandoned industrial buildings, and political corruption.[3] Not anymore. Today, Somerville is hot, funky—the place where "hipsters," the young adults whom Richard Florida of the University of Toronto labeled the "creative class"[4]—want to live.[5]

The change began when metropolitan Boston's transit system was extended to Somerville's Davis Square. It got a big boost when Joseph Curtatone became mayor.

In 2003, when Curtatone first ran for mayor, he pledged to bring CitiStat to the city. As an alderman, Curtatone chaired the finance committee and knew how much the city spent for each line item but had been unable to learn what the city was getting for these expenditures. "It used to drive me up the wall," he recalled. "We didn't know how we were performing." The city's managers, he continued, "really couldn't justify" their spending.[6]

TABLE 13-1. Somerville Is Not Baltimore, Some Comparative Data, 2000

City	Square miles	Population	Population density[a]	Population ages 25 to 44 (percent)
Baltimore	92	650,000	7,000	30
Somerville	4.2	77,000	18,000	40

Source: U.S. Census Bureau. All data rounded to two significant figures.
a. Population density is in residents per square mile.

After his election, Curtatone visited Baltimore. He was particularly impressed when, during a CitiStat session about abandoned cars, Mayor Martin O'Malley asked the staff to overlay the abandoned car map with a map of gang activity. The close visual juxtaposition of the two maps immediately got Curtatone's attention.

Curtatone did more than observe a few CitiStat sessions and listen to the standard briefing. He also went around the city, talking to city employees to learn how it worked. And he tried to benefit from Baltimore's mistakes, paying less attention when told what *to* do than when told, "whatever you do, don't do this."[7]

Still, Somerville is not Baltimore. They are old cities, yet quite different. Somerville is the densest municipality in Massachusetts, and the 18th densest in the United States. In Baltimore and in the United States, the median age is about 35. For Somerville, it is 31; many residents are young adults. (See table 13-1.)

Given these obvious differences (and others), Curtatone could not simply copy Baltimore's CitiStat. To exploit the advantages of Baltimore's leadership strategy, he had to understand *how* O'Malley's approach worked, appreciate its obvious and subtle features, and then *adapt* them to fit his city's characteristics and capabilities, plus his performance purposes. To improve city services in Somerville, Curtatone needed to create his own, unique SomerStat.

SomerStat plus ResiStat

In several obvious ways, Somerville's SomerStat is different from Baltimore's Citi-Stat. For example, Curtatone did not create a special room. SomerStat meetings are held in a small conference room that serves multiple purposes. In the room, there are maybe a dozen people: a couple of SomerStat staff, the finance director, others from the mayor's office, and one or two people from the reporting agency. The room does have a podium, a projector, and a screen. But the portable screen and projector are removed after each session.

Moreover, Curtatone made several explicit choices that were different from O'Malley's. First he made sure that the SomerStat staff had direct access to all of the city's information systems and databases. Then he made, for what is a very small city, a major investment in analytic capacity; the initial SomerStat staff of two gradually grew to five and, eventually, to seven. Third, the day before each meeting, the SomerStat staff sends a draft of their slides to the department head (providing an opportunity to correct any factual errors). Then, by midnight, the staff sends the final materials to the department head, the mayor, and his key aides for budget and personnel.

Still, SomerStat is obviously a variant of PerformanceStat. It looks very familiar. Although Somerville's smaller scale demanded adaptations, SomerStat is built on the strategy's core leadership principles and key operational components: data and analysis, meetings and learning, deficits and targets, feedback and follow-up, persistence and leadership . . . the entire package.

In over a decade as mayor, Curtatone sought to adapt PerformanceStat to the performance challenges he faced. In particular, Curtatone created ResiStat "to bring SomerStat into the community to extend the SomerStat problem-solving discussion to Somerville residents."[8] Curtatone has held semiannual ResiStat meetings in each of the city's seven wards. And ResiStat has its own listserv with over 5,000 subscribers who ask questions about city services—everything from tree removal and replanting to the completion of street-improvement projects.[9]

Again: How much of this is new? Innovative? Mayors who want to be reelected hold community meetings. So Curtatone brings data to his meetings. Big deal.

The locals, however, aren't quite this cynical. The *Somerville Patch*, which calls itself "an on-line community-specific news and information platform," reports that, after "resident concerns" are raised at ResiStat, "SomerStat analysts then research those issues, return to the community with data, and then gather resident input on how to best address the problem."[10] One local realtor (who seeks to promote the city) called ResiStat "Your Wicked Awesome Somerville Resource."[11]

Indeed, ResiStat is part of Curtatone's effort to ensure that SomerStat remains after he leaves office: "We want citizens to have that expectation"—that city government will continue to focus on service delivery.[12]

Somerville is "the best run city in Massachusetts," concluded Thomas Keane, a former member of the Boston city council. It is "outperforming its much bigger and wealthier neighbors," wrote Keane—"almost embarrassingly so." With the combination of SomerStat and 311, Keane observed, Somerville "actually treats its citizens like customers and holds itself accountable to them." This is "amazing stuff," concluded Keane, "an example of just how good—inspiring even—local government can be."[13]

Avoiding Mindless Mimicry

Curtatone could have simply copied O'Malley. After all, both Somerville and Baltimore are cities. They have the same basic responsibilities and tasks. They pick up trash and fill potholes. They put out fires and catch muggers. It isn't that Baltimore is a city, while Somerville is a derivatives regulator or a baseball team. In the galaxy of human organizations, Baltimore and Somerville are very similar.

Moreover, both Curtatone and O'Malley focused on the same purpose: improving the operational effectiveness of city agencies (which in the galaxy of human purposes are very similar).

So why didn't Curtatone just imitate O'Malley? NYPD's CompStat was the model for police. And Baltimore's CitiStat was the model for cities. Both were certified winners—of Harvard's award for "Innovation in American Government." A police department couldn't get in trouble for duplicating the original CompStat. Curtatone couldn't be criticized for replicating the original CitiStat. Why think when you can clone?

Actually, even cloning isn't easy. As Eli Silverman of the John Jay College of Criminal Justice has observed: "Attendance at a Compstat meeting, while a useful introduction, does not provide adequate preparation for introducing and establishing Compstat." Consequently, he argued, efforts to replicate CompStat "are frequently based on a superficial understanding of its proper development, implementation, and many dimensions" with the result that "some Compstats may be viewed as 'Compstat Lite.'" Jack Maple called them "knock-off versions."

In a classic article on "institutional isomorphism," Paul DiMaggio of Princeton and Walter Powell of Stanford described and explained the human habit of organizational imitation:[14] The world is an uncertain place. Thus changing something that has proven successful elsewhere is dangerous; the adaptation might fail. Copying the success is much safer.[15]

For example, how could Curtatone know whether his adaptation of Baltimore's approach would work? But Baltimore's did work (or, at least, appeared to work, which for a mayor faced with uncertainty is almost the same thing). When the choice is between the known and the unknown, why not choose the known? Moreover the arbiters of professional competence (can you get any better than Harvard?) have put Baltimore's version on a pedestal. To be recognized as among the avant-garde of municipal leaders, a mayor could simply copy Baltimore. No thinking required.

Indeed, too many public agencies and government jurisdictions have engaged in such mindless mimicry. Observe a version of CompStat or CitiStat or

AnythingStat. Listen to a brief briefing about its most explicit (and thus explicable) features. Ask a few questions particularly about the (budgetary) cost. Go home. Copy faithfully. If the CitiStat you visited had two screens, you need two screens. If the CompStat you attended displayed maps with dots on these screens, you need maps with dots. If the SomethingStat you visited had a podium, you need a podium.

But *how* do screens, maps, and podiums contribute to better results? What are the causal connections between PerformanceStat's principles and components and the results it is designed to produce? How do the leadership behaviors of PerformanceStat contribute to better results? Indeed, what are these results? What is the underlying purpose? What are the performance deficits that need to be fixed next?

These questions may never get asked. For, observed DiMaggio and Powell, organizations face "an inexorable push towards homogenization." Because organizations seek to establish their legitimacy, they continued, "the concept of institutional isomorphism is a useful tool for understanding the politics and ceremony that pervade much modern organizational life."[16]

What happens, however, if the new MimicStat doesn't quickly produce unambiguously better results? The imitators want their MimicStat to produce visible results—and now. Yet, performance improvements never happen quickly. Meanwhile, all of those meetings—to say nothing of the preparation for those meetings—consume time: "Maybe we don't need to meet biweekly like Baltimore." "Maybe we only need to meet monthly." "Oops. A crisis. Have to cancel tomorrow's session."

Without any clear, established, underlying purpose, MimicStat slowly dissipates.

No Model, No Template, No One Best Way

DiMaggio and Powell suggested three sources of institutional isomorphism. The first is "coercive isomorphism" from "formal and informal pressures exerted on organizations by other organizations upon which they are dependent." The second is "mimetic processes"; the uncertainty about how to solve a (perhaps undefined) problem prompts organizations to mimic others. The third is "normative pressures" driven by professional standards.

For PerformanceStat, I have observed no example of coercive isomorphism, except when a jurisdiction or agency decides to create its own PerformanceStat and then requires its own subunits to do the same.[17] And none of the multitude of professional organizations in the United States for either jurisdictions or policy agencies have sought to encourage (let alone pressure) their members to adopt this strategy.[18] PerformanceStat has spread almost exclusively through mimetic processes, in which one organization tries to mimic—and perhaps to also learn from—another.

Unfortunately, for a leadership strategy, mimicry is difficult. Each strategy is designed to achieve a specific purpose in specific circumstances. Thus any copying will be inherently superficial. To take advantage of the PerformanceStat potential, an organization's leadership team must develop a subtle appreciation of the strategy's core leadership principles and key operational components so that it can adapt them to its own purposes, resources, and circumstances. To create their own ParformanceStat strategy, the members of the leadership team must think, adapt, learn, think some more, adapt some more. . . .

PerformanceStat is not a model. There is no template. If Frederick Winslow Taylor were still alive, he could not define "the one best way" to create and run a PerformanceStat (though he would certainly try). There is not even a "best practice."[19] Instead, there may be numerous "better practices"[20]—or what Eugene Bardach of the University of California–Berkeley called "smart practices."[21] There is no reason to believe (except that Taylor's ideas have slipped serendipitously into our collective subconscious) that there exists a one best way to create every PerformanceStat.

PerformanceStat doesn't just *permit* adaptation. It *demands* adaptation. An effective CitiStat for Baltimore can't be identical to an effective one for Somerville, let alone identical to an effective one (AmesStat) for Amesbury, Massachusetts, with only 16,500 residents.

Any adaptation starts with the purpose: What are we trying to accomplish? What are our key performance deficits? What targets should who achieve by when? Only after the members of the leadership team have made these core choices can they craft the rest of their strategy. The leadership team can't start with data. They can't start with podiums, projectors, and screens. They have to start with purpose. Then they have to define what their next level of success will look like, how they will measure progress, and how they will motivate people.

If You've Seen One PerformanceStat, You've Seen One PerformanceStat

Both New York's CompStat and Los Angeles's CompStat were created under the leadership of William Bratton. They are not identical. They are similar in all the visual and superficial ways: data and maps, meetings and questions. An observer can't miss the similarities. Still they are different.

NYPD's CompStat today is different from its CompStat of 1994. Today's CompStat in Los Angeles is different from its original. Both have evolved as these agencies mitigated some performance deficits and were confronted with new ones—and as their leadership teams learned what was effective in what circumstances and thus adapted their strategy.

Maryland's StateStat isn't the same as Baltimore's CitiStat, even though StateStat was created when Martin O'Malley moved from being mayor of Baltimore to being governor of Maryland, and when Matthew Gallagher simultaneously moved from being director of CitiStat to become the director of StateStat.

For any leadership strategy to be effective, learning and adaptation are necessary. As Howard Gardner suggested, the test of the learning is whether the adaptation works: "An individual understands a concept, skill, theory, or domain of knowledge to the extent that he or she can apply it appropriately in a new situation."[22]

No PerformanceStat is identical to any other. New York City's different AgencyStats—JobStat, ChildStat, TEAMS, and STARS—are all descendants of CompStat. Still, no two of these offspring are identical. They can't be. Each leadership team designed its adaptation to achieve its own purposes. Each must cope with its own performance deficits. Each must build on its own sources of available data. Each must reflect its own competences and culture.

To create an effective PerformanceStat, a leadership team needs to design each individual component of the strategy and ensure that, collectively, they work in concert. How to do this is never obvious. The macro framework—and its micro components—may be conceptually comprehensible. Unfortunately, as the avant-garde architect Ludwig Mies van der Rohe reminded us, "God is in the details."[23]

The details matter. They matter a lot. How they are crafted, organized, deployed, and coordinated affects performance. No organization can hope to clone another's PerformanceStat. All the leadership team can do is learn from one or several examples. Then, adapt.

Learning by Groping Along

In one way, however, Somerville did follow Baltimore. When Curtatone hired Stephanie Hirsch to be the first director of SomerStat, he wanted her to hold two or three meetings by the end of the month. "Just start," Curtatone told Hirsch. "The content can evolve."[24] Neither Baltimore nor Somerville did a lot of planning. To improve city services, they just started.[25] They employed the managerial philosophy described as "Get it up and running and then fix it."[26]

Curtatone and Hirsh could have created a comprehensive strategic plan. They could have analyzed every department. They could have surveyed the CitiStat literature. They could have created a commission, hired a consultant, engaged citizens in brainstorming. A year later, they would still not have produced the perfect PerformanceStat (if such a thing exists). Humans miss things, misjudge people, overestimate the importance of some factors, underestimate the relevance of others. Mistakes are inevitable.

So Curtatone and Hirsch just started. Given Hirsch's experience working on CompStat at the Boston Police Department, she didn't start from zero; she benefitted from BPD's mistakes, learning, and adaptations. Still mistakes happened. For example, in addition to the SomerStat meetings, Curtatone was also holding biweekly, one-on-one meetings with his department heads. Then, at a SomerStat meeting, a department head revealed an unknown agreement with the mayor. The one-on-one meetings were soon eliminated so that all agreements were made at SomerStat sessions and known to all. Indeed for over a decade, Curtatone and SomerStat have been learning and adapting.

By just starting, those who seek to create their own PerformnceStat will certainly make mistakes. Mistakes facilitate learning. By just starting, people make their mistakes more quickly. The accelerated visibility of these quick mistakes creates opportunities to learn more quickly. Those developing a PerformanceStat don't have to wait months to discover what is working and what isn't. They get feedback quickly and evolve quickly. They learn what fits their organization. They learn what helps to achieve their purposes. Then they adapt their strategy to ensure that it improves performance.

This is "management by groping along."[27] Think of it as "learning by groping along."

Aim, Fire, Learn, Ready

In their best seller, *In Search of Excellence,* Tom Peters and William Waterman argued that successful organizations have "a bias for action," and thus that the old military drill of "ready, aim, fire" is too deliberate. Instead, they concluded, the sequence should be "ready, fire, aim."[28]

But why is "aim" the last step? For any organization—private, public, or non-profit—the initial emphasis should be on the "aim"—on the purpose it is trying to accomplish. How can the organization fire without aiming? Without a target it is trying to hit? Indeed, how can the organization get ready until it has determined what it is getting ready to accomplish?

Unfortunately, getting ready can take a lot of time: You have to worry about this problem. You have to plan for that contingency. And don't forget about this dilemma, . . . complication, . . . threat. . . . Of these many worries, however, which are really important? Which sound significant but turn out to be trivial? It's hard to tell. Before you have established your purpose, it is very hard to tell.

That's why it is so instructive to take aim at your target, fire off an initial shot, and see what happens. This first shot creates an immediate opportunity for learning. It illuminates what is significant and what it trivial. It eliminates the hand-wringing and the don't-forget-about-this discussions. It reveals what performance deficits the organization needs to fix next. Unless the organization is lucky (or omniscient), it won't hit its target with its first shot. Still, from this miss, it can *learn* what adaptations it needs to make and how to better get ready.

In its effort to produce results, government doesn't get just one shot. After it aims and fires, it analyzes the results, learns from this analysis, does better at getting ready, then aims and fires again. It isn't just: Aim and Fire. It's: Aim, Fire, Learn, Ready. [29] Then Aim and Fire again.

And learn more. A public agency has to take multiple shots. It has to keep on shooting. Thus, for a leadership team that is truly seeking to improve performance, a more accurate description of the sequence is:

Aim, Fire, Learn. Ready, Aim, Fire, Learn more. Ready better, Aim, Fire, Learn even more. . . . [30]

Senge's Five Learning Disciplines

In *The Fifth Discipline,* MIT's Peter Senge argued that a "learning organization" is "continually expanding its capacity to create its future." Such an organization, he continued, is constantly practicing the five "disciplines of learning":

1. *Systems thinking* is a discipline for seeing wholes [not just "isolated parts"] . . . for seeing interrelationships rather than things, for seeing patterns of change rather than static "snapshots." . . . to help us see how to change them effectively. [31]
2. *Personal mastery* is the discipline of continually clarifying and deepening our personal vision, of focusing our energies, of developing patience, and of seeing reality objectively. [32]
3. *Mental models* are deeply ingrained assumptions, generalizations, or even pictures or images that influence how we understand the world and how we take action. [33]

4. *Shared vision* is the answer to the question, "What do we want to create?" . . . it provides the focus and energy for learning.[34]
5. *Team learning* is the process of aligning and developing the capacity of a team to create the results its members truly desire.[35]

To Senge, these are not models but "disciplines": "They are more like artistic disciplines than traditional management disciplines." Moreover, he emphasizes, "Practicing a discipline is different from emulating 'a model.'"[36]

For business, on which Senge focuses, mastering these disciplines is hard. For government, it is even harder.

—How can public employees engage in systems thinking if they only see their own little part, never the whole?

—How can public employees devote time to personal mastery when their work is driven by rules and the fear of punishment for minor errors?

—How can public employees think critically about their own mental models while trying to survive on a battlefield of dueling assumptions?

—How can public employees develop a shared vision when different stakeholder groups are each aggressively campaigning to make its own vision dominant?

—How can public employees foster team learning if their colleagues are uninterested in personal learning?

How can the public-sector leadership team ever hope to create a learning organization?[37] After all, learning requires experimentation. Yet, as Senge observed, "business has a freedom to experiment [that is] missing in the public sector."[38]

NYPD as a Learning Organization

Can a PerformanceStat leadership strategy foster a learning organization? Barry Sugarman of the University of Massachusetts examined NYPD's CompStat strategy, looking "closely at key components of the structural reforms and how they work together to yield improved results." He identified six such components: "reframing the mission, redefining management roles, accountability, the information system, the CompStat meetings, and effective top leadership."[39]

Sugarman wrote of the many benefits of "the regular meetings of precinct commanding officers (COs) with the top brass to review their crime fighting plans (using the new data), to improve coordination of specialized police resources, and to assess their results."[40] He emphasized how these meetings contribute to his other components:

The CompStat meeting helps NYPD to become less fragmented. . . . It provides better information sharing across the many barriers of this huge bureaucracy—including outside partner agencies which attend. For middle managers, it provides unprecedented direct access to many senior managers—instead of being restricted to sending them memos through the chain of command that result in long-delayed (cautious) written responses, with no chance to clarify on either side. . . . It is the master classroom for on-the-job training and coaching, supervised in person by the top authority figures; it is also a place for peer learning among middle managers. . . . For senior managers the regular CompStat meeting plus their small follow-up meeting right afterward provides a regular overview of all operations, and problems needing their special attention. It is also a showcase of rising talent. It is their "continuing education" with data from many parts of the agency. It also gives top brass a bully pulpit or megaphone to send edicts across the agency, and a stage to recognize and honor outstanding performers at any rank.[41]

Dennis Smith made a similar observation. CompStat, he wrote, helped to accelerate "the process of learning what does and does not work," to expedite the task of "widely disseminating the lessons," and to create "accountability for learning from experience." For example, to reduce drug-related crime, NYPD "carefully monitored interventions through analysis and CompStat meetings, expanded those that worked and discarded those that didn't."[42]

Sugarman's examination of CompStat focused on "the role of top managers as change leaders in directly supervising middle managers as they both learned their challenging new roles." Indeed, leadership, teaching, *and* learning are core to Sugarman's analysis. He described NYPD's innovation as an "explicit, data-based, process of planning, acting, and learning from experience." The meeting, he observed, "was designed by the same senior executives who then implemented it for several years, teaching participants how they wanted roles to be played."[43]

To Sugarman, CompStat wasn't just operational mechanics. "Equally essential was changing the ways of thinking that accompany and shape action." Specifically, he noted the importance of CompStat's underlying purpose: "NYPD's reform introduced a lot of new pressure for performance, but it was accompanied by a new sense of purpose and pride among the rank and file." For police officers, he wrote, it "opened the possibility of a new pride in their work."[44]

Concluded Sugarman: "NYPD's reform and improved results is a good example of a whole organization learning to create a better way to do its work and accomplish its mission."[45] PerformanceStat has the potential—but only the potential—to help create a learning organization.

Loving or Overcoming "the Competency Trap"

Still, a public agency doesn't need too much learning. Without a PerformanceStat strategy, a police department could figure out how to break up drug gangs effectively, a public works department could figure out how to fill potholes efficiently, and a child-welfare agency could figure out how to investigate allegations of child abuse speedily.

Once an agency learns how to hit its established targets, what's next? The agency could seek to develop an entirely different strategy with the potential for doing a significantly better job at achieving the real purpose for breaking up drug gangs, filling potholes, or investigating abuse allegations. Or the agency could continue to be very efficient at these functional tasks but do little to prevent the emergence of new drug gangs, new potholes, or new child abusers.

The agency has proven to the world that it is competent. It has earned recognition for its mastery of a task with which most other jurisdictions struggle. Why change? Why not simply tweak some operating procedures, retune the allocation of resources, and increase production by another 5 percent? The agency would get credit for this too.

This is the "competency trap."[46] The organization has demonstrated its competence. It gets credit for this competence. It wants to avoid putting its reputation at risk. Indeed, any halfway effective organization can get lulled into the "competency trap." Noted Sugarman: "Often one generation's reform/renewal results in institutionalizing a new and weighty tradition which precludes further, radical renewals to meet later challenges."[47]

For the leadership team of a public agency, getting "caught" in a competency trap is comfortable. If most stakeholders are mostly satisfied, if no one is seriously demanding change, what's not to like? "Other agencies are getting beat up for their incompetence, and ours is Exhibit A (there being no Exhibit B) of how government *can be* effective." Why bother experimenting with an unproven strategy that might be significantly better at achieving the agency's real purpose, when there exists a real possibility that the experiment will screw everything up?

Exploitation or Exploration?

James March calls this the tension between "exploration and exploitation in organizational learning." Should the agency *exploit* its existing knowledge, making some small improvements that are marginally (but not spectacularly) better? Or should it *explore* new possibilities, looking for qualitatively different strategies that might produce some dramatic performance improvements (or nothing but failure)? By exploiting only its existing knowledge, the organization may lock itself in to a less-than-optimal strategy. At the same time, some (many? most?) efforts to explore new possibilities will fail, and even a successful exploration will initially reduce performance as the organization works out the inevitable kinks. Amy Edmondson and Sara Singer of the Harvard Business School have labeled this "the worse-before-better problem."[48]

Once an organization is achieving (or almost achieving) its existing (or revised) target, it has little incentive to experiment with new strategies. Yet, a focus strictly on marginal improvements may undermine an opportunity to truly learn. Only if the new target is a "stretch target"—one that cannot be achieved simply by working a little harder or a little smarter—will the organization have an incentive to explore new strategies—to learn from its failures as well as its successes.

If an organization seeks to improve the performance of a unit with a routine task (for example, filling potholes) it makes sense, suggested Edmondson and Singer, "to measure performance against quality and efficiency standards." Unfortunately, they continue, "policies that reward compliance with specific targets or procedures encourage effort toward those measures but may thwart efforts toward innovation and experimentation." Thus, if improving performance requires experimentation with entirely different procedures for filling potholes, or perhaps with materials very different from asphalt, or even with entirely different policies toward highway maintenance, the city needs to give its public works team the freedom to experiment *plus* the freedom to fail. As Edmondson and Singer wrote, "practices involved in organizing to learn include promoting rather than reducing variance, conducting experiments rather than executing prescribed tasks, and rewarding learning rather than accuracy."[49]

To Chris Argyris, also of Harvard, this willingness to question fundamental assumptions about purposes, policies, and practices marks the difference between single-loop and double-loop learning. Single-loop learning employs feedback documenting how far the organization is from its target to adjust its strategy to move closer to its target. If the organization has a reasonable strategy and if it is close to its target, single-loop learning can be quite effective. If a public agency is seeking to break up *a few more* drug gangs, fill *a few more* potholes, or investigate *a few more* child abusers, single-loop learning will hit the target.

If, however, the leadership team recognizes that it is not coming close to hitting its target, or if it concludes that an entirely different target would best help it to accomplish its purpose, or if it changes its basic purpose (which requires a major change in the nature of the target), the feedback of single-loop learning that exploits existing knowledge and produces some marginal improvements will be completely inadequate. Now the leadership team is forced to challenge its own basic assumptions, to look for data that offer new insights, to reflect on the implications of the data it is receiving, to rethink the assumptions that underlie the activities in its current repertoire, and to experiment with approaches that would once have been unfathomable. To Argyris, this is double-loop learning.[50]

A PerformanceStat strategy can do either. It can help an organization learn how to continually make the marginal adjustments necessary to make small, continuous improvements. Or it can help the organization jump off its slow-but-steady treadmill and learn how to produce qualitatively different and more significant results.[51]

Learning Ain't Easy

Unfortunately, learning is difficult. It's difficult for individuals. It's difficult for teams. And, as Senge observed, "teams, not individuals, are the fundamental learning unit in modern organizations."[52]

It isn't easy to learn from success. What exactly caused the success? How much was due to innovative strategy, brilliant leadership, and creative implementation? To outside forces? To luck? Separating out the various causes of any effect is complicated.

It isn't easy to learn from failure.[53] Was that *really* a failure? Or just a low level of success? If it was a failure, was it a failure in strategy? In leadership? In implementation? Or were the real causes uncontrollable events and uncooperative people?

Learning from either success or failure requires the analytical capacity to identify and test potential causes. In addition, human factors—our human psychological predilections and our organizational norms—inhibit our ability to learn from failure.

Nevertheless, concluded Edmondson and Mark Cannon of Vanderbilt, organizations can develop a conscious ability to learn, even from failure. Their recommendations include: creating "information systems to capture and organize data," training people to analyze these data, and holding meetings to review and examine the data.[54] Sound familiar?

In addition, Edmondson suggested how to overcome the human and social frailties that contribute to our propensity to ignore or dismiss evidence of failure. To help organizations identify and learn from failures, she advocated creating "team psychological safety": "a shared belief that the team is safe for interpersonal risk taking" or "a sense of confidence that the team will not embarrass, reject, or punish someone for speaking up." Of course PerformanceStat meetings that brutally criticize failure do precisely the opposite. "A team's history matters in shaping psychological safety," wrote Edmondson; it can foster "an unwillingness to question the team goal for fear of sanction by management."[55]

Such "threats to self-esteem," Cannon and Edmondson argued, inhibit the ability of people to recognize their own failures. To "reenforce psychological safety," they recommended policies such as "blameless reporting systems" and "publicizing failures as a means of learning." They also suggested training managers in "group dialogue and collaborative learning" so they can conduct "learning-oriented discussions." Certainly some who chair PerformanceStat sessions could "be more effective in generating learning from the heated discussions often produced when failures are analyzed."[56]

From Exploitation to Exploration

If a government jurisdiction or public agency needs to do its first-level, routine tasks (for example, filling potholes) more efficiently and effectively, it doesn't need too much experimentation. A high-pressure PerformanceStat strategy can drive an agency to make these essential, first-order improvements and hit its efficiency and effectiveness targets.

But once the organization has achieved significant success by creating the competences necessary to produce basic, first-order results, the leadership team may want its PerformanceStat strategy to create a major, second-order jump in performance. The organization may be unable, however, to do so simply by exploiting existing competences. It may need to experiment with qualitatively different strategies. This experimentation may require the leadership team to make significant adjustments in its PerformanceStat approach to operating, learning, and improving.

This experimentation may also require the leadership team to create Edmondson's "team psychological safety" by reducing the pressure on subunits to achieve targets that are incrementally above current performance. For example, will a team from the Public Works Department that is hitting its pothole-filling targets be willing to risk the failure that may result from exploring an unproven approach to filling potholes or from experimenting with a road surface that might (but only might) defeat the annual pothole invasion? Maybe not. On the current scorecard, the team is winning.

Consequently, if a leadership team wants to use a PerformanceStat strategy to create a significantly better way to deal with potholes, it can't just pressure the department to ratchet up performance by another 5 percent. It has to encourage experimentation. And it can only do this if it is willing to establish that failure—missing a target—is not automatically punished but is valued *if* it results from intelligent, purpose-focused experimentation.

Of course, the leadership team does not have a monopoly on the incentives. Others (drivers? journalists? citizens?) may not tolerate experimental failure. Moreover the leadership team does not control a subunit's implicit values. Consequently, the leadership team has a limited ability to encourage subunits to experiment. Still Edmondson and her colleagues "found that individuals under high evaluative pressure were less likely to experiment when normative values and instrumental rewards were inconsistent in supporting experimentation. In contrast, individuals under low evaluative pressure responded to inconsistent conditions with increased experimentation."[57]

When should a leadership team apply pressure to improve performance? When a subunit isn't even worrying about performance or isn't trying to achieve its explicit targets, pressure might be very useful. But once a subunit has demonstrated both its commitment to achieving its targets and its competence in doing so, once it has revealed an ability to fully *exploit* its existing knowledge, it may be time to back off. It may be time to reduce the pressure on the subunit to achieve an incremental improvement against its established measure of success.[58] It may be time to encourage the subunit to *explore* new ways to achieve its purpose. Getting this balance right is never easy.

Shaping the Performance (and Learning) Challenge

How do organizations learn? For a firm in the production business, the dominant concept has been the "learning curve." This graph presents a downward sloping line revealing that as the total number of units produced grows (and thus the firm's experience in production also grows), the cost per unit declines. Somehow, someone in the firm is learning something that improves its efficiency. This is "learning by doing."

Kazuhiro Mishina of Kobe University took a closer look. He found a rich lode of World War II data on Boeing's production of the B-17, the Flying Fortress. As predicted, as production increased, direct labor hours per plane dropped from 71 worker-years in September 1941 to 8 worker-years in December 1944.[59] Is this learning by doing?

Mishina developed an alternative hypothesis: "learning by new experiences." And his analysis of the B-17 production data supported this explanation. Yes, over three-plus years, Boeing did accumulate experience producing the plane. But, concluded Mishina, "the source of learning is new experiences that scaling-up of effective capacity entails."[60]

Boeing wasn't just continually producing planes, and then, in the next quarter, producing the same number of planes. As demand increased, Boeing was continually scaling up capacity. Doing the same thing over and over again—producing one plane, and a second plane, and then another—did not require anyone to learn. No one had to do anything differently. Boeing, however, was faced with a stretch target. If the rate of production was to dramatically increase, everyone couldn't just work a little harder and a little smarter. Boeing would have to do things differently—a lot of things differently, some things very differently. Achieving a dramatic increase in production required managers "who coordinate the various aspects of the plant operations" to learn how to better organize the work. It was these "core managers"—not the front-line supervisors—who were, essentially, forced to learn.[61]

This was "learning by stretching," concluded Mishina: "There is no learning where there is no challenge."[62] The leadership challenge is to shape the performance challenge and thus the learning challenge. By creating a very specific target, the leadership team can pressure the operating units to *exploit* their existing knowledge to make a series of marginal improvements. By creating a stretch target, however, the leadership team can pressure the operating unit to *experiment* with new ways of hitting this target. By emphasizing the underlying purpose as well as the target, the leadership team can pressure the operating units to *explore* new ways of achieving this purpose—and thus to create new knowledge.

The PerformanceStat Meeting as a Learning Opportunity

Actually, the leadership team could start this exploring at its second Performance-Stat meeting:

> We are doing things a little differently this time. We learned from our first sessions and decided to make some small changes plus one bigger one. We expect to make more changes. In fact, if you have any suggestions about how to improve this process, please let us know. Here's the first change, suggested by Dusteen Ortez from Public Works. . . .

The leadership team needs to learn how to experiment, to help others learn how to experiment, and to help everyone learn to tolerate the inevitable failures.

The leadership team will have to start simple by cobbling together its initial approach from ideas it picked up from the PerformanceStats it visited and from what it read and was told. Then, it will have to consciously experiment with these leadership principles and operational components to create its own unique adaptation. At the same time, the leadership team will be trying to articulate the purposes it is trying to achieve, the routine tasks that it wants done more efficiently and effectively, and the initial performance targets it wants to achieve.

While trying to get the routine tasks done more efficiently and effectively, the jurisdiction's or agency's leadership team will need to simultaneously encourage innovation in how it accomplishes its purposes. It can start with a generic approach. Soon, however, it will have to experiment with some unique adaptations. All the while, it is trying to learn, trying to use its PerformanceStat meetings to discover what is actually going on.

Meanwhile it wants to continually and consciously rethink the operational components of its PerformanceStat strategy as well as their implementation. To whom should it give what responsibilities and what discretion? Under what circumstances should it modify what targets? What new kinds of data does it need? How does who analyze it? What style should who use to conduct the meetings? What feedback do people need and what form should it take? What kind of competences do what subunits and individuals need, and how can we help develop them? How does the leadership team demonstrate its commitment to this (necessarily evolving) strategy?

Learning how to create an effective PerformanceStat strategy takes a lot of experimentation—multiple failures—and a lot of adaptation. As Robert Sutton emphasizes, "creativity results from using old ideas in new ways, places, or combinations."[63]

Back to Question Zero: What Are We Trying to Accomplish?

If the performance purpose is clear and specific, understood and accepted, then the strategies and tactics for producing improved results can evolve while everyone keeps focused on accomplishing that purpose.

14

Thinking about Cause and Effect

How can public executives identify the causal impact of their leadership efforts when they cannot observe how these activities affect the behavior of people who directly create results?

> Nothing in the quantum-mechanical theory of radioactivity explains how a subatomic particle performs its magic and makes its way through impenetrable walls.
> GEORGE GREENSTEIN, Amherst College[1]

> To explain is to provide a mechanism, to open up the black box and show the nuts and bolts, the cogs and wheels of the internal machinery.
> JON ELSTER, Columbia University[2]

In 2006, the Scottish Executive (now called the Scottish Government) released a report on six experiments with a CitiStat strategy: "What Do We Measure and Why? An Evaluation of the CitiStat Model of Performance Management and Its Applicability to the Scottish Public Sector."[3] As I read the report, I was surprised. Public executives in Scotland seemed to understand the complex, causal behaviors and appreciate the subtle nuances of Baltimore's CitiStat leadership strategy significantly better than many in the United States.

U.S. public executives who worked so much closer to Baltimore did copy the visible features of CitiStat: data, projectors, meetings. Yet, they often failed to figure out the underlying cause-and-effect relationships that can contribute to the potential effectiveness of this leadership strategy. Consequently, many never adopted—let alone adapted—many of the core leadership principles and key operational components that contribute to the PerformanceStat potential.

Why did these neighbors miss many of the principles and components? Why did the visitors from across The Pond get it?

When I asked the people from Scotland, their answer was obvious—and explained a lot. Scotland had not merely flown a single observer to Baltimore, who, during a morning visit, watched a meeting or two and got a brief briefing. Instead, Scotland had sent an entire team to spend an entire week in Baltimore. The members of the team observed a variety of CitiStat sessions. They talked with people in the mayor's office and in city agencies. They spent five days poking around, trying to soak up what people were doing and grasp what was really going on. One member of the team even took a side trip to Somerville, Massachusetts to learn about SomerStat.[4]

Most public officials who seek to create their own CitiStat do make a visit to Baltimore—a quick one. They watch a session, maybe two, get the standard briefing from a CitiStat staffer, and ask a few questions (mostly about cost—the cost to their budget, not the cost to their time). Their questions answered, they leave thinking that they fully understand this leadership strategy.

They may have seen quite a lot. Yet, they may comprehend very little.

Explicit Knowledge about "*What?*"

Like Baltimore, most public agencies and governmental jurisdictions that have created their own PerformanceStat welcome visitors.[5] But what, exactly, do these visitors *learn?*

What these visitors *see* is the room, the people, the questions and discussion, the data, the technology used to project the data. Maybe even some analysis. What, however, do they *learn?*

Mostly, I think, these visitors learn that PerformanceStat is pretty simple. What they observe does not appear to be particularly complex. They have seen it all before: meetings, data, questions. They may have used data in their own meetings. Nothing much new here.

What may well be different, however, is the technology. This is new. The projectors used to display data, maps, and photographs are designed to get everyone's attention—to ensure that everyone in the room is concentrating on the same information. The technology also gets the attention of visitors. This is cool. How much more technologically *avant-garde* can public management get? The visibility of the technology helps explain why visitors focus their initial questions on it: "*What* kind of software did you buy?" "*What* did it cost you for all this technology?"

After these easy questions about technology and cost are answered, the visitors shift their attention to operational details: "*What* kind of data do you collect?" "*What* software do you use? "*What* is the frequency of your meetings?" These "*What?*" questions are explicit. They demand an explicit response. Thus, most presentations about any PerformanceStat do the same. They focus on the explicit. They anticipate and answer the "*What?*" questions.

Thus, the visitors acquire the explicit knowledge about technology and operations. They learn that PerformanceStat is quite simple, standard stuff—plus some IT extras: "This is easy. We can do this." What could be easier to copy than these visible, explicit components of PerformanceStat? No wonder that CompStat, CitiStat, and other SimpleStats have been subjected to so much mindless mimicry.

Tacit Knowledge about "*How?*"

Unfortunately, unless they are willing to spend a week poking around, the visitors to any PerformanceStat are unlikely to be exposed to the tacit knowledge about *how* the behavior of the leadership team affects the performance of people and subunits. Indeed, they won't learn enough to ask. Thus, neither the questions, the answers, nor the formal presentations give much attention to the causal "How?" question. "*How?*" does a PerformanceStat work?

> *How* does your PerformanceStat leadership strategy help your organization to produce better results?

Yet this tacit knowledge of cause-and-effect is what creates the true potential to improve performance.

Unfortunately, the tacit knowledge about the causal effects of the leadership behaviors underlying any PerformanceStat is illusive. As Michael Polanyi has observed about our (collective and individual) tacit knowledge: "We can know more than we can tell."[6] Those who have created an effective PerformanceStat strategy are no better at this telling than the rest of us.

Those who have created an effective PerformanceStat understand much more about their leadership strategy than they can convey in their briefings and answers to questions. They have accumulated—individually and collectively—an abundance of tacit knowledge about *how* their different leadership behaviors influence the organizational culture and operational activities that they hope will produce the results they seek and thus achieve the purposes that they have chosen to pursue. Still, they can't explain this tacit knowledge in mere words.

The dependence of an effective PerformanceStat on the tacit knowledge of the members of the leadership team explains why I call it a "leadership strategy"— why it can't work as a mechanistic system. A system is based on explicit knowledge. It can be fully explained in words and, thus, can be copied. A management *system*—an email *system;* a personnel *system*—comes with a set of procedures that codify and explain. The system's technology—be it an electronic technology or a human technology—can be replicated faithfully by different organizations in different circumstances. A leadership strategy, however, is much more subtle. It cannot be reduced to a replicable template. It is not a policy or a reform. It is based on tacit knowledge that must be learned from detailed observation—even better through apprenticeship and experimentation.

When an individual or team seeks to employ another's leadership strategy, it needs to figure out how to adapt the strategy's core leadership principles and key operational components to their own purposes and circumstances. Mindless mimicry of the mechanics will accomplish little. Adaptation of the operational components is essential. Such adaptation requires, however, a sophisticated understanding of the core leadership principles.

The essential role of tacit knowledge in developing an effective Performance-Stat leadership strategy is both significant and unfortunate. Certainly an effective PerformanceStat depends on the intelligent application of some formal, explicit knowledge about operation mechanics. But an effective PerformanceStat—indeed, any effective management or leadership strategy—also requires a subtle appreciation of complex causal behaviors. No wonder that so many efforts to create a new CompStat, or Citistat, or any other PerformanceStat are little more than MimicStats.

Unfortunately, even when we go looking for the tacit knowledge of leadership, our empirical search for specific causes and our understanding of their effects are shaped by our own theories about causal connections. As Sir John Lubbock wrote over a century ago, "What we do see depends mainly on what we look for."[7] And each of us, given our background and interests, looks for different things. Noted Lubbock: "In the same field the farmer will notice the crop, geologists the fossils, botanists the flowers, artists the coloring, sportsmen the cover for game."[8] People with different theories about behavioral causation will search for entirely different behavioral specifics. They will go looking for different causal relationships and—not surprisingly—find them.

The Search for Effective Policies: Answering the "*Whether?*" Question

Does any new policy work? Before an agency or jurisdiction decides whether to replicate a policy employed elsewhere, it wants to know *whether* it works. Fortunately, social science has a method for answering the policymaker's "*Whether?*" question: the double-blind, randomized (placebo-controlled) experiment (see chapter 9). For example, what can public policymakers do to learn if a "negative income tax" works—if it accomplishes its purpose? An answer to this "*Whether?*" question can be obtained by conducting an experiment.[9]

Such an experiment can be expensive and time consuming. It is necessary to clearly specify the policy. It is necessary to implement the policy for some people and deny it to others. It is necessary to collect a variety of data. It may be necessary to wait a long time before expecting to find an impact. Nevertheless, if designed carefully, the experiment can determine *whether* or not the policy works. Then, if the policy works, and if its key components have been clearly specified—that is, the knowledge of the policy's components is very explicit— then other jurisdictions and agencies can faithfully replicate the policy.

The Search for Causal Behaviors: Answering the "*How?*" Question

"*How?*" however, does any leadership strategy—including PerformanceStat— work? What is the theory: if not explicit, then at least implicit; if not directly mechanistic, then at least indirectly causal? *How* might a PerformanceStat strategy produce better results? What exactly are the potential causal connections between the behaviors of a chief executive and his or her leadership team and the results they are trying to produce?[10]

For a public executive—someone who seeks to produce specific results by implementing a leadership strategy employed in another organization—answering the "*How?*" question is essential.[11] After all, this executive's circumstances are different, and thus the formal operational machinery of another executive's leadership strategy may not have the same causal effect on employees, subunits, and collaborators, and thus will not automatically produce similar (or any) results. Unless the public executive understands *how* another's leadership strategy causes improved performance, he or she will be unable to figure out *how* to adapt the strategy's leadership behaviors to new circumstances.

Unfortunately, social science lacks an experimental method to answer the executive's "*How?*" question. Even if the experiment answers the "*Whether?*" question with a "yes," it usually fails to answer the question posed by Mario Bunge, the McGill physicist whose research has also focused on the philosophy of science: "How does it work?" The answer to this "*How?*" question establishes what Bunge calls "the mechanism(s) that makes the system in question tick." To Bunge, "a mechanism is one of the processes in a concrete system that makes it what it is."[12]

For a policy, a mechanism would provide an explanation that connects key features of the policy to its consequences. It establishes (1) *what* features of the policy have an effect (either deterministically or stochastically), and (2) *how* these effective features—individually and interactively—contribute to the resulting effects.[13]

Similarly, for a leadership strategy, a mechanism would provide an explanation that connects key behaviors taken by the leadership team to the consequences they are seeking to produce. It establishes (1) *what* leadership behaviors have influence (either deterministically or stochastically) on the actions of the organization, and (2) *how* these leadership behaviors—individually and interactively—contribute to these actions. Here the "organization" would include not only the formal, governmental entity and the people who work in it, but also all of the other individuals, informal collections of individuals, formal organizations, and functioning collaboratives whose behavior can influence the desired results.

The Missing "*How?*" in Physics and Engineering

For engineers to use knowledge from physics, they usually do not have to answer the "*How?*" question. Sir Isaac Newton's law of gravitation was both mathematically precise and operationally useful:

$$F = G \frac{m_1 \times m_2}{r^2}.$$

In Newton's formula, F is the force of gravitational attraction between two objects with masses m_1 and m_2 that are separated by the distance r. G is the universal gravitational constant (which has yet to be measured precisely).

Physicists may find their inability to accurately measure the value of G frustrating, and their inability to specify it theoretically disappointing. Still, none of this invalidates the practical utility of Newton's formula. To use it, engineers do not need to know *how* gravity works.[14]

The same applies to quantum mechanics. "The theory is profoundly mysterious. It gives a detailed set of instructions for calculating subatomic processes, yet fails to provide the slightest comprehension of *how* these processes take place," writes Greenstein. "Nothing in the quantum-mechanical theory of radioactivity explains *how* a subatomic particle performs its magic and makes its way through impenetrable walls" (emphasis added).[15]

The Missing "*How?*" in Medicine

For doctors to use knowledge from biology and chemistry, they usually do not have to answer the "*How?*" question. For a proven treatment, how it works is interesting but not essential. It is only necessary to answer the "*Whether?*" question: We only need to know whether the treatment works. To do this, it is necessary to specify the treatment explicitly and completely. Then, to answer the "*Whether?*" question, medical research employs the gold standard for comparisons: the double-blind, randomized, placebo-controlled experiment. If done properly, this experimental approach can eliminate all but one of the alternative explanations.

The classic example is the experiment conducted in 1954 to determine whether the polio vaccine developed by Jonas Salk was effective (see chapter 9). This experiment answered the "*Whether it works?*" question, with a convincing "yes." Thus, to ensure the effective use of the vaccine, it is only necessary to specify the components of the vaccine plus the timing and procedures for its use. It would be nice to understand *how* the polio vaccine works, but doctors who prescribe it need not understand the science. They simply need to use the identical vaccine in an identical way. The production and delivery of the vaccine are based on explicit knowledge. Very straightforward.

The Causal "*How?*" in Public Management and Leadership

For public executives, however, answering the "*How?*" question is absolutely essential. There is no leadership formula, no leadership vaccine. Any leadership strategy involves multiple behaviors each of which is difficult to specify. There is no single "treatment"—nothing that can be as easily specified (or as routinely delivered) as a vaccine. Moreover, leadership behaviors do not function individually but interact with each other (in ways that may not be clear). Finally, any specific leadership behavior may have different effects with different people, in different circumstances, and in the pursuit of different purposes. Thus, when public executives develop a leadership strategy, they have to figure out which behaviors will have the desired effects on which people, in which circumstances, in the pursuit of which purposes.[16]

Moreover, our knowledge about management and leadership is primarily tacit. It cannot be unequivocally codified in the forms we use for explicit knowledge: words, numbers, equations, codes, manuals, patents. Management and leadership fall into what Polanyi calls an "ineffable domain"—"the area where the tacit predominates to the extent that articulation is virtually impossible."[17] This is why so many management textbooks are so general; they consist primarily of unobjectionable aphorisms that provide no useful guidance in any particular circumstance. It is why it is so difficult for managers to adapt best-practice formulas to their own, specific purposes.

Thus, because a management or leadership strategy does not consist of well-specified components that can be implemented simply and consistently in a wide variety of circumstances, those who seek to adopt it must be able to answer Bunge's question: "How does it work?" Even if an only slightly complicated management strategy could produce a definitive (or conditional or tentative) "yes" in the *whether* experiment, implementing it elsewhere still requires an understanding of the *causal how.* Employing this successful strategy in a different circumstance, organization, or political environment will necessarily involve not just adoption but also adaptation—usually significant adaptations.

Thus, an executive who seeks to employ another's leadership strategy needs to understand *how* this strategy works. This executive needs to understand *how* the strategy's leadership behaviors affect the actions of people who will produce the desired results. Without this tacit knowledge, this executive will be unable to get his or her organization to "tick" effectively.

The Search for Mechanisms

Scientists and philosophers have long sought to identify both physical and social mechanisms and to explain how they work. "Science explains in terms of mechanisms," writes Bunge. Peter Hedström of Oxford University and Petri Ylikoski of the University of Tampere have written: "mechanisms and mechanism-based explanations have attracted a great deal of attention in the social sciences as well as in the philosophy of science."[18]

Mechanisms, report Hedström and Richard Swedberg of Cornell University, "usually are unobserved analytical constructs . . . that provide hypothetical links between observable events."[19] "A mechanism is an irreducibly causal notion," argue Hedström and Ylikoski; it "provides a how-possible explanation; it tells us how the effect could in principle be produced."[20]

To explain evolution, Charles Darwin proposed his theory of natural selection containing two important mechanisms: (1) inheritable variations, combined with (2) the struggle for survival. To explain the wealth of nations, Adam Smith proposed his theory of the invisible hand, for which the key mechanism was every individual's desire to be wealthier. In both cases, the mechanisms are intentional but individual; each individual, seeking survival or wealth, develops a personal strategy for achieving it. Thus, the phenomenon that is explained results from the aggregated but uncoordinated impact of multiple individuals carrying out their own, individual intentions; both mechanisms work without any individual's calculated effort at overall guidance.

Leadership behaviors are also intentional. But leaders seek to achieve their intentions not only directly through their own actions but also indirectly by consciously attempting to influence the actions of others. The intention of public leaders is not to personally survive or to become personally wealthier but to achieve a public purpose. The leader is attempting to accomplish a specific purpose by making a deliberate, conscious, calculated attempt to affect the behavior of others. Thus, there are two steps in the causal explanation: (1) How do specific leadership behaviors have an impact on the thinking and actions of others? and (2) How do these others think and act to help achieve the desired result? In the next chapter, I seek to identify the first set of causal mechanism(s): How do the multiple behaviors of a PerformanceStat leadership team explain individual and organizational reactions?

If the PerformanceStat leadership strategy is to have any validity, there must exist at least one such mechanism connecting leadership behavior to the thinking and actions of others. After all, as Hedström and Ylikoski write, "the absence of a plausible mechanism linking X to Y gives us a good reason to be suspicious of the relation being a causal one."[21] If we cannot identify some plausible mechanisms linking the behaviors of a PerformanceStat leadership strategy to what individuals and organizations do, we would need to conclude that the strategy has no impact.

The Clunky Metaphor of the Black Box

To understand *how* a PerformanceStat leadership strategy might produce better results, I have tried to look inside Jon Elster's black box—to identify the "nuts" and "bolts," to understand the "cogs" and "wheels" of this "machinery." Of course, this metaphor is all wrong. There are no nuts or bolts, no cogs, no wheels. Indeed, there is no machinery—though the analogy is attractive—indeed, reassuring.[22]

After all, the metaphor suggests not only that there exists such machinery but also that, if we are clever enough, our mind's eye can penetrate the blackest of these mechanistic boxes. It permits us to infer that if leaders are only brilliant enough, they can somehow (perhaps with some superpower x-ray vision) discern the organization's machinery chugging away, cogs whirling and wheels spinning. Moreover, it permits us to infer that if such leaders spend enough time thinking—and if they understand the applicable formulas of organizational engineering—they can figure out what the nuts and bolts hold together and how the turning of specific cogs and the rotating of particular wheels directly affect the thinking and actions of people and teams.

Indeed, behind the machinery metaphor lies the hint that really smart and resourceful leaders—by selecting carefully and using properly the appropriate nuts, bolts, cogs, and wheels—can create higher performing black boxes. This analogy is reminiscent of Max Weber's description of a bureaucracy as a machine that "reduces every worker to a cog in this machine and, seeing himself in this light, he will merely ask how to transform himself from a little into a somewhat bigger cog."[23] Inside the organizational black box, the humans are the cogs.

Yet, despite our human propensity for mechanical metaphors, we cannot really open up and observe the action of the cogs in a PerformanceStat machine—or in any other leadership strategy. For one thing, there is no leadership machine. And to the extent that we are in love with this metaphor, we still need to accept that this "machine" does not exist inside a single box—be it black or green or pink. For example, the CompStat "machine"—if you insist on imagining it in this way—is spread all over New York City (and into adjacent jurisdictions as well) and includes not only what goes on inside the "black box" of the New York Police Department. For crime everywhere is affected not only by the individual and collective behavior of the police, but also by the personal behavior of individual citizens and by their collective behavior in their neighborhoods. If there exists a black box for NYPD's CompStat, it is very large with millions of cogs and wheels rotating and counter-rotating each other in very complex and undecipherable ways.

CompStat—indeed, any PerformanceStat—is not a machine. Rather it is a "complex, adaptive system."[24] This is not a formal, structural "system" created by the leadership team. Rather, it is the informal, inherent "system" of human interactions and adaptations of the various people who are somehow connected to the effort to improve performance. The cops and the bad guys, for example, are not only interacting with each other, but also adapting their strategies in response to the behavior of the others. The cops—having identified patterns in, for example, burglaries—create new strategies to capture the burglars and prevent future burglaries. The burglars, in response, adapt their modus operandi, or develop new targets, or engage in different crimes. In turn, the cops adapt . . . . The interactions among cops and crooks is a very complex and continuously adaptive system with multiple feedback loops.

Thus, the challenge facing the leadership team is not to build some new, fabulous machine. Rather it is to work with the existing people, relationships, and structures—injecting some conscious purposes, creating some specific targets, inspiring with public recognition, devoting time while remaining persistent . . . all the while analyzing data, asking questions, scrutinizing reports, in an effort to learn whether their leadership behaviors are introducing new feedback loops that foster adaptations that help to achieve the purposes.

Leadership Behaviors as Plausible Explanations

Thomas Schelling of the University of Maryland proposed that "a social mechanism is a plausible hypothesis, or a set of plausible hypotheses, that could be the explanation of some social phenomenon, the explanation being in terms of interactions between individuals and other individuals, or between individuals and some aggregate."[25] No nuts or bolts. No cogs or wheels. Just "a plausible hypothesis," or "a set of plausible hypotheses," that "could be the explanation." "*Could be.*"

In this spirit, I offer a set of 16 hypotheses that *could be* an explanation for the interactions created by a PerformanceStat leadership strategy that improves performance. (See table 14-1 and chapter 15.) As Hedström and Swedberg argue, "Explanations of most concrete social events or states require resort[ing] to several elementary mechanisms: one is not enough."[26]

Each of these 16 hypotheses describes a behavior of the organization's leadership team and how it has (or might have) an impact on middle managers, front-line supervisors, and front-line employees. Each seeks to explain *how* these interactions change the thinking and actions of both individuals and groups that *could*, in turn, affect organizational performance. Each is one item in what Hedström and Ylikoski call "the toolbox of possible causal mechanisms."[27]

Not even 16 causal explanations can capture all of the subtle behaviors of a leadership strategy let alone their multiple interactive effects.[28] Each of the 16 is but one possible analytical construct. Yet, note Hedström and Swedberg, such analytical abstractions are both necessary and desirable:

> It is through abstractions and analytical accentuation, however, that general mechanisms are made visible. But these abstractions also distort by their very nature the descriptive account of what actually happened, by accentuating certain aspects of the situation and by ignoring others.[29]

Thus, the real question about any of these 16 abstractions (or any other abstraction about PerformanceStat) is whether what it accentuates and what it ignores helps scholars and executives understand the causal features of the strategy—and whether it helps executives adopt and adapt their own approach.

The leadership team can influence department heads, middle managers, front-line supervisors, and front-line workers to improve performance by consciously and consistently employing these 16 potentially causal behaviors. These leadership behaviors do not, however, directly *cause* improved performance. Instead, it is the reactions of individuals and groups that produce the enhanced results.

No one of these 16 behaviors would be sufficient to cause a significant improvement in performance. Moreover, they neither function independently

TABLE 14-1. Sixteen Causal Leadership Behaviors of the
PerformanceStat Leadership Strategy

Leadership behaviors	Cause	Individual and organizational reactions
1 Clarifying and reiterating purpose	Keeps	Focuses people on accomplishments
2 Analyzing data	Reveals	Performance deficits
3 Creating targets	Specifies	What needs to be accomplished
4 Making assignments	Defines	Performance deficits to be fixed
5 Devoting resources and time	Dramatizes	Commitment
6 Holding meetings	Focuses	Attention
7 Requesting and discussing reports	Ensures	Assignments are taken seriously
8 Asking questions	Promotes	Personal responsibility
9 Following up	Creates	Feedback that suggests adjustments
10 Distributing comparative data	Helps	Teams honestly appraise performance
11 Scrutinizing positive deviants	Facilitates	Learning
12 Recognizing accomplishments	Confirms	Success is possible and valued
13 Reproving the recalcitrant	Gets	Everyone's attention
14 Telling stories	Fosters	Results-oriented culture
15 Abetting evaluations	Breeds	Individual and team motivation
16 Remaining persistent	Demonstrates	This isn't going away

nor are they mutually exclusive. Rather, they interact with and reinforce each
other, creating causal impacts through a variety of feedback loops. Collectively,
they serve to ensure that everyone in the organization recognizes both what needs
to be done next and what his or her responsibility is for getting this done. All
serve to establish and maintain an emphasis on results and performance.

To be effective, the members of the leadership team need to possess the personal and institutional capacity to behave in a way that induces (though never
compels) individuals, teams, and agencies to establish their own performance-
focused culture and to engage in the kind of day-to-day results-producing activities that the leadership team seeks.[30]

Conjecturing on the Unobservable

Unfortunately, although we can observe an organization's leadership team engaging in these behaviors, we cannot observe *how* these behaviors affect what others do. The operational obscurity of these mechanisms is disappointing but
predictable. "Most of reality is unobservable," argues Bunge, who applies this

observation to mechanisms: "Typically, mechanisms are unobservable, and therefore their description is bound to contain concepts that do not occur in empirical data." Indeed, he continues, "most mechanisms are concealed, so that they have to be conjectured."[31]

We can conjecture that holding meetings (Behavior 6) can focus everyone's attention on what is most important, but we cannot observe any individual's attention being focused (or diffused) by a meeting. We can speculate that scrutinizing the positive deviants (Behavior 11) can facilitate everyone's learning, but we cannot peer inside any single individual's brain to observe whether any such learning is going on. Every one of the suggested individual and organizational reactions that *could be* explained by these 16 leadership behaviors cannot be directly observed; or if this reaction were to have a visible manifestation, we are still forced to conjecture that the leadership behavior is a contributing cause.

These hypotheses emerge from my observations, at various PerformanceStats, of a variety of different leadership behaviors that, when employed consciously and creatively, *could* help to improve the results produced by any organization. Given what we know about how humans function, interact, and respond in organizations, these causal behaviors *could* help us understand *how* the various opaque, enigmatic, ambiguous, and contingent strategies that fit my definition (in chapter 3) of PerforamnceStat might influence people to help improve performance.

I have observed multiple leadership teams in agencies and jurisdictions employing each of these behaviors. I have observed the conduct and culture of subunits, their middle managers, and (sometimes even) their front-line supervisors and front-line workers. Have each of these 16 always induced precisely the desired changes in the application of formal procedures and in the human effort behind informal practices? Of course not. Sometimes there is resistance, even insubordination. Still, by reproving the recalcitrant (Behavior 13) while remaining persistent (Behavior 16), the insolent and mutinous can be isolated. And by recognizing accomplishments (Behavior 12), others can be recruited to the task of producing better results.

These hypotheses are also based on the research about how humans behave and function in organizations. Thus, they are also derived from what Eugene Bardach calls "smart practice analysis," a "sort of reverse engineering." This involves taking apart not just the organization but what people are doing inside that organization and trying "to figure out the clever trick that makes it work so well." Of course, as Bardach emphasizes, this kind of analysis is much easier for an engineer and involves "a complex process of theoretical reasoning."[32] Bardach's smart practice analysis has the potential to help us understand the causal connection between leadership behavior and organizational performance.

Emphasizing Purpose; Motivating People

The first 4 of these 16 behaviors dramatize the purposes to be pursued, highlight the performance deficits to be fixed, specify the results to be produced, and identify who needs to do what. The latter 12 are designed to motivate individuals and teams to make these improvements.[33]

These 12 behaviors seek to move people not just to *work harder* (though for some front-line supervisors and workers that might be the major concern). They are also designed to encourage individuals, teams, and agencies to experiment with ways to *work creatively* by experimenting with different tactics and by reallocating resources. They seek to encourage everyone to *work differently*—to replace their rule-obsessed behavior with a performance perspective; to get them to focus on accomplishing their organization's purpose by achieving their targets.

Underlying the first four behaviors is the assumption that the jurisdiction or agency is, indeed, capable of improving its performance. Underlying the other 12 behaviors is the assumption that the leadership team can affect the behavior of subunit managers, middle managers, and front-line workers. Underlying all 16 behaviors is the assumption that the leadership team possesses the intellectual and interpersonal competences to implement them.

None of these 16 behaviors is new. Each has been employed by numerous leaders, in numerous organizations, in numerous circumstances. What makes a public-sector PerformanceStat strategy worthy of our attention is that its leadership team employs them creatively, consistently, coherently, and constantly.

Necessary? Sufficient? Helpful?

If an organization's leadership team engages in all 16 of these behaviors, will performance improve? Maybe. Maybe not. These behaviors are neither individually nor collectively deterministic. Numerous factors affect an organization's ability to produce results—many of which the leadership team is unable to influence. Over several years, these managers might be able to make some progress. Yet without the support of their superiors, or the flexibility in the deployment of resources, or the cooperation of powerful interests, progress may be slow. Even when employed creatively, diligently, and persistently, these 16 leadership behaviors may not be sufficient to guarantee significant improvements in performance. As Bunge warns: "There are no universal mechanisms, hence no panaceas."[34]

A team of automotive engineers may know how to design and build a six-speed transmission, and a fuel injector, and a camshaft, and a clutch, and an alternator, and a differential, and a. . . . All of these are essential components of an automobile. Nevertheless, even if the engineering team can design and build every component from front bumper to tail pipe, it may still be unable to design and build a complete, working car. For a functioning automobile not only moves forward and backward and around turns; it is also easy to drive—indeed, pleasant to drive. A complete car has multiple features—from engine efficiency to passenger comfort. A complete, functioning automobile is more than a collection of independent parts. Those multiple parts have to work together in synergy—to release the potential energy stored in the gasoline and direct this kinetic energy to accomplish something useful: moving people where they want to go, safely and swiftly.

The same applies to any PerformanceStat. The members of an organization's leadership team need to know not only how to create targets, ask questions, and tell stories. They need to know how to employ these 16 behaviors in a way that reflects the purposes they are trying to achieve, the performance deficits that they face, and the political and organizational circumstances within which they must work. They need to be able to engage in these behaviors so that they reinforce each other—so that, like the multiple parts of the automobile, they work together in synergy. They need to engage in these multiple behaviors to release the "potential energy" stored in the organization (and its collaborators) and direct this "kinetic energy" to accomplish something useful: producing results that achieve public purposes.

What would happen if an organization's leadership team engaged in none of these 16? This counterfactual suggests the relevance of these leadership behaviors.[35] For in the absence of any of them, we would attribute any improvement in performance to outside or random effects. Given what we know about the behavior of humans in organizations, managers who eschew all 16 of these causal behaviors are unlikely—even if they build a fancy room with the latest technology—to produce better results.

What if a leadership team employed 15 of the 16? Would that improve performance? Maybe. Maybe not. As always, it all depends. Indeed, the answer could depend on a lot of things—for example, how well the organization was performing before the leadership team decided to seek better results, the nature of the key performance deficits, and the relevance of the missing behavior to these performance deficits.

Individually and collectively these 16 behaviors are not sufficient. Still, some may be necessary. But which ones? Or which ones in what combination? And in what circumstances? None of this is obvious.

Moreover, the quality of each behavior counts. How often—and in what ways—do public managers need to clarify and reiterate their purpose to have an impact on performance? The intensity and frequency of such repetition depends on how well the organization has already internalized this purpose. How many questions do public managers need to ask to get a subunit manager to take personal responsibility for subunit performance? Again, it all depends. For example, how much personal responsibility has each subunit manager already assumed? Some may need only a few questions; others may require pointed and persistent questioning.

Or suppose the members of a leadership team only pretend to employ these behaviors. For example, suppose they ask only trivial or irrelevant questions of subunit managers. Or suppose they are completely incompetent—unable to clarify their purpose or to create relevant targets. Or suppose their persistence consists solely of holding a regular series of ritualistic, *pro forma* meetings? Such questions, purposes, targets, or meetings will accomplish little.

There might be other causal behaviors of leadership that are not on this list. Nevertheless, these 16 do appear to be individually and collectively important. If an organization's leadership team does not engage in any of them, we would not expect performance to improve, but rather to deteriorate. Conversely, to improve performance, an organization's leadership team would need to adapt creatively and employ intelligently many (though perhaps not all) of these 16 leadership behaviors that *could* have a causal effect on people and organizations.

Maybe none of these leadership behaviors is absolutely *necessary*. Certainly none is *sufficient*. Individually and collectively, however, the 16 could be very *helpful*.

15

Appreciating Leadership's Causal Behaviors

How can what leadership behaviors of a PerformanceStat strategy have what causal impacts on organizational and individual behavior— and thus actually produce better results?

The mayor saying it should happen isn't enough.
STEPHANIE HIRSCH, First SomerStat Director[1]

There is nothing so practical as a good theory.
KURT LEWIN, Founder of Social Psychology[2]

In 1937, Luther Gulick and Lyndall Urwick published their classic *Papers on the Science of Administration.* In the opening essay, Gulick—a leader in the effort to make public administration more, well, scientific—asked: "What is the work of the chief executive? What does he do?" Gulick's answer was POSDCORB, an acronym for: Planning, Organizing, Staffing, Directing, Co-Ordinating, Reporting, and Budgeting. Into these seven "functional elements," Gulick argued "can be fitted each of the major activities and duties of any chief executive."[3] Impressive.

Still, Gulick's list of the chief executive's activities and duties neglects something important: leadership. His vision of public administration is quite mechanical: "Organizing," for example, is about "the formal structure of authority through which work subdivisions are arranged, defined and co-ordinated" (with no acknowledgment of the multiple, informal relationships upon which even the most hierarchical of organizations must rely to get things done). "Directing" is "the continuous task of making decisions and embodying them in specific and general orders and instructions and serving as the leader of the enterprise." This

261

"leader" does not set targets nor delegate discretion; he issues orders and gives instructions. All very clinical. Gulick's government is populated by automatons. Thus leadership is unnecessary.

These seven activities may be helpful. Still, Gulick offers no causal suggestion about how any of the seven works to create any desired consequences. Indeed, six are quite detached from the challenge of producing results. The one exception is "planning," which to Gulick "is working out in broad outline the things that need to be done and the methods for doing them to accomplish the purpose set for the enterprise." His chief executive has no role in thinking through any of the nuances of that purpose (let alone in setting targets for achieving it). The purpose is given by others, clear and obvious. To accomplish this purpose, Gulick's executive focuses on methods that will, presumably, be communicated through orders and instructions.

Today, many administrative functions have deteriorated into exercises in compliance. Organizations follow formal procedures and reporting requirements with little attention to how they might help (or hinder) the ability to produce results. Moreover, although Gulick describes the chief executive as "the leader of the enterprise," he offers no hint about *how* that chief executive might exercise leadership.

Nevertheless, there do exist leadership "behaviors": *personal behaviors* of the leadership team that can help everyone understand and appreciate the purposes to be achieved and the results to be produced. These behaviors can also motivate individuals, teams, and agencies to improve performance. These behaviors are human activities, not impersonal systems. They are the words and deeds that members of a leadership team employ to achieve the PerformanceStat potential.

Behavior 1: Clarifying and reiterating the purpose can keep everyone focused on what is to be accomplished.

> By repeating and repeating the public purpose that the organization is responsible for achieving, the leadership team can ensure that, in their pursuit of detailed tasks and specific targets, people do not forget their overarching mission.

Regular and frequent PerformanceStat meetings provide a perfect opportunity to remind everyone of the purposes they and their organization are trying to achieve. Too often, the daily tasks and operational routines displace the organization's real purpose that these tasks and routines are supposed to achieve. Thus, a major challenge of leadership is to ensure that people do not forget their real purpose.

Clarifying and reiterating the purpose is, however, more than a defense against forgetfulness. It has positive consequences. As Richard Hackman observed:

"People seek purpose in their lives and are energized when an attractive purpose is articulated for them."[4] A public organization—almost by definition—has an attractive purpose, perhaps several attractive purposes. By clarifying and reminding everyone of these purposes, public executives can give meaning to the organization's work and energize people.

(In chapter 4, I examined the importance of purpose; consequently, this section is short. For the other behaviors that I have already discussed in detail, I also provide only a brief summary here. For the remaining behaviors, however, I thoroughly examine their causal effect, drawing on lessons from social psychology and organizational behavior.)

Behavior 2: Analyzing data can reveal significant performance deficits.

> By analyzing very current performance data, the leadership team can discern and highlight the performance deficits that the organization needs to eliminate or mitigate.

Lots of public agencies have lots of performance measures. Dozens, perhaps hundreds, of measures. A visitor from Mars could easily conclude that many governments have established a rule: "More measures are better."

As a political strategy, reporting more measures may make sense. Some measures will suggest performance has improved. For these gains, agency managers will take credit. Some measures will suggest performance has deteriorated. For these failures, the managers can blame others. Next year, when different measures improve, the managers can say: "See, we worked on those, and they got better." As for those that got worse, they can again blame others.

To actually improve performance, however, an organization needs to fix the performance deficits that are preventing it from producing better results. No organization can simultaneously create improvement on a hundred different measures. For most public agencies, attempting to simultaneously ratchet up performance on even 10 dimensions may be too much. Leaders have to choose. They have to decide which one or two performance deficits they need to fix next and then set the targets to get them fixed.

Which measures are really important? Which measures need to be improved next? Which measures can reveal—through an increase or decrease—whether or not the organization has eliminated, or at least mitigated, one of its key performance deficits? Time to call out the cavalry: the analysts armed with their data. Actually, for a small agency, one skilled analyst can work wonders. Larger organizations with multiple responsibilities will need more, but not an entire regiment. Initially, a small squad will do fine.

Give them a data dump and ask: "What are our different performance deficits?" These analysts may not possess the organization-wide perspective necessary to select the performance deficits on which the organization should focus next. Still, they should possess the analytical skills necessary to nominate candidates. When people applied for a job as a SomerStat analyst, Stephanie Hirsch would give them a data set and ask: What can you learn from these data?

Identifying performance deficits is an analytical task. Choosing the one(s) on which to focus is a leadership responsibility.

Behavior 3: Creating targets can specify exactly what needs to be done by when.

> *By evolving, in consultation with subunit managers, specific, challenging, consequential performance targets for each subunit to achieve, the leadership team can not only identify the results to be produced but also motivate agencies, individuals, and teams to produce them.*

Targets can be inspiring. They can challenge human egos. Targets aren't merely lofty yet amorphous aspirations. They are specific, concrete purposes. They define what is to be done. An attractive purpose can energize people, and an attractive purpose articulated as a specific target can energize people to do what is necessary to attain it. Achieving this purpose can provide a sense of accomplishment.

To accomplish something, a PerformanceStat leadership team needs to motivate improvements in both individual and collective performance. Well-structured targets—particularly targets for teams—can do precisely that. Both individuals and teams perform better when challenged by specific targets. Over the past 40 years, research—beginning with the work of Edwin Locke of the University of Maryland and Gary Latham of the University of Toronto—has demonstrated that setting targets has a significant impact on performance.[5]

Thus, an effective motivational tactic is setting performance targets that are specific, challenging, consequential, and broadly agreed upon.

1. *Specific* targets: An organization can always set vague goals (not real targets). To motivate people to accomplish something significant, it helps to set *specific* targets. Such targets create an unambiguous standard of performance for an agency and can create such standards for subunits and individuals.

2. *Challenging* targets: An organization can always set targets that are easy to achieve.[6] To motivate people to accomplish something significant, it helps to set challenging targets. Stephen Harkins of Northeastern University and Richard Petty of Ohio State University report that people are more likely to try harder when the task is difficult than when it is easy.[7]

3. *Consequential* targets: An organization can always set targets that only the organization's cognoscenti value. To motivate people to accomplish something significant, it helps to set targets that reflect citizen concerns. As the research of Adam Grant of the Wharton School reveals, people have a "prosocial motivation": They will work harder if their target possesses some social significance.[8]

4. *Broadly agreed upon* targets: An organization can always set targets that only the top executives think are important. To motivate people to accomplish something significant, it helps if the targets are not merely imposed on subunits, but suggested (or, at least, agreed to) by key people in these subunits. Indeed, those who head subunits sometimes even anticipate requests for new targets and offer some before they are imposed.[9]

Performance targets do not magically improve performance. Public agencies can create targets and yet fail to pursue them with energy and intelligence.[10] The leadership team needs to provide its people with the necessary operating capacity and to support their targets with other leadership behaviors.

Behavior 4: Making specific operational assignments can define who needs to fix which performance deficits next.

By developing a series of operational tasks that are directly linked to the organization's purpose and its targets, the leadership team can focus the efforts of subunit managers and front-line employees on the next steps for eliminating or mitigating specific performance deficits.

Some performance targets are daily, operational, output assignments. For example, fill all potholes in 48 hours. For such targets, data can be collected frequently—weekly, or even daily. Other performance targets are outcomes to be achieved over years or decades. For example, the Washington Traffic Commission established "Target Zero": zero highway deaths and serious injuries in 2030.[11]

For targets all along this spectrum, there are performance deficits that must be fixed before the target can be achieved. To be able to fill every pothole in 48 hours, a city's public works department may need new equipment. Or, it may need to redesign its operational routines. Once the relevant managers have agreed to this target, they need to think analytically about what performance deficits are preventing them from achieving it. Then, having identified what needs to be fixed, they need to assign an individual or team to fix each.

Sometimes, the link between target and deficit will be clear. It may even be clear who should eliminate or mitigate it. Not all targets, however, are directly operational. Yes, to achieve the target, an organization has to fix deficiencies in its operations. Still, the organization may not actually *produce* the result that the target measures. For example, no public agency in the state of Washington "produces" a reduction in deaths. A variety of state and local agencies do directly or indirectly help to reduce fatalities. So *who* should do *what* by *when* to ensure that by 2030 nobody in Washington dies from a traffic accident? It may not even be obvious *what* should be done. And even if the tasks are obvious, who should do each task may not be.

Setting a long-term outcome or output target and monitoring it often is not enough. The organization needs to analyze its data to identify key performance deficits. It needs to determine the specific tasks that, when completed, will help eliminate or mitigate each deficit. Then, it needs to give *specific* people these *specific* operational assignments to be completed by *specific* dates.

Behavior 5: Devoting resources and time to PerformanceStat can dramatize the chief executive's personal commitment to improving performance.

> *By investing significant resources in an analytic staff and assigning these individuals and other members of his or her leadership team to spend significant time on PerformanceStat, a chief executive demonstrates a serious, personal commitment to improving performance.*

John Ehrlichman, President Richard Nixon's domestic policy adviser, worried that cabinet secretaries, once appointed, would fail to remain loyal to the president and his agenda. "We only see them at the annual White House Christmas party," observed Ehrlichman; "they go off and marry the natives."[12] This organizational parochialism of subunit managers is not unique to the Nixon Administration. Indeed, it is not a government problem; it is a large-organization problem. Any executive with multiple and diverse responsibilities faces this challenge: "How do I get everyone to understand what I really want to accomplish?"

The chief executive can write and distribute memos, post a mission statement on walls, and give speeches. Who pays attention? Who thinks these communications represent core concerns of the chief executive (and not the pretty words of some intern in the communications office)?

What people really want to know is: Where is the chief executive investing discretionary resources? In government, most resources are fixed. Even an elected chief executive cannot easily reallocate them to other purposes (or even to other tasks to achieve the same purpose). Still, some resources are moveable. And people carefully watch what the chief executive does with those few scarce resources over which he or she does have discretion. By investing significant resources to build a talented, dedicated PerformanceStat staff; to establish a series of regular, frequent, integrated PerformanceStat meetings; and to require subunit managers and key members of his or her leadership team to participate in them; a chief executive is sending a clear signal. Everyone gets it: PerformanceStat is important.

Moreover, everyone in a large organization has a simple test for determining whether the chief executive cares about something:

> The chief executive really cares, if and only if he or she spends the most valuable resource of any public official—his or her personal time and the personal time of his or her top staff. If an executive does not invest any time in a problem, policy, program, or agency, everyone quickly figures out that—despite the rhetoric—the executive does not really care.

After all, every public executive—like every human—has exactly 168 hours in every week. No more. No less. And, at midnight on Saturday, those 168 hours are spent—gone. No one can put a few hours in the bank for another week; no one can borrow a single hour from a friend. Every week, every human has precisely the same time budget: 168 hours. Consequently, how an executive spends his or her time—and the time of the leadership team—sends unambiguous signals about what he or she thinks is important.

Alfred Ho of the University of Kansas analyzed the value that mayors place on performance measurement and observed, "If elected executives and legislators are not interested in performance measurement, managers may easily lose their enthusiasm about the tool because they do not see any payoff from their time investment and effort to collect and report the data."[13] In Baltimore for over a decade, three mayors, through the investment in biweekly CitiStat meetings, have dramatized that performance was high on their agenda and thus needed to be high on the agenda of every city agency.[14]

For any PerformanceStat to be effective, the leadership team must make a big time commitment.

Behavior 6: Conducting meetings can focus everyone's attention on what is most important.

By conducting an ongoing series of regular, frequent, integrated meetings, members of the leadership team can keep everyone focused both on the important macro purposes and on the essential actions and activities necessary to achieve these purposes.

No one likes meetings. Everyone goes to meetings. Meetings serve a variety of purposes. They resolve differences, establish priorities, make assignments, check on progress. . . . The list of reasons for holding meetings is long. So is the list of meetings that anyone must attend.

Thus, performance-focused managers do not schedule meetings carelessly. By holding another meeting, they are consuming that most valuable of resources: time that people could spend on other purposes. By regularly scheduling PerformanceStat meetings, by ensuring that the leadership team participates in these meetings, a chief executive is sending a powerful message: This is *really* important.

In Washington, D.C., Victor Prince was Mayor Fenty's director of CapStat. When Prince heard Fenty tell a caller on his VIP Blackberry (Fenty usually carried three) that he couldn't talk because he was in the middle of a CapStat meeting, Prince concluded that Fenty had decided that his CapStat was effective. The person who called was obviously important enough for the mayor to answer; but the CapStat meeting was even more important.

Behavior 7: Requesting and discussing frequent reports on progress can ensure that targets and assignments are taken seriously.

By asking subunit managers to report regularly and frequently in a quasi-public meeting on the status of their assignments, on their progress toward achieving their performance targets, and on their strategies for overcoming their performance deficits, the leadership team can remind everyone that these responsibilities are important.

Many assignments are made. Fewer are completed. Public employees have many bosses—direct superiors, other high-ranking officials, legislators, interest group officers, citizens—all of whom believe that they are entitled to make assignments. Their employees, however, cannot complete them all.

Thus, they triage. Perfectly reasonable. But do their triage choices make sense? Have they focused on the assignments that will help their organization fix its important performance deficits? Who knows? No one . . . unless someone asks for a progress report.

The need to make a progress report next week or next month can quickly affect an individual's triage decisions. Anyone who has to report back—in front of superiors, peers, and subordinates—on whether an assigned task has been completed is likely to put that task at the top of the to-do list. And, if the task is an essential prerequisite for others to complete their tasks, finishing it becomes even more imperative.

Bureaucracies produce reports, which, observed Anthony Downs, have three purposes:

1. "to inform high-level officials about what is happening";
2. "to remind each subordinate that he must meet certain performance standards";
3. to encourage subordinates "to carry out the desired performance—or at least to report having done so" through "the fear of punishment for failure."[15]

Of course, if the superiors never look at the reports (or never communicate that they have), subordinates will quickly learn to ignore them, thus subverting Downs's three purposes.

The approach to reporting employed by an effective PerformanceStat differs, however, from the usual bureaucratic routine. Traditional reports are annual or, at best, quarterly, available weeks or months after the reporting period. These sizable documents are so dense that not even a dedicated data wonk will read them. Moreover, the sheer volume of the data inhibits anyone's ability to determine what is going on. (Many dashboards that governments post on the web are mere data dumps.)[16] The traditional method of reporting neutralizes the impact of Downs's three purposes. "The normal way of functioning," reports an official in the Finnish Ministry of Finance, is that people "receive the report and they put it on the shelf."[17] Not just in Finland.

For an effective PerformanceStat, however, reports are frequent. They contain very current data. They include comparisons—with previous periods, with specific performance targets, and, perhaps, with similar subunits—thus providing a basis for judging whether performance is up or down. Moreover, agency managers report personally in response to direct questions from superiors, in front of peers and subordinates. To achieve Downs's three purposes, personal reporting at a quasi-public meeting can be very effective.

Behavior 8: Asking questions of individuals can promote personal responsibility.

By directly questioning specific subunit managers and their subordinates about their progress, the leadership team can establish in them a sense of personal responsibility for completing their assignments, achieving their targets, and improving performance.

Data and performance deficits. Targets and operational assignments. Meetings and reports. For a PerformanceStat leadership strategy, these are all essential. None, however, guarantees that any individual—subunit director, middle manager, front-line supervisor, or front-line worker—feels personally responsible for achieving a particular performance target or completing a specific assignment.

Public executives who seek to produce real results need a way to establish *who* is responsible for *what:* Which specific individual is responsible for which specific endeavors that will contribute to the desired results?

At an effective PerformanceStat session, direct questioning establishes this personal responsibility. These questions are not raised in a phone call, an email, or a memo circulated to a few people. At a PerformanceStat session, each question is addressed directly to a specific person who, at many PerformanceStat meetings, is standing at a podium while everyone else sits. The direct question identifies—for everyone in the room—who is responsible: "Have *you* completed your assignment?" Knowing that you will be asked this question two weeks from today at 8:30 in the morning in a room full of people can focus the mind. Managers who know that they will be asked this question in even a month or a quarter can't leave a PerformanceStat meeting saying, "Whew. I don't have to worry about this for a while."

Sometimes, the question is not asked of the subunit director but of another manager in the subunit. At least for large organizations, the subunit is usually represented not just by its director but by several other managers. Thus, questions can be addressed not only to the subunit director who is standing at the podium. They can be addressed to anyone, who can also be called to the podium.

These other agency managers were in the room during the last meeting—indeed, during all of last year's meetings. The chief executive and the PerformanceStat staff have learned their names. They know who is responsible for what. They remember what questions they asked at the last meeting and at the meeting before that, and at. . . . They remember who answered which ones satisfactorily, and whose answers required more follow-up.

Thus, each question is direct in two ways: first, because it is directed at a specific assignment, and second, because it is directed at a specific individual. Indeed, when members of the leadership team ask an individual a question, they may ask the individual to stand—to even come to the podium. When they ask a question, they leave no doubt who is personally responsible for answering it.

Moreover, a subunit manager can facilitate the process of identifying who within his or her unit is the responsible individual. The manager may call this individual to the podium. In fact, the subunit manager may step aside, leaving this individual standing at the podium alone. In doing so, the agency head clearly dramatizes which subordinate is responsible. Al Foxx, who served as director of Baltimore's department of transportation and then its department of public works, often did precisely this.

The podium and the questions—specific questions directed to specific individuals—clarify responsibility. The subunit head is responsible for every aspect of the subunit's performance. Every member of the subunit's management team also has personal responsibility for those aspects of performance for which his or her unit must make a contribution. Effective PerformanceStat sessions focus attention on each individual's specific, personal responsibility.

"In Western civilizations it is commonly believed that being identified as the source of one's accomplishments and errors has an important effect on performance," wrote three social psychologists: Kip Williams, Stephen Harkins, and Bibb Latané. Williams, Latané, and their colleagues conducted a couple of experiments in which the subjects thought that their own, individual effort could or could not be identified. They found that "when individual outputs are always identifiable (even in groups), people consistently exert high levels of effort, and if their outputs are never identifiable (even when alone), they consistently exert low levels of effort." "Identifiability," they conclude, is "an important, albeit complex, psychological variable and appears to have great implications for human motivation and performance."[18]

An effective PerformanceStat strategy seeks to establish each manager's "identifiability."

Behavior 9: Following up frequently on targets and assignments can create feedback that suggests adjustments.

By following up regularly on targets and assignments, the leadership team can generate feedback that compares progress with objectives and thus reveals whether the current approach needs to be modified or revamped and, perhaps, what kind of changes might produce better results.

In addition to the reports and questions, PerformanceStat meetings provide regular feedback. The data, the reports, the questions and answers, plus the leadership team's personal observations create the basis for feedback about how well the agency is doing.[19]

The leadership team can convey this feedback through complaints or compliments. To do so, they can draw on their own experience, or on information received from others, on data in the latest performance report, or on photos, projected on a screen, that document continuing problems. Moreover, the influence of this feedback can be significant. Jeffrey Pfeffer reports "impressive evidence that feedback, even in the absence of goal setting, can impact behavior."[20]

Behavior 10: Distributing comparative data widely can help every team appraise, without delusions, its own performance.

> By distributing data that compare the results produced by subunits with similar responsibilities, the leadership team can ensure that each subunit has an honest, realistic appreciation of how its performance compares with that of its peers.[21]

Large public agencies divide operational responsibilities among a variety of subunits—usually giving each responsibility for a particular geographic area. A school department divides responsibility for teaching students into different schools and different classes. U.S. government departments divide responsibilities into 10 (or so) regions.

Does each subunit know how well it is performing? Has each subunit duped itself into believing that it is at least above average—if not absolutely superior? Or does each possess the information necessary to make a realistic assessment of how well it is doing? If the managers for every subunit can assume that they are at least above average, they have little reason to try to improve. If, however, they frequently get data that compare the performance of every subunit, they will know where they stand on the organization's performance ladder. They will know which units are hitting their targets and which are not, which are making improvements and which are not.

The Bar Chart and The List (see chapter 11) are two simple ways to distribute comparative data. Both reward—with recognition and prestige—the high-performing units and their managers (see Behavior 12). And they both reprove—with peer embarrassment—the low-performing units and their managers (see Behavior 13). These two simple feedback practices can motivate unit managers who value peer esteem to focus on producing results.

Behavior 11: Scrutinizing the positive deviants can facilitate everyone's learning.

By identifying subunits that are achieving significant success and by analyzing and explaining the causes of their achievements, the leadership team can help other subunits learn how they too can improve performance.

To achieve a new performance target—for a higher level of performance or a new kind of performance—an organization must learn. It needs to do something new—something it has not done before. Thus, the organization needs to experiment with new ways to achieve the new target.

The Bar Chart or The List identifies not just the subunits that are underperforming but also the positive deviants—those subunits that have improved significantly. Unless, they are purely lucky (which the next round of comparative data is apt to expose), these subunits are doing something different—something that has helped them achieve their targets; something from which others could benefit.

Will the positive deviants want to share their knowledge? Not necessarily. Thus, in addition to creating incentives for experimentation, the leadership team needs to create incentives for successful experimenters to explain what they have learned (see appendix C). Only if these positive deviants share their knowledge will the entire organization benefit.

The positive deviants will be able to explain what they have done operationally. Unfortunately, they may not be able to explain *how* their new approach works. They may not fully understand the cause-and-effect relationships underlying their new, and apparently effective approach. As Carla O'Dell and Jackson Grayson of the American Productivity and Quality Center have lamented: "If only we knew what we know."[22]

Thus, there may be a puzzle to solve: What is the cause of the positive deviants' success? The analysts may have to examine the data. They may have to investigate not only what positive deviants are doing operationally, but also *how* these new operations create better results.

Behavior 12: Recognizing accomplishments publicly can confirm that success is both possible and valued.

By publicly and demonstratively recognizing meaningful accomplishments with intrinsic rewards for subunits, their employees, and their managers, the leadership team can demonstrate that significant successes can be achieved and are valued.

Matthew Gallagher has emphasized that the meetings he has chaired in Baltimore and Maryland separate "the contenders from the pretenders."[23] At many PerformanceStat meetings, I have a difficult time following the conversation. Even if I am familiar with the organization, even if I have previously been to some of its PerformanceStat meetings, the acronyms and code words are still whizzing over my head. Nevertheless, even I can separate the contenders from the pretenders. The answers to the questions combined with the body language tell all. If a subunit has not hit its targets, even a visitor can tell whether its managers have thought analytically and creatively about their performance tasks—whether they are seriously striving to make their approach work.

The answers offered in this quasi-public setting are quite revealing. Everyone in the room gets it. Everyone can figure out who is performing and who isn't. Everyone can discern who is trying and who isn't. Everyone can identify who accepts the need to improve performance as legitimate and who believes that everything has been and continues to be just fine.

Moreover, the questions and answers themselves provide the first level of reward. Like most of the public sector's significant rewards, they convey status. The answers to questions reveal—to everyone in the room—who is competent and who isn't. They reveal whose performance is truly outstanding, whose is acceptable, and whose is nonexistent. Some praise does help, but it doesn't need to be excessively exuberant. Indeed, one way to provide the top performers with an extra, intrinsic reward of internal prestige is to ask them to explain their strategies in formal training sessions for others.[24] In any organization, an honest, public compliment for what everyone recognizes as a job well done conveys status. Such status provides all sorts of benefits—including social capital that creates deference and warrants flexibility in making future strategic and tactical choices

Public executives are limited by the number and size of the extrinsic rewards that they can offer. Intrinsic rewards, however, are available with hardly any limits. PerformanceStat meetings provide an immediate opportunity to recognize those who warrant such intrinsic rewards.

Creative public executives realize that they also possess some extrinsic rewards—inexpensive ways to recognize a job well done. "I was talking with some executives from the business community," Martin O'Malley reported when he was mayor of Baltimore, "and one of them asked, 'Were those garbage men in your Orioles box the other night?'" Replied O'Malley, "Yes."[25]

The mayor of Baltimore has a box for all Baltimore Orioles' baseball games, and it comes with food and drink (and not just lemonade). At CitiStat meetings, O'Malley's leadership team was always looking for outstanding performers to whom they could give these tickets. On that night at Orioles Park, while business executives sat in one box, the next box was occupied by an excellent team from the city's Department of Public Works. Do you think they kept this game secret from their families and coworkers? Do you think they have forgotten the game?

Behavior 13: Reproving the recalcitrant can get everyone's attention.

By regularly questioning subunit managers about their lack of analytical insight, operational effectiveness, or strategic coherence, the leadership team can ensure that everyone in the organization understands that ineffectiveness (as well as indifference, incompetence, and insubordination) are unacceptable.

A leadership team that is making a significant, deliberate effort to improve performance cannot tolerate subunit managers who resist either actively or passively. Indifferent, incompetent, or insubordinate behavior by subunit managers automatically undermines the morale—and the motivation—of everyone else.

Fortunately, PerformanceStat meetings provide an opportunity to dramatize that such behavior is unacceptable, to reprove the recalcitrant, and to punish the saboteurs. To do so, the leadership team can simply ask follow-up questions, and more follow-up questions, and then even more follow-up questions. For the inability to provide adequate answers is personally and professionally embarrassing.

Some public employees believe it is unacceptable to embarrass a member of the team. Although "naming and shaming" is used in some organizations to punish and deter deviant behavior, some people find it unsavory when employed within their own agency.[26] In a small community, it strikes them as "unfair."

Suppose, however, that a subunit manager has been unable to answer a question about his or her own responsibilities. Suppose a manager has made no effort to improve performance. Suppose a manager asserts—data and evidence to the contrary—that everything is just fine. Suppose while others diligently work to improve performance, a manager ignores or even undermines these efforts. Does such a recalcitrant deserve to be treated the same as those who are struggling to improve? Is it "fair" to treat someone who is pursuing the organization's purposes and targets with commitment with the same respect as those who ignore them? Does not an organization's own integrity require its leadership to ask *all* of the organization's managers about what actions they have taken to complete their assignments, to eliminate their performance deficits, to achieve their targets?

The questioning at a PerformanceStat session need not be relentless. Effective follow-up merely needs to be "persistent." There is nothing unethical about asking a follow-up question—"Has this task been completed yet?"—and continuing to ask this question until the answer is a clear "yes." Will a manager who answers with a "no"—or an equivocation—be embarrassed? Undoubtedly. Who, however, *caused* this embarrassment? The questioner? Or the answerer?

Creating a target is a leadership responsibility—an ethical responsibility. Is the target *fair?* Can the managers, given their resources, be reasonably expected to achieve it by the target date? Are the targets created with *integrity?* Are different managers given targets of equal difficulty and significance?

Conducting the follow-up is also an ethical responsibility. Is the follow-up questioning done with *respect?* Are the words and the tone of the conversation *courteous?* Is the inquiry about a missed deadline handled with *compassion?* Are the explanations of extenuating circumstances treated with appropriate consideration for the challenges facing the manager?

Asking follow-up questions about important assignments designed to fix consequential performance deficits is an essential task of leadership—an ethical task. Failing to follow-up would be—given the importance of the underlying purpose—an ethical lapse.

Behavior 14: Telling stories can foster a results-focused culture.

> *By frequently telling stories about employees whose exemplary work significantly improved performance (and occasionally about the incompetent or indolent who undermined these efforts), the leadership team can validate the meaning underlying everyone's work and foster a results-focused culture.*

Thirty years ago, the idea of organizational culture first invaded the private sector and then government. "This culture stuff is great," said one business executive to another as they left a compelling seminar. "Get me a culture by Monday."[27]

Unfortunately, this executive already had a culture—and, undoubtedly, it was subtle and deep. This executive was not going have a new one by Monday. Observed John DiIulio, then a member of the White House staff, about U.S. government agencies: "Organizational cultures are among the hardest substances known to humankind." To his rule, DiIulio offered only one exception: "diamonds."[28]

Also unfortunately, most public agencies have not a results-focused culture, but a rule-obsessed one. After all, if civil servants follow the rules, it is hard to get in trouble. Yet, if civil servants follow all of the rules, it is hard to improve performance. The rules limit the discretion and flexibility that agencies need to improve their performance.

Edgar Schein of MIT defined organizational "culture" as "a pattern of shared basic assumptions that the group learned as it solved its problems of external adaptation and internal integration, that has worked well enough to be considered valid and, therefore, to be taught to new members as the correct way to perceive, think, and feel in relation to those problems."[29] Within most governments, there is little opportunity to earn meaningful rewards for positive contributions but multiple opportunities to incur serious penalties for some major or minor error.[30] Thus, many civil servants believe that one important problem is how to stay out of trouble. To solve this problem, the dominant culture teaches them to follow the rules assiduously.

To Caren Siehl of the Thunderbird School of Global Management and Joanne Martin of Stanford, culture is "the glue that holds an organization together." It consists of values, forms, and strategies: "the core values of the organization" that "define the basic philosophy or mission"; the forms that provide the "indirect, implicit, and subtle means of value transmission" including stories and rituals; and the strategies that managers use to reinforce the "underlying values of preferred culture."[31]

From this perspective, Kurt Lewin's strategy for replacing a rule-based culture with a results-focused one would be to:

1. "Unfreeze" the old core values that emphasize staying out of trouble by undermining the validity of the old stories (which told how people got into trouble only when they didn't follow the rules and how they stayed out of trouble when they did) and the old rituals that reinforced these stories.
2. "Move" the organization by establishing how the new behaviors do improve performance and providing real recognition for those who produce results.
3. "Freeze" the organization at the new level through new assumptions about the importance of performance, combined with new stories and new rituals that convey the values of the results-focused culture.

In many ways, an organization's stories define its culture. They provide the metaphors that explain how people should and should not behave. They illustrate what does and doesn't work. Stories convey the behaviors that are desirable and acceptable, objectionable and intolerable. They are an effective way to indoctrinate new members. Stories that are "told and retold," wrote Anne Khademian, "help newcomers understand what is important . . . and why." They help people "learn the language, rules of thumb, and understandings of the organization."[32]

Everyone tells stories to educate the newcomers. Front-line workers use them to prevent their new colleagues from becoming disruptive rate-breakers. But the organization's leadership team can also tell stories to communicate what they are trying to accomplish—or, as Philip Selznick put it—to convey "the institutional embodiment of purpose." Such stories—or what Selznick terms "socially integrating myths"—"are efforts to state, in the language of uplift and idealism, what is distinctive about the aims and methods of the enterprise."[33]

When front-line employees are telling stories to their colleagues, and when a leadership team is telling them to everyone in the organization, both are seeking to establish organizational norms—but not necessarily the same norms. Front-line workers may recount stories whose message undermines those from the leadership team. Thus, these leaders need to be strategic and energetic in establishing the validity and significance of *their* stories.

Fortunately, the PerformanceStat leadership strategy provides a built-in ritual for conveying these stories: the regular, frequent, integrated meetings. To many visitors, these meetings may appear to focus on the data; yet they are also about the stories. Many of these stories will be about failures of units or individuals to complete an assigned task, or to miss an opportunity to eliminate a performance deficit. Effective leaders, however, are always looking for stories to tell about middle-managers and front-line workers who did something extraordinary (or even quite ordinary) that had an extraordinary (or ordinary) impact on results.

In the competition over the validity of contradictory stories, the leadership team is at a disadvantage. Others are telling their stories to their colleagues every day. The leadership team, however, is able to tell its stories to a wide internal audience much less frequently. Thus, to keep everyone focused on what is to be accomplished, the members of the leadership team need to keep telling and retelling their stories. They need to identify an ongoing series of individuals and their actions to serve as real examples of how everyone in the organization can contribute to better performance. In addition to these heroes, they need to be sure that the malfeasors and misfeasors are not ignored, that stories about their sloth and its consequences become another defining myth.

The challenge is to freeze the results-focused culture while leaving it open to learning, adaptation, and improvement.

Behavior 15: Abetting everyone's implicit evaluation of everyone else can breed individual and team motivation.

By creating an environment in which everyone present at the PerformanceStat meetings will implicitly (and perhaps explicitly) evaluate everyone else who is present, the leadership team can motivate agencies, individuals, and teams to engage in results-focused behavior.

PerformanceStat sessions are not just *venues* for telling stories. They *become* stories. Participants easily remember what happened at the last meeting—what happened a month ago or a year ago. And if what happened was particularly remarkable—particularly commendable or particularly reprehensible—it will itself become a story.

Everyone in the room is observing the discussion—the questions asked; the answers given. At the same time, they are replaying in their heads the last meeting's questions and answers for which the current discussion is a follow-up. They know why today's questions are being asked. They are attentive to the answers being given. Simultaneously, they are evaluating these answers—and the person offering them. Indeed, at every PerformanceStat session, every individual's performance is being evaluated not just by the leadership team. As the team questions, praises, and reproves, everyone else is silently doing the same.

Every individual who is called upon to speak is constantly being evaluated by everybody else. These evaluations are informal, personal, implicit, never spoken. Still, we humans cannot help ourselves; we are always evaluating others. And this evaluation—both explicit (as expressed in a follow-up question or comment) and implicit (silently by others in the room)—is what creates the stress for which CompStat, CitiStat, and multiple PerformanceStats are known. Everyone knows that everyone else is watching. And evaluating.

Moreover, the research in social psychology suggests that evaluation can significantly enhance performance.[34] This motivation does not depend on a formal evaluation. The impact comes from the visibility to others of the individual's performance, which introduces the potential for evaluation.[35] When individuals stand up in front of others and answer questions about what their organization has done (and not done), everyone in the room has a chance to evaluate them.

The resulting stress—the desire to be perceived as competent by superiors, peers, and subordinates—can motivate better performance. But too much stress can suppress it. This relationship, first introduced a century ago by psychologists Robert Yerkes and John Dodson,[36] is described as an "inverted U."[37] As the stress first increases, so does performance; but as the stress continues to increase the performance curve peaks and then declines. Unfortunately, there exists no unique, discoverable peak that is the same for all people, for all tasks, in all circumstances. Thus, for any manager, it is not obvious when an evaluation creates too much pressure and thus begins to erode performance. Still, if there has been little or no pressure to improve performance, an initial increase in stress is apt to move most people *up* the Yerkes-Dodson curve.

The evaluations that occur in a PerformanceStat room not only create stress. They also inflict punishment. This punishment may be a sharp rebuke, a mild reprimand, a pointed question, a subtle inquiry, a sarcastic comment. Or it could simply be yet another, polite (but specific), follow-up question. It may be expressed in words or conveyed in tone and body language. Rarely will the punishment be a formal critique placed in the employee's file. Still, to move from a rule-obsessed to a results-focused culture, punishment of the recalcitrant may be essential. Charles O'Reilly of Sanford and Barton Weitz of the University of Florida conclude that the "appropriate use of sanctions may be perceived by [other] employees as legitimate and may be conducive to the development of productive group norms."[38] If indolent behavior goes unpunished—thus suggesting that it is acceptable—it can itself become the norm.

Each manager is, of course, being evaluated not just at the PerformanceStat sessions. Every manager is being evaluated by coworkers every day. These coworkers may, however, use criteria that are not identical—maybe even antithetical—to those of the leadership team. Consequently, a PerformanceStat leadership strategy will have little impact on front-line workers who never attend the meetings *unless* the directors of the various subunits use the same criteria at their own internal SubunitStat sessions. Unless leadership's results-oriented culture penetrates down to each working team, a PerformanceStat strategy will not create any evaluation or stress among those who do the real work and thus may have little impact on the day-to-day operations.

Behavior 16: Remaining persistent can prove that PerformanceStat isn't going away.

> *By making PerformanceStat a formal part of organizational life and assiduously adhering to the practices that they have established, members of the leadership team can demonstrate that their performance strategy is neither superfluous nor ephemeral.*

Another new chief executive. Another new management scheme. What's new?

The permanent civil service has seen it all before. New chief executive; new stuff—new rhetoric, new systems, yet another best-practices hammer from the airport bookstore.[39]

They've dealt with a series of these newbies. Some, they've educated. Others, they've fought. Others, they've simply ignored. Regardless, every "We-Be" assumes that the newbies—and their new ideas—will soon be gone.

In some jurisdictions, the permanent civil servants refer to the political appointees as the "tourists" and to themselves as the "residents." Elsewhere, they talk about themselves as the "We-Bes": "We be here before you're here; we be here after you're here."

They all know: "This, too, shall pass." As Abraham Lincoln observed of this maxim about transience: "How chastening in the hour of pride!"[40] For unless the new executive is persistent with his or her new PerformanceStat, its hour of pride will be short.

For too many new efforts to produce better results with an approach mimicking some of the characteristics of PerformanceStat, the hour of pride has, indeed, been short. With an initial burst of enthusiasm, technology is purchased to collect and project data. Analysts are hired to scrutinize these data. Meetings are held. The room is full.

Without any loss in timing, the shiny new hammer has made its entrance again with its usual flair. Everyone approves. We're all in mid-air. Isn't this bliss?

But where are the targets? The assignments? Where are the reports? The questions? Where is the follow-up? The recognition for improved performance? Where is the reproof for indifference—for recalcitrance? What is a better result? Indeed, what is the purpose?

For this new hammer, what counts as a nail?

Soon, the new hammer doesn't look so shiny. This hammer's hour of pride has quickly passed. It's yet another farce.

Stephanie Hirsch observed: "The mayor saying it should happen isn't enough."[41] So what is enough? Nothing really. Producing results is hard, and improving performance requires continuous effort. Nothing is ever enough. Unless the leadership team is constantly engaged, the focus on results will quickly atrophy.

If the chief executive and the leadership team are not persistent—if they don't demonstrate that their PerformanceStat is not going away—none of the other 15 causal behaviors will have much impact. They might as well send in the clowns. Indeed, maybe they're them.

16

Making the Leadership Commitment

What does the leadership team of a governmental jurisdiction or public agency need to do to ensure that the organization is able to realize the PerformanceStat potential?

"Thinking things up is not the same as making things happen."
THEODORE LEVITT, Harvard Business School[1]

"There is nothing more difficult to execute, nor more dubious of success, nor more dangerous to administer than to introduce a new order of things."
NICCOLÒ MACHIAVELLI, *The Prince*[2]

In 1993, Congress enacted and President Bill Clinton signed the Government Performance and Results Act or GPRA, which sought to "improve Federal program effectiveness and public accountability by promoting a new focus on results." It was also designed to "help Federal managers improve service delivery, by requiring that they plan for meeting program objectives."

That's an interesting juxtaposition of words: "help . . . by requiring." If the members of the leadership team of any organization conclude that improving the delivery of its services would benefit from the creation of a plan, can't they just do it?

Of course, the word "help" doesn't capture the spirit of this legislation. After all, Congress used this string of four letters only once. In contrast, it used the words "require," "required," or "requirement" 20 times. GPRA was not about *helping*. It was about *requiring*.

GPRA *required* each federal agency to create a five-year "strategic plan" with "a comprehensive mission statement" plus "general goals and objectives, including outcome-related goals and objectives." It *required* each agency to create an annual "performance plan" containing "performance goals" that are "objective, quantifiable, and measurable." It *required* this plan to include "performance indicators" for "measuring or assessing the relevant outputs, service levels, and outcomes." GPRA also *required* each agency to produce a "performance report" that includes "actual results for the three preceding fiscal years" plus "actual program performance achieved compared with the performance goals."[3]

That's a lot of "help."

Congress is, unfortunately, in a difficult position. It can require a federal agency to do a lot of different, specific things. It cannot, however, require it to take any of these things seriously. Indeed, if the members of the leadership team of a public agency take performance seriously, they do not need legislation to "help" or "require" them to create goals, plans, and reports. They would just do it. Conversely, if agency executives have too many other demands and worries, they can give all such hoop-jumping requirements to an intern.

In 2010, Congress passed and President Barack Obama signed the GPRA Modernization Act.[4] In this legislation, the word "help" disappeared. But the words "require," "required," and "requirements" made 55 appearances—that's nearly a 200 percent improvement. Indeed, this is "an act to require quarterly performance assessments of Government programs for purposes of assessing agency performance and improvement." The new, improved GPRA still required agencies to create strategic plans, performance plans, performance goals, performance indicators, and performance reports. It also required the director of the Office of Management and Budget (OMB) to "coordinate with agencies to develop the Federal Government performance plan."

The modernized GPRA also introduced "priority goals." From its "performance goals," each agency is now required to select its "priority goals." Moreover, the director of OMB is required to "develop priority goals to improve the performance and management of the Federal Government." In the new legislation, the words "goal" or "goals" appeared 151 times, nearly triple the 56 times it was used in the original. How about that for performance improvement?

Furthermore, for each of its performance goals, an agency is required to identify a "goal leader" who is "responsible for the achievement" of the goal. Similarly, for each of OMB's priority goals, the federal performance plan has to "identify a lead Government official who shall be responsible for coordinating the effort to achieve the goal."

Finally, the act requires the director of OMB to conduct a quarterly performance review with the "lead government official" for each governmentwide priority goal. Similarly, the head of each agency is required to meet quarterly with the "goal leader" for each of its own priority goals.

In requiring, for each priority goal, the creation of a "goal leader" and a "lead government official," Congress is obviously looking for someone to hold accountable. Since GPRA was modernized, public executives in Washington may have been tripping over each other to be identified as a "goal leader" or as a more prestigious "lead government official." Or, they may have all gone into hiding, believing that the only possible reward for being a "goal leader" is the opportunity to be held publicly accountable at a televised Congressional hearing.

Congress did recognize that missions, plans, goals, indicators, and measures do not—all by their miraculous selves—automatically produce better results. To improve performance, government also needs leadership, active leadership, human leadership.

Congress, however, can't require leadership.

The Essential Role of the Leadership Team

What improves performance? Politicians and academics, think tanks and management gurus have offered a panoply of changes to the formalities of government. The possibilities include legislative reforms, executive orders, data systems, and management models. All have been suggested. All have been tried. Most contain useful ideas. Sometimes they produce some successes. Sometimes they do not. Regardless of what those who create the various formalities believe or promise, neither legislative reforms, nor executive orders, nor data systems, nor management models will magically improve performance.

Without the full engagement of an organization's leadership team, none will have—can have—much impact. If the operational objective is to improve the performance of a public agency, and if the analytical objective is to understand how the performance of a public agency improves, the appropriate focus is not reforms, or orders, or systems, or models. The focus of analysis should be the behaviors of the leadership team. Without the clear commitment and active engagement of the leadership team, the formalities will have little impact.

Why? Because the members of the leadership team are the humans who implement these formalities. They undertake the essential tasks that drive improvements in performance. They:

Articulate the organization's purpose;
Identify the organization's performance deficits;
Set the targets for eliminating or mitigating those deficits;
Identify the initial strategies for achieving these targets;

Decide what data need to be collected and analyzed;

Initiate the problem-solving discussions to determine what strategies are
working, what ones are not, and why;

Help the organization learn;

Motivate people to contribute significantly to the effort; and

Follow up to ensure that commitments have been fulfilled.

Reforms, orders, systems, and models cannot make these things happen. Only people can.

These people are real leaders. They might be the people at the top of the organization's formal hierarchy—those traditionally charged with these responsibilities. But their formal status does not make them leaders. It only gives them the opportunity to exercise leadership.[5]

They are not, however, the only ones. If a governor does not want take on these leadership responsibilities, a department head can. If a cabinet secretary avoids them, an agency director can take them up. Others—people with a purpose—can simply take up the responsibility for producing results. In the process, they exercise leadership.

Unfortunately, reforms, orders, systems, and models do not convert people with impressive titles into leaders. These formalities can designate who must report on compliance with which requirements. They can convince agencies to install a data system or copy a management model. Such formalities cannot, however, require people to do any of these tasks with the intelligence, creativity, subtlety, and commitment that will have a real impact on performance.

Creating the Illusive Synergy

PerformanceStat isn't all that different. And yet it is. Yes: An effective PerformanceStat employs a variety of well-established leadership strategies and management tactics. It includes purpose and targets, responsibility and discretion, data and analysis, meetings and questions, feedback and follow-up, learning and adaptation. With the exception of the technology, none of these components is all that new or different or impressive.

What is new is the *personal commitment* of the leadership team to producing results—the *analytical and comprehensive combination* of various performance-enhancing activities into a coherent macro strategy whose individual components reinforce each other synergistically to produce improved results. The members of the leadership team don't just want a few better results. They don't just want to improve performance a notch or two. They want to introduce Machiavelli's "new order of things." They seek to build a permanent results-focused mindset and the future operational capacity necessary to continually ratchet up performance.

Every individual component of a PerformanceStat leadership strategy makes an individual contribution to improved results. The leadership team does not, however, implement each component in isolation. The feedback is connected to the targets. The targets are connected to the performance deficits. The performance deficits are connected to the data. The data are connected to the analysis. The analysis is connected to the meetings. The meetings are connected to the follow-up. And everything is connected to purpose.

Underlying the successes (and the failures) in improving performance is the behavior of a leadership team. Its members have (or have not) dedicated themselves to achieving specific public purposes, they have developed a strategy that matches their circumstances, and they have figured out how to motivate their organization to focus on producing results. They have committed themselves to creating a comprehensive and synergistic combination of activities, to learning how they work (or don't work), and, as they learn, to making the necessary adaptations.

They don't just want a few better results today. They want to introduce a new, results-focused "order of things." They are Peter Drucker's monomaniacs with a mission.

Enemies to the New Order of Things

PerformanceStat can be different because the leadership team is committed to deploying a collection of mundane managerial mechanisms in a synergistic combination designed to introduce "a new order of things." This commitment to managerial synergy is what distinguishes an effective PerformanceStat leadership strategy from halfhearted, short-lived pretenders that produce nothing but cynicism. The members of the leadership team are demanding results not just from their organization and their subordinates but also from themselves. They are telling citizens to expect results.

Unfortunately, not everyone in the organization immediately signs on to this commitment. The leadership team may be able get away with focusing on results. The rest just want to stay out of trouble. They have their own priorities that may be completely unrelated to the leadership team's purposes. Many may never have been pressed to produce results. Others have experienced some past managerial pretension about performance only to observe how quickly it was replaced by another infatuation. They have seen it before. They know where it ends. Nowhere.

Moreover, many public agencies have their own cultures and subcultures. They have clans whose values and beliefs, combined with subtle and ritualized sanctions, establish what is acceptable and what is not. And the values and beliefs of these cultures and clans can be dysfunctional. In the police departments of New York and Los Angeles, in the city governments of Baltimore and Somerville, indeed in other agencies and jurisdictions whose leadership created a PerformanceStat strategy, this dysfunction became obvious. These clans were quite tolerant of collective and individual behavior that was inconsistent with the organization's purpose.

Different organizations might have different cultures, but one problem common to many large organizations (public, nonprofit, and for-profit) is simple indifference. Too many employees don't care. Too many don't care whether they do the job right, whether they do the job on time, whether they do the job completely. They don't care how they treat citizens. They simply don't care. Moreover, a strong and pervasive subculture combined with peer pressure for conformity[6] limits the ability of agency managers to persuade employees to care.

Thus, if the members of the leadership team are serious about their commitment to producing results and improving performance, they have "to introduce a new order of things." They can't be content with "thinking things up"; they have to commit to "making things happen."

Still, Machiavelli's warning about the difficulty and danger is real and serious. For, he explained, a new order of things will create both allies and enemies, but not with equal intensity: "He who introduces it has all those who profit from the old order as his enemies, and he has only lukewarm allies in all those who might profit from the new."[7] Those who might profit from a new, performance-driven government are its citizens. Yet, they might not be even lukewarm allies. They might not even understand that they are allies. And if these citizens were allies (whether lukewarm, quite warm, or very hot), they would not know how to support the new order. Meanwhile, those who profited from the old order are quite capable of resisting.

To produce results and improve performance, the members of the leadership team face a variety of obstacles. With few active allies, they confront dedicated adversaries. With constraints on their ability to influence the behavior of public employees, they face competitive influences from the existing culture. With limited ability to reward cooperative behavior, they seek to impose new responsibilities on these employees.

To introduce a new results-focused order of things, the leadership team needs a strategy. A PerformanceStat strategy can help—but only if the team makes a full, *leadership* commitment.

Disrupting Complacency

Most of the time, most people in most organizations are mostly satisfied:

> "We're working as hard as we can."
> "Given the circumstances, we're doing a good job."
> "Sure, some people complain but most people are satisfied, and we have too many people telling us what we can and can't do."
> "If the budget shop would give us the funds we asked for, we could do a better job; but they won't, so we can't."

In many organizations, the classic response is: "Sure, we want to do better, but given our circumstances and constraints, there's no way that can happen."

This claim is hard to rebut. The historical record does not suggest that the agency can do significantly better. Similar agencies in similar jurisdictions are not doing much better. And, if such agencies do exist, there is still a well-practiced and quite plausible counter: "If we had their [fill in a resource], we could produce [fill in a result]." Or simply: "They are weird."

Such complacent thinking is not a government problem. It is a large organization problem. People in the private sector can also become complacent, concluding that (1) their business is doing quite well, and (2) circumstances prevent them from doing much better. There is, however, one important difference: Competition—a cheaper product, an improved product, a different product—can force the business to go out of business. The public agency, however, continues on. In government, Dutch Leonard of Harvard's Kennedy School is wont to say, "Mediocrity is sustainable." Thus, many people in many public agencies set for themselves a modest performance target (or vague performance goal) all quite consistent with the available "facts." Complacency is attractive.

An executive who wishes to improve performance has to disrupt this complacency. For this purpose, a crisis can be valuable. It tells the world that the organization's performance is inadequate. It tells the organization that the world knows this. A crisis is an indisputable signal that things have to change. A crisis disrupts complacency.

So does a performance target, a stretch target, an unreasonable target.

It Can't Be Done

In 1933, when President Franklin D. Roosevelt first proposed the Civilian Conservation Corps (CCC), every member of his cabinet told him: It can't be done.

The United States was facing its worst economic crisis ever. Still the new president's senior executives told him that it can't be done.

Fortunately, Roosevelt was undeterred by such pragmatic considerations. Indeed, explained Jonathan Alter in his book on Roosevelt's first hundred days, "FDR's obliviousness to theories of pragmatism was a blessing, for while his solution was practical, his means of getting there were not, or so thought those around him." On March 21, 1933, only 17 days after taking office, Roosevelt outlined his idea, reported Alter, "in a message to Congress designed to tell the country that relief and job creation were on the way." FDR wanted to get young men working—and quickly. Still, "for all sorts of logistical reasons," Alter continued, the President "was told repeatedly that this was simply impossible."[8]

FDR had a stretch target: He wanted 250,000 young men working in the national forests that very summer. His message to the Department of Labor and its secretary, Frances Perkins, reported Alter, was straightforward: "Do it now and I won't take any excuses." Then, continued Alter, "after setting this seemingly unrealistic target, FDR worked on the gearing to make it happen."[9] In fact, it happened very quickly. On April 17, the Forest Service opened its first camp. By June 29, the CCC had 270,000 men in 1,300 camps.[10] Zero to 270,000 in a hundred days.

"It can't be done." Whenever a public executive thinks about setting a specific target, let alone a true stretch target—he or she will hear these four words. Although most public executives may lack the personal determination, managerial skills, and political savvy that FDR had acquired through a half-century of personal adversity, executive experience, and leadership challenges, they can still develop his professional commitment to a specific result.

Roosevelt was, of course, being unreasonable. Yet, as George Bernard Shaw explained, unreasonableness is essential: "The reasonable man adapts himself to the world; the unreasonable one persists in trying to adapt the world to himself. Therefore all progress depends on the unreasonable man."[11]

William Bratton was unreasonable. So was Martin O'Malley. So is every public executive who establishes a stretch target. They will all be told: "It can't be done."

Learning from the Dissimilar

Congress cannot require leadership. It cannot require learning. It cannot require public executives to learn from what is happening in their own organization, which (presumably) they know quite well. Certainly Congress cannot force public executives to learn from circumstances that appear to be very different.

As a young scholar, Woodrow Wilson used a now-famous metaphor to explain how governments in the United States could employ management ideas from European monarchies:

> If I see a murderous fellow sharpening a knife cleverly, I can borrow his way of sharpening the knife without borrowing his probable intention to commit murder with it; and so, if I see a monarchist dyed in the wool managing a public bureau well, I can learn his business methods without changing one of my republican spots. He may serve his king; I will continue to serve the people; but I should like to serve my sovereign as well as he serves his.

Wilson stressed that strategies from elsewhere "must be adapted," while urging Americans "not to be frightened at the idea of looking into foreign systems of administration for instruction and suggestion."[12]

Unfortunately, many public officials are frightened at the idea of learning from circumstances that appear to be different. Not only did Tony Bovaird and Elke Löffler discover that many people believe: "Nothing new works and, if it works somewhere else, it must be because they are weird." They also learned that many have concluded, "We can only learn from places that are *just like us.*"[13] Yet, to learn to improve, public executives have to look to different jurisdictions and agencies. If people can only learn from places that are "just like us," they can never learn. For no organization will ever find another that is *"just like us."*

When a public executive explains that another organization has accomplished something significant, he or she is told: "Yes, but. . . ." "Yes, but their circumstances are different." To which Shaw had yet another retort: "People are always blaming their circumstances for what they are. I don't believe in circumstances. The people who get on in this world are the people who get up and look for the circumstances they want, and, if they can't find them, make them."[14]

Anyone who can't get something done (or who won't try to get something done) can always blame unfavorable circumstances. Thus, to produce significant results, a public executive needs to be unreasonable. Jack Maple certainly was: "The leadership's [NYPD's] goals sometimes border on the unreasonable because that's the only way to ensure at least reasonable results."[15]

Moving the Unmovable

Jeffrey Pfeffer and Robert Sutton identified a number of "dangerous half-truths" about organizations. One is that "organizational change invariably takes a long time, is hard to accomplish, and is best if done slowly." This self-fulfilling idea, they argued, "is a big reason why profound change is so rarely attempted." Yet, change does not have to take a long time. In fact, they wrote, "organizations can change remarkably fast when the right conditions are in place." Organizations, they observed, "are surprisingly adaptive and can change quickly and easily."[16]

Pfeffer and Sutton identified four conditions that make change possible:

1. People are dissatisfied with the current situation, provoking them to question how they are doing things. "Stretch goals" can "generate a sense of striving and dissatisfaction with the status quo."

2. People are clear about the direction in which they need to move. "Being specific about the few things that matter most is a hallmark of effective leadership."

3. People are convinced—through the confidence (indeed, overconfidence) of the leadership team—that the change will succeed. "Talented individuals are more likely to want to work on things that look as if they are going to be successful, and to the extent that more talent and support gets attracted to projects, the projects will be more successful."

4. People accept that the change will be messy and that the leadership team considers the inevitable mistakes, confusion, and anxiety as problems to be fixed, as well as opportunities for learning. These problems are not malfeasances for which it is necessary to assign blame. The leadership team needs to "prepare people to confront and live with ambiguity."

If these conditions don't exist, they argue, the leadership team needs to create them.[17]

Exploiting Small Wins

A stretch target not only creates a specific purpose. It also disrupts complacency, forcing people to confront their own "dissatisfaction" with the organization's and their own performance. Yet this stretch target can only be achieved through significant changes in behavior that require experimentation, failure, and learning. How will people ever gain the confidence that Pfeffer and Sutton think is essential for them to succeed? Karl Weick of the University of Michigan has an answer: "a strategy of small wins."

Weick asked why public problems are so unsolvable and concluded: "People often define social problems in ways that overwhelm their ability to do anything about them." As an alternative, Weick proposed that we reformulate "social issues as mere problems . . . as a series of controllable opportunities of modest size that produce visible results." These individual successes "may seem unimportant," he wrote. Still, "a series of wins at small but significant tasks," he continued, "reveals a pattern that may attract allies, deter opponents, and lower resistance to subsequent proposals."[18]

To Weick, a "small win" is "a concrete, complete, implemented outcome of moderate importance." Moreover, because each result is visible, it possesses "immediacy, tangibility, and controllability." Then, "once a small win has been accomplished, forces are set in motion that favor another small win."[19]

For the leaders of a public agency who seek to produce results, the lesson is clear: Don't try to immediately jump to the top of the performance mountain. Don't try to produce international peace and harmony by the end of the fiscal year. Instead, create both an overall stretch target and a series of intermediate performance targets each of which will move the organization one step closer to accomplishing its purpose.

Ratcheting up performance is an addiction strategy: Create a stretch target. Then break it down into a series of incremental targets that people can hit relatively quickly and easily. Get them hooked on success. Give them an opportunity to earn that adrenaline rush that comes from accomplishing something worthwhile, and then give them the challenge of accomplishing even more.

When a public agency is ratcheting up its performance, each small win creates not just a sense of accomplishment; it also establishes a new and higher plateau— a new baseline from which to ratchet up to the next level.

From Operational Production to Collaborative Outcomes

When Martin O'Malley launched CitiStat, he focused on getting city agencies to simply do their primary jobs. To learn how to make their adaptation of CompStat work, O'Malley's leadership team had to focus on the basics: Baltimore upgraded the city's 311 phone system, created the CitiTrack database, and set specific targets for each service request.

Baltimore's classic target was the 48-hour pothole guarantee. When citizens called 311 to request that a pothole be filled, they were told that it would be done in 48 hours. Then O'Malley's leadership team monitored and motivated city employees to ensure that these targets were met. As a result, city employees filled the potholes quickly. And citizens noticed! Calling city hall actually produced the desired result. Thus, the number of pothole calls to 311 jumped significantly (see chapter 7).

A few years later, when Joseph Curtatone was elected mayor of Somerville, he took his leadership team to visit Baltimore and CitiStat. Soon, Curtatone had

SomerStat and 311 up and running. Curtatone, too, focused first on delivering basic city services.

Yet others complained: What's the big deal? So they can fill potholes. Weren't they always supposed to do that? If a city were really innovative, it would invent something to eliminate the need to ever again fill potholes. Perhaps. But isn't that what the private sector is supposed to do so well? Rust-belt mayors would rush to buy a magic elixir that would banish potholes.

Meanwhile, some mayors who have learned to use their PerformanceStat to fix basic service delivery—to fill potholes, trim trees, and eradicate graffiti—broadened their use of the strategy.

In November 2012, one of Baltimore's CitiStat meetings had nothing to do with potholes. It focused on Mayor Stephanie Rawlings-Blake's "Vacants to Value" (V2V) effort to clean up and redevelop vacant and abandoned buildings, to increase property values, and to attract businesses and residents.[20] Rawlings-Blake is the city's third mayor to employ CitiStat to achieve her purposes. But her V2V requires more than getting city employees to do their tasks properly and promptly. Thus, the CitiStat room was overflowing with 50 managers from five departments—Housing, Transportation, Planning, Recreation and Parks, and Police—as well as the Bureau of Solid Waste. Each has responsibilities for the V2V outcomes that require them to collaborate with others.

Four days later in Somerville—at a meeting on Youth SystemStat—the story was similar. This SomerStat session focused on the various public and civil-society systems that "shape outcomes relating to children and youth." One such outcome is: "Young people succeed throughout their academic career and graduate from high school prepared to succeed in life." Producing this outcome is not the sole responsibility of one city agency. It, too, requires collaboration.

PerformanceStat 1.0, 2.0, and 3.0

Both Baltimore and Somerville advanced from PerformanceStat 1.0, to PerformanceStat 2.0, and now to PerformanceStat 3.0.

PerformanceStat 1.0 is about *creating operational effectiveness*. It requires managers and employees—with the leadership team's prodding—to do the basic tasks promptly and properly. It is about production: getting the primary outputs done on time.

PerformanceStat 2.0 is about *redesigning primary functions*. It requires managers and employees—with the leadership team's prodding and guidance—to rethink how they accomplish their purposes. It is about identifying new, innovative ways to produce the standard outputs.

PerformanceStat 3.0 is about *creating outcomes*. It requires managers and employees from *multiple* agencies—with the leadership team's prodding, guidance, and analytical engagement—to figure out who needs to collaborate with whom to produce the desired outcomes. It is about assigning priorities to outcomes and then motivating everyone to learn how best to achieve them.

When governmental jurisdictions and public agencies graduate from PerformanceStat 1.0, to 2.0, and then to 3.0, they move from ProductionStat, to OutputStat, to CollaborationStat.[21] Before they can make such collaboration work, however, they have to learn to fix the potholes.

Purpose, Ego, and Motivation

Effective public executives seek to tap the egos of key staff and agency directors. These executives recruit them with the promise that their work will be professionally interesting, socially worthwhile, and personally rewarding. Explaining the impact of their PerformanceStat strategy, public executives promise people that they will be engaged in an exciting innovation in management and leadership. They seek to convince potential recruits that they will have an opportunity to earn a sense of true accomplishment that they might not get working for another organization. To make a PerformanceStat strategy effective, an executive needs to enlist people who seek a consequential challenge and then give it to them. Without such a recruitment strategy, an executive will not have people with the egos and talents necessary to ratchet up performance. Anthony Downs has proposed the "Law of Progress Through Imperialism." which simply states: "The desire to aggrandize breeds innovation."[22] To improve performance, an agency manager needs at least a small, latent desire to aggrandize.

After all, the significant results sought by any real PerformanceStat cannot be achieved by merely working harder. To truly improve performance, people will need to work smarter—a lot smarter. Attempting to work smarter is, however, a more perilous undertaking. Working harder is straightforward: Continue to employ current practices; just do them faster, better, cheaper. Working smarter, however, involves uncertainty: Maybe this new approach is actually dumber? At the beginning, there will be multiple opinions about whether this "smarter" approach is really smarter—or dumber, more expensive, or downright pernicious.

Moreover, working smarter conflicts with working harder. Time devoted to figuring out how to work smarter incurs an opportunity cost: less time to work harder. Thus, humans tend to focus on working harder, for it can show immediate if small improvements. Actually, getting people to work harder—to implement their basic tasks with dedication and energy—is often the correct first step. Usually, people will consider trying to work smarter only after they have exhausted the benefits of working harder.

A focus on improved implementation of current approaches may, however, inhibit people from considering how to work smarter. It may harden personal and organizational commitments to existing approaches. It may reinforce both the formal operating procedures and informal norms that sustain established approaches. For example, Malcolm Sparrow, Mark Moore, and David Kennedy argued that police departments that measure their performance by the time it takes them to respond to 911 calls lock themselves into a technology, a set of operational tactics, and an approach to policing that prevents them from thinking about different purposes and different strategies.[23]

In a bureaucracy, concluded Downs, creativity is neither natural nor inevitable: "the quasi-alien nature of creativity means that special incentives are required within a bureau to promote the generation, adoption, and acceptance of important innovations."[24] PerformanceStat can help create these incentives.

Herbert Simon argued that any organization's "top supervisors" affect the "organization's work" by "'influencing' rather than 'directing'" the "decisions and behavior" of the "intermediate supervisors" and "the operative employees."[25] PerformanceStat is one strategy for influencing public employees. And because these employees function in a bureaucracy (and thus are difficult to influence), effective PerformanceStat meetings are frequent opportunities to influence a large number of people. Like the data, the meetings are not an end in themselves; they do not themselves produce any results. Still, executives can use these meetings to influence not only employees' short-run behavior but also their long-run socialization. Frequent PerformanceStat meetings are one way to influence the culture of public agencies. These meetings are integrating activities that bring together the performance purpose and the performance deficits, the data and the analysis, the assignments and the reports, the questions and the feedback, the comparative data and the stories, the recognition and the reproofs.

Performance Technology and Performance Politics

"Performance measurement" and "performance management"—these two phrases are often used interchangeably by both public managers and university scholars. The implicit (never stated) assumption is: If you get the measures right, the management stuff is automatic or simple.

Thus, "performance measurement" and "performance management" are presented as a technocratic undertaking. Get the measures right, and the rest will follow. And getting the measures right is obviously a technical task to be delegated to the measurement technocrats.

No one is ever this blunt. None of this is ever said. It is simply implicit—an assumption so obvious that it need not be stated. No need to discuss it.

Thus in many governmental jurisdictions, the task of improving performance is given to the budget shop.[26] These technocrats know how to manage the budget numbers. They are good at this. They are particularly good at saying "no." (If you don't learn how to say "no," you don't last long in a budget shop.) Unfortunately, these technocrats know little about leadership or management. When it comes to motivating people, saying "no" and accounting prowess are not particularly helpful. As CitiStat director Christopher Thomaskutty once noted: "If we gave CitiStat to the budget office, the primary measure of performance would be dollars saved."

The budget office is certainly a political office. Decisions about what agencies get how much money for what programs are political decisions. But these political decisions are different from deciding what targeted results should be produced by when. And setting targets is different from motivating people to achieve them.

For several decades there has been much talk about performance budgeting. But what is performance budgeting? Does it mean that an agency's budget contains some performance measures, which someone may scan at the end of the fiscal year? Or does it mean that an agency's budget contains some performance targets, which will be used to help determine how much funding the agency will get next year? If so, what does a municipality do when the fire department doesn't make its performance targets? Cut its budget?

Government budgets are political. They reflect how much the body politic wants to invest to achieve different public purposes. If the schools are doing quite well and the fire department is not, a municipality could quite reasonably choose to spend *more* on fire and *less* on schools.

Certainly the failure of a municipal fire department to hit its performance targets is relevant. It suggests that someone needs to do something to fix the department. Who, however, should do what? Fixing the fire department might require a new leadership team. It might require a new fire-fighting strategy, or a new fire-prevention strategy. The department's inability to achieve its targets does not reveal who should do what. Determining exactly what needs fixing requires analysis. This analysis might reveal that improving the fire department's performance to a satisfactory level will require *more* funding. It might suggest all the fire department needs to do is reallocate its existing resources. Or the analysis might expose wasteful spending and uncover an opportunity to both reduce costs and improve performance.

The performance office is also a political office. It makes very political decisions. It decides (1) what results to achieve by when and (2) how to mobilize and deploy the available human, financial, and other resources to produce these results.

Any real PerformanceStat is about more than the technicalities of measurement—much more. It is not about performance systems. It is about performance leadership. And also about performance politics.

A Performance Target Is a Political Target

Few public executives put improving performance at the top of their own political agendas. Those who do, however, make their targets public. By doing so, they make a commitment that is both personal and political. For once a public executive makes a public commitment to achieving a specific target by a specific date, he or she has made a personal and political commitment.

This is dangerous. The public executive who establishes an explicit, public, performance target is painting a bull's-eye on his or her back. The executive is establishing a basis for criticism—indeed, multiple bases for personal and political criticism.[27] No wonder a governor once told his department heads: "Never put a number and a date in the same sentence."[28]

Because, the selection of a performance target is not at all technical, the choice is a judgment call—a political call. It will always be open to debate. And this debate will be political. Why would any chief executive want to encourage an open debate about his or her personal intelligence, let alone his or her personal commitment to serving the public?

Politics is, of course, how a society makes important choices about the purposes and strategies to which it will allocate its scarce resources. When Rudolph Giuliani was elected mayor of New York, to make good on his campaign promise to do something about crime, he appointed William Bratton as police commissioner. When Martin O'Malley was elected mayor of Baltimore, to make good on his campaign promise to improve basic services, he created CitiStat to ensure that his department heads did precisely that. These elected executives made a personal commitment to produce specific results.

These two mayors selected results they would pursue in consultation with citizens during their campaigns for office. Then, having won, they and their politically appointed executives were committed—explicitly and publicly—to the results they promised.

Outcomes and Outputs—Responsible for Which?

What kind of target should a public executive choose? An outcome? An output? It all depends. It depends on the kind of data that are available to provide feedback to help improve performance. Sometimes an outcome can be achieved quickly and is easily measurable. In this case, an outcome target may make sense. But sometimes the real outcome will not be achieved for years, or is hard to specify and measure, or is hard to attribute to the work of the organization. In such situations, an output target may make sense. If the targeted output is designed to fix an important performance deficit, achieving this target will help to achieve the desired outcome.

Daily, police get both outcome data (crimes reported) and output data (arrests made). Moreover, they can relatively quickly—not just over decades but within years or even months—affect both their arrest output and the crimes-reported outcomes. These data tend to be pretty reliable (compared with a lot of public-sector data) and can be monitored by citizens. Thus, police executives who seek to improve performance can use both output and outcome data. After all, citizens care about both.

Daily, the public works department can get output data: potholes filled. Public works can also get outcome data : smoothness of the roads, commute times. Such outcome measures can, however, be subjective and open to debate. In contrast, the data on potholes filled can be very accurate, very observable, very connected to the department's work, and directly related to a common citizen concern. In this situation, short-run output data supported by longer-run outcome data may make the most sense.

Those who use output data need to answer their own *"How?"* question: *"How* will better outputs help to create better outcomes?" Sometimes the output-outcome connection is direct: Filled potholes create smoother streets (and fewer front-end realignments). Sometimes the output-outcome connection is less obvious: Higher test scores might (or might not) help create productive employees and responsible citizens.

Thus, using the output of test scores to measure a school system's performance creates a controversy. Some argue that the tests fail to capture what they want their schools to accomplish. Others, while recognizing the inadequacies of test scores, insist that they provide the best data that can be collected. Then they try to both create better tests and use the data more creatively to identify key performance deficits.

These choices are subjective. They are political. As Dennis Smith observed, "What constitutes an outcome is a value judgment, and in a democracy values are always contested terrain."[29]

Citizen Expectation and Citizen Satisfaction

Targeting a big jump in performance has significant advantages. It gets everyone's attention. It gets employees' attention. It gets citizens' attention. And, as paradoxical as it may sound, a public agency may actually benefit if citizens have high expectations for performance.

Gregg Van Ryzin of Rutgers University explored how citizens evaluate the performance of urban services—specifically the services provided by New York City (including such basics as police, schools, road conditions, and the cleanliness of streets). Obviously, citizens who reported that the city's performance was low were less satisfied than citizens who reported that performance was high. But citizens' prior expectations also influenced their satisfaction. Citizens who reported that their prior expectations were low but who rated actual city performance as high were *less* satisfied than those who reported both high expectations and high performance. As for citizens who reported low performance, those who had high prior expectations were still more satisfied than those with low expectations.[30]

Thus, wrote Van Ryzin, "cultivating low expectations—in the sense of warning citizens to expect less in the face of budget constraints or service cuts—may not be an optimal public relations strategy for managers of public services, even in difficult times." Indeed, he noted, "even given low performance, citizen satisfaction would suffer less if citizen expectations remained high." Of course, he continued, "the best outcome, in terms of satisfying citizens, would be to encourage high expectations while also delivering high levels of performance." Thus, Van Ryzin suggested "that urban managers should seek to promote not only high-quality services, but also high expectations among citizens."[31] Still, promoting high expectations requires a leadership commitment.

The Complication of Commitment

"Commitment is the only general explanation for sustained differences in the performance of organizations," wrote Pankaj Ghemawat of the IESE[32] Business School at the University of Navarra. Commitment, he argued, seems "to be both sufficient and necessary to explain sustained difference in the performance of organizations."[33]

Ghemawat is not alone in his conclusion about the necessity of commitment. Research, reported Denise Rousseau, reveals "the critical role of top management commitment." From a survey of research on organizational behavior, Rousseau concluded: "it is a truism that top management commitment promotes productivity improvement."[34] From an analysis of research on the use of management-by-objectives, Robert Rodgers and John Hunter (then of the University of

Kentucky and Michigan State, respectively) found "that when top-management commitment was high, the average gain in productivity was 56%" compared with only a 6 percent gain when the commitment was low.[35]

André de Wall and Harold Counet of the Maastricht School of Management sought "to identify the main problems that can be encountered during the implementation and use of a performance management system [PMS]" in the private sector. Their research revealed "the crucial role [that] commitment—on all levels of the organization—plays in achieving a successful PMS." And they emphasized "the importance of management being a role model"—consistent and visible.[36]

Most of these analyses of the link between commitment and performance do not concern government. Ghemawat, for example, focused exclusively on the for-profit sector. Thus by "sustained differences in performance," he meant profits that were consistently higher than those of both direct competitors and other businesses in general. So it isn't obvious that commitment, as Ghemawat analyzed it, is essential for a public agency or governmental jurisdiction.

At the same time, governments often lack what Ghemawat meant by "commitment"—"the tendency of organizations to persist with their broad courses of action or strategies" or, more simply "the tendency of strategies to persist over time." He argued that "a strategy embodies commitment to the extent that, if adopted, it is likely to persist." Indeed, there are several reasons that governments are unlikely to follow Ghemawat's prescription for persistence.[37]

First, public executives tend to have a shorter tenure than those in business. In the United States, elected chief executives can think no more than four years into the future, and their appointed department heads may have even shorter time horizons. They all know that their successor—even a successor from the same political party—may dismantle their key initiatives.

Moreover, these executives, and their strategies, are constantly challenged not only by the "loyal opposition" in the legislature but also by a variety of stakeholder organizations that perceive of the strategy as disadvantaging them. And minor scandals and internal errors—mistakes that would never disrupt a business firm's commitment to its core strategy—can undermine a public executive's strategic commitment.

From evolutionary biology, Ghemawat drew on the concept of "punctuated equilibrium" to describe the "strategic continuity" of business firms as "punctuated by brief periods of radical change."[38] In many public agencies, unfortunately, strategies have little equilibrium and lots of punctuation. Government executives are buffeted by a multitude of pressures to which they are obligated to respond. These pressures complicate any effort to define a strategy and undermine the operating freedom necessary to make a true commitment.

Bureaucratic inertia certainly ensures that many things in government do persist: rules and procedures, routines and rituals, customs and protocols. None of these things should be confused with strategy. They are important. They help implement—or obstruct—strategy. They help a public agency guarantee fairness and spend funds legally. But they are not connected to a larger public purpose.

Yet to produce real results, public executives need to make a real commitment. Performance will not improve quickly—and not just because of bureaucratic inertia. For the organization needs to figure out *how* it will improve performance. In some cases, some organizations may be able to improve some results relatively quickly. Indeed, it makes sense to employ Weick's "strategy of small wins" to get some early successes and learn from them. But these small wins will (by definition) be small. The big wins will come later—only after many small wins. Even if a big win is actually an accumulation of a series of small wins, the small wins will take time to accumulate.

Performance Leadership Requires a Dangerous Commitment

No organization can improve its performance if it has no responsibility for its performance. No organization can influence results if it lacks the means for producing those results. No organization will make a specific improvement in performance until its leadership team commits itself to a specific improvement.

Some public officials might find it convenient to assert—and to have society believe—that outside forces, not what they and their organization do, control results. If everyone accepts that a school district cannot influence the academic skills of its students, if everyone accepts a health department cannot affect the well-being of citizens, their executives gave a great job. For no one can criticize them or their organization for failing to improve the education of children or the health of citizens. And, if they are criticized, these officials can simply recite the convenient retort. "It's not our fault. It's society's fault. These people have a social disease."

Conversely, creating a PerformanceStat leadership strategy is dangerous. For in doing so, the members of the leadership team are throwing away one of the all-time great excuses. They have surrendered the right to say: "It's not our fault. It's society's fault." They have no place to hide.

Superficially, PerformanceStat appears to be about data and accountability—a system with data and computers. At its core, however, PerformanceStat is about the responsibility to achieve specific public purposes. For public executives, embracing this responsibility is dangerous.

To realize the PerformanceStat potential, public executives have to make an explicit—and thus very dangerous—commitment.

Eight Possible Societal Explanations for Crime Decline

In chapter 4, I examined two policing explanations for the drop in crime in the United States and in New York City: More Cops, and Innovative Policing. In this appendix, I examine eight societal explanations.[1]

Explanation 1: Randomness

At a CompStat meeting in another city, I heard one cop say: "Crime goes up; crime goes down." This commander of one of the city's police zones offered a common explanation: Crime levels? The police have little to do with it.[2] Wrote Alfred Blumstein of Carnegie Mellon University, "Although there have been [over time] sharp swings up and down, it is striking how trendless these two crimes [murder and robbery] are."[3] John Donohue of Stanford Law School writes that "with all of the random factors that influence the amount of criminal conduct, it is virtually impossible to fully explain or precisely predict the crime rate at any point in time."[4]

There is, however, a plausible, statistical explanation for what happened in the United States and New York that reflects the inherent randomness of the world. The technical term is "regression toward the mean."[5] (For anyone who has ever taken a statistics course, this explanation should come quickly to mind; if not, your instructor should, retroactively, lower your grade.)

From 1960 to 1990, violent crime in the United States more than quadrupled: from 161 crimes per 100,000 population in 1960 to 730 in 1990.[6] In New York City, the violent-crime rate peaked in 1990 at 2,384—triple the U.S. average. Indeed, in 1990, New York City's crime rate was one of the nation's big outliers.

Thus, anyone familiar with "regression toward the mean" could expect that the U.S. crime rate would "regress" down toward its traditional mean, and that New York City's rate would decline toward its own (and the U.S.) mean. (Conversely, for a city in which the crime rate was significantly below its historical level, statisticians would expect it to regress upward toward its traditional mean.) Indeed, whenever data reveal that a problem has become worse, public officials are apt to make some big changes and then to ride the advantages they will get from regression toward the mean.[7]

Regression toward the mean would tend to have the biggest impact in cities with crime rates furthest from the mean. In 1990, New York had a violent-crime rate of 2,384 crimes per 100,000 population. Of the 33 other U.S. cities with populations over half a million, only six—Baltimore, Chicago, Dallas, Detroit, Los Angeles, and Washington, D.C.—had rates higher than New York's.

For New York and four of the six other cities whose 1990 violent-crime rate was greater than New York's, the drop in the violent-crime rate from 1990 to 2000 was greater than the drop for the United States as a whole. (See table A-1.) But if this were regression toward the mean, it was not universal. Baltimore saw no drop in its violent crime, and Detroit's decline was just 14 percent. Moreover, New York's drop was off the scale: while the violent-crime rate dropped 45 percent in Dallas, and 43 percent in Los Angeles and Chicago, it dropped 60 percent in New York. By 2000, New York City's rate of violent crime was also below that of 15 of the other 33 cities with populations greater than 500,000—the 6 in table A-1, plus Albuquerque, Boston, Houston, Jacksonville, Memphis, Milwaukee, Nashville, Philadelphia, and Portland (Oregon).

Certainly, regression toward the mean could explain why the crime rate dropped in many cities and in the United States too. It does not, however, appear to explain why New York's crime rate dropped so much faster.

Donohue emphasized; "there will always be random events that escalate the rate of crime, such as innovations in illegal drug markets, and, similarly, random events that tend to depress it, such as bad weather." It is essential, he continued, not to "confuse fluctuations with trends," but to distinguish "stable trends from temporary fluctuations."[8]

For 1950 through 1997, argued Donahue, there were two long-term trends in the U.S. murder rate: a significant growth from 1950 to 1977 (averaging 4.4 percent per year) followed over the next two decades by a much slower downward trend (averaging 0.6 percent annually). But over the last half decade of this period, the murder rate dropped much more significantly. In 1998, Donahue wrote: there are "large short-term variations around the long-term trends" and thus, "there is not enough information to refute the view that we are currently experiencing a benign short-term fluctuation around the long-term trend in crime."[9]

Some are prepared to dismiss New York City's drop in crime as random luck.

TABLE A-1. Large-City Violent-Crime Rates, 1990 and 2000[a]

Jurisdiction	1990	2000	Change 1990 to 2000	
			Absolute change	Percent change
New York	2,384	945	−1,439	−60
Los Angeles	2,405	1,360	−1,045	−43
Baltimore	2,438	2,458	20	1
Dallas	2,438	1,350	−1,088	−45
Washington, D.C.	2,458	1,507	−951	−39
Detroit	2,699	2,325	−374	−14
Chicago	2,842	1,606	−1,236	−43
United States	730	507	−223	31

Source: FBI, Uniform Crime Reports, Bureau of Justice Statistics (http://bjsdata.ojp.usdoj.gov/ucrdata).

a. Includes New York City plus the other six large (>500,000 population) cities with 1990 violent-crime rates greater than New York's. Violent crimes include murder, rape and sexual assault, robbery, and assault. Crime rates are per 100,000 residents.

Explanation 2: Demographic Shifts

Who commits crimes? Answer: young males. If a city has an increase in the number of young males, crime might go up. Conversely, if it has fewer young males, crime might go down.

Here's where the fight starts, with Steven Levitt leading the charge. He is not the only one to suggest that the legalization of abortion had consequences for both population and crime. Still, Levitt has been vocal in asserting a "causal link between legalized abortion and crime"[10] and attracting, quite naturally, dissent and criticism.[11] In *Freakonomics,* his language was quite explicit: "Norma McCorvey [the "Jane Roe," of *Roe* v. *Wade*] had a far greater impact on crime than did the combined forces of gun control, a strong economy, and innovative policing strategies."[12]

Moreover, Levitt emphasized that three years before the Supreme Court legalized abortion, New York did so, and since then "New York City has had abortion rates among the highest of anywhere in the nation." The "link" between an increase in the rates of abortion and a later decrease in crime, he argued "provides further evidence against the argument that there is an unexplained crime decline in New York City that can be attributed to policing strategy."[13]

Zimring, however, dissents: In 1970, abortion was legalized in New York State, not just in New York City. In the city, the homicide rate declined almost

TABLE A-2. Number of Persons under Correctional Supervision, 1980, 1990, 2000

Year	State or federal prison	Local jail	Parole	Probation	Total
1980	319,598	183,988	220,438	1,118,097	1,842,100
1990	743,382	405,320	531,407	2,670,234	4,350,300
2000	1,316,333	621,149	723,898	3,826,209	6,445,100

Source: Bureau of Justice Statistics, "Key Facts at a Glance: Correctional Populations" (http://bjs.ojp.usdoj.gov/content/glance/tables/corr2tab.cfm).

continuously throughout the 1990s, dropping 73 percent over the decade. In the rest of the state, however, it first increased and by 2000 was down just 25 percent (a drop not as large as the national average). These data, he argued, "suggest that city-level rather than state-level changes were the likely cause of the extra decline in homicide."[14]

Explanation 3: More Criminals in Prisons

This explanation is straightforward. During the 1980s, and then again in the 1990s, the United States locked more people up, incapacitating some bad guys and (perhaps) deterring others. From 1980 to 1990, the population of state and federal prisons more than doubled as did the population of local jails. (See table A-2.) Moreover, during that decade, the number of people on parole or probation also doubled. In the 1990s, the incarcerated population continued to grow, though not as fast. So did the number of people on parole or probation.

Indeed, "the one factor that dominates all others in terms of predicted impact on crime," wrote Levitt, "is the growth in the prison population."[15] He concluded that "incarcerating one additional prisoner reduces the number of crimes by approximately fifteen per year."[16]

Not everyone agrees that this explanation "dominates" the others. Using data from California, Zimring and Gordon Hawkins, also from the University of California, found that confining an additional prisoner for one additional year reduced the actual felonies committed by three and a half below what would otherwise be predicted, and that 90 percent of this reduction was for burglary and larceny. In contrast, they concluded, the "evidence for significant prevention was weak to negligible for robbery, homicide, assault, and auto theft."[17]

In a book chapter titled "The Limited Importance of Prison Expansion," William Spelman of the University of Texas argued: "The violent crime rate would have dropped, anyway, at almost the same time." He attributed a quarter of the drop in violent crime to incarceration policies. For most of the crime drop, he credited "improvements in the economy," plus "changes in the age structure" as "the baby boom was followed by a baby bust" and "other social factors."[18]

Explanation 4: The Decline in the Use of Crack Cocaine

In the mid-1980s, the crack form of cocaine attracted so many users that public-health professionals called it an "epidemic."[19] In 1991, of the 14 million U.S. males aged 18 to 25, roughly 655,000 had used crack at least once, and 188,000 had done so in the past year.[20] With this epidemic of crack, goes this explanation, came an epidemic of crime and violence.

With crack in demand, selling it became a lucrative business. Crack was cheap and could be purchased on the street in a single-hit size. The combination of these two characteristics meant lots of sales, requiring lots of sellers. So the wholesalers recruited lots of retailers, who tended (for several reasons[21]) to be juveniles.

Because the crack business was so lucrative, it also became dangerous. Buyers and sellers could get free crack by robbing other buyers and sellers. But those in the business could not ask the police for protection. Consequently, explained Alfred Blumstein, the retailers would "carry guns for self-protection, largely because that industry uses guns as an important instrument for dispute resolution." This behavior produced, observed Blumstein, an "'arms race' among young people" that created "a major escalation of the violence."[22]

If criminologists can agree on anything, it is that the rise in the use of crack cocaine in the 1980s contributed to that decade's rise in crime and that the decline in its use in the 1990s contributed to that decade's crime decline—in both New York City and the United States. Benjamin Bowling of King's College London concluded that "among the most convincing explanations for the rise and fall of New York murder in the last decades of this [twentieth] century is the simultaneous rise and fall of crack cocaine."[23]

Okay: This view isn't that unanimous.[24] But it comes as close to being "unanimous" as anything will ever be in criminology.

Explanation 5: Economic Growth

If the economy is improving, creating more and better jobs, the criminal business may not look as appealing as its legitimate alternatives. Like all humans, explained Jeff Grogger of the University of California, "young men are responsive to wage incentives." He sought to estimate the effect of wages on youth crime and concluded that "falling real wages [particularly for young males] may have been an important determinant of rising youth crime during the 1970s and 1980s."[25]

During the 1980s, the unemployment rate for those 16 to 19 years old (the age at which a male is apt to enter the criminal profession) was consistently in the mid to high teens. From July 1990 through October 1997, it never dropped below 15 percent.[26] Moreover, from 1979 to 1988, Grogger reported, "real wages paid to males 16 to 24 years old dropped by 22 percent. In 1993, however, they began to rise, and were up 4 percent by 1997. "For several reasons," however, Grogger argued, "it seems unlikely that wages played the leading role in reversing the rise in violence": the violence started to drop before wages started to rise, and "a 4 percent rise in wages is not enough to explain the magnitude of the reduction in violence."[27]

Zimring isn't so sure: "The economic circumstances of the 1990s were good news on the crime front, but the magnitude of the aggregate impact on crime rates of all the positive economic trends is very much an open question."[28]

Explanation 6: Social Services for the Victims of Domestic Violence

The previous two explanations—the rise and fall of crack, and the fall and rise of the economy—could help explain the drop in crime by the most crime-prone members of society: young males. But what about the drop in crime for those who are older? A trio of scholars—Laura Dugan of the University of Maryland, Daniel Nagan of Carnegie Mellon, and Richard Rosenfeld of the University of Missouri—noted that the "rates of homicide involving 'intimate partners'— spouses, ex-spouses, boyfriends, girlfriends—have declined substantially over the past 25 years." From 1976 to 1996, the intimate-partner homicide rate dropped by approximately 30 percent, from 1.3 victims per 100,000 population to 0.9. Over the same two decades, they found, "the intimate-partner homicide victimization rate for married 20- to 44-year-old African-American men dropped by an astonishing 87%, from 18.4 to 2.4 per 100,000."[29]

Why? As usual, there exist multiple (and sometimes conflicting) explanations. Victimization rates, hypothesized causes, and observed impacts of policies and services can differ depending on whether the individual is married or unmarried, male or female, black or white. Still, in one summary, Rosenfeld noted that this research "found the greatest declines in intimate partner homicides over the last 25 years occurred in those cities with the largest drops in marriage rates, the largest increases in divorce rates, and the most rapid growth in shelters and legal advocacy programs for domestic violence victims."[30]

Explanation 7: Collective Efficacy

Some have suggested that improved citizenship, increased volunteerism, and community organizations have enhanced some communities' "collective efficacy." Individuals and associations, they argue, have directly and indirectly fostered the collective action of community crime prevention. Friedman argued that "ordinary people" are a "causal factor." They are "a major force for safer communities" and, through their "collective, grassroots efforts," have had "an impact on the national crime and violence statistics."[31] Robert Sampson of Harvard wrote that "*community-level variations in social control contribute to varying crime rates*" (emphasis in the original).[32]

Sampson and his colleagues developed the concept of "collective efficacy": the shared capacity of the residents of a neighborhood to work together to solve community problems and to maintain social control by enforcing their collective norms. Collective efficacy, Sampson wrote, consists of two parts: "*social cohesion* (the 'collectivity' part of the concept) and *shared expectations for control* (the 'efficacy' part of the concept)." Sampson's examples for exercising this control include "sharing information about other children's behavior, willingness to intervene in preventing acts such as truancy and street-corner 'hanging' by teenage peer groups."[33]

Neither Sampson nor his colleagues argued that a rise in collective efficacy during the 1990s contributed specifically to that decade's drop in crime. But they certainly believed that enhanced collective efficacy could help explain differences in crime rates among communities.[34] Indeed, Friedman was quite specific: "Neighborhood residents, acting together through community organizations, have made a serious contribution to the decline in violent crime."[35]

Peter St. Jean of the University of Buffalo was not so sure. From a study of a community in Chicago, he found that city blocks with high collective efficacy were "predominantly matched with low crime." But, "low collective efficacy blocks were just as likely to be crime coldspots as to be hotspots." Thus, although high collective efficacy may help reduce crime, a community that lacks it is not destined to have high crime.[36]

Explanation 8: The (Fall and) Rise of Institutional Legitimacy in Society

Institutions, "the patterned, mutually shared ways that people develop for living together," wrote Gary LaFree of the University of Maryland, "are arguably the most important of all human creations."[37] He has suggested that "social institutions begin to develop whenever the interpretation of routine human actions comes to be mutually shared."[38] From this perspective, LaFree argued, "changes in the legitimacy of social institutions provide the most promising explanation" for the rise of crime after World War II (particularly in the 1960s) and for "the crime bust of the 1990s."[39]

LaFree focused on six institutions that, he argued, accrued increased legitimacy during the 1990s. He paired three "traditional institutions" (political, economic, and familial) with three "newer, social institutions" (criminal justice, education, and welfare) that "have become increasingly important during the postwar years":

"Political trust" with "criminal justice support";
"Economic well being" with "welfare support"; and
"Family organization" with "educational support."

Then, he concluded, the "stabilization in the legitimacy of political, economic, and family institutions, and investments in criminal justice, education, and welfare eventually produced downward pressure on crime rates." They did this in "three interrelated ways": they lowered the motivation of individuals to commit crimes; they created "effective controls" that suppressed criminal behavior; and they protected individuals from criminals.[40]

Operational Issues for Regular PerformanceStat Meetings

Since humans first formed tribes millennia ago, we have held meetings. Not much new here (except the lighting is from electricity, not a fire): Get folks together. Hash out what's to be done. Follow up to make sure they do it. What's the big deal? Not much. Yet, to create a series of meetings that can achieve the PerformanceStat potential, a leadership team needs to make some operational choices, thinking about how to adapt the room, schedule, and participation to the culture of their organization while focusing on the results they seek.

These meetings need to be a regular part of organizational life. All subunit managers need to take these meetings just as seriously as they take other core responsibilities, such as creating a budget or hiring key personnel. The location, timing, and participation of these meetings need to be regular. Such continuity establishes that these meetings are how the organization ensures that all operational units are thinking analytically about improving their performance.

Room

Where are the meetings held? Some organizations (such as the New York Police Department and Baltimore) created a room for precisely this purpose. The technology, seating, and podium are built in. Many organizations use a conference room, setting up the tables, projectors, and screens before each meeting and taking them down afterwards. While the Los Angeles Police Department was building its new headquarters, it conducted its weekly CompStat meetings in a large room that it rented at the LA Mart (a huge building for wholesalers and trade shows to display furniture). Each Wednesday morning LAPD staff rolled in their technology, set up their computers with three projectors and three screens. In the afternoon, they dismantled everything, only to return on the following Wednesday.

How are people arranged in the room? Does the subunit director stand at a podium facing the chief executive's leadership team? Do the subunit's key managers stand or sit behind the director? Or does the chief executive's leadership team sit at one long table facing the subunit's director and managers who sit at a parallel long table? Or does everyone sit around a U-shaped arrangement of tables with the screen at the open end? Where do you put the screen(s) so that everyone can see them?

There is no perfect design of the room. I have observed multiple variations. Nevertheless, one of the core choices is whether the subunit managers will stand at a podium or sit at a table. This choice has obvious implications for how exposed the subunit's top manager feels.

Timing

When are the meetings held? The timing needs to be regular—perhaps quarterly, maybe monthly, or even biweekly. In Baltimore, an agency's CitiStat session happens every 14 days at precisely the same time (every other Thursday, for example, at 8:30 a.m.). While Martin Horn was commissioner, the Department of Correction regularly held its TEAMS meetings at 8:00 a.m. on the last Thursday of the month, and the Department of Probation held its STARS session at 9:00 a.m. the next day. Obviously, the meetings can be held no more frequently than updates on the data and with enough of a delay after a reporting period so both headquarters and subunits have time to analyze the data.

Regardless of their frequency, the meetings need to be regular. Subunit directors and managers need to know that after some well-established period of time, they will appear at the next PerformanceStat meeting. And they need to know that they will again be dealing with the same members of the organization's leadership team, who will again be asking questions—perhaps the same questions, certainly related questions.

After all, the objective of these PerformanceStat meetings is to engage all subunits in the task of improving performance. The leadership team seeks not obsequious compliance, but full, engaged, energetic dedication, which regular, frequent meetings encourage.

In *The Evolution of Cooperation,* Robert Axelrod of the University of Michigan concluded that one way to promote cooperation between two individuals is to ensure that they know they will meet each other again. Indeed, Axelrod argued, it helps to ensure that they will have interactions that are durable and frequent. If subunit directors and managers expect to interact only rarely and infrequently with the organization's leadership team, they will feel little need to produce any specific result. They can reason, "who knows what these guys will be interested in the next time?" Observed Axelrod, "frequent interactions help promote stable cooperation."

Participation

Who attends and participates? Again, consistency is important. The room needs to include those who can contribute analysis, knowledge, and resources. That's why most effective PerformanceStat meetings include someone from budget, from personnel, and from information technology—people whose staff agencies will need to contribute resources if the decisions are to be implemented.

What about the subunits themselves? Whom should they bring? Just the subunit manager and the top deputy? Or should the subunit come with a delegation of, say, a couple dozen? There are at least two arguments for having the subunit's management team in the room.

First, when a question is asked, it helps to have in the room the person who knows the answer. This might be the subunit's director, or a subordinate. Moreover, this person might be the one who will implement any decision; so it might help to solicit his or her thoughts before it is made.

Second, it may help to have a dozen or two of the subunit's top people hear firsthand about the chief executive's purposes and concerns. If only a few people from the subunit attend, those who don't may wonder whether the attendees' reports reflect their own concerns, not those of the chief executive. When Horn held his TEAMS meetings, he would formally address the warden whose facility was being discussed; but he was consciously and explicitly sending a message to everyone in the room.

In Baltimore, Kimberly Flowers brought her entire Recreation and Parks management team to her biweekly CitiStat meeting. She wanted to ensure that all two dozen of them realized that she wasn't just inventing the mayor's priorities. Flowers wanted them to get the message directly from the mayor's leadership team. "Everyone in the agency has to get it," Flowers said. "That's why I bring so many people with me." Indeed, through the regular PerformanceStat meetings, the chief executive has an excellent opportunity to get his message down into his organization—to people the chief executive would otherwise rarely see.

In Australia, where the states (not the cities) are responsible for policing, the state of Queensland is bigger than Alaska. It would be terribly expensive to have the key commanders from the eight regions (and 30 districts) in the Queensland

Police Service come to Brisbane (the capital) every other week for its Operational Performance Reviews (its version of CompStat). So the Queensland Police Services created a schedule reflecting its circumstances. Each region has just two OPRs per year: one in Brisbane; one in its region. The focus of these meetings is on the region's districts, which are the smallest units that can allocate resources; and the meetings in Brisbane last for two days. Moreover, by traveling to the regions, the commissioner can deliver his message to the field officers who might otherwise not learn his priorities.

Managing the Discussion

Some PerformanceStat sessions begin with a review of the recent period's data with analytical observations. Others start with introductions, a few formalities, even ceremonies or commendations, perhaps a couple of informal updates, or simply with an open introductory question.

At Probation, Commissioner Horn usually started STARS by ostentatiously turning off his cell phone, introducing guests, offering a few words of praise, and noting some recent developments or problems, and perhaps asking for some help. Then he would turn to the assistant commissioner sitting in the middle of the table across from him, the manager in charge of operations in one of the city's boroughs, and simply say: "Commissioner [Lorene] Gilmore, tell me about Queens"; "Commissioner [Gineen] Grey, how are the children doing in Brooklyn?"[1] This gave the subunit director the opportunity to report on a success or two, praise individuals or teams, or raise a problem with which the borough needed some help. This, however, was not show-and-tell. Horn was clearly in charge of the entire session. And when data tables were projected on the screen, Horn was the one leading everyone through the numbers and their implications.

Sometimes Horn would drill down into the specifics: "Tell me about the three felonies," he said to Jonnie Mae Howard, chief of the juvenile services branch in Manhattan. This led to a detailed discussion of a juvenile who was stealing cell phones from other juveniles and to another who was grinding up aspirin and selling it as cocaine. "I appreciate this kid's entrepreneurship," said Horn to laughter. But, he continued, "does this kid realize that he could be dead?"[2]

Although PerformanceStat meetings have a reputation for focusing on the macro trends as revealed in the data, most meetings quickly focus on specific micro problems. In this case, Horn concentrated on a few specific juveniles who had committed felonies, including the cell-phone thief whom Horn described as "scary." Such discussions can produce a specific solution to the specific problem as well as create subtle (or not so subtle) guidance for how others should approach similar problems.

The First Follow-Up

Any PerformanceStat session needs to conclude with some specific tasks. Who is to accomplish what by when? The next meeting could begin with these follow-up items.

Moreover, the specifics of these tasks cannot be left to individual memories. They need to be communicated unequivocally to everyone who participated in the meeting. In Baltimore, this is done by the CitiStat analyst assigned to the agency. By 5:00 p.m. after a CitiStat session, the analyst sends the agency director a memo, outlining what commitments the agency needs to fulfill by when—with specific emphasis on what needs to be done by the next meeting.

The Motivational Consequences
of Feedback and Rewards

The Bar Chart and The List create two types of comparisons. First, such feedback creates *absolute* comparisons. From the data, individuals will observe: "I am achieving my target," or "I am not achieving my target." Second, the feedback also creates *relative* comparisons—what the social psychologist Leon Festinger called "social comparisons."[1] From the data, individuals may observe: "I am doing better than these people" or "I am not doing as well as those people."

Sometimes, team targets work better than individual targets.[2] Moreover, if the data are distributed for *both* teams and individuals within teams, the comparison fosters even better performance,[3] which may be the result of intragroup competition.[4]

The Motivational Consequences of Comparisons

Such comparisons can be either encouraging or discouraging, motivating or demotivating. In some circumstances, people who learn they are below the median produce more while those above the median produce less.[5] Indeed, the research on the motivational impact of social comparisons has produced conflicting conclusions and implications.[6] Jerry Suls of the University of Iowa and his colleagues concluded that "exposure to someone who is superior to oneself can lead either to positive or negative evaluations because such exposure suggests (a) that one is relatively disadvantaged and (b) that one could improve."[7] Circumstances can affect people's response to performance feedback.

People in similar circumstances can be inspired by others who are performing better. Joanne Wood of the University of Waterloo reported that people "tend to adopt the performance standards of others who are similar on surrounding dimensions . . . imitating others who are similar on dimensions that are related to performance." An upward social comparison can be inspiring. Yet, it can also be threatening. But which? Wood observed: "Evidence suggests that when similar others are competitors, upward comparisons are aversive, but when they are not competitors, their superior performance is inspiring (or irrelevant)."[8]

Zero-Sum Competition

Sometimes, as in an athletic competition, not everyone can be successful. Kevin Williams of the State University of New York at Albany and his colleagues report that college track-and-field athletes who fail to achieve their initial goals tend to revise them downward *if* they conclude that their failure was due to uncontrollable and stable factors (the difficulty of the goal; their own ability). In contrast, if they conclude that their failure was due to controllable or unstable factors (strategy, effort, or luck), they will not lower their goal, but rather seek to work harder or smarter.[9] But one of these uncontrollable factors is the form of competition; track-and-field athletes are engaged in a zero-sum game; an individual athlete's ability to achieve any goal depends on the quality of the competitors. On The List, most athletes do not end up in column A.

Information and Rewards

Two aspects of organizational circumstances can significantly affect the motivation created by feedback. First, what is the precise nature of the performance information? Second, what kinds of rewards—both extrinsic and intrinsic—are available to whom for what levels of performance?

The specificity of the performance *information* can affect how people respond. Is each unit given information only about its level of performance? Or is each unit given information about how *all* the other units are performing? If so, is each unit given information only about the distribution of the performance of the other units? Or are they told which units are performing at each level? The more detailed the comparative feedback a unit receives about how it is performing, the greater the ability of that unit to gauge how easy or difficult it will be to improve both absolute and relative performance.

The nature of the *rewards* that individuals or units can receive for different levels of performance also affects how they respond. Do all of the rewards— both extrinsic (a bonus) and intrinsic (the sense of accomplishing something significant)—go to the single, top performer? Or does each individual or unit have an opportunity—by achieving its own target—to receive a reward? Or does the reward system require that most units (and thus most people) end up being labeled as losers?

Are the units competing against each other? Or is each unit competing against its own target? The first can produce cutthroat competition. The second can produce "friendly competition."[10]

Consider how several possible combinations of the availability of information and the availability of rewards affect behavior:

Situation #1: *Reward:* Only the top performer wins the reward (which may be either extrinsic or intrinsic). *Information:* A unit is simply told it is well above, slightly above, slightly below, or well below the median. *Behavior:* The social comparison may motivate all units—except those told that they are well above the median—to stop working.

Situation #2: *Reward:* Every unit that achieves its own target wins the reward (extrinsic or intrinsic). *Information:* Every unit is, at least, told how well it compares with its target. *Behavior:* The units that conclude that they can, with a reasonable amount of effort, achieve their target are apt to work to achieve it; units that are so far below the target that they cannot possibly achieve it may decide not to bother. Units that are well above their target may conclude that they can slack off and still achieve the reward.

Situation #3: *Reward:* Every unit that achieves its target wins the extrinsic or, at least, most obvious and visible reward, but those who also do particularly well in particular dimensions win an intrinsic reward (or perhaps, depending on how well they do, several different intrinsic rewards). *Information:* The same as Situation #2. Every unit at least knows how well it compares with its target. *Behavior:* Those near or well below their target are apt to behave as they did in Situation #2, but those well above the target may decide not to slack off.

Situation #4: *Reward:* Every unit that achieves its target wins the extrinsic or most obvious and visible reward; and if every unit achieves its target, everyone gets an *extra* reward. *Information:* Every unit knows precisely how well all units are doing compared with their targets. *Behavior:* Every unit has an incentive to help every other unit to achieve its target.

If everyone has a chance to win the formal, extrinsic reward (Situations 2, 3, and 4), the well-performing units have no incentive to withhold their performance strategies from others. Moreover, one way to provide extra, intrinsic rewards (in terms of internal prestige and personal sense of accomplishment) to the top performers—the "positive deviants"—is to ask them to explain their strategies in formal training sessions to their colleagues.[11]

Causal Contributors to the Missing Competences

Producing results in government requires managers who possess a breadth of competences. No one individual needs to possess all of them. But an organization's leadership team does need the capacity for numerate reasoning, analytical thinking, strategic conceptualization, organizational implementation, political savvy, motivational leadership, and the basic, operational capacity to get the job done.

This imposing list contains many competences that many public managers fail to acquire. Why? The absence of these competences has, I think, four contributors: (1) the reason why people enter public service; (2) the professional training they receive; (3) the type of daily work they do; and (4) the nature of bureaucratic life.

The Public-Service Choice

Most people choose a public-service profession to do it, not to analyze it. Few people become teachers because they want to analyze data to determine what teaching strategies are most effective for which students. They become teachers to teach—to help children learn and grow. Few people become firefighters to analyze data to determine what fire-fighting strategies are most effective for which kinds of fires. They become firefighters to fight fires—to help maintain public safety. Those who choose to work in child welfare do so to help children—to save children's lives.

Those who choose public service get their professional kicks from doing it—not from thinking about it philosophically or analyzing it abstractly. If they don't like doing it, they find another profession.

The Limits of Traditional Professional Training

Second, they are trained to do it—not to analyze it. Every public-service profession has its collection of best practices, evolved from years of professional work, that everyone needs to know. For every common (and not so common) situation, the profession has "learned" what works best and has encoded these lessons in textbooks and iconic myths.

Professional curricula focus on what to do—on the accepted professional practices and established standards. When fire cadets enroll in the fire academy or when experienced firefighters take a specialized course, they will learn the same practices that their colleagues have already learned. People who go to the fire academy will be taught to do what firefighters do—not how to analyze the effectiveness of what they do. When those who seek a career in child welfare enroll in a university social service school, they will be taught the latest clinical diagnoses and the accepted practices for treating them.[1]

With rare exceptions, the first job for most public-service professionals will require little analytical work. Primarily, these entry-level jobs require mastering the organization's Standard Operating Procedures (SOPs) for dealing with disruptive students, kitchen fires, or parental abuse. Such SOPs can be written into the formal policy manual or adopted informally by the professional culture. Either way, these conventions, practices, and routines create the basis for operations. In a new situation, no one has to rethink what to do; all that has already been established and internalized.

Sure, as preprofessionals they took some management-oriented courses in budgeting or personnel, and perhaps even a course that sought to convey the tacit knowledge required to motivate humans to accomplish public purposes. Some of the bolder preprofessionals may take a graduate course or two in analytical methods—techniques that they may use to challenge the effectiveness of some practices. Still, within the profession, many will be quite comfortable with the existing orthodoxy. With the profession's repertoire firmly established, most of its members will not analyze (and thus implicitly challenge) the effectiveness of its standard routines. The few who do may be quickly labeled as cranks.

The Daily Work of Public-Service Professionals

Third, when they take their first, entry-level job, public-service professionals won't be asked to conduct much analysis. They will be asked to simply do it. Doing it doesn't mean analyzing it. Doing it means doing what was taught in the academy or graduate school. It means following the accepted practices. It means taking cues from experienced pros.

From the organization's baseline practices, each neophyte will evolve his or her own professional repertoire, including a few modifications from official practice. With experience, he or she will amend a few of the accepted practices to deal with a unique problem that he or she has confronted frequently enough to have learned what works personally. Primarily, however, each professional's repertoire will be based on the profession's accepted practices.

As these professionals show the ability to accept more responsibility, they will be given additional assignments, though rarely analytical assignments. They are more apt to be given more demanding versions of the same assignments. They may be promoted from front-line worker, to front-line supervisor, to first-level manager. Still the profession's basic routines for dealing with its basic problems will remain substantially unchanged. The problems (and thus the headaches) just get bigger. And, those who continue to be good at solving their profession's standard problems by employing its standard routines are continually promoted.

The Nature of Organizational (Bureaucratic) Life

The fourth contributor to the absence of analytical and leadership competences in many large public organizations is the fundamental nature of bureaucratic life. Large organizations (public, private, and nonprofit) are built to ensure consistency. If everyone is analyzing data, if everyone is entitled to extract his or her own lessons from the data, and if everyone is authorized to act on the lessons that he or she has derived from the data, the consistency that large organizations require is compromised.

The true deviants will try to create their own innovative "skunkworks."[2] To maintain control,[3] the guardians of organizational consistency seek to track down and exterminate these deviants. If the guardians fail to do so, an epidemic of discretion might contaminate even the most compliant.

Large organizations seek to eliminate inequities, to prevent mistakes, and to control confusion by imposing organization-wide consistency on accounting forms, personnel practices, and operating procedures.[4] In such an organization, central headquarters has also seized the responsibility for producing results—for deciding not just what results to produce but also how to produce them. Headquarters creates standard operating procedures for producing results, and as long as a subunit follows these SOPs, it can't get in trouble because it failed to achieve the desired results. After all, this subunit did precisely what headquarters told it to do. If, however, someone failed to follow one of these procedures (even if the decision was results focused and analytically based) that someone (and thus the entire unit) can be in trouble.

A few eccentric mavericks will recognize the orthodoxy's perverse ramifications for performance, but they may lack the ability to make a convincing analytical case for changing established doctrine.

Notes

Acknowledgments

1. William James, *The Varieties of Religious Experience* (New York: W. W. Norton, 1902, 1961), p. xvii.

2. Quoted in Thomas L. Friedman, "Courageous Arab Thinkers," *New York Times,* October 19, 2003.

Preface

1. Jim Algie, "U.S. Government Can't Seem to Accomplish Anything," *Owen Sound Sun Times,* April 14, 2010 (www.owensoundsuntimes.com/2010/04/14/us-government-cant-seem-to-accomplish-anything/).

2. Ray Pawson, "Evidence Based Policy: The Promise of 'Realist Synthesis,'" *Evaluation* 8, no. 3 (July 2002): 346.

3. Åge Johnsen, "Why Does Poor Performance Get So Much Attention in Public Policy?" *Financial Accountability and Management* 28, no. 2 (May 2012): 122, 125, 138, 122, 134.

Chapter One

1. Quoted in David Remick, "The Crime Buster," *New Yorker,* February 24 and March 3, 1997, p. 100.

2. Peter F. Drucker, *Adventures of a Bystander* (Piscataway, N.J.: Transaction Publishers, 2009), p. 255.

3. Jack Maple (with Chris Mitchell), *The Crime Fighter* (New York: Doubleday, 1999), p. 31.

4. William Bratton (with Peter Knobler), *Turnaround: How America's Top Cop Reversed the Crime Epidemic* (New York: Random House, 1998), p. 223.

5. Maple, *The Crime Fighter,* p. 32.

6. CompStat? What does this word mean? Where does it come from? What does it stand for? Even among those in the NYPD who developed and nurtured it, there are disagreements. It could stand for "Computer Statistics" or "Comparative Statistics." Maple wrote, "Nobody can be sure which" (Maple, *The Crime Fighter,* p. 33). Mayor Rudolph Giuliani said CompStat was "short for Computerized Crime Comparison Statistics." Who knows?

A credible story—credible because it reflects the reality of organizational life rather than some neat, sanitized explanation that is invented long after the deed—comes from Tom Steinert-Threlkeld:

> Gene Whyte, John Brancato, Richard Mehia, and John Yohe wanted to go home, before the weather turned impenetrable. But Brancato, now a narcotics detective, had to save the file the New York City policemen were working on. So the four-man band had to come up with a name, first.
>
> They had eight characters to work with. This was January 1994, and their computer used 5.25-inch floppy disks to store data and used the now-ancient Disk Operating System that Microsoft had originally re-branded to instruct standard IBM-type personal computers how to work.
>
> So someone called out "CompStat." It could be interpreted to mean Computer Statistics. Or Comparative Statistics. Or even Comparative Computer Stats. It didn't matter.
>
> What did matter was getting home.

Sounds like they had their priorities right.

See Tom Steinert-Threlkeld, "CompStat: From Humble Beginnings," *Baseline Magazine,* September 2002 (www.baselinem ag.com/c/a/Past-News/CompStat-From-Humble-Beginnings/2/). The source for Guiliani's version of the meaning of CompStat is a press release for a speech he gave on May 13, 1997, to the International CompStat Conference: "Innovative Computer Mapping Program Has Reduced Crime to Its Lowest Levels in 30 Years" (www.baselinemag.com/c/a/Past-News/CompStat-From-Humble-Beginnings/).

7. Bratton, *Turnaround,* pp. 194, 202.

8. David Weisburd and others, *The Growth of Compstat in American Policing* (Washington: Police Foundation, April 2004), p. 1.

9. George L. Kelling and William H. Sousa, Jr., *Do Police Matter? An Analysis of the Impact of New York City's Police Reforms,* Civic Report 22 (New York: Manhattan Institute, December 2001), p. 2.

10. William F. Walsh, "Compstat: An Analysis of an Emerging Police Managerial Paradigm," *Policing: An International Journal of Police Strategies & Management* 24, no. 3 (2001): 347–62. Reprinted in Roger G. Dunham and Geoffrey P. Alpert, *Critical Issues in Policing: Contemporary Readings* (Long Grove, Ill.: Waveland Press, 2010), pp. 197–211.

11. Dall W. Forsythe, "Pitfalls in Designing and Implementing Performance Management Systems," in *Quicker, Better, Cheaper: Managing Performance in American Government,* ed. Dall W. Forsythe (Albany, N.Y.: Rockefeller Institute Press, 2001), p. 540.

12. Mark H. Moore, "Sizing Up CompStat: An Important Administrative Innovation in Policing," *Criminology and Public Policy* 2 (July 2003): 469–94.

13. These awards are made annually by the Ash Institute for Democratic Governance and Innovation at Harvard University's John F. Kennedy School of Government (www. innovations.harvard.edu/awards.html?id=3716).

14. The classic analysis of this process is Everett M. Rogers, *Diffusion of Innovations,* 5th ed. (New York: Free Press, 2003).

15. Weisburd and others, *The Growth of Compstat in American Policing,* p. 6. Weisburd and his colleagues sent a survey to the 515 police agencies with 100 or more sworn officers. Of these, 445 returned the survey, with 145 (or 32.6 percent) saying they had implemented a CompStat-like program and another 114 (or 25.6 percent) saying they were planning to do so. See also Shaila K. Dewan, "New York's Gospel of Policing by Data Spreads across U.S.," *New York Times,* April 28, 2004, p. A1.

16. Christopher Swope, "The ComStat Craze," *Governing* 12 (September 1999): 40–43.

17. Note that some people use the term "ComStat" (without the *p*). Some use all capital letters, "COMPSTAT." Still others only capitalize the *C:* "Compstat." To avoid the confusion of different organizations using different terms, I shall be consistent when describing the general idea of CompStat or CitiStat or PerformanceStat or AgencyStat or JurisdictionStat. That is, I will capitalize two letters: the first letter, and the *S* in the "Stat" suffix. When, however, I am referring to a particular organization's example, I will use its own unique spelling. When I am quoting someone, I will use whatever spelling is in the quote.

18. Los Angeles Police Department (www.lapdonline.org/search_results/content_basic_view/6363).

19. Philadelphia Police Department (www.ppdonline.org/hq_compstat.php). These same words are also employed by the police department in the town of Jupiter, Florida (www.jupiter.fl.us/jpd/compstat.cfm).

20. Columbia, South Carolina, Police Department (www.columbiapd.net/process.htm).

21. Escondido, California, Police Department (http://police.escondido.org/compstat-dac.aspx).

22. Minneapolis Police Department (www.minneapolismn.gov/police/statistics/police_about_codefor).

23. John Dorriety, "CompStat for Smaller Departments," *Law and Order* 53 (June 2005): 100–05. This article also describes Maple's four principles.

24. Maple's four principles were found (1) on the CompStat web page of the Sandy Springs, Georgia, Police Department (www.sandyspringspolice.org/index.aspx?NID=99), (2) on the CompStat web page of the West Vancouver Police Department in British Columbia (www.wvpd.ca/index.php?option=com_content&view=article&id=21), (3) on the CompStat web page of the Shawnee Police Department (www.shawneeok.org/Public Safety/Police/AboutComStat.asp), (4) in the spring 2006 newsletter (vol. 15, no. 1) of the Township of Burlington (www.twp.burlington.nj.us/nltrspr06.pdf), and (5) on the CompStat web page of Warwick Township (www.warwicktownship.org/warwick/cwp/view.asp?a=3&q=549356).

25. In addition to Winnipeg, a few other police agencies use the term "CrimeStat" rather than CompStat. These include the New York State Division of Criminal Justice Services, and police departments in Orangeburg, South Carolina; Mundelein, Illinois; and Shelby, North Carolina. CrimeStat is also the name of a "spatial statistics" software package used for "the analysis of crime incident locations" that was developed with the support of the U.S. Institute of Justice (http://nij.gov/nij/maps/crimestat.htm). Nevertheless, the complete PerformanceStat, CompStat, CrimeStat strategy, which requires both data and analysis (see chapters 3 and 4), also requires real human leadership to motivate real people to improve performance.

26. Winnipeg Police Service (http://winnipeg.ca/crimestat/about/whatisit.aspx).

27. Washington Highway Patrol (www.wsp.wa.gov/information/docs/saf/weberseav. pdf). Former Highway Patrol chief Ronal W. Serpas further described Maple's principles as "four key, yet very simple, strategies" (www.wsp.wa.gov/information/docs/saf/cabinet.pdf).

28. Lorraine Mazerolle, Sacha Rombouts, and James McBroom, "The Impact of CompStat on Reported Crime in Queensland," *Policing: An International Journal of Police Strategies and Management* 30, no. 2 (2007): 237–56, at 238.

29. Simon Kelly, "Reviews Credited with Crime Reduction," *Police Bulletin* 298 (October 2005): 29 (www.police.qld.gov.au/Resources/Internet/services/reportsPublications/documents/Bulletin_298_P2930.pdf).

30. Louis R. Anemone and Francis E. Spangenberg, "Building on Success: TrafficStat Takes the NYPD's CompStat Method in a New Direction," *Police Chief* 67 (February 2000): 26. The NYPD took a similar approach to its support services, creating FleetStat, CentralRecordsStat, PropertyStat, and PrintStat.

31. Louisiana State Police Troop C, "'TrafficStat': A Comprehensive Traffic Safety Initiative," January 3, 2003 (www.lsp.org/pdf/troopctrafficstat.pdf).

32. For its Traffic Safety Program, the Ontario Provincial Police lists five principles of "Result Driven Policing":

1. Focused Traffic Initiatives
2. Timely and accurate statistical information
3. Effective police strategies and tactics
4. Rapid deployment of personnel and resources
5. Relentless follow-up, reaction and assessment

See Ontario State Police, *2007 Provincial Business Plan* (Orillia, Ont.: Ontario State Police, 2007) (www.ontla.on.ca/library/repository/ser/226827/2007.pdf).

33. Rebecca Webber and Gail Robinson, "Compstatmania," *Gotham Gazette,* July 7, 2003 (www.gothamgazette.com/article/issueoftheweek/20030707/200/432).

34. Paul E. O'Connell, *Using Performance Data for Accountability: The New York City Police Department's CompStat Model of Police Management* (Washington: Pricewaterhouse-Coopers Endowment for the Business of Government, August 2001), pp. 21–24.

35. Dennis C. Smith and William J. Grinker, *The Transformation of Social Services Management in New York City: "CompStating" Welfare* (New York: Seedco, 2005), p. 19.

Swati Desai, "Performance Management at the Human Resources Administration—Job-Stat," in *Performance Management in State and Local Government* (Albany, N.Y.: Nelson A. Rockefeller Institute of Government, 2005), pp. 44–57.

36. As far as I can tell, BET-STAT no longer exists. It did, however, on July 19, 2006 (www.nycotb.com/viewPage.cfm/?page=25).

37. Compstatmania did not last forever, and not all of these AgencyStats have survived. Indeed, some of them might never, despite their name or claim, have had the characteristics of a true PerformanceStat.

38. In January 1996, *Time* magazine was preparing a cover story on the drop in crime in New York City. Mayor Giuliani thought, Cool. My picture will be on the cover of *Time*. But when the January 15 issue hit the streets, the cover (with the words "Finally We're Winning the War Against Crime. Here's Why") featured a police car in front of which was standing the trench-coated police commissioner. Three months later Bratton was the city's *former* police commissioner. He had been commissioner for twenty-seven months. In Los Angeles, Bratton served as police chief from 2002 to 2009—more than seven years. In January 2014, Bratton returned to NYPD as Mayor Bill de Blasio's new police commissioner.

39. Rudolph Giuliani, press conference, New York, May 31, 2007 (www.politicaldebate zone.com/2007/12/03/giuliani-ad-facts-%E2%80%9Cpromise%E2%80%9D-2/).

40. Public Law 111-352.

41. Public Law 103-62.

42. U.S. Government Accountability Office, *Data-Driven Performance Reviews Show Promise but Agencies Should Explore How to Involve Other Relevant Agencies,* GAO-13-228 (2013).

43. Martin O'Malley, speech, October 3, 2008 (www.gov.state.md.us/speeches/081003. asp).

44. CitiStat/Tenets, city government, Baltimore, Maryland (www.baltimorecity.gov/ Government/AgenciesDepartments/CitiStat/Tenets.aspx).

45. CitiStat/Tenets, city government, Baltimore, Maryland (www.ci.baltimore.md.us/ government/citistat/tenets.php).

46. CitiStat/Tenets, city government, Baltimore, Maryland (www.baltimorecity.gov/ Government/AgenciesDepartments/CitiStat/Tenets.aspx).

47. Karen Branch-Brioso, "Slay Hopes Baltimore Model Will Boost City Efficiency," *St. Louis Post-Dispatch,* July 1, 2001, p. E1.

48. Francis X. Clines, "Baltimore Uses a Databank to Wake Up City Workers," *New York Times,* June 10, 2001, p. A11.

49. Lance Dickies, "Moving Up, Talking Fast and Borrowing Good Ideas," *Seattle Times,* March 12, 2004, p. B6.

50. Joan Scales, "Mayor Playing with Fire," *Irish Times* (Dublin), July 12, 2004, p. 13.

51. David Snyder, "Baltimore Mayor Has National Reach; Critics Say Record of O'Malley Untested," *Washington Post,* August 10, 2003, p. C1.

52. Neal Peirce, email to the author and others, January 17, 2004.

53. Full disclosure: I did the site visit for this award (January 29–30, 2004), which means I am not merely an observer of this award but was a participant in the selection process.

54. Charles Bens, "CitiStat: Performance Measurement with Attitude," *National Civic Review* 94 (Summer 2005): 78.

55. Neal Peirce, "Regional Efficiency?," January 19, 2004 (http://citistates.com/archives/45/).

56. Sam Allis, "Baltimore Tutorials," *Boston Globe,* September 29, 2002, p. A2.

57. Mark Thompson, "Wonk 'n' Roller," *Time,* April 25, 2005, p. 20.

58. In some counties the word "CountyStat" has been solely about law enforcement. This is true of the CountyStat run by the sheriff's office in Harford County, Maryland, and of the one run by the district attorney of Westchester County, New York.

59. Bratton, *Turnaround,* p. 167.

60. William J. Harkins, Jr., "Mobile CitiSmart," Mobile, Alabama (www.cityofmobile.org/citism art/CitiSmartBasicsNov10.ppt).

61. Clifton Peoples, Jr., "CitiStat Puts Union Township on the Road to More Effective Government," *New Jersey Municipalities* 85 (April 2008), p. 9.

62. "Gov. Gregoire Signs Bill to Make Government More Accountable, Including GMAP and Performance Audits," press release, State of Washington Governor's Office, May 11, 2005 (www.governor.wa.gov/news/news-view.asp?pressRelease=78&newsType=1).

63. Improvement Service, *A Review of UK and International Public Sector Performance Frameworks & Approaches,* ImprovementService.org, January 2008, p. 31 (www.improvement service.org.uk/library/download-document/1708-a-review-of-uk-and-international-public-sector-performance-management-frameworks-and-approaches/).

64. Worcester Regional Research Bureau, *CompStat and CitiStat: Should Worcester Adopt These Management Techniques?,* Report 03-01 (Worcester, Mass., February 18, 2003), pp. 3–4.

65. Economy League of Greater Philadelphia, "Best Practices: Baltimore's CitiStat," July 20, 2007 (http://economyleague.org/node/183).

66. Lawrence Singer, *Local Criminal Justice Board Effectiveness,* Ministry of Justice Research Series, Office for Criminal Justice Research, United Kingdom, February 2008, p. ii (http://webarchive.nationalarchives.gov.uk/20100505212400/http://www.justice.gov.uk/publications/docs/local-criminal-justice-board.pdf).

67. Jerry Ratcliffe, *Intelligence-Led Policing* (Cullompton, U.K.: Willan Publishing, 2008), p. 76.

68. Vince E. Henry, *The Compstat Paradigm: Management Accountability in Policing, Business and the Public Sector* (Flushing, N.Y.: Looseleaf Law Publications, 2002), p. 45.

69. Paul E. O'Connell, *Using Performance Data for Accountability: The New York City Police Department's CompStat Model of Police Management* (Washington, D.C.: PricewaterhouseCoopers Endowment for the Business of Government, August 2001), p. 13.

70. Jon M. Shane, *What Every Chief Executive Should Know: Using Data to Measure Police Performance* (Flushing, N.Y.: Looseleaf Law Publications, 2007) p. 196.

71. Christopher Dickey, *Securing the City: America's Best Counterterror Force—The NYPD* (New York: Simon & Schuster, 2009), p. 104.

72. Dean Dabney, "Observations Regarding Key Operational Realities in a Compstat Model of Policing, *Justice Quarterly* 27, no. 1 (February 2010): 28. Dabney does not, however, directly attribute the four principles to Maple.

73. These include the testimony of Governor Martin O'Malley before a subcommittee of the U.S. Senate Committee on Homeland Security and Government Affairs, July 24, 2008 (www.hsgac.senate.gov/download/072408-omalley); a presentation by Detective III Jeff Godown, the Officer-in-Charge of the CompStat Section of the Los Angeles Police Department to the Southwest Chapter of the International Association of Law Enforcement Planners (www.ialepsw.com/Compstat%20Docs/Compstat_Presentation.ppt); a presentation by Samuel Clark of the Baltimore CitiStat Staff (www.apse.org.uk/presentations/08/12/dec08_pn seminar/Session%201%20Samuel%20Clark.pdf); and a report on "ServiceStat" to the Town Board by Brian X. Foley, supervisor of the Town of Brookhaven, New York, on June 14, 2007 (www.brookhaven.org/LinkClick.aspx?filetick et=o%2BVM363yLbU%3D&tabid=190&mid=779).

74. These include William F. Walsh, "Compstat: An Analysis of an Emerging Police Managerial Paradigm," *Policing: An International Journal of Police Strategies & Management* 24, no. 3 (2001): 347–62; Anthony Allan Braga, *Problem-Oriented Policing and Crime Prevention* (Monsey, N.Y.: Criminal Justice Press, 2002), p. 112; Graeme Drummond and others, "Market Orientation Applied to Police Service Strategies," *International Journal of Public Sector Management* 13, no. 7 (2000): 571–87; Russ Linden, "How Do You Create a Culture of Accountability?," *Virginia Review,* May/June 2004 (www.vareview.com/linden/collection.asp?date=MJ04); and Charles R. Swanson, Leonard Territo, and Robert W. Taylor, "Police Administration: Structures, Processes, and Behavior: Policing Today" (http://static.schoolrack.com/files/65146/587912/0135121264pp2.ppt).

75. Tim Newburn, *Criminology* (Uffculme, U.K.: Willan Publishing, 2007), p. 621.

76. For example, the Geographic Technologies Group (located in Goldsboro, N.C.) and Bishop Rock Software (located in California) emphasize Maple's four principles on their web advertising (www.geotg.com/ProductMarketing/New%20Case%20Studies/City%20of%20Laredo,%20Texas.pdf; www.bishoprocksoftware.com/).

77. Mathias Consulting (Santa Rosa, Calif.) emphasizes how the four principles can be used "in fighting healthcare fraud" (http://mathiasconsulting.com/node/388).

78. Ellen Perlman, "'STAT' Fever," *Governing,* January 2007, pp. 48–50.

79. Not all of these efforts at improving performance in public agencies and government jurisdictions were significant. Many lacked several or more of the core leadership principles or key operational components (see chapter 3) that contribute significantly to the PerformanceStat potential. Some were not serious and soon atrophied or disappeared. Some that had produced some significant results were terminated (such as Washington, D.C.'s CapStat) when the chief executive who created it was replaced by a less than enthusiastic successor.

80. Wallace Sayre, long of Columbia University, is reported to have articulated the following law: "Public and private management are fundamentally alike in all unimportant

respects." One of the important respects in which they are not at all alike concerns the challenge of improving performance. When it comes to producing results, public executives face a variety of problems that can be much more challenging than those facing business executives. These differences may include (depending on the agency) ambiguity and disagreements about purposes, inflexible budgetary and personnel systems, an army of accountability holders prepared to criticize them for even small mistakes, unrealistic expectations for quick improvements, and a greater disconnect between employees' extrinsic rewards and the organization's purposes. Sayre is quoted in Graham T. Allison, "Public and Private Management: Are They Fundamentally Alike in All Unimportant Respects?," *Proceedings of the Public Management Research Conference* (U.S. Office of Personnel Management, February 1980), pp. 27–38.

81. Elaine Kaufman died in December 2010. Elaine's closed in May 2011.

82. Douglas Martin, "Jack Maple, 48, a Designer of City Crime Control Strategies," *New York Times,* August 6, 2001.

Chapter Two

1. Brian Meyer, "CitiStat Begins Tracking of Operations," *Buffalo News,* June 17, 2006.

2. Editorial, "In Our View—Monitoring Agencies; State Government's Accountability Enhanced," *The Columbian,* May 19, 2005.

3. Rob Gurwitt, "Bratton's Brigade," *Governing* (August 2007): 32–41.

4. Heather MacDonald, "The NYPD Diaspora: Former New York Cops Bring Cutting-Edge, Effective Policing to Beleaguered Communities," *City Journal* 18, no. 3 (Summer 2008): 22–31.

5. Many of the ***Stats listed in chapter 1 were never for real—or quickly deteriorated into something that was not at all real.

6. Daniel Meyerson, *The Linguist and the Emperor: Napoleon and Champollion's Quest to Decipher the Rosetta Stone* (New York: Ballantine Books, 2004).

7. Jerry Ratcliffe, *Intelligence-Led Policing* (Cullompton, Devon, U.K.: Willan Publishing, 2008), p. 76.

8. Ibid.

9. For a long-winded, discussion of "accountability," see Robert D. Behn, *Rethinking Democratic Accountability* (Brookings, 2001). Or just read chapter 1.

10. Jon M. Shane, "Compstat Process," *FBI Law Enforcement Bulletin* 74, no. 4 (April 2004): 13. His quote is from a page on the Philadelphia Police Department's website (retrieved May 6, 2003) that is no longer active.

11. Queensland Police Service, *Multicultural Strategic Directions 2008–2012, With Action Plan 2008–2009,* p. 18 (www.police.qld.gov.au/Resources/Internet/services/reportsPublications/documents/Strategic Directions statements 2008-12 Att 2.pdf).

12. Francis X. Clines, "Baltimore Uses a Databank to Wake Up City Workers," *New York Times,* June 10, 2001.

13. Jessee Jannette, *COMPSTAT for Corrections* (Irvine, Calif.: Center for Evidence-Based Corrections, University of California, December 2006), pp.1, 3, 8.

14. Dean Dabney, "Observations Regarding Key Operational Realities in a Compstat Model of Policing," *Justice Quarterly* 27, no. 1 (February 2010): 28, 33, 30.

15. Joel Samaha, *Criminal Justice,* 7th ed. (Belmont, Calif.: Wadsworth Publishing, 2005), pp. 213, 214, 216.

16. *CompStat* is also the nickame for the journal *Computational Statistics,* and the title of the proceedings for the annual conference on computational statistics.

17. Rudolph W. Giuliani, Testimony before the House Committee on Government Reform, Thursday, March 13, 1997, Cannon House Office Building, Washington D.C. (http://home.nyc.gov/html/records/rwg/html/97a/reform.html).

18. Phyllis Parshall McDonald, "Information Technology and Crime Analysis," in *Information Technology and the Criminal Justice System,* edited by April Pattavina (Thousand Oaks, Calif.: Sage, 2005), p. 129.

19. Gerard Shields, "City Figures to Improve Efficiency," *Baltimore Sun,* November 19, 2000, p. 1B.

20. Liz Bowie, "'Stat' Coming to City Schools," *Baltimore Sun,* December 27, 2001, p. 1B.

21. Sarah Sacheli, "Francis Vows More Openness at City Council," *The Star* (Windsor, Canada) September 23, 2003.

22. "The State of the City: Masiello Views the Good While Ignoring the Bad in His Annual Speech," *Buffalo News,* February 4, 2004, p. C4.

23. Brian Meyer, "Mayor to Unveil System to Track Problems," *Buffalo News,* March 1, 2004.

24. Rachel DiCarlo, "Baltimore Mayor Martin O'Malley Is Speaking at the Convention Tonight. Is He a Rising Star in Democratic Politics?" *Daily Standard,* Irish Times blog, July 28, 2004 (www.weeklystandard.com/Content/Public/Articles/000/000/004/395vcyct.asp).

25. Joan Scales, "Mayor Playing with Fire," *Irish Times* (Dublin), July 12, 2004, p. 13.

26. Cathy Sharp, Jocelyn Jones, and Alison M. Smith, *What Do We Measure and Why? An Evaluation of the Citistat Model of Performance Management and Its Applicability to the Scottish Public Sector* (Edinburgh: The Scottish Executive, Office of Chief Researcher, 2006), p. 1.

27. Perri 6, "It's America, Where You Stand Up to Be Accountable: How Can Public Bodies Improve Their Services?" *The Guardian,* March 24, 2004 (www.guardian.co.uk/society/2004/mar/24/epublic.technology9).

28. Noah Weiss, "Government by Numbers: How CitiStat's Hard Data and Straight Talk Saved Baltimore," *Stanford Social Innovation Review* 5, no. 1 (Winter 2007): 68.

29. Michael Cross, "Public Domain," *The Guardian* (London), March 4, 2004, p. 17.

30. "How to Torture Your Contractors," *The Times* (London), March 9, 2004, Features; Public Agenda 4.

31. Eddie Barnes, "US Trip Is Chance to Learn from the Charismatic Mayor," *Scotland on Sunday,* April 4, 2004, p. 13.

32. Clines, "Baltimore Uses a Databank to Wake Up City Workers."

33. Neal Peirce, "A More-Efficient Approach to Governing Our Cities," *Seattle Times,* January 19, 2004.

34. Gerard Shields, "City Figures to Improve Efficiency," *Baltimore Sun,* November 19, 2000, p. 1B.

35. Christopher Swope, "Restless for Results," *Governing,* April 2001, p. 22.

36. Sam Allis, "Baltimore Tutorials," *Boston Globe,* September 29, 2002, p. A2.

37. Charles Bens, "CitiStat: Performance Measurement with Attitude," *National Civic Review* 94, no. 2 (Summer 2005): 78–79.

38. Lenneal Henderson, *The Baltimore CitiStat Program: Performance and Accountability* (Washington, D.C.: IBM Endowment for the Business of Government, 2003), pp. 7, 6, 12.

39. The Abell Foundation, "Abell Salutes: "CitiStat" Making Baltimore City Government More Responsive," *Abell Report* 15, no. 1 (January 2002): 8, 1.

40. The Abrahams Group, "Somerville CitiStat Performance Management" (www.theabrahamsgroup.com/SomerStat.htm).

41. Fred Siegel and Van Smith, "Can Mayor O'Malley Save Ailing Baltimore?" *City Journal* 11, no. 1 (Winter 2001): 74.

42. Perri 6, "Re-Wiring Decision Making for Local Government, Not Local Administration," *eGov Monitor,* March 18, 2004 (http://www.egovmonitor.com/features/perri6.html).

43. Perri 6, "Re-Wiring Local Decision Making," March 18, 2004 (www.localgov.co.uk/index.cfm?method=news.detail&id=7879). For more details, see Perri 6, *Rewiring Local Decision Making for Political Judgment* (London: New Local Government Network, 2004).

44. "DPSS Total Accountability, Total Success," Department of Public Social Servics, Los Angeles County, California website (www.ladpss.org/dpss/dpsstats/default.cfm).

45. DPSSTATS, "DPPS Total Accountability, Total Success," March 17, 2011 (dpss.lacounty.gov/dpss/pdfs/factsheet.pdf).

46. Swati Desai, "Performance Management at the Human Resources Administration—JobStat," in *Performance Management in State and Local Government* (Albany, N.Y.: The Nelson A. Rockefeller Institute of Government, 2005), p. 47.

47. Russell M. Linden, *Leading across Boundaries: Creating Collaborative Agencies in a Networked World* (San Francisco, Calif.: Jossey-Bass, 2010), p. 220.

48. Washington State Government, "About GMAP" (www.accountability.wa.gov/main/about.asp).

49. Brian Meyer, "CitiStat Begins Tracking of Operations," *Buffalo News,* June 17, 2006, p. D3.

50. Editorial, "Mayor for Life," *St. Louis Post-Dispatch,* February 22, 2009, p. B2

51. Richard A. Webster, "Police Slow to Provide Online Info on Crimes in N.O." *New Orleans CityBusiness,* February 23, 2009.

52. Editorial, "In Our View—Monitoring Agencies; State Government's Accountability Enhanced," *The Columbian,* May 19, 2005.

53. Accountability is a fancy philosophical word. Operationally, however, the implications are clear: The accountability holdees "recognize that, if someone is holding them accountable, two things can happen. When they do something good, nothing happens, but when they screw up all hell can break loose." Behn, *Rethinking Democratic Accountability,* p. 3.

54. Clifton Peoples, Jr., "CitiStat Puts Union Township on the Road to More Effective Government," *New Jersey Municipalities* 85, no. 4 (April 2008): 8.

55. Silvia Gullino, "Urban Regeneration and Democratization of Information Access: CitiStat Experience in Baltimore," *Journal of Environmental Management* 90, no. 6 (May 2009): 2012–19.

56. *Informing Our Nation: Improving How to Understand and Assess the USA's Position and Progress* (Washington, D.C.: U.S. Government Accountability Office, November 2004), p. 116.

57. Teresita Perez and Reece Rushing, *The CitiStat Model: How Data-Driven Government Can Increase Efficiency and Effectiveness* (Washington, D.C.: Center for American Progress, April 2007), pp. 1, 3.

58. Economy League of Greater Philadelphia, "Best Practices: Baltimore's CitiStat," July 20, 2007 (http://economyleague.org/node/183).

59. "CountyStat 2009 Quarter 1 Report" (www.montgomerycountymd.gov/content/EXEC/stat/pdfs/2009firstquarterreport.pdf).

60. The Auditor General, *Priorities and Risks Framework: A National Planning Tool for 2006/07 NHSScotland Audits* (Edinburgh, Scotland: Audit Scotland, September 2006), p. 16 (www.audit-scotland.gov.uk/docs/health/2006/prf_0607_nhsscotland.pdf).

61. National Health Service, "NHS Highland Annual Review 2007—Action Plan," Appendix 2, pp. 1–2.

62. Winnie Hu, "Child Welfare Agency, Spurred by 7-Year-Old's Death, Plans Data System Like Police Departments," *New York Times,* March 24, 2006.

63. Ibid.

64. Diane Cardwell and Sewell Chan, "Mayor Fills 2 Positions Overseeing Welfare," *New York Times,* April 12, 2006.

65. Sewell Chan, "Open Abuse Investigations Increase at Child Agency," *New York Times,* June 1, 2006.

66. Leslie Kaufman, "After 7-Year-Old's Death, Agency Monitors Cases More Aggressively," *New York Times,* December 11, 2006.

67. Ray Rivera, "Agency Lags in Protecting Children, Report Says," *New York Times,* August 10, 2007.

68. Mosi Secret, "Children's Services Leader Leaving after 7 Years," *New York Times,* July 26, 2011.

69. "Prevent, Prepare, and Protect: Regional Crime Fighting and Counterterrorism," *Government Technology,* November 2005 (http://media.govtech.net/custompubs/Oracle 1105/GT05_ORACLE_November.pdf).

70. Mark Friedman, Phil Lee, Adam Kuecking, and Andrew Boyd, *ResultsStat™ Overview*, (Bethesda, Md.: Results Leadership Group, 2009), p. 1 (http://resultsleadership.org/services/documents/rs_overview5.pdf).

71. Worldwide Law Enforcement Consulting Group, Inc., "The 'CompStat' Program" (www.worldwidelawenforcement.com/CompstatProgram.htm).

72. There are numerous versions of this parable with different numbers of blind men. I'm going with six, the number in John Godfrey Saxe's poem, "The Blind Men and the Elephant." *The Poems of John Godfrey Saxe,* complete edition (Boston: James R. Osgood and Company, 1873), pp. 135–36.

73. Frank C. Mish, executive ed., *Merriam-Webster's Collegiate Dictionary,* 10th ed. (Springfield, Mass.: Merriam-Webster, 1996), p. 374.

74. R. E. Brown, J. P. Butler, J. J. Godleski, and S. H. Loring, "The Elephant's Respiratory System: Adaptations to Gravitational Stress," *Respiration Physiology* 109, no. 2 (August 1997): 177–94.

75. Two examples of such behavioral analyses are: George M. McKay, *Behavior and Ecology of the Asiatic Elephant in Southeastern Ceylon* (Washington, D.C.: Smithsonian Institution Press, 1973); and Bruce A. Schulte, "Social Structure and Helping Behavior in Captive Elephants," *Zoo Biology* 19, no. 5 (2002): 447–59

76. Richard P. Feyman, *The Pleasure of Finding Things Out* (Cambridge, Mass.: Perseus Publishing, 1999), p. 4.

77. Frank A. Beach, "The Descent of Instinct," *Psychological Review* 62 (November 1955): 403.

Chapter Three

1. Michael Polanyi, *The Tacit Dimension* (New York: Doubleday, 1967), p. 4.

2. *Ecclesiastes* 1: 9 (King James Version).

3. Ibid.

4. Using a similar phrase, "performance gap," Downs was quite explicit about this: "The concept of a performance gap is essential in explaining what causes bureaus to change. No bureau will alter its behavior pattern unless someone believes that a significant discrepancy exists between what it is doing and what it 'ought' to be doing." Anthony Downs, *Inside Bureaucracy* (Brookings, 1967), p. 191.

5. Robert Balfanz, Liza Herzog, and Douglas J. Mac Iver, "Preventing Student Disengagement and Keeping Students on the Graduation Path in Urban Middle-Grades Schools: Early Identification and Effective Interventions," *Educational Psychologist* 42, no. 4 (2007): 223–35.

6. Education pays: in 2012, workers with a less than a high school diploma had an unemployment rate of 12.4 percent—or 50 percent above the unemployment rate of those with a high school diploma (and nearly double the average unemployment rate

of 6.8 percent). Moreover, their weekly median earnings of $471 were less than three-quarters of those with a high school diploma and less than 60 percent of the earnings for all workers. Bureau of Labor Statistics, "Employment Projections" (www.bls.gov/emp/ep_chart_001.htm).

7. Mark Moore offered a more nuanced purpose for a police department: it should not only reduce crime but also reduce fear—which, he emphasized, is not the same thing: Mark H. Moore with Anthony Braga, *The "Bottom Line" of Policing: What Citizens Should Value (and Measure!) in Police Performance* (Washington: Police Executive Research Forum, 2003); Mark H. Moore and Robert C. Trojanowicz, "Policing and the Fear of Crime," *Perspectives on Policing* no. 3 (Washington: National Institute of Justice, 1988).

8. Still, the dots themselves do not prescribe what kind of resources to deploy or what strategy to use when deploying them.

9. John F. Timoney, *Beat Cop to Top Cop* (University of Pennsylvania Press, 2010), p. 212.

10. Ibid., p. 209.

11. County of Los Angeles, Department of Mental Health, "Strategic Plan: Goals and Strategies," May 26, 2010 (http://file.lacounty.gov/dmh/cms1_165743.pdf).

12. Arresting a suspect does not complete the work of a government's criminal justice agencies—let alone of the police. Indeed, if the police have failed to collect adequate evidence (or collected it improperly), an arrested—and guilty—suspect may go free.

13. The first word in this name—"*Uniform* Crime Reports"—is misleading. These data are collected by over 750,000 individual state and local police officers, plus another 120,000 individuals in agencies of the U.S. government. Each of them is given an explicit definition for each category of crime, yet each exercises much discretion when employing these definitions

14. Eli B. Silverman, "Compstat's Innovation," in *Police Innovation: Contrasting Perspectives,* edited by David Weisburd and Anthony A. Braga (Cambridge University Press, 2006), p. 275.

15. Jack Maple (with Chris Mitchell), *The Crime Fighter* (New York: Doubleday, 1999), p. 93.

16. Elsa Walsh, "Miami Blue: The Testing of a Top Cop," *New Yorker,* March 5, 2007, p. 52.

17. Robert Moran, "Crime Reviews Will Be Closed," *Philadelphia Inquirer,* October 27, 2006, p. B2.

18. Quoted in Susan Barnes-Gelt, "Hiring New Cops Foolish," *Denver Post,* November 17, 2005, p. B-7. The official name of Denver's CompStat was Command Operations Review and Evaluation, or COPE.

19. Hackman and Wageman reached a similar conclusion about the implementation of Total Quality Management in business. "Rhetoric is winning out over substance," they wrote. "What many organizations are actually implementing is a pale or highly distorted

version of what [W. Edwards] Deming, [Kaoru] Ishikawa, and [Joseph] Juran laid out." Too often, they emphasized, "it is the difficult-to-implement portions of the program that are being finessed or ignored and the rhetoric that is being retained." J. Richard Hackman and Ruth Wageman, "Total Quality Management: Empirical, Conceptual, and Practical Issues," *Administrative Science Quarterly* 40 (June 1995): 338.

20. Los Angeles County Department of Mental Health homepage (http://dmh. lacounty.gov/wps/portal/dmh).

21. November 30, 2005.

22. William Bratton (with Peter Knobler), *Turnaround: How America's Top Cop Reversed the Crime Epidemic* (New York: Random House, 1998), pp. 202, 194.

23. Government Performance and Results Act of 1993, P. L. 103-62; 107 Stat. 285.

24. GPRA Modernization Act of 2010, P. L. 111-352, 124 Stat. 3866.

25. For more than you want to know about holding-other-people-accountable, see: Robert D. Behn, *Rethinking Democratic Accountability* (Brookings, 2001).

26. Michael Power, *The Audit Explosion* (London: Demos, 1994); Michael Power, *The Audit Society: Rituals of Verification* (Oxford University Press, 1999); Michael Power, "The Audit Society—Second Thoughts," *International Journal of Auditing* 4, no. 1 (March 2000): 111–19.

27. Frederick Herzberg, "One More Time, How Do You Motivate Employees," *Harvard Business Review* 46, no 1 (January-February, 1968): 53–62.

28. Given my definition, unless the agency or jurisdiction is actively engaged "in an effort to achieve specific public purposes," it is not using a PerformanceStat strategy.

29. Polanyi, *The Tacit Dimension*, p. 4.

30. The astute reader will observe that I am trying to do precisely what I assert is extremely difficult to do: To explain tacit knowledge in explicit words. You wondered why the book is so long?

31. For a discussion of the tacit knowledge of riding a bicycle, see Robert D. Behn, "On the Responsibility of Helping Others to Learn the Tacit Knowledge of Leadership," *Bob Behn's Public Management Report* 4, no. 9 (May 2007).

32. Before you deliver this lecture, you should read: J. P. Meijaard, Jim M. Papadopoulos, Andy Ruina, and A. L. Schwab, "Linearized Dynamics Equations for the Balance and Steer of a Bicycle: A Benchmark and Review," *Proceedings of the Royal Society A* 463, no. 2084 (August 8, 2007): 1955–82.

33. George A. Akerlof, "The Market for 'Lemons': Quality Uncertainty and the Market Mechanism," *Quarterly Journal of Economics* 84 (August, 1970): 488.

34. Gresham didn't even invent his own, original law, so he might as well get credit for this one too.

35. Robert D. Behn, "On the Value of Creating Esteem Opportunities," *Bob Behn's Public Management Report* 1, no. 9 (May 2004).

36. H. L. Mencken, *A Mencken Chrestomathy: His Own Selection of His Choicest Writing* (New York: Vintage, 1982), p. 443.

Chapter Four

1. Nathan Glazer, "The Hard Questions: Unsolved Mysteries," *New Republic* 216, no. 25, June 23, 1997, p. 29. "Perhaps government has been working less on social theory and more on resolving urgent problems through direct action," observed Glazer, though he also emphasized that "the changes we are seeing go beyond any governmental action."

2. Mark A. R. Kleiman, *When Brute Force Fails: How to Have Less Crime and Less Punishment* (Princeton University Press, 2009), p. 106.

3. Steven D. Levitt, "Understanding Why Crime Fell in the 1990s: Four Factors That Explain the Decline and Six That Do Not," *Journal of Economic Perspectives* 18, no. 1 (Winter 2004): 163.

4. Richard Rosenfeld, "The Case of the Unsolved Crime Decline," *Scientific American* 290, no. 2 (February 2004): 82.

5. Bruce D. Johnson, Andrew Golub, and Eloise Dunlap, "The Rise and Decline of Hard Drugs, Drug Markets, and Violence in Inner-City New York," in *The Crime Drop in America,* edited by Alfred Blumstein and Joel Wallman, 2nd ed. (Cambridge University Press, 2005), p. 164.

6. Garen Wintemute, "Guns and Gun Violence," in *The Crime Drop in America,* edited by Blumstein and Wallman, p. 45.

7. Wenxuan Yu and Bryon E. Price, "CompStat and Crime Reduction," in *Battleground: Criminal Justice,* edited by Gregg Barak, vol. 1 (A-L) (Westport, Conn.: Greenwood Press, 2007), p. 90.

8. Andrew R. Gimber, "The Effect of Policing Strategies: Evidence from the USA," *Economic Affairs* 27, no. 4 (December 2007): 17. Alfred Blumstein and Joel Wallman, "The Recent Rise and Fall of American Violence," in *The Crime Drop in America,* edited by Blumstein and Wallman, p. 1.

9. Richard Rosenfeld, "Crime Decline in Context," *Contexts* 1, no. 1 (Spring 2002): 25.

10. John E. Conklin, *Why Crime Rates Fell* (Boston, Mass.: Allyn and Bacon, 2003), p. vii.

11. Gary LaFree, "Social Institutions and the Crime 'Bust' of the 1990s," *Journal of Criminal Law & Criminology* 88, no. 4 (Summer 1998): 1325.

12. Franklin E. Zimring, *The Great American Crime Decline* (Oxford University Press, 2007).

13. Steven D. Levitt and Stephen J. Dubner, *Freakonomics: A Rogue Economist Explores the Hidden Side of Everything* (New York: Harper Perennial, 2009), p. 118.

14. All of these crime data come from the National Archive of Criminal Justice Data of the Bureau of Justice Statistics (U.S. Department of Justice) and are based on the FBI's annual Uniform Crime Reports (http://bjs.ojp.usdoj.gov/dataonline/).

15. Not everyone agrees: Baumer and Wolff conclude that New York City's "uniqueness has been exaggerated." Eric P. Baumer and Kevin T. Wolff, "Evaluating Contemporary

Crime Drop(s) in America, New York City, and Many Other Places," *Justice Quarterly* (forthcoming).

16. The rehabilitative strategies include: education and vocational training, individual psychotherapy, individual and group counseling, changes in the institutional environment to create a more therapeutic community, medical treatment, sentence length and the level of institutional security, and probation and parole. Douglas Lipton, Robert Martinson, and Judith Wilks, *The Effectiveness of Correctional Treatment: A Survey of Treatment Evaluation Studies* (New York: Praeger, 1975).

17. Robert Martinson, "What Works?—Questions and Answers about Prison Rreform," *Public Interest*, no. 35 (Spring 1974): 25, 48, 49 [italics in original]. Bratton and Maple's approach to reducing crime did not depend on rehabilitation, which Martinson suggested, is derived from the "social disease" explanation for crime: "Our present treatment programs are based on a theory of crime as a 'disease'—that is to say, as something foreign and abnormal in the individual which can presumably be cured." Continued Martinson, "This theory may well be flawed." Ibid., p. 49.

18. Martinson offered one caveat: "It is just possible that some of our treatment programs are working to some extent, but that our research is so bad that it is incapable of telling." Ibid., p. 49.

19. James McGuire and Philip Priestley, "Reviewing 'What Works': Past, Present, Future," in *What Works: Reducing Reoffending: Guidelines from Research and Practice*, edited by James McGuire (Chicester: John Wiley & Sons, 1995), p. 7. The "consensus that 'nothing works' " made it to Australia, observed Dixon and Maher, where it was applied not just to rehabilitation but to policing in general. "What worked in New York" was CompStat: "managerial reform, deployment based on strategic analysis of criminal intelligence and statistics and the introduction of a new way of operating." David Dixon and Lisa Maher, "Policing, Crime and Public Health: Lessons for Australia from the 'New York Miracle,'" *Criminal Justice* 5, no. 2 (May 2005): 120, 124.

20. Not everyone believes that "nothing works" should be the universal default. Ray Pawson and Nick Tilley, "What Works in Evaluation Research?" *British Journal of Criminology* 34, no. 3 (Summer 1994): 291–306. They argued "that the quasi-experimental paradigm has resulted in moribund evaluation, being itself a contributing factor to the 'nothing works' lament," and wrote that "everyone now regards Martinson's infamous conclusion on corrections programs as being based on ridiculously over-stringent expectations" (p. 291).

21. The world can't be purely random, with absolutely nothing having any impact on anything. If this were true—if nothing ever worked—entropy (the level of disorder in our physical and social worlds) would constantly increase (though heat from the sun provides an external source of physical energy). See Rudolf Clausius, William Thomson (Lord Kelvin), and the Second Law of Thermodynamics.

22. By 2010 in policing, Reiner reports, "there was explicit rejection of the earlier 'nothing works' pessimism." Robert Reiner, *The Politics of the Police*, 4th ed. (Oxford University Press, 2010), p. 13.

23. Scholars, practitioners, and journalists have, of course, proposed many more than 10 explanations. I focus on the 10 that I think warrant the most serious attention. For each, I provide only a brief description that, inevitably, fails to capture the subtlety and nuance of the reasoning offered by its advocates. For more detailed explanations, see the references cited in these notes. For a comprehensive analysis of many of these competing explanations, see: Zimring, *The Great American Crime Decline.*

24. Violent Crime Control and Law Enforcement Act of 1994, P. L. 103–322, pp. 13, 19.

25. Government Accountability Office, *Community Policing Grants: COPS Grants Were a Modest Contributor to Declines in Crime in the 1990s* (Washington: U.S. Government Accountability Office, October 2005, Report GAO-06-104), summary and p.12.

26. Edward R. Maguire, Jeffrey B. Snipes, Craig D. Uchida, and Margaret Townsend, "Counting Cops: Estimating the Number of Police Departments and Police Officers in the USA," *Policing: An International Journal of Police Strategies & Management* 21 no. 1 (1998): 115.

27. John E. Eck and Edward R. Maguire, "Have Changes in Policing Reduced Violent Crime? An Assessment of the Evidence," in *The Crime Drop in America,* edited by Blumstein and Wallman, p. 215.

28. "The size of police agencies in the United States is undoubtedly growing. . . . Unfortunately, historically inaccurate methods of counting police make it difficult to know by how much." Eck and Maguire, "Have Changes in Policing Reduced Violent Crime?" p. 216.

29. Citizens Budget Commission, *Preserving Police Services in Tough Fiscal Times* (New York: Citizens Budget Commission, December 2002), pp. 7, 8 (www.cbcny.org/sites/default/files/report_policeservices_12042002.pdf).

30. Eck and Maguire, "Have Changes in Policing Reduced Violent Crime?" p. 217.

31. John L. Worrall and Tomislav V. Kovandzic, "Police Levels and Crime Rates: A Complete Instrumental Variables Approach," *Social Science Research* 39, no. 3 (May 2010): 515. They also note "the reverse causality problem." Maybe "governments alter police levels in response to crime" (p. 506).

32. Zimring, *The Great American Crime Decline,* p. 79.

33. In 1994, the uniformed employees in NYPD (plus the Transit Authority and the Housing Authority Police) totaled 37,918. In 2000, the number was 40,285. Citizens Budget Commission, *Preserving Police Services in Tough Fiscal Times* (New York: Citizens Budget Commission, December 2002), p. 7 (www.cbcny.org/sites/default/files/report_policeservices_12042002.pdf). In January 2010, New York City's Office of Management and Budget forecast that NYPD's uniformed force for June 30, 2010 would be 33,217. *The Financial Plan of the City of New York, Fiscal Years 2010-2014: Full-Time and Full-Time Equivalent Staffing Levels* (New York: City of New York Office of Management and Budget, January 2010), p. 27.

34. Franklin E. Zimring, *The City That Became Safe: New York's Lessons for Urban Crime and Its Control* (Oxford University Press, 2012), p. 1.

35. Matthew J. Hickman and Brian A. Reaves, *Local Police Departments 2000* (Washington: Bureau of Justice Statistics, 2003), p. 1. Brian A. Reaves, *Local Police Departments 2007* (Washington: Bureau of Justice Statistics, 2010), p. 8.

36. Dennis C. Smith and William J. Bratton, "Performance Management in New York City: Compstat and the Revolution in Police Management," in *Quicker, Better, Cheaper: Managing Performance in American Government,* edited by Dall W. Forsythe (Albany, N.Y.: The Rockefeller Institute Press, 2001), p. 453.

37. William J. Bratton, "Crime Is Down in New York City: Blame the Police," in *Zero Tolerance: Policing a Free Society,* edited by Norman Dennis, 2nd ed. (London: IEA Health and Welfare Unit, 1998), pp. 29–43.

38. Both community policing and CompStat decentralize responsibility and authority: community policing decentralizes to the cop on the beat; CompStat decentralizes to the precinct commander. NYPD's leadership concluded that the precinct commander not the beat cop was best positioned to solve problems: Louis Anemone, one of Bratton's key NYPD executives, explained:

> Experience has taught NYPD that there is no one more capable of determining the best way to solve local problems than the man or woman who commands the precinct. Certain models of community policing give the role of 'all-purpose problem solver' to the cop on the beat. However, most officers on patrol lack the expertise, authority or network of connections necessary to handle problems on their own. . . . It is the precinct commander who has personal familiarity with the neighborhood and its issues . . . [and] the experience, knowledge, authority and resources required to build a multi-member team to successfully address a problem over the long term.

Louis R. Anemone and Francis E. Spangenberg, "Building on Success: TrafficStat Takes NYPD's CompStat Method in a New Direction," *Police Chief* 67, no. 2 (February 2000), pp. 23–24.

39. For a debate over the value of problem-oriented policing, see: John E. Eck, "Science, Values, and Problem-Oriented Policing: Why Problem-Oriented Policing?" and Anthony A. Braga and David Weisburd, "Problem-Oriented Policing: The Disconnect between Principles and Practice," both in *Police Innovation: Contrasting Perspectives,* edited by David Weisburd and Anthony A. Braga (Cambridge University Press, 2006), pp. 117–32 and 133–52.

40. Herman Goldstein, "Improving Policing: A Problem-Oriented Approach," *Crime & Delinquency* 25, no. 2 (April 1979): 236, 238, 236.

41. Herman Goldstein, *Problem-Oriented Policing* (New York: McGraw-Hill, 1990). For another take on the problem-oriented approach, see Malcolm K. Sparrow, *The Character of Harms: Operational Challenges in Control* (Cambridge University Press, 2008).

42. For a debate over the value of community policing, see Welsey G. Skogan, "The Promise of Community Policing," and Stephen Mastrofski, "Community Policing: A

Skeptical View," in *Police Innovation,* edited by Weisburd and Braga, pp. 27–43 and pp. 44–73.

43. Community Policing Consortium, *Understanding Community Policing: A Framework for Action* (Washington: Bureau of Justice Assistance, Office of Justice Programs, U.S. Department of Justice, August 1994), pp. 13, 14.

44. Malcolm K. Sparrow, "Implementing Community Policing," *Perspectives on Policing,* no. 9 (November 1988), National Institute of Justice, U.S. Department of Justice, p. 1.

45. Bratton, "Crime Is Down in New York City," p. 34.

46. James Q. Wilson and George L. Kelling, "Broken Windows," *Atlantic Monthly* 249, no. 3 (March 1982), p. 31.

47. Ibid., p. 30.

48. Ibid., pp. 32, 34.

49. Ibid., p. 38.

50. It has also been called "zero tolerance" policing: Benjamin Bowling, "The Rise and Fall of New York Murder: Zero Tolerance or Crack's Decline?" *British Journal of Criminology* 39, no. 4 (Autumn 1999): 531–54. Judith A. Greene, "Zero Tolerance: A Case Study of Police Policies and Practices in New York City," *Crime & Delinquency* 45, no. 2 (April 1999): 171–87. Andrea McArdle and Tanya Erzen (eds.), *Zero Tolerance Quality of Life and the New Police Brutality in New York City* (New York University Press, 2001). Bratton, however, found the zero-tolerance phrase "troublesome." He argued that it "smacks of over-zealousness," "communicates to political leaders and the general public an unrealistic view of what police can accomplish," "is not credible to trouble-makers," and "as a slogan [it] belies the complexity of police work." Bratton, "Crime Is Down in New York City," pp. 42, 43.

51. For more on broken-windows, see: George L. Kelling and Catherine M. Coles, *Fixing Broken Windows: Restoring Order and Reducing Crime in Our Communities* (New York: Free Press, 1996).

52. In the war against graffiti on public transit, David Gunn was a hawk. I first met him on Saturday, October 22, 1983 at the Hilton Hotel in Philadelphia, when he was the general manager and chief operations officer of SEPTA, the Southeastern Pennsylvania Transportation Authority. Gunn was scheduled to give a major conference talk, "How to Revitalize a Public Agency," which I was to moderate. Arriving a little late (but in time to speak), Gunn apologized. He had ridden one of SEPTA's trolleys to the hotel, and the car was decorated with graffiti. This was before the advent of cell phones; so when Gunn got to the hotel, he found a pay phone and called SEPTA to have the trolley taken out of service immediately.

53. Nathan Glazer, "On Subway Graffiti in New York," *Public Interest,* no. 54 (Winter 1979): 8.

54. Kelling and Coles, *Fixing Broken Windows,* pp. 115–17.

55. William Bratton with Peter Knobler, *Turnaround: How America's Top Cop Reversed the Crime Epidemic* (New York: Random House, 1998), pp. xxiv, 144, 152, 159.

For a debate on the value of broken-windows policing, see: William H. Sousa and George L. Kelling, "Of 'Broken Windows,' Criminology, and Criminal Justice," and Ralph B. Taylor, "Incivilities Reduction Policing, Zero Tolerance, and the Retreat from Coproduction: Weak Foundations and Strong Pressures," in *Police Innovation,* edited by Weisburd and Braga, pp. 76–97 and 98–114. For another critique, see: Bernard E. Harcourt, *Illusion of Order: The False Promise of Broken Windows* (Harvard University Press, 2001).

56. Glazer, "The Hard Questions," p. 29. "Perhaps government has been working less on social theory and more on resolving urgent problems through direct action," observed Glazer, though he noted, "the changes we are seeing go beyond government action."

57. Michael Lipsky, *Street-Level Bureaucracy: Dilemmas of the Individual in Public Services* (30th Anniversary Expanded Edition) (New York: Russell Sage Foundation, 2010), pp. 13, 14.

58. Zimring, *The City That Became Safe,* p. 145.

59. Bratton, "Crime Is Down in New York City," p. 43.

60. Zimring, *The City That Became Safe,* p. 150. "The reason that a devotion to the across-the-board strict enforcement of public order offenses didn't contribute to the [New York City] crime decline is that it never happened," p.147.

61. Anthony A. Braga and David L. Weisburd, *Policing Problem Places: Crime Hot Spots and Effective Prevention* (Oxford University Press, 2010), p. 9.

62. For a debate on CompStat's value, see: Eli B. Silverman, "Compstat's Innovation," and David Weisburd, Stephen D. Mastrofski, James J. Willis, and Rosann Greenspan, "Changing Everything So That Everything Can Remain the Same: Compstat and American Policing," both in *Police Innovation,* edited by Weisburd and Braga, pp. 267–83 and 284–301.

63. Smith and Bratton, "Performance Management in New York City," pp. 455, 457.

64. Lorraine Mazerolle, Sacha Rombouts, and James McBroom, "The Impact of CompStat on Reported Crime in Queensland," *Policing: An International Journal of Police Strategies and Management* 30, no. 2 (2007), pp. 237, 251.

65. Marilyn Chilvers and Don Weatherburn, "The New South Wales 'Compstat' Process: Its Impact on Crime," *Australian and New Zealand Journal of Criminology* 37, no. 1 (April 2004), p. 44. For three reasons, their analysis cannot provide "definitive evidence": the short period for which data were available (NSW suspended OCR in early 2000 for the Sydney Olympics, though it has since resumed); a change in NSW's police commissioner; and structural changes in the department (p. 45).

66. Richard Rosenfeld, Robert Fornango, and Eric Baumer, "Did Ceasefire, CompStat, and Exile Reduce Homicide?" *Criminology & Public Policy* 4, no. 3 (August 2005), p. 419.

67. Quoted in Eric Pooley and Elaine Rivera, "One Good Apple," *Time,* January 15, 1996.

68. Given that none of these six strategies are mutually exclusive and assuming that there is only one version of each strategy, a police department has a total of $2^6 = 64$ different possible combinations. Given, however, the variations of each strategy, the actual number of possible combinations is much higher.

69. Any experiment requires the ability to deny the treatment to the control group. Because each of these treatment strategies is an "idea" (not something physical like a vaccine), it is impossible to prevent the leaders of a control-group precinct from learning about it, concluding that it might help, and then implementing something like it. See chapter 14.

70. In the United States, concluded one study, "there may be as many as 14,628 local police agencies . . . 3,156 sheriffs' agencies . . . 3,280 special police agencies." (Don't forget the state police.) Maguire and others, "Counting Cops," pp. 106, 107, 108.

71. Braga and Weisburd, *Policing Problem Places,* pp. 36, 240.

72. Zimring, *The City That Became Safe,* pp. 227, 142, 143.

73. In 1994 and 1995, in addition to creating CompStat, NYPD created eight different *policing* strategies—Police Strategy No 1: Getting Guns Off the Streets of New York; Police Strategy No 2: Curing Youth Violence in the Schools and on the Streets; Police Strategy No 3: Driving Drug Dealers out of New York; Police Strategy No 4: Breaking the Cycle of Domestic Violence; Police Strategy No 5: Reclaiming the Public Spaces of New York; Police Strategy No 6: Reducing Auto-Related Crime in New York; Police Strategy No 7: Rooting Out Corruption; Building Organizational Integrity; Police Strategy No 8: Reclaiming the Roads of New York. All are available from the National Criminal Justice Reference Service.

74. Rosenfeld, "The Case of the Unsolved Crime Decline," p. 82.

75. Warren Friedman, "Volunteerism and the Decline of Violent Crime," *Journal of Criminal Law & Criminology* 88, no. 4 (Summer 1998), p. 1455.

76. Rosenfeld, "Crime Decline in Context," p. 31.

77. Jeremy Travis, "Foreword" [to a "Symposium: Why Is Crime Decreasing?"], *Journal of Criminal Law & Criminology* 88, no. 4 (Summer 1998), p. 1173.

78. Quoted in John Tierney, "Prison Population Can Shrink When Police Crowd Streets," *New York Times,* January 25, 2013 (www.nytimes.com/2013/01/26/nyregion/police-have-done-more-than-prisons-to-cut-crime-in-new-york.html?pagewanted=all&_r=0).

79. Andrew R. Gimber, "The Effect of Policing Strategies: Evidence from the USA," *Economic Affairs* 27, no. 4 (December 2007), p. 22.

80. Kleiman, *When Brute Force Fails,* p. 106.

81. Ibid., p. 106.

82. Jack Maple (with Chris Mitchell), *The Crime Fighter* (New York: Doubleday, 1999), p. 148.

Chapter Five

1. Friedrich Nietzsche, *The Wanderer and His Shadow* (1880), in Friedrich Nietzsche, *Human, All Too Human: A Book for Free Spirits,* translated by R. J. Hollingdale (Cambridge University Press, 1996), p. 360. The full quotation is: "Forgetting our objectives.— During the journey we commonly forget its goal. Almost every profession is chosen and commenced as a means to an end but continued as an end in itself. Forgetting our objectives is the most frequent act of stupidity."

2. James Q. Wilson, "The Bureaucracy Problem," *Public Interest* no. 6 (Winter 1967): 8.

3. William Bratton (with Peter Knobler), *Turnaround: How America's Top Cop Reversed the Crime Epidemic* (New York: Random House: 1998), p. 194.

4. John Buntin, "William J. Bratton: Solid Brass," *Governing,* November 2007, p. 30.

5. Eric Pooley and Elaine Rivera, "One Good Apple," *Time,* January 15, 1996.

6. Phyllis Parshall McDonald, *Managing Police Operations: Implementing the New York Crime Control Model—CompStat* (Belmont, Calif.: Wadsworth, 2002), p. 2.

7. Buntin, "William J. Bratton," p. 30.

8. David H. Bayley, *Police for the Future* (Oxford University Press, 1994), p. 3.

9. James Q. Wilson, *Varieties of Police Behavior: The Management of Law and Order in Eight Communities* (Harvard University Press, 1968), p. 63.

10. Lance Montauk and Virginia L Morrison, "Crime, Confidentiality, and Clinical Judgment," *The Lancet* 364, supplement 1 (December 18, 2004): s46.

11. Martín Sánchez Jankowski, "Ethnography, Inequality, and Crime in the Low-Income Community," in *Crime and Inequality,* edited by John Hagan and Ruth D. Peterson (Stanford University Press, 1995), p. 80.

12. George Elliott Howard, "Alcohol and Crime: A Study of Social Causation," *American Journal of Sociology* 74, no. 1 (July 1918): 62.

13. Quoted by Lawrence Rosen, "The Creation of the Uniform Crime Report: The Role of Social Science," *Social Science History* 19, no 2 (Summer 1995): 216–17.

14. Benjamin Bowling, "The Rise and Fall of New York Murder: Zero Tolerance or Crack's Decline?" *British Journal of Criminology* 39, no. 4 (Autumn 1999): 550.

15. Nancy Ritter, ed., "LAPD Chief Bratton Speaks Out: What's Wrong with Criminal Justice Research—and How to Make It Right," *National Institute of Justice Journal* no. 257 (June 2007): 29, 30.

16. "Chief's Message," *The Beat* LV, no. 1 (January-March 2009): 2.

17. Richard Winton, "Bratton is Sworn in for Second Term—The Chief Cites LAPD Achievements under His Leadership and Vows Crime Will Keep Falling," *Los Angeles Times,* October 26, 2007 (http://articles.latimes.com/2007/oct/26/local/me-bratton26).

18. Ritter, ed., "LAPD Chief Bratton Speaks Out," p. 30.

19. In addition to "rules," wrote Allison, public organizations have "standard operating procedures." They also have "routines" that bundle these rules and procedures together, and these routines collectively make up an organization's "repertoire." Graham T. Allison, *The Essence of Decision: Explaining the Cuban Missile Crisis* (Boston: Little, Brown and Company, 1971), chapter 3 (particularly p. 83).

20. Elie Abel, *The Missile Crisis* (Philadelphia: J. P. Lippincott, 1966), p. 156. Eight months later, however, McNamara got the final word: Anderson was not reappointed as chief of naval operations.

21. Frederick Winslow Taylor, *The Principles of Scientific Management* (New York: W. W. Norton, 1967 [1911]), particularly pp. 25-26.

22. These crime data come from the Bureau of Justice Statistics (U.S. Department of Justice) and are based on the FBI's annual Uniform Crime Reports (http://bjs.ojp.usdoj. gov/dataonline/).

23. Jack Maple with Chris Mitchell, *The Crime Fighter* (New York: Doubleday, 1999), p. 249.

24. Martin O'Malley, "Remarks at the Baltimore Stat Summit," September 10, 2008 (www.governor.maryland.gov/speeches/080910b.asp).

25. To Wilson, a "production organization" is one "in which both 'outputs' and 'outcomes' can be observed." But Wilson used the words "outputs" and "outcomes" differently than I and others do. I think of an "output" as what happens at the border of the organization—the results that government actually produces, such as criminals arrested. In contrast, an "outcome" is a societal consequence beyond this border—such as citizen safety—that government *and* other societal forces affect only indirectly. This distinction between an output and an outcome isn't always clear, if only because the border of governmental responsibility isn't always clear.

To Wilson, "observable outputs" are "the activities of [IRS] auditors, [of USPS] letter sorters, [and of Social Security Administration] claims processors." The corresponding "observable outcomes" are "taxes collected, mail delivered, [and] checks received." For a motor vehicle agency, he wrote, the outputs are "clerks working" and the outcomes are "licenses received." Yet, given that the purpose for licensing drivers and vehicles is to improve highway safety, I think the "outcomes" for the motor vehicle agency are highway accidents, injuries, and deaths prevented (though others share responsibility for this outcome). James Q. Wilson, *Bureaucracy: What Government Agencies Do and Why They Do It* (New York: Basic Books, 1989), pp. 159–63.

Thus, as I and (I think) most scholars use the words, Wilson's "production organization" is one in which both (1) the internal "*activities*" and (2) the production "*outputs*" can be observed. By this definition, most of the departments of most cities are what Wilson calls a "production organization."

Pollitt makes a similar distinction: "a 'production' task such as the issuing of driving licenses is standardizable, predictable, and measurable in ways that a 'coping' task such as mental health counseling is not." Christopher Pollitt, "Performance Management in Practice: A Comparative Study of Executive Agencies," *Journal of Public Administration Research and Theory* 16, no. 1 (January 2006), p. 29.

26. Quoted by Neal Peirce, "A More-Efficient Approach to Governing Our Cities," *Seattle Times,* Monday, January 19, 2004 (http://community.seattletimes.nwsource.com/ archive/?date=20040119&slug=peirce19).

27. In February 2012, a three-year-old boy in Townsend, Massachusetts, called 911 when his grandmother had a seizure. See "3-Year-Old Townsend Boy Lauded for Saving 'Nana'" (www.boston.com/news/local/massachusetts/articles/2012/02/29/3_year_old_townsend_boy_lauded_for_saving_nana/).

28. A four-year-old called 911 for help with arithmetic, honest (www.hark.com/clips/yqmmjfzynr-math-homework-911-call).

29. Lorraine Mazerolle and others, "Managing Citizen Calls to the Police: The Impact of Baltimore's 3-1-1 Call System," *Criminology & Public Policy* 2, no. 1 (November 2002): 97–124.

30. Cities that use the one-call-to-city-hall phrase include: Tuscaloosa, Chicago, Fort Wayne, Somerville (Massachusetts), Detroit, Rochester (New York), and Akron. Miami-Dade County, Florida, has a single 311 system for all 35 incorporated municipalities as well as the unincorporated areas.

31. Paul J. Cosgrove, "Beyond the Beltway," a presentation at the "Big City/County Conference," McLean, Virginia, March 31, 2008 (http://media.centerdigitalgov.com/CenterEvents/Presentations/Beyond_the_Beltway_2008/cosgrave_slides.ppt).

32. David R. Eichenthal, "Using 311 Data to Measure Performance and Manage City Finances," *Government Finance Review* (August, 2008): 46–50.

33. The relevant information includes a street address that can identify the location of the pothole or graffiti. But what about graffiti inside a city park for which there is no street address? For a while in Baltimore, this was a problem. Chris Yakaitis, "All Signs Point to Confusion at Park: City Can't Quickly Fix Problems It Struggles to Locate, Visitors Say," *Baltimore Sun,* June 12, 2006, pp. 1B, 5B.

34. Open Baltimore website, CitiStat, WaterStat data (https://data.baltimorecity.gov/CitiStat/CitiStat-Water-Stat-1-30-2013/26dk-zcnp).

35. Open Baltimore website, CitiStat (https://data.baltimorecity.gov/browse?category=CitiStat&utf8=%E2%9C%93).

36. Interview with Schlanger, January 29, 2004.

37. Since Baltimore created its 48-hour pothole-repair guarantee, other cities have made similar (if not always as firm) commitments: Buffalo, Cleveland, Denver, Golden (Colorado), Indianapolis, Kansas City, Miami (Ohio), Moline (Illinois), San Francisco, St. Louis, Seattle.

38. W. Eric Martin, "Point of Contact," *Government Technology,* May 12, 2004 (www.govtech.com/gt/articles/90220?id=90220&full=1&story_pg=1).

39. "Mayor Sheila Dixon's 2007 Inaugural Address," January 18, 2007 (www.msa.md.gov/megafile/msa/speccol/sc3500/sc3520/014400/014499/html/inaugural_jan07.html).

40. Michael Dresser, "After the Snow, a Profusion of Potholes: Snow-Removal Crews Shift to Filling In Craters," *Baltimore Sun,* February 18, 2010 (http://articles.baltimoresun.com/2010-02-18/features/bal-md.cm.potholes18feb18_1_snow-removal-secondary-roads-richard-hooper).

41. Carl Campanile, "Top City Gripes: Potholes, Dirty Street and Noise," *New York Post,* June 23, 2005, p. 16. Survey Research Unit, School of Public Affairs, Baruch College, "Neighborhood Problems and Quality of Life, Spring 2005, Special Report 7" (a survey conducted in collaboration with Citizens for NYC). In this survey, property crime ranked 13th; violent crime was 20th. This survey was not a random sample, but of selected community leaders. When Citizens for NYC conducted the survey again in

2006, potholes had dropped from first to sixth on the list. Property crime dropped one notch to 14th; youth violence or gangs was 16th, and violent crime had dropped to 24th. Survey Research Unit, School of Public Affairs, Baruch College, "Neighborhood Problems and Quality of Life, Spring 2006, Special Report 11" (a survey conducted in collaboration with Citizens for NYC).

42. Indianapolis hasn't created a better way to fill potholes. Between May and October, however, it sealed roadway cracks that may later become potholes between November and April. As with all infrastructure, preventive maintenance helps. Paul W. Taylor, "Pothole Principles: Preventing Small Problems from Growing Bigger Takes on Significance in Today's Economy," *Governing* 23, no. 8 (May 2010): 8.

43. City and County of Honolulu, "Mayor Reports Progress in His War on Potholes," Press Release M-25, March 30, 2005.

44. Matthew D. Gallagher, "CitiStat: Bringing a New Level of Efficiency and Effectiveness to Baltimore City's Water Utility," in *Management Innovation in U.S. Public Water and Wastewater Systems,* edited by Paul Seidenstat, Michael Nadol, Dean Kaplan, and Simon Hakim (Hoboken, N.J.: John Wiley & Sons, 2005), p. 295.

45. Anderson Cooper 360 Degrees program, CNN transcript, September 11, 2008 (http://premium.cnn.com/TRANSCRIPTS/0809/11/acd.01.html).

46. Christopher Swope, "Flakes of Danger: The One Thing a Big-City Mayor Can't Afford to Do Is Mishandle Snow Removal," *Governing* 22, no. 3 (December 2008): 60.

47. Quoted in Donna Slack, "When Dealing with Snow, All Storms Are Political," *Boston Globe,* December 23, 2008, p. B4.

48. Although Baltimore County completely surrounds the City of Baltimore, the county provides no services within the city. Rather, the city also functions as a county, delivering the services that are delivered in the rest of Maryland by counties. For example, the City of Baltimore has a health department. Most U.S. cities (except for those, such as New York and San Francisco, which are also counties) do not have a health department. Thus, the City of Baltimore provides more services than a typical U.S. city.

49. Deborah Lamm Weisel, *Graffiti,* Problem-Oriented Guides for Police; Problem-Specific Guides Series, Guide no. 9 (Washington, D.C.: Center for Problem-Oriented Policing, Office of Community Oriented Policing Services, U.S. Department of Justice, August 2004), p. 3.

50. This is the "broken-windows theory" of Kelling and Wilson. One case of graffiti has the same impact as "one unrepaired broken window [which] is a signal that no one cares"—and thus that the neighborhood is unsafe. George L. Kelling and James Q. Wilson, "Broken Windows: The Police and Neighborhood Safety," *The Atlantic* (March 1982), p. 31. See also George L. Kelling and Catherine M. Coles, *Fixing Broken Windows: Restoring Order and Reducing Crime in Our Communities* (New York: Free Press, 1996).

51. Weisel, *Graffiti,* p. 35.

52. During 2009, the 311 service requests (SRs) for graffiti removal averaged 474 per month. But during the first seven months, the average was 560; while during the final

three months it was 353. For 2010, the average was 347 per month. Then, in 2012, it jumped to 717 per month. What caused these changes in the volume of graffiti SRs? The answer isn't obvious. These data depend on crew performance, on data-entry practices, and on SR definitions and categories, all of which can change over time, as the people learn and responsibilities change. For example, these data reflect 311 SRs, which are assigned to Public Works and are the most frequent graffiti SR. The second most common are the "proactive" SRs created by the crews themselves. At both the beginning and the end of each shift, each graffiti crew is supposed to ride the "gateways"—the major streets leading into the city—and when they find some graffiti to immediately abate it. But do these proactive SRs get entered accurately? Not necessarily always. Also, graffiti in the city's parks was originally the responsibility of the Department of Recreation and Parks, for which there was a separate SR. But before Sharkey arrived, this responsibility was shifted to Public Works, and eventually, the SRs were merged into one. Similarly and also before Sharkey arrived, Public Works took over responsibility for graffiti on school grounds and buildings (in trade for one of the school system's trucks).

Finally, the changes could reflect citizen perception of the city's competence. In 2009, it took the city 3.3 days, on average to abate a case of graffiti that was called in to city hall, and during the first seven months of the year, the average was 3.8 days. In 2010, however, the crews improved their efficiency and the average number dropped by more than a full day to 2.1 days. Thus, if citizens saw that the city was acting on their calls to 311—and acting promptly—they might be encouraged to make more requests. For more on this see chapter 7.

53. Wilson's four types of public agencies are: production, procedural, craft, and coping. Wilson, *Bureaucracy*, p. 159.

54. Pollitt, "Performance Management in Practice," p. 29.

55. Anthony Downs, *Inside Bureaucracy* (Brookings, 1967), p. 209.

56. "About the Agency," FEMA website (www.fema.gov/about-agency).

Chapter Six

1. Philip Selznick, *Leadership in Administration: A Sociological Interpretation* (New York: Harper & Row, 1957), p. 143.

2. Peter H. Schuck, "Controlling Administrative Discretion," in *Foundations of Administrative Discretion*, edited by Peter H. Schuck, 2nd ed. (New York: Foundation Press, 2004), p. 175.

3. This material is from an interview with Karen Kent, then director of DPSSTATS at the Los Angeles County Department of Public Social Services, on September 24, 2008.

4. This is not a government problem. It is a large organization problem. Large businesses have it too.

5. Here I use Downs's definition of both a "bureau" (a.k.a. bureaucracy) and a "bureaucrat." A bureaucracy has four key characteristics: (1) "it is large"; (2) "a majority

of its members are full-time workers who depend upon their employment in the organization for most of their income"; (3) these workers are hired, retained, and promoted based on "some type of assessment" of their past and future performance, not on personal characteristics (religion, political connections, and so on) or election; and (4) "the major portion of its output is not directly or indirectly evaluated in any markets external to the organization." A "bureaucrat" is anyone whose employment possesses these four characteristics. Anthony Downs, *Inside Bureaucracy* (Brookings, 1967), pp. 24–26.

By this definition, almost everyone employed by a government is a bureaucrat who works in a bureaucracy. The exceptions are elected officials and perhaps a few of their political aides. By this definition, the members of LADPSS's DPSSTATS staff and Baltimore's CitiStat staff are "bureaucrats" for they are selected, retained, and promoted almost exclusively on the basis of their performance. Many political appointees are, by Downs's definition, bureaucrats; for if they fail to perform up to the elected official's expectations, they could be moved to a different job in which either their performance was at least adequate (in which case he would still be a Downsian "bureaucrat") or in which performance was irrelevant to employment (in which case he would not be a "bureaucrat").

6. Max Weber, *From Max Weber: Essays in Sociology,* translated and edited by H. H. Gerth and C. Wright Mills (Oxford University Press, 1946), pp. 196–98; Downs, *Inside Bureaucracy;* James Q. Wilson, *Bureaucracy: What Government Agencies Do and Why They Do It* (New York: Basic Books, 1989).

7. Yes, Rousseau, in a survey of research on organizational behavior, found "a new era of flexible, lateral forms of organizing" and a "weaker role of hierarchy." She was, however, focusing almost exclusively on business firms. And although such firms must treat people (primarily employees and customers) fairly, this is a constraint not a purpose. In government, however, treating people (employees and citizens) fairly is a fundamental value. And to ensure that they treat people fairly, government agencies employ more and more-detailed rules and rely on hierarchies to ensure that those rules are followed. Denise M. Rousseau, "Organizational Behavior in the New Organizational Era," *Annual Review of Psychology* 48 (1997): 516, 519.

8. Weber thought "speed" was a characteristic of bureaucracy only because he compared it with the "collegiate, honorific, and avocational forms of administration" of earlier centuries. Today, we tend to think of governmental bureaucracies as "slow" because we compare them with entrepreneurial firms and informal networks (though corporate bureaucracies can be slow too).

9. Weber, *From Max Weber,* p. 214.

10. Quoted by Reinhard Bendix, *Max Weber: An Intellectual Portrait* (University of California Press, 1960), p. 421.

11. Johan P. Olsen, "Maybe It Is Time to Rediscover Bureaucracy," *Journal of Public Administration Research and Theory* 16, no. 1 (January 2006): 2, 8, 5.

12. Although the phrase "the one best way" is predominantly attributed to Frederick Winslow Taylor (it is even the title of a biography of Taylor), it was actually coined by Frank and Lillian Gilbreth (better known as the authors of and the parents in the original

Cheaper by the Dozen). See, for example, Brian Price, "Frank and Lillian Gilbreth and the Motion Study Controversy, 1907–1930," in *A Mental Revolution: Scientific Management since Taylor,* edited by Daniel Nelson (Ohio State University Press, 1992), pp. 58–76.

For an example of the Gilbreths' frequent use of the phrase, see: Frank B. Gilbreth and Lillian Moller Gilbreth, *Motion Study for the Handicapped* (London: George Routledge & Sons, 1920), particularly p. 93, where they write of "our quest of the one best way to do work." The biography of Taylor is: Robert Kanigel, *The One Best Way: Frederick Winslow Taylor and the Enigma of Efficiency* (New York: Viking, 1997).

13. Ann Gerhart, "Charm City's Mr. Charming; Mayor O'Malley Cheers Baltimore On," *Washington Post,* March 10, 2000, pp. C1, C7.

14. The original research that produced social-psychology's concept of "diffusion of responsibility" was motivated by the failure of 38 bystanders to help Kitty Genovese as she was attacked and killed late one night in 1964 on the streets of Queens. Latané and Darley hypothesized that if each of the 38 had thought no other person was around, he or she would have been more likely to have helped in some way. They and others conducted a variety of laboratory experiments to test and validate this hypothesis. John M. Darley and Bibb Latané, "Bystander Intervention in Emergencies: Diffusion of Responsibility," *Journal of Personality and Social Psychology* 8, no. 4 (April 1968): 377–83; Latané and Darley, "Group Inhibition of Bystander Intervention in Emergencies," *Journal of Personality and Social Psychology* 10, no. 3 (November 1968): 215–21; Latané and Darley, *The Unresponsive Bystander: Why Doesn't He Help?* (New York: Appleton-Century-Crofts, 1970).

Although "diffusion of responsibility" was originally (and has been primarily) employed to explain whether people will help in an emergency situation, it has been adapted to circumstances in which people may or may not decide to put some effort into contributing to the solution of a problem. For example, Yechiam and Barron concluded that it also applied to whether people respond to online requests for assistance or advice. Latané, Williams, and Harkins experimented with collective efforts in nonemergency situations, surveyed other research, found similar behavior, and suggested: "If a person is a member of a group that is the target of social forces from outside the group, the impact of these forces on any given member should diminish in inverse proportion to the strength, immediacy, and number of group members." Eldad Yechiam and Greg Barron, "Learning to Ignore Online Help Requests," *Computational & Mathematical Organization Theory* 9, no. 4 (December 2003): 327–39. Bibb Latané, Kipling Williams, and Stephen Harkins, "Many Hands Make Light Work: The Causes and Consequences of Social Loafing," *Journal of Personality and Social Psychology* 37, no. 6 (June 1979): 823.

Moreover, without any reference to this literature, O'Toole notes that the "diffusion of responsibility" has been "a matter of concern for public-sector ethicists." Laurence J. O'Toole, Jr., "Treating Networks Seriously: Practical and Research-Based Agendas in Public Administration," *Public Administration Review* 57, no. 1 (January/February 1997): 45–52.

15. Latané and others, "Many Hands Make Light Work," p. 822.

16. See, for example, William G. Ouchi, "Markets, Bureaucracies, and Clans," *Administrative Science Quarterly* 25, no. 1 (March 1980): 134.

17. Robert D. Behn, *Rethinking Democratic Accountability* (Brookings, 2001), p. 15.

18. Weber, *From Max Weber*, p. 228.

19. Downs, *Inside Bureaucracy*, p. 143.

20. Robert D. Behn, "Do Goals Help Create Innovative Organizations," in *Public Management Reform and Innovation: Research, Theory, and Application*, edited by H. George Frederickson and Jocelyn Johnston (University of Alabama Press, 1999), p. 83. Apparently, professional athletes also have this problem with their new coaches: "It takes some doing for players to refrain from adopting a "we-be" attitude toward coaches— we-be here before you and we-be here after you." See Albert Bandura, *Self-Efficacy: The Exercise of Control* (New York: W. H. Freeman & Company, 1997), p. 402.

21. Robert K. Merton, "Bureaucratic Structure and Personality," *Social Forces* 18, no. 4 (May, 1940): 565.

22. Government could, of course, be treating citizens both fairly (that is, equally) and poorly. Everyone—not just some—could get identically horrid service.

23. For the importance of rules in a bureaucracy, see: Downs, *Inside Bureaucracy*, pp. 59–61; Steven Kelman, *Unleashing Change: A Study of Organizational Renewal in Government* (Brookings, 2005), pp. 10–16; Weber, *From Max Weber*, pp. 216–21; Wilson, *Bureaucracy*, particularly chapter 18, pp. 333–45.

24. Following the rules can be a measure of success even if these rules were neither enacted by the legislature nor promulgated by a jurisdiction-wide regulatory agency but were formulated internally in response not to any external pressure but simply to the habit and comfort that can evolve from a reliance on rules reflecting organizational culture and norms. For example, Kelman reported being "repeatedly surprised [by] how many common procurement practices are not mandated by the [jurisdiction-wide] procurement regulations, but come from a procurement culture that has developed in contracting offices [within individual agencies]." Steven Kelman, *Procurement and Public Management: The Fear of Discretion and the Quality of Government Performance* (AEI Press, 1990), p. 25

25. For a discussion of the impact of organizational culture, see Anne M. Khademian, *Working with Culture: How the Job Gets Done in Public Programs* (Washington, D.C.: CQ Press, 2002); Edgar H. Schein, *Organizational Culture and Leadership*, 2nd ed. (San Francisco: Jossey-Bass Publishers, 1992); Wilson, *Bureaucracy*, pp. 90–110; William G. Ouchi and Alan L. Wilkins, "Organizational Culture," *Annual Review of Sociology* 11 (1985): 457–83.

26. Schein, *Organizational Culture and Leadership*, p. 12.

27. Khademian, *Working with Culture*, p. ix.

28. See William G. Ouchi, "A Conceptual Framework for the Design of Organizational Control Mechanisms," *Management Science* 25, no. 9 (September 1979): 833–48; and Ouchi, "Markets, Bureaucracies, and Clans," pp. 129–41.

29. For a discussion of organizational culture in fire departments, see: Karen K. Myers, "A Burning Desire: Assimilation into a Fire Department," *Management Communication Quarterly* 18, no. 3 (February 2005): 344–84.

30. Ouchi, "A Conceptual Framework for the Design of Organizational Control Mechanisms," pp. 838, 844, 845.

31. Ibid., p. 833.

32. Denise M. Rousseau, *Psychological Contracts in Organizations: Understanding Written and Unwritten Agreements* (Newbury Park, Calif.: Sage, 1996); Rousseau, "Organizational Behavior in the New Organizational Era," pp. 515–46.

33. Rousseau, "Organizational Behavior in the New Organizational Era," p. 521.

34. Alvin W. Gouldner, "The Norm of Reciprocity: A Preliminary Statement," *American Sociological Review* 25, no. 2 (April 1960): 161–78.

35. Rousseau, "Organizational Behavior in the New Organizational Era," p. 521.

36. Ouchi, "A Conceptual Framework for the Design of Organizational Control Mechanisms," p. 838.

37. William J. Bratton, "Crime Is Down in New York City: Blame the Police," in *Zero Tolerance: Policing a Free Society,* edited by Norman Dennis, 2nd ed. (London: IEA Health and Welfare Unit, 1998), pp. 37, 35.

38. Ibid., p. 37.

39. Jack Maple, with Chris Mitchell, *The Crime Fighter* (New York: Doubleday, 1999), p. 23.

40. Bratton, "Crime Is Down in New York City," pp. 36, 37.

41. Ibid., p. 37.

42. Ibid., p. 38.

43. Maple with Mithcell, *The Crime Fighter,* p. 33.

44. For examples and analyses of discretion in criminal justice, see: George L. Kelling and Catherine M. Coles, *Fixing Broken Windows: Restoring Order and Reducing Crime in Our Communities* (New York: Free Press, 1996), chapter 5, particularly pp. 169–93. Lloyd Ohlin and Frank J. Remington, *Discretion in Criminal Justice: The Tension between Individualization and Uniformity* (State University of New York Press, 1993).

45. Kelman, *Procurement and Public Management,* pp. 3, 9, 14.

46. Schuck, "Controlling Administrative Discretion," p. 175.

47. For more on our fear of discretion (and its inevitability), see: Behn, *Rethinking Democratic Accountability,* pp. 87–96. For a discussion of "the fear of discretion" at the United Nations and the "trade-off [that] exists between process accountability and performance accountability in international organizations," see: Tim Balint, Sarah Schernbeck, and Simone Schneider, "Performance Accountability in the UN Secretariat—The Conflictual Way toward More Flexibility," *Public Administration and Development* 29, no. 5 (December 2009): 352–61.

48. Kate Stith, "The Arc of the Pendulum: Judges, Prosecutors, and the Exercise of Discretion," *Yale Law Journal* 117, no. 7 (May 2008): 1422. The fear of discretion is

not, however, purely a modern phenomenon. See: Daniel R. Ernst, "Ernst Freund, Felix Frankfurter and the American Rechtsstaat: A Transatlantic Shipwreck, 1894–1932," *Studies in American Political Development* 23, no. 2 (October 2009), 171–88.

49. Kate Stith and José A. Cabranes, *Fear of Judging: Sentencing Guidelines in the Federal Courts* (University of Chicago Press, 1998), p. 169.

50. Ibid., p. 169.

51. Schuck, "Controlling Administrative Discretion," p. 175.

52. Barry Sugarman, "Organizational Learning and Reform at the New York City Police Department," *Journal of Applied Behavioral Science* 46, no. 2 (June 2010): 164.

53. Neil Carter, "Performance Indicators: 'Backseat Driving' or 'Hands Off' Control?" *Policy and Politics* 17, no. 2 (1989): 136.

54. Peter Drucker, "Managing the Public Service Institution," *Public Interest*, no. 33 (Fall 1973): 57–58.

55. Peter F. Drucker, "The Deadly Sins in Public Administration," *Public Administration Review* 40, no. 2 (March/April 1980): 103.

56. Selznick, *Leadership in Administration*, p. 143.

57. Dean Esserman, "How to Decentralize Control and Get Police Officers to Love Their Jobs," *Heritage Lectures* 707 (June 1, 2001), delivered at the Heritage Foundation, February 28, 2001, pp. 2, 6, 7.

58. Ibid., p. 4.

Chapter Seven

1. Tony Bovaird and Elke Löffler, "Lessons from Europe: Innovations in Rural Service Delivery," Proceedings of the 2005 National Rural Affairs Conference, Castle Green Hotel, Kendal, Cumbria, United Kingdom, February 24, 2005 (www.defra.gov.uk/rural/pdfs/voice/nrac/2005-february/day1-tony-bovaird.pdf).

2. Garrett Hardin, "The Cybernetics of Competition: A Biologist's View of Society," *Perspectives in Biology and Medicine* 7 (Autumn, 1963): 81.

3. Mitchelle Krupa, "New Orleans City Hall Dysfunction Leaves Specialist 'Shocked,'" *The Times-Picayune*, March 3, 2011 (www.nola.com/politics/index.ssf/2011/03/new_orleans_city_hall_dysfunct.html). See also David Osborne and Ted Gaebler, *Reinventing Government: How the Entrepreneurial Spirit Is Transforming the Public Sector* (Reading, Mass.: Addison Wesley, 1992).

4. For details on the series of BlightSTAT meetings, see www.nola.gov/Code-Enforcement/BlightStat/. New Orleans also created several specialized PerformanceStats, including: QualityOfLifeStat, which focused on frequently reported, citywide concerns such as abandoned vehicles, illegal dumping, and streetlight outages; BottomLineStat, which focused on revenue collection and cost containment; and Req2CheckStat (for Requisition to Payment), which focused on the city's contracting for services.

5. Quoted in Ellen Lee and David Marcello, co-chairs, "Blight: Transition New Orleans Task Force," presented to Mayor-Elect Mitch Landrieu, City of New Orleans, April 2010, p. 8 (www.transitionneworleans.com/SiteContent/Static/Documents/Blight.pdf).

6. Allison Plyer and Elaine Ortiz, "Benchmarks for Blight," Greater New Orleans Community Data Center, October 27, 2010, p. 7.

7. Lee and Marcello, "Blight," p. 11.

8. "Mayor Unveils Comprehensive Blight Eradication Strategy: Administration Aggressively Aims to Reduce 10,000 Blighted Properties in 3 Years," City of New Orleans Press Release, September 30, 2010 (www.nola.gov/PRESS/City Of New Orleans/All Articles/ MAYOR UNVEILS COMPREHENSIVE BLIGHT ERADICATION STRATEGY/).

9. BlightSTAT, "Blight Strategy, City of New Orleans," PowerPoint, September 30, 2010, p. 6 (BlightStrategyPowerpoint093010.pdf).

10. Ibid., p. 34.

11. Ibid., p. 15. Both "tax lien sales" and "expropriation" were part of the original plan. Yet, Landrieu, Kopplin, and Wise soon determined it was most efficient and effective to use "code lien foreclosures."

12. Ibid., "2011 Budget, Special Presentation to City Council, Blight Reduction," November 1, 2010 (Blight_presentation_110110-1.pdf).

13. Private communication, July 30, 2012.

14. Louisiana has a strong property-rights law. If an owner fails to pay real estate taxes, government cannot easily take control of the property. Instead, it simply sells the debt to a private debt collector.

15. Charlie London, "BlightStat 33," blog April 12, 2012 (http://fsjna.org/2012/04/ blightstat-33/).

16. Fox 8 news report, "Blighted Properties to Be Auctioned in New Orleans," July 18, 2012 (www.fox8live.com/story/18951350/city-of-new-orleans-announces).

17. Allison Plyer and Elaine Ortiz, "Benchmarks for Blight: How Much Blight Does New Orleans Have?" Greater New Orleans Community Data Center, August 21, 2012.

18. Wise observed (personal communication, September 28, 2012) that "the best possible measure we have is the Postal Service data, but it's imperfect." Indeed, in both September 2010 and March 2012, the Greater New Orleans Community Data Center used data from the U.S. Postal Service for "blighted addresses or empty lots plus vacant but habitable homes"; Plyer and Ortiz, "Benchmarks for Blight," newsletter, October 27, 2010, p. 2; Plyer and Ortiz, "Benchmarks for Blight,"newsletter, August 21, 2012, p. 4. But between September 2010 and March 2012, the Postal Service did not collect these data. During this period, the Landrieu administration simply used its own activity data.

19. Even if the output or outcome data show an improvement over historical trends, this does not prove that a PerformanceStat leadership strategy had anything to do with the improvement. Something else could have been the cause. Or the "improvement" could have been purely random. More in chapter 14.

20. Martin O'Malley, "PerformanceStat: Measuring Priorities, Progress and Results," written testimony before the U.S. Senate Budget Committee field hearing, July 12,

2010, p. 2 (www.budget.senate.gov/democratic/index.cfm/files/serve?File_id=4cd4ece2-e5ec-4a81-8e1c-0d72e55dcda7).

21. Los Angeles County Quality and Productivity Commission, Department of Mental Health STATS Award Application for the 23rd Annual Producing and Quality Awards Program, Los Angeles County, p. 3 (http://qpc.co.la.ca.us/cms1_136291.pdf).

22. For this metric, the target was 65 percent.

23. Los Angeles County Quality and Productivity Commission, "Department of Mental Health STATS Award Application," p. 3. See also: Program Support Bureau, Quality Improvement Division, *Quality Improvement Handbook* (Los Angeles: Los Angeles County Department of Mental Health, 2010), p. 29 (http://psbqi.dmh.lacounty.gov/QUALITY IMPROVEMENT/QI Handbook June10-2010.pdf).

24. Los Angeles County Quality and Productivity Commission, "Department of Mental Health STATS Award Applicaton," p. 1.

25. Paul Arns, Robin Kay, and Marvin Southard, "Implementing Performance-Based Management in Public Mental Health Systems," presentation at the 21st Management Institute of the National Network for Social Work Managers, April 29–30, 2010, Fordham University, New York, p. 18 (https://socialworkmanager.org/data/PaulArns.pdf).

26. DCWatch, online magazine, Washington, D.C., www.dcwatch.com/mayor/070111.htm.

27. Cathleen Everett, "Civic Leadership: Dan Tangherlini," *Milton Magazine,* Fall 2007, p. 3 (www.milton.edu/news/upload/magazine_fall07.pdf).

28. Quoted in Michael Neibauer, "Fenty's CapStat Comes with Hard Deadlines," *Washington Examiner,* January 31, 2007 (http://washingtonexaminer.com/fentys-capstat-comes-with-hard-deadlines/article/75748).

29. Thomas M. Anderson, "Best Cities 2010: Washington, D.C.: People and Companies Are Relocating to Our Nation's Capital and Number-Three Pick for Best Cities for the Next Decade," *Kiplinger's Personal Finance,* July 2010 (www.kiplinger.com/magazine/archives/best-cities-2010-washington-dc.html).

30. Nikita Stewart, "Fenty's Legacy, Like His Tenure, May Be Marked by Polarizing Views," *Washington Post,* December 25, 2010 (www.washingtonpost.com/wp-dyn/content/story/2010/12/25/ST2010122502136.html?sid=ST2010122502136).

31. Peter Harkness, "Despite Corruption Concerns, D.C. Improves Services," *Governing,* March 2011.

32. Harry Jaffe, "Adrian Fenty: His Own Worst Enemy?" *Washingtonian,* March 2010 (www.washingtonian.com/articles/people/15092.html).

33. "Adrian Fetny: The Jerk D.C. Needs. Why You Should Vote for an Unpopular Mayor," *Washington City Paper,* September 10, 2010 (www.washingtoncitypaper.com/articles/39709/2010-endorsements).

34. Paul Schwartzman and Chris L. Jenkins, "How D.C. Mayor Fenty Lost the Black Vote—And His Job," *Washington Post,* September 18, 2010 (www.washingtonpost.com/wp-dyn/content/article/2010/09/18/AR2010091804286.html).

35. CapStat, District of Columbia website, http://capstat.oca.dc.gov/Performance Indicators.aspx (discontinued).

36. Jaffe, "Adrian Fenty: His Own Worst Enemy?"

37. Jonetta Rose Barras, "Fenty Builds to the End," *Washington Examiner*, December 26, 2010 (http://washingtonexaminer.com/local/dc/2010/12/fenty-builds-end).

38. Nikita Stewart and Tim Craig, "Fenty's Approach Leaves Council Members Fuming," *Washington Post*, November 1, 2009 (www.washingtonpost.com/wp-dyn/content/article/2009/10/31/AR2009103102235.html?hpid=dynamiclead).

39. Black Voices, "Adrian Fenty, Former D.C. Mayor, Has No Regrets One Year Out of Office," *Huffington Post*, September 29, 2011 (www.huffingtonpost.com/2011/09/28/a-year-after-being-voted-_n_986135.html?view=print&comm_ref=false).

40. The quotes in this section are from a presentation that Gallagher delivered at Harvard's Kennedy School of Government on March 12, 2008.

41. Office of Legislative Audits, "Audit Report: Department of State Police" (Annapolis, Md.: Maryland General Assembly, Department of Legislative Services, February 2007), pp. 1, 11, 12.

42. Governor's Office of Crime Control and Prevention, "Maryland's Comprehensive State Crime Control and Prevention Plan, 2009-2011" (January 15, 2009), p. 33 (www.goccp.maryland.gov/documents/crime-plan09-11.pdf).

43. Sameer Sidh, personal communication, February 28, 2012.

44. Kimberly A. C. Wilson, "O'Malley Gives Potholes Priority in a Campaign to Fix Streets Fast," *Baltimore Sun*, March 21, 2001. Baltimore had yet to launch its 311 phone system, so residents had to send an email to pothole@baltimorecity.gov or call 410-POTHOLE (http://articles.baltimoresun.com/2001-03-21/news/0103210196_1_potholes-fix-omalley).

45. Baltimore conducts CitiStat meetings on a two-week cycle; thus it aggregates data by two-week periods.

46. For the first four months of FY 2010 (July through October, 2009) New York City reported that the "average time to close a pothole work order where [a] repair was done" was 5.9 days, up from 2.8 for the same four months in the previous year. Michael R. Bloomberg, Edward Skyler, and Jeffrey A. Kay, "The Mayor's Management Report, Preliminary Fiscal 2010" (New York: Mayor's Office of Operations, 2010), p. 57.

47. These six words—"everything is connected to everything else"—have been written and spoken by academics and sages, politicians and scoundrels. Examples include: Environmentalist Barry Commoner, *The Closing Circle: Nature, Man, and Technology* (New York: Knopf, 1971); Physicist Albert-László Barabási, *Linked: How Everything Is Connected to Everything Else and What It Means for Business, Science, and Everyday Life* (New York: Plume, 2002); Biochemist Bill (William E. M.) Lands, "Everything Is Connected to Everything Else," *Journal of Biological Chemistry* 286, no. 51 (December 2011): 43589–595; Canadian designer Bruce Mau, *Massive Change* (London: Phaidon Press 2004), p. 97; Revolutionary Vladimir Ilich Ulyanov (a.k.a. Lenin).

48. M. Mitchell Waldrop, *Complexity: The Emerging Science at the Edge of Order and Chaos* (New York: Simon & Schuster, 1992).

49. Garrett Hardin, "The Cybernetics of Competition: A Biologist's View of Society," *Perspectives in Biology and Medicine* 7 (Autumn, 1963): 81, emphasis in the original.

50. Public executives have another option: ignore management and focus on policy. If they will only be around for a few years—not enough time to have a detectable impact on results—they can try to establish a new policy through legislation or regulation. They can put this policy on their resumes and leave it to their successors to make it work.

51. Robert D. Behn, "On Why All Public Executives Need to Re-Introduce the Missing Feedback into Most Logic Models," *Bob Behn's Performance Leadership Report* 10, no. 7 (March 2013).

52. Robert D. Behn, "Management by Groping Along," *Journal of Policy Analysis and Management* 7, no. 4 (Fall 1988): 643–63. Robert D. Behn, *Leadership Counts: Lessons for Public Managers* (Harvard University Press, 1991), pp. 127–50.

53. In large organizations, lethargy is the default. About employment policy, William Monat of Northern Illinois University wrote: "There is almost an institutional or organizational conspiracy working against the faithful translation of policy intent into operational policy." Numerous policy initiatives, he observed, have fallen "victim to imbedded organizational traditions and biases as well as organizational lethargy born of a reluctance to embark on uncertain ventures that promised no real organizational reward and appeared to contain vague organizational risks." William R. Monat, "The Once and Future Revolution: Manpower Policy in the United States," *Public Administration Review* 30, no. 1 (January/February 1970): 75.

54. Bovaird and Löffler, "Lessons from Europe."

55. For a discussion of the problem of sorting out cause and effect when multiple histories are possible, see: Nassim Nicholas Taleb, "A Mathematical Meditation on History," in *Fooled by Randomness: The Hidden Role of Chance in Life and in the Markets*, 2nd ed., pp. 43–69 (New York: Random House, 2005). Stephen Jay Gould makes a similar point in his Gedankenexperiment on "replaying life's tape." Rewind the evolutionary "tape of life" back to the time of the Burgess Shale, erasing everything; then replay this evolutionary tape again, and see if it produces the same collection of species. Gould believes that "any replay of the tape would lead evolution down a pathway radically different from the road actually taken." Stephen Jay Gould, *Wonderful Life: The Burgess Shale and the Nature of History* (New York: W. W. Norton, 1989), p. 51.

Chapter Eight

1. George Bernard Shaw, *Man and Superman: A Comedy and a Philosophy* (New York: Brentano's, 1905), p. 37 (Act I, spoken by John Tanner, M.I.R.C., Member of the Idle Rich Class.).

2. J. Richard Hackman, *Leading Teams: Setting the Stage for Great Performances* (Harvard Business Press, 2002), p. 104.

3. Mel Shestack and Sayre Ross, eds., *How'm I Doing? The Wit and Wisdom of Ed Koch* (New York: Lion Books, 1981).

4. Jane Clemen, Dianna Kirkwood, Bobbi Schell, with Daniel Myerson, *The Town That Lost a Ton: How One Town Used the Buddy System to Lose 3,998 Pounds . . . and How You Can Too!* (Naperville, Ill.: Source Books, 2002).

5. Dennis C. Smith, "Making Management Count: A Case for Theory-and-Evidence-Based Public Management," *Journal of Policy Analysis and Management* 28, no. 1 (Summer 2009): 498.

6. Alice M. Rivlin, *Systematic Thinking for Social Action* (Brookings, 1971), p. 143.

7. In the late 1920s, the International Association of Chiefs of Police created a committee on Uniform Crime Records, which established the categories of crime and system of voluntary reporting to the national government. The U.S. federal government did not decide what kind of data local police departments should (or would have to) collect. Instead, the leaders of these departments made a set of choices that formed the basis of today's FBI Uniform Crime Reporting (UCR) program. Committee on Uniform Crime Records, International Association of Chiefs of Police, *Uniform Crime Reporting, A Complete Manual for Police,* 2nd ed. (New York: J. J. Little and Ives Company, 1929). Louis N. Robinson, "History of Criminal Statistics (1908–1933)," *Journal of Criminal Law and Criminology* 24, no. 1 (May-June, 1933): 125–39; Saran Ghatak, "The Whole Extent of the Evil: Origin of Crime Statistics in the United States, 1880–1930," *Journal of Historical Sociology* 21, no. 1 (March 2008): 30–54.

8. There is, of course, nothing particularly "uniform" about the FBI's uniform crime reports. The FBI has definitions for each crime and provides guidelines for classifications. But the decisions about how to classify a crime are made by nearly 17,000 local police departments—often by the officer who goes to the scene and submits a report. And there is little reason to believe that all police officers across the country are collectively—or, indeed, individually—consistent in how they classify identical or merely similar crimes.

9. Jack Maple (with Chris Mitchell), *The Crime Fighter* (New York: Doubleday, 1999), p. 30.

10. Ibid.

11. Ibid., p. 113.

12. Overtime may be a minor performance issue. Yet, I have been struck by how many governments perceive that they have an overtime problem. Indeed, I suspect that the problem is real, persistent, and widespread. After all, to a front-line supervisor, overtime is an important tool. If an employee calls in sick, the supervisor sees overtime as an obvious solution. Even if these supervisors exceed their overtime budget, they are not apt to be punished severely—at least not as severely as they would be punished if they failed to fill the operational gap created by an absent employee.

13. Charles V. Euchner and Stephen J. McGovern, *Urban Policy Reconsidered: Dialogues on the Problems and Prospects of American Cities* (New York: Routledge, 2003), p. 32.

14. Robert D. Behn, *What All Mayors Would Like to Know about Baltimore's CitiStat Performance Strategy* (Washington: IBM Center for the Business of Government, 2007), p. 38.

15. In the short run, reducing overtime might hinder service delivery. But by focusing on controlling overtime, O'Malley could motivate agency managers to think seriously about how they managed their budgets and how they deployed their people. And if a manager failed to do either, it would soon become obvious, signaling that this manager needed to be replacved.

16. Marshall W. Meyer and Vipin Gupta, "The Performance Paradox," in *Research in Organizational Behavior,* vol. 16, edited by Barry M. Staw and L. L. Cummings (Greenwich, Conn.: JAI Press, 1994), pp. 310, 322.

17. Byron Sharp, Erica Riebe, John Dawes, and Nick Danenberg, "A Marketing Economy of Scale   Big Brands Lose Less of Their Customer Base than Small Brands," *Marketing Bulletin* 13 (May 2002): 1–8. See also, Ajay K. Kohli, N. Venkatraman, and John H. Grant, "Exploring the Relationship between Market Share and Business Profitability," in *Research in Marketing,* vol. 10, edited by Jagdish N. Sheth (Greenwich, Conn.: JAI Press, 1990), pp. 113–33. For a meta-analysis of 276 studies of the relationship between market share and profitability, see David M. Szymanski, Sundar G. Bharadwaj, and P. Rajan Varadarajan, "An Analysis of the Market Share-Profitability Relationship," *Journal of Marketing* 57, no. 3 (July, 1993): 1–18.

18. Denise M. Rousseau, "Organizational Behavior in the New Organizational Era," *Annual Review of Psychology* 48 (1997): 525.

19. Stuart E. Jackson, *Where Value Hides: A New Way to Uncover Profitable Growth for Your Business* (New York: Wiley, 2006), pp. 15, 16.

20. A newer performance measure designed to capture all of a baseball player's contribution to his team is WARP for Wins Above Replacement Player. For any player, this measure asks: How many more games would a team win with this player compared with how many it would win with a replacement player "of a caliber so low that they are always available in the minor leagues" (www.baseballprospectus.com/glossary/index.php?search=WARP).

21. Interview, December 3, 2010.

22. From the FAA's statement of mission, vision, and values on the FAA website (www.faa.gov/about/mission/)

23. The Aviation Safety Reporting System (ASRA), created in 1976, is voluntary, confidential and anonymous, and (to ensure its independence) is operated by the National Aeronautics and Space Administration.

24. Employing near-miss data to help identify performance deficits has been used in medicine. A variety of hospitals have created near-miss reporting regimes. For example, see: Paul Barach and Stephen D. Small, "Reporting and Preventing Medical Mishaps: Lessons from Non-Medical Near Miss Reporting Systems," *British Medical Journal* 320, no. 7237 (March 18, 2000): 759–63; Rachel Sorokin, Jennifer L. Claves, Gregory C. Kane, and Jonathan E. Gottlieb, "The Near Miss Resident Conference: Understanding

the Barriers to Confronting Medical Errors," *Seminars in Medical Practice* 5, no. 1 (March 2002): 12–19; Erin DuPree, Loraine O'Neill, and Rebecca M. Anderson, "Achieving a Safety Culture in Obstetrics," *Mount Sinai Journal of Medicine* 76, no. 6 (December 2009): 529–38. Lucian L. Leape, "Reporting of Adverse Events," *New England Journal of Medicine* 347, no. 20 (November 14, 2002): 1633–38.

In 2000, the U.S. Department of Veterans Affairs contracted with NASA to develop the "Patient Safety Reporting System" or PSRS (similar to ASRA), which "invites every-one who works in a healthcare facility to voluntarily report any events or concerns that involve patient safety" (www.psrs.arc.nasa.gov/faq.html#accept_anonymous_reports).

These practices are not completely uncontroversial. For a discussion of the differ-ent incentives for reporting near misses in aviation and in medicine, see: Charles H. Andrus, Eduardo G. Villasenor, John B. Kettelle, Randolph Roth, Allison M. Sweeney, and Nathaniel M. Matolo, "'To Err Is Human': Uniformly Reporting Medical Errors and Near Misses," *Journal of the American College of Surgeons* 196, no. 6 (June 2003): 911–18.

25. Robert D. Behn, "On Why Public Officials Need to Remember That There Is No Perfect Performance Measure," *Bob Behn's Public Management Repor* 6, no. 6 (February 2009).

26. The public-management literature on unintended and perverse consequences is long and critical. For example: Sandra van Thiel and Frans L. Leeuw, "The Performance Paradox in the Public Sector," *Public Performance & Management Review* 25, no. 3 (March 2002): 267–81.

27. William Atkinson, Charles (Skip) Wolfe, Jennifer Hamborsky, Lynne McIntyre, eds., *Epidemiology and Prevention of Vaccine-Preventable Diseases,* 11th edition (Atlanta, Ga: The Centers for Disease Control and Prevention, 2009), p. 166. See also, John C. Watson, John A. Pearson, Lauri E. Markowitz, Andrew L. Baughman, Dean D. Erdman, William J. Bellini, Roy C. Baron, and David W. Fleming, "An Evaluation of Measles Revaccination among School-Entry-Aged Children," *Pediatrics* 97, no. 5 (May 1996): 613–18.

28. T. Jacob John and Reuben Samuel, "Herd Immunity and Herd Effect: New Insights and Definitions," *European Journal of Epidemiology* 16, no. 7 (June 2000): 601–06.

29. Donald T. Campbell, "Assessing the Impact of Planned Social Change," in *Social Research and Public Policies: The Dartmouth/OECD Conference,* edited by Gene M. Lyons, (Public Affairs Center, Dartmouth College, 1975), pp. 35, 36, 37. Donald T. Campbell, "Assessing the Impact of Planned Social Change," *Evaluation and Program Planning* 2, no. 1 (1979): 85.

30. Michael J. Bowers, Robert D. Wilson, and Richard L. Hyde, Letter to Gov-ernor Nathan Deal, June 30, 2011 (http://graphics8.nytimes.com/packages/pdf/us/Volume-1.pdf).

31. Mark Toor, "Survey: Retired Cops Say NYPD Crime Stats Fudged," *The Chief,* July 13, 2012 (http://thechiefleader.com/content/tncms/assets/v3/eedition/2/ba/2ba21060-2129-5126-a531-ab332697f0f6/4ffb40e75b194.flash.swf). For a more detailed account, see John A. Eterno and Eli B. Silverman, *The Crime Numbers Game: Management by*

Manipulation (Boca Raton: CRC Press, 2012). Bratton dissented. See: William Bratton, "Crime by the Numbers," *New York Times,* February 17, 2010, p. A23.

In July 2013, NYPD released a report by two former federal prosecutors, David Kelley and Sharon McCarthy, who found that "A close review of the NYPD's statistics and analysis demonstrates that the misclassification of reports may have an appreciable effect on certain reported crime rates." The authors also wrote: "Even considered in light of the committee's findings, the accomplishment of the N.Y.P.D. in reducing crime compared with 20 and even 10 years ago is indeed historic." David N. Kelley and Sharon L. McCarthy, *The Report of the Crime Reporting Review Committee to Commissioner Raymond W. Kelly Concerning CompStat Auditing* (New York Police Department, April 8, 2013), pp. 49, 54 (www.nyc.gov/html/nypd/downloads/pdf/public_information/crime_reporting_review_committee_final_report_2013.pdf).

32. Yang Jisheng, *Tombstone: The Great Chinese Famine 1958–1962* (New York: Farrar, Straus and Giroux, 2012), pp. 12, 74.

33. Frank Dikötter, *Mao's Great Famine: The History of China's Most Devastating Catastrophe, 1958–1962* (New York: Bloomsbury, 2010), p. 130. The problem wasn't just pressure to achieve the quotas. There was also the imposition of an absurd production plan on people who lacked the necessary operational capacity.

34. William L. Riordon, *Plunkitt of Tammany Hall* (New York: E. P. Dutton & Co., 1963), pp. 3–6.

35. Ruth Mitchell, *Testing for Learning: How New Approaches To Evaluation Can Improve American Schools* (New York: Free Press, 2007), pp. 22, 61.

36. Daniel Koretz, "Using Multiple Measures to Address Perverse Incentives and Score Inflation," *Educational Measurement: Issues and Practice* 22, no. 2 (summer 2003), p. 25.

37. New York City Department of Correction website (www.nyc.gov/html/doc/html/stats/doc_stats.shtml). During his six-and-a-half years as correction commissioner (January 2003 to August 2009), Martin Horn managed to cut stabbings and slashings in half: from 40 per year in fiscal years 2003 and 2004 to averaging 20 per year during his last two years in office.

38. From remarks delivered by Horn at Harvard's Kennedy School of Government, April 14, 2008.

39. Neil Carter, Rudolf Klein, and Patricia Day, *How Organisations Measure Success: The Use of Performance Indicators in Government* (London: Routledge 1992), pp. 49–50.

40. Ibid., p. 50. When Carter first laid out this typology, he introduces the dial or prescriptive indicator, the tin opener or descriptive indicator, and a "negative or proscriptive indicator"—but without mentioning the "alarm bell." Neil Carter, "Performance Indicators: 'Backseat Driving' or 'Hands Off' Control?" *Policy and Politics* 17, no. 2 (1989), p. 135.

41. Carter, Klein, and Day, *How Organisations Measure Success,* p. 50.

42. Ibid., pp. 153, 86.

43. Robert D. Behn, "Why Measure Performance? Different Purposes Require Different Measures," *Public Administration Review* 63, no. 5 (September/October 2003): 595. I am not the only one to suggest this purpose: The "2013–2014 Student/Parent Handbook of St.

Clair [Missouri] High School" notes (p. 2): "The St. Clair Community will expect that every SCHS graduate possess the skills necessary to become productive employees and responsible citizens" (http://stclair.fesdev.org/vimages/shared/vnews/stories/ 477e986032308/ SCHSHandbook 2013-2014.doc). This same purpose has also been established at the university level. The Tennessee Board of Regents in "Charting a Course," its strategic plan for 2010–15, stated (on page 12): "Improving access and completion rates in higher education can improve the lives of Tennesseans only to the degree that students acquire and retain knowledge, skills and abilities they need to become productive employees and responsible citizens" (www.tbr.edu/WorkArea/linkit.aspx?LinkIdentifier=id&ItemID=6819).

44. DPSS explains that "DPSSTATS, implemented in April 2005, is an innovative management tool that creates a forum for Executive Management and key managers across the Department to review current and comprehensive data so that swift, effective decisions could be made to enhance the Department's operations to better serve the more than 2 million residents of Los Angeles County that are served by this Department" (http://dpss.lacounty.gov/dpss/dpsstats/default.cfm).

45. HRA website (www.nyc.gov/html/hra/html/about/about.shtml).

46. DPSS website (www.ladpss.org/about/).

47. Kay E. Sherwood, "Managing the Welfare System with JobStat," in *Managing Welfare Reform in New York City,* edited by E. S. Savas (Lanham, Md.: Rowman & Littlefield, 2005), p. 116.

48. Interview, May 31, 2012.

49. If a municipality contributes some funding for a social service program, its officials make some of these decisions.

50. HRA website (www.nyc.gov/html/hra/downloads/pdf/dekalb.pdf).

51. HRA website (www.nyc.gov/html/hra/downloads/pdf/facts/trends/job_placment. pdf).

52. To outsiders, some measures are less obvious: to ensure that it can check to see if it needs to adjust the benefits of a client who has been placed in a job, HRA requires that the vendor that places a client in a job report the placement within one week of when the participant starts working. For 2012, each HRA job center had a 90 percent completion-rate target, with 80 percent being the minimally acceptable level.

53. Bureau of Contract and Technical Services, *Caseload Characteristics Report* (Los Angeles County Department of Public Social Services, March 2013) (www.ladpss.org/ dpss/ISS/pdf/2013/CaseloadCharMar2013.pdf).

54. Bureau of Contract and Technical Services, *Statistical Report* (Los Angeles County Department of Public Social Services, May 2013) (http://dpss.lacounty.gov/dpss/ISS/ pdf/2013/STAT_05-13_Reduced_Combined_w_link.pdf).

The latest *Caseload Characteristics Report* and *Statistical Report* are at http://dpss. lacounty.gov/dpss/ISS/default.cfm.

55. "DPSSTATS Process," fact sheet dated March 17, 2011 (http://dpss.lacounty.gov/ dpss/dpsstats/pdfs/factsheet.pdf). The full description of "Performance Measures" on this fact sheet is:

DPSSTATS maintains an inventory of more than 200 different performance measures. The measures come from a variety of sources including, Performance Counts!, Department Head Goals, managers' MAPP goals, State or Federal standards, or current Departmental priorities. New measures are constantly being developed and explored through the STATS process. Divisions may recommend measures for themselves or for other operations in the Department. The measures chosen for a particular meeting are determined by the Chief Deputy and the Assistant Directors.

While the measures reviewed at STATS often change, a set of core measures for Line offices (All Application Processing, CalFresh Error Rate, and Medi-Cal Redetermination Processing) are reviewed prior to each Line meeting and presented in a separate document at the start of the meeting. District Directors that meet all of the applicable core measures are recognized with stars on their nameplates for each meeting where they have achieved the established targets.

56. Earning a "star" might not appear to be a very significant reward. Nevertheless, it establishes status—performance status—among the local offices and thus is (to many) both prized and pursued.

57. For example, the meeting to set the measures for January 2009 was held in mid-November 2008. Kent sat down with her staff to think about what the measures might be. Then they met with Ansell to decide what measures to recommend (at a meeting the following week) to the department's leadership, which gave the final approval.

58. A good example is DPSS's effort to determine whether a local office was providing relatively equivalent service to people with disabilities, as measured by the average hours of service per client provided by each employee in each office. The question was not whether different offices were providing equivalent service; for a variety of reasons, different offices might have quite different clientele. Rather, DPSS wanted to know whether different workers in the same office were providing roughly equivalent service.

Conceptually, this question isn't complicated. Still, it may not be obvious what the averages represent: What are they averaged over? What is in the denominator? And what kind of comparisons should or could you make? And what might be a desirable or unacceptable distribution?

For this example, consider an office with just two workers (A and B). What should this office's distribution look like? Assuming that the cases are randomly assigned and that no single case is so weird or so large that it dominates a worker's average, both should have roughly the same average hours worked per client. Both should have approximately the same percentage of hours worked per client in the 41-50 hour range, and approximately the same percentage in the 71-80 hours range. If in any office, individuals work significantly different average hours per case—some very high; some very low—some of the workers are not following California's Hourly Task Guidelines (HTG).

The issue is the differences among the workers *within* the same office—not differences *between* offices. Yet at one DPSS meeting (September 25, 2008), several people found this distinction confusing.

59. "California State Association of Counties (CSAC)—Challenge Awards 2011, Executive Summary: LACDMH STATS: Success through Performance-Based Management" (www.counties.org/images/users/1/Los Angeles 324.pdf).

60. Paul Arns, Robin Kay, and Marvin Southard, "Implementing Performance-Based Management in Public Mental Health Systems," Presentation at the 21st Management Institute of the National Network for Social Work Managers, April 29–30, 2010, Fordham University, New York, N.Y., p. 18 (https://socialworkmanager.org/data/PaulArns.pdf).

61. Ibid., p. 30.

62. Ibid., p. 32.

63. Many who receive inpatient psychiatric care are doing so involuntarily. The courts have determined that they are a danger to themselves, a danger to others, or have a "grave disability," defined under California's Lanterman-Petris-Short Act (Section 5150 of the California Welfare and Institutions Code) as: "A condition in which a person, as a result of a mental disorder (or impairment by chronic alcoholism), is unable to provide for his (or her) basic personal needs for food, clothing or shelter." For these people, a release from inpatient care may be very disruptive. Thus, to ensure an effective transition, it helps to get a newly released patient quickly connected to outpatient care.

64. Christopher Pollitt, "Performance Management in Practice: A Comparative Study of Executive Agencies," *Journal of Public Administration Research and Theory* 16, no. 1 (2006): 30–33.

65. Behn, "Why Measure Performance?" pp. 586–606; Alfred Tat-Kei Ho, "Accounting for the Value of Performance Measurement from the Perspective of Midwestern Mayors," *Journal of Public Administration Research and Theory* 16, no. 2 (2006): 222.

66. For performance "measurement," the operational question is: "How can we measure what we are doing?" For performance "management," the operational question is: "What are our important performance deficits, and what is our strategy for eliminating or mitigating a few of the most important?" For performance "leadership," the operational question is: How do we motivate everyone in our organization—and our collaborators, too—to pursue our strategy with intelligence, creativity, and persistence and thus to eliminate these few important performance deficits.

Chapter Nine

1. Charles A. Lave, and James G. March, *An Introduction to Models in the Social Sciences* (New York: Harper & Row, 1975), p. 2. Also see Steven Bernstein, Richard Ned Lebow, Janice Gross Stein, and Steven Weber, "God Gave Physics the Easy Problems: Adapting Social Science to an Unpredictable World," *European Journal of International Relations* 6, no. 1 (March 2000): 43–76.

2. Quoted in Irving John Good, ed., *The Scientist Speculates: An Anthology of Partly-Baked Ideas* (New York: Basic Books, 1962), p. 15.

3. John Maynard Keynes, *The General Theory of Employment, Interest, and Money* (New York: Harcourt, Brace, and Company, 1936), p. 383.

4. Oliver Wendell Holmes, "The Law as a Profession," *American Law Review* 20 (January-February 1886), pp. 741–42. Lecture delivered at Harvard University, February 17, 1886.

5. Carl Becker, "Everyman His Own Historian," Becker's presidential address to the American Historical Association, December 29, 1931, *American Historical Review* 37, no. 2 (January 1932), p. 232.

6. Gary T. Marx, "Of Methods and Manners for Aspiring Sociologists: 37 Moral Imperatives," *American Sociologist* 28, no. 1 (March 1997): 102–05.

7. James J. Heckman, "Micro Data, Heterogeneity and the Evaluation of Public Policy" (Part 1), *American Economist* 48, no. 2 (Fall 2004): 4.

8. Peter M. Blau, *The Dynamics of Bureaucracy: A Study of Interpersonal Relations in Two Government Agencies,* 2nd ed. (University of Chicago Press, 1963), p. 6.

9. For an example, see Lloyd S. Etheredge, *The Case of the Unreturned Cafeteria Trays* (Washington: American Political Science Association, 1976).

10. Christopher Pollitt, "Performance Management in Practice: A Comparative Study of Executive Agencies," *Journal of Public Administration Research and Theory* 16, no. 1 (2006): 34.

11. Milford H. Wolpoff, "Comment on 'Hypothesis Testing in Paleoanthropology,' by D. Pilbeam and J. R. Vaisnys," in *Paleoanthropology: Morphology and Paleoecology,* edited by Russell H. Tuttle (The Hague: Mouton, 1975), p. 15.

12. Robert Parker, *Cold Service* (New York: G. P. Putnam's Sons, 2005), p. 185.

13. Quoted in Good, ed., *The Scientist Speculates,* p. 15.

14. David N. Cicilline, "Inaugural Address," January 6, 2003 (http://providenceri.com/sites/default/files/file/Mayors_Office/speeches/Mayor-Cicilline%27s Inaugural-Address.pdf).

15. Interview, May 5, 2005.

16. Rob Gurwitt, "A Fragile Peace in Providence," *Governing,* December 2009, p. 25.

17. Interview, January 13, 2012.

18. The Forestry Division had a four-year backlog on tree-trimming requests. A year-and-a-half later, the backlog was gone. Ellen Perlman, "'Stat' Fever: The Practice of Collecting Data to Monitor and Improve Government Performance Continues to Gain Momentum and Evolve," *Governing,* January 2007, p. 50. At the same time, the city saved money on its contract for removing dead and diseased trees. From ProvStat's analysis of its data, the city provided more information to potential bidders, which lowered the cost of one contract by approximately $100 per tree, and over $30,000 for the contract. Gregory Smith, "Council Questions Achievements of ProvStat," *Providence Journal,* July 12, 2004.

19. Interview, January 13, 2012.

20. Interview, May 17, 2005.

21. Perlman, "'Stat' Fever," p. 50.

22. Interview, May 17, 2005.

23. Ibid., and interview, December 3, 2010.

24. Interview, May 17, 2005, and presentation at the Seminar on Transition and Leadership for Newly Elected Mayors, at Harvard University, November 29, 2007.

25. Paul Meier. "The Biggest Public Health Experiment Ever: The 1954 Field Trial of the Salk Poliomyelitis Vaccine," in *Statistics, A Guide to the Unknown,* edited by Judith M. Tanur and others (San Francisco: Holden-Day, 1975), pp. 12, 11.

26. Editorial, "The Salk Poliomyelitis Vaccine," *American Journal of Public Health* 45, no. 5 (May 1955): 676.

27. For a description of how this randomization was done, see Thomas Francis, Jr. and others, "An Evaluation of the 1954 Poliomyelitis Vaccine Trials," *American Journal of Public Health* 45, no. 5, (May 1955, pt. 2): 4–5.

28. I have carefully chosen these (hypothetical) precinct numbers. They no longer exist.

29. For an example, see: Robert D. Behn, *Leadership Counts: Lessons for Public Managers* (Harvard University Press, 1991), pp. 106–07 and 123–24.

30. For a description of the concept of positive deviance, see Jerry Sternin and Robert Choo, "The Power of Positive Deviance," *Harvard Business Review* 78, no. 1 (January 2000): 14–15; Richard T. Pascale, Mark Millemann, and Linda Gioja, *Surfing the Edge of Chaos: The Laws of Nature and the New Laws of Business* (New York: Three Rivers Press, 2000), pp. 175–81, 222, 284; Gretchen M. Spreitzer, and Scott Sonenshein, "Toward the Construct Definition of Positive Deviance," *American Behavioral Scientist* 47, no. 6 (February 2004): 828–47; David R. Marsh and others, "The Power of Positive Deviance," *British Medical Journal.* 329, no. 7475 (November 13, 2004): 1177; Richard Tanner Pascale and Jerry Sternin, "Your Company's Secret Change Agents," *Harvard Business Review* 83, no. 5 (May 2005): 73–81.

31. For those unfamiliar with this cultural icon, visit www.cartalk.com.

32. Maple described Yohe as the "one person in the crime analysis division who's ready to knock down walls to pull together the crime data we need." Jack Maple, with Chris Mitchell, *The Crime Fighter: Putting the Bad Guys Out of Business* (New York: Doubleday, 1999), p. 107.

33. Tod Newcombe, "Crime Drops 38 Percent in New York City," *Government Technology* 10, no. 3 (March 1997): 18–19. Also cited in Bernard E. Harcourt, *Illusion of Order: The False Promise of Broken Windows* (Harvard University Press, 2001) p. 98.

34. Steven Johnson, *The Ghost Map: The Story of London's Most Terrifying Epidemic and How It Changed Science, Cities, and the Modern World* (New York: Riverhead Books, 2006). For a dissent from the significance of Snow's role, see: Howard Brody, Michael Russell Rip, Peter Vinten-Johansen, Nigel Paneth, and Stephen Rachman, "Map-Making and Myth-Making in Broad Street: The London Cholera Epidemic, 1854," *Lancet* 356,

no. 9223 (July 1, 2000): 64–68. Actually, mapping the incidence of disease began half a century earlier. See: Lloyd G. Stevenson, "Putting Disease on the Map: The Early Use of Spot Maps in the Study of Yellow Fever," *Journal of the History of Medicine* 20, no. 3 (July 1965): 226–61; Frank A. Barrett, "Finke's 1792 Map of Human Diseases: The First World Disease Map?" *Social Science & Medicine* 50, nos. 7-8 (April 2000): 915–21.

35. William Bratton (with Peter Knobler), *Turnaround: How America's Top Cop Reversed the Crime Epidemic* (New York: Random House: 1998), p. 99.

36. Maple with Mitchell, *The Crime Fighter*, p. 128.

37. Today, even citizens have access to local crime maps. Several nongovernmental organizations have established relationships with local police departments to put their crime maps on the web: CrimeReports.com (http://crimereports.com); The Omega Group (www.crimemapping.com); and SpotCrime (www.spotcrime.com).

38. A seminar at Harvard's Kennedy School of Government, Saturday, October 6, 2010.

39. The word "analysis" comes from the Greek αναλύω, one meaning of which is "to resolve into its elements."

40. Even when using a map, the analyst needs to think carefully about the appropriate level of disaggregation. Mark Monmonier observed that for a choropleth map—one that uses different colors, shades, or patterns to indicate the level of some variable (such as crime) for different subareas—the level of disaggregation can be important. If the map simply consists of one dot for each incident—a crime or a case of cholera—the disaggregation is complete. But if the mapmaker decides to aggregate the data into subareas (because, for example, this analyst believes that there are simply too many individual dots to be useful) the choice of the boundaries of these subareas can be important. From Snow's map of the cholera dots, Monmonier used the streets near the Broad Street pump to draw boundaries and aggregate the data in three different ways. Different aggregations produced different impressions, but all three "diluted the Broad Street cluster." Monmonier noted that "aggregation involves not only areal units but also time, disease classification, and demography" and how those choices are made affects what the data reveal or conceal. "Clearly one map is not sufficient," emphasized Monmonier, "although one good map can signal the need for a more detailed investigation." That is the objective of any first-cut analysis: to find something that suggests "the need for a more detailed investigation." Mark Monmonier, *How to Lie with Maps* (University of Chicago Press, 1991), pp. 22–23, 141–43.

41. One of the worst things that could happen to the PerformanceStat strategy would be for it to be kidnapped by the ISO cabal. If the International Organization for Standardization (ISO) gets hold of this innovative leadership strategy, it will standardize everything. Nothing will be left but a template.

42. Malcolm K. Sparrow, *The Character of Harms: Operational Challenges in Control* (Cambridge University Press, 2008), pp. 8, 11, 9.

43. Ibid., pp. 68, 149. See also Malcolm K. Sparrow, *The Regulatory Craft: Controlling Risks, Solving Problems, and Managing Compliance* (Brookings, 2000), p. 132.

44. David Ignatius, "Two Attacks Highlight Counterterrorism's Bureaucratic Bog," *Washington Post,* January 6, 2010, p. A15 (www.washingtonpost.com/wp-dyn/content/article/2010/01/05/AR2010010502986.html).

45. Sparrow, *The Character of Harms,* pp. 14, 9.

46. Read Montague, *Why Choose This Book? How We Make Decisions* (New York: Dutton, 2006), p. 108.

47. Louis Pasteur, *La Vie de Pasteur,* edited by Rene Vallery-Radot (Paris: Librairie Hachette, 1900), p. 88.

48. Gary Klein, *Sources of Power: How People Make Decisions* (MIT Press, 1998), chapter 4 ("The Recognition-Primed Decision Model"), particularly pp. 33, 40, 35, 31.

Chapter Ten

1. Jack Maple, *Crime Fighter: How You Can Make Your Community Crime-Free* (New York: Doubleday, 1999), p. 93.

2. Michael Barber, *Instruction to Deliver: Fighting to Transform Britain's Public Services* (London: Methuen Publishing, 2008), pp. 44–45.

3. The department has 10 jails on Rikers Island and, elsewhere in the city, 6 detention centers and hospital prison wards.

4. Horn left Correction in August 2009. For FY 2009, the department had a daily inmate population of 13,362 and annual admissions of 99,939 (www.nyc.gov/html/doc/html/stats/doc_stats.shtml). In December 2008, the department had 1,460 civilian employees and 9,393 uniformed employees. New York City Office of Management of Budget, "The Financial Plan of the City of New York, Full-Time and Full-Time Equivalent Staffing Levels, Fiscal Years 2009–2010" (January 2009), pp. 33–34. Since then, inmate population and admissions, and staffing have dropped.

5. In New York City, correction officers need 60 college credits (21 of which can be earned at the Department of Correction Academy) or a high school degree and either two years of full-time service in the military or as a police officer. "Notice of Examination: Correction Officer" (www.nyc.gov/html/doc/downloads/pdf/0517_001_1.pdf). In contrast, probation officers need a college degree, plus a graduate degree in social work, law, psychology (or other related field); or two years of full-time casework or counseling; or one year of full-time work in probation; or a bachelor of social work plus one year of full-time casework or counseling. Notice of Examination: Probation Officer" (www.nyc.gov/html/dcas/downloads/pdf/noes/201000142000.pdf).

6. In December 2008, eight months before Horn left, the probation department had 1,195 employees. NYC Office of Management of Budget, "The Financial Plan of the City of New York," p. 54. Since then, staffing levels have dropped.

7. On Google, the two words "citistat baltimore" generated 17,100 hits. The three words "citistat baltimore accountability" generated 7,600 hits (or 44 percent of the 17,100 total), while "citistat baltimore learning" produced 4,050 hits (or 24 percent of the 17,100).

8. This behavior is similar to how people behaved in the famous experiment in which they were asked to carefully count the number of basketball passes by one of two teams. Many participants were so focused on their counting that they missed a gorilla walking between the two teams. Daniel J. Simons and Christopher F. Chabris, "Gorillas in Our Midst: Sustained Inattentional Blindness for Dynamic Events," *Perception* 28, no. 9 (1999), pp. 1059–074; Christopher Chabris and Daniel Simons, *The Invisible Gorilla: How Our Intuitions Deceive Us* (New York: Crown Publishers, 2010).

9. Every elected executive needs someone to manage operations: a chief of staff, a secretary of administration. The elected executive has multiple responsibilities: meeting with stakeholders, courting legislators, cutting ribbons. Thus, middle managers might find it easier to deceive the elected chief executive about a subunit's performance deficits than the individual who runs the jurisdiction.

10. I figured this out before I learned that O'Malley and Enright were friends since their student days together at Gonzaga College High School.

11. Eric Pooley and Elaine Rivera, "One Good Apple," *Time,* January 15, 1996.

12. Greg Donaldson, "Captain Midnight," *New York,* April 23, 2001.

13. David Remnick, "The Crime Buster," *New Yorker,* February 24, 1997, p. 96.

14. William K. Rashbaum, "Retired Officers Raise Questions on Crime Data," *New York Times,* February 7, 2010, p. 1.

15. Remnick, "The Crime Buster," p 96.

16. This description appears in two books: Leonard Levitt, *NYPD Confidential: Power and Corruption in the Country's Greatest Police Force* (New York: Thomas Dunne Books, 2009), p. 69. William Bratton (with Peter Nobler), *Turnaround: How America's Top Cop Reversed the Crime Epidemic* (New York: Random House, 1998), p. 237.

17. Pooley and Rivera, "One Good Apple."

18. For an alternative concept of "accountability," see Robert D. Behn, *Rethinking Democratic Accountability* (Brookings, 1991).

19. One journalist, in an article about crime, NYPD's CompStat, and the "fudging" of crime data, reported the views of a variety of experts and then turned to "The Wire" for "a more realistic view." Honest! David Von Drehle, "Why Crime Went Away," *Time,* February 22, 2010.

20. Christopher Hood describes efforts to improve performance in Britain as "target and terror regimes." Christopher Hood, "Gaming in Targetworld: The Targets Approach to Managing British Public Services," *Public Administration Review* 66, no. 4 (July/August 2006), pp. 515–21.

21. Nevertheless, at any meeting designed to analyze—and thus evaluate—individual or group performance, those whose performance is being examined may perceive more

criticism than praise. Even independent observers can perceive this tendency. For example, a group of scholars from the University of Houston, in an experiment on the effectiveness of feedback, found "that management in some cases seemed to focus much more on small amounts of negative productivity information rather than on the much larger amount of positive information," which "had the effect of making those meetings a somewhat punishing experience for unit members rather than a positive experience." Robert D. Pritchard and others, "Effects of Group Feedback, Goal Setting, and Incentives on Organizational Productivity," *Journal of Applied Psychology* 73, no. 2 (May 1988), p. 354.

22. Christopher Swope, "Restless for Results," *Governing,* April, 2001, pp. 20–23.

23. Mayor Martin O'Malley, "Baltimore Citistat," PowerPoint (http://frank.mtsu.edu/~famcom/spring02/omalley.ppt).

24. Anthony Barksdale is real. He should not be confused with the fictional Avon Barksdale, a drug dealer in "The Wire."

25. Benjamin Bowling, "The Rise and Fall of New York Murder: Zero Tolerance or Crack's Decline?" *British Journal of Criminology* 39, no. 4 (Autumn 1999), pp. 545–46.

26. I take detailed notes.

27. Quoted in Larisa Benson, "What Makes Washington State's GMAP Program Tick?" Paper prepared for the 28th annual research conference of the Association for Public Policy Analysis and Management, Madison, Wisconsin, November 2–4, 2006, p. 4.

28. Research over several decades revealed "that 60% to 75% of the employees in any organization—no matter when or where the survey was completed and no matter what occupational group was involved—report that the worst or most stressful aspect of their job is their immediate supervisor." Robert Hogan, Gordon J. Curphy, and Joyce Hogan, "What We Know about Leadership: Effectiveness and Personality," *American Psychologist* 49, no. 6 (June 1994), p. 494. Imagine how much more stressful it is to deal with an immediate supervisor in the quasi-public setting of a PerformanceStat meeting.

29. Or maybe this dread comes from years spent as a student worrying about being asked a question in class. Thomas and Brown explain "why a student panics when she is called on in class." It is because "even if she knows the answer to the question," the student is being asked to expose in public what had been until that moment a very private activity [her own learning]." Douglas Thomas and John Seely Brown, *A New Culture of Learning: Cultivating the Imagination for a World of Constant Change* (Seattle: Create Space, 2011), p. 58.

30. The Pew Center on the States reports: "At traditional staff meetings, employees sit around a table and discuss agency issues on an agenda. At Compstat, the agenda is the performance of individual staff members and their units. . . . Once in the spotlight, the supervisor provides an update on progress during the past week. Top department managers, seated together at a head table, ask questions about trends and developments based on their knowledge and interpretation of data. This practice creates enormous incentives for supervisors to have already identified problems and creative solutions, especially those that involve partners in the room and in the community." William Burrell and Adam

Gelb, *You Get What You Measure: Compstat for Community Corrections, Public Safety Policy Brief,* no. 1, July 2007, Pew Center on the States.

31. Maple, *Crime Fighter,* pp. 62, 78, 185.

32. Philip B. Gove, ed., *Webster's New Dictionary of Synonyms* (Springfield, Mass.: G. & C. Merriam Company, 1968), pp. 676, 383.

33. Robert D. Behn, *The Seven Big Errors of PerformanceStat* (Cambridge, Mass.: Rappaport Institute for Greater Boston and the Taubman Center for State and Local Government, Policy Brief, February 2008).

34. This point reflects conversations both with those who have created something that they would like to think has the impact of a real PerformanceStat as well as with others who have decided against doing so. Many view *any* PerformanceStat as synonymous with brutal embarrassment and want nothing to do with it. When Mayor Rudolph Giuliani tried to introduce LearnStat into the New York City School system, Jill Levy, president of the union representing the city's principals and assistant principals, disagreed: "We are about education, not about numbers and cases and criminals," said Levy. "All this will do is heighten the fear and blame and drive the good principals out of the system." Abby Goodnough, "For Schools in a Torpor, Shock Therapy; Education May Soon Face the Same System of Accountability as Police," *New York Times,* April 22, 2001 (www.nytimes.com/2001/04/22/ nyregion/for-schools-torpor-shock-therapy-educators-may-soon-face-same-system.html.)

35. Kimberly Flowers, January 29, 2004, and September 21, 2004.

36. Jeff Godown, Wednesday, November 5, 2008.

Chapter Eleven

1. Henry Louis Mencken, *A Mencken Chrestomathy: His Own Selection of His Choicest Writings* (New York: Vintage, 1982 [1949]), p. 617.

2. Dennis C. Smith, "Making Management Count: A Case for Theory-and-Evidence-Based Public Management," *Journal of Policy Analysis and Management* 28, no. 1 (Summer 2009): 500.

3. Anthony Downs, *Inside Bureaucracy* (Brookings, 1967), pp. 158, 163–64. Downs suggests two ways that organizations can break the ossification: by creating a new organization to deal with a complex and novel "urgent task"; or by reorganizing (pp. 160–61 and 165–66). But the tasks conducted by a centuries-old city such a Baltimore are hardly novel. And Downs's second way for a city to shake up its ossified agencies—through reorganization—has its own, well-known disadvantages.

4. Herbert Simon, "Rationality as Process and as Product of Thought," *American Economic Review* 69, no. 4 (May 1978): 15.

5. Herbert A. Simon, "Designing Organizations for an Information-Rich World," in *Computers, Communication, and the Public Interest,* edited by Martin Greenberger (Johns Hopkins University Press, 1971), pp. 40–41.

6. Even people with M.D.s don't always show up for their appointments. Dr. Mehmet Oz—the cardiothoracic surgeon who hosts a medical-advice television show—did not follow the instructions of his own gastroenterologist for his colonoscopy. Mehmet Oz, "What I Learned from My Cancer Scare," *Time* (June 27, 2011), pp. 34–39.

7. Marshall H. Becker and Lois A. Maiman, "Sociobehavioral Determinants of Compliance with Health and Medical Care Recommendations," *Medical Care* 13, no. 1 (January 1975): 10.

8. David L. Sackett and J. C. Snow, "The Magnitude of Compliance and Noncompliance," in *Compliance in Health Care,* edited by R. Brian Haynes, D. Wayne Taylor, and David L. Sackett (Johns Hopkins University Press, 1979), pp. 11–22.

9. The following articles explicitly emphasize the importance of "persistent follow-up": Susan Harding, "Chronic Cough: Practical Considerations," *Chest* 123, no. 3 (March 2003): 659–60; Jacob J. Lokich, "Secondary Uncommon Solid Neoplasms in Cured Hodgkin's Disease and Follow-Up of the Original B-DOPA Chemotherapy Patient Group," *American Journal of Clinical Oncology* 13, no 3 (June 1990): 247–50; E. M. López-Tomassetti Fernández and others, "Recurrence of Inflammatory Pseudotumor in the Distal Bile Duct: Lessons Learned from a Single Case and Reported Cases," *World Journal of Gastroenterology* 12, no. 24 (June 28, 2006): 3938–943.

10. Steven Gan, Katherine Wilson, and Paul Hollington, "Surveillance of Patients Following Surgery with Curative Intent for Colorectal Cancer," *World Journal of Gastroenterology* 13, no. 28 (July 28, 2007): 3816.

11. Manoj Pawar, "5 Tips for Generating Patient Satisfaction and Compliance," *Family Practice Management* 12, no. 6 (June 2005): 46.

12. The classic references include Joel B. Cohen and Dipankar Chakravarti, "Consumer Psychology," *Annual Review of Psychology* 41 (1990): 243–88; Daniel Kahneman, *Attention and Effort* (Englewood Cliffs, N.J.: Prentice-Hall, 1973); John G. Lynch and Thomas K. Srull, "Memory and Attentional Factors in Consumer Choice: Concepts and Research Methods," *Journal of Consumer Research* 9, no. 1 (June 1982): 18–37; George Miller, "The Magic Number Seven, Plus or Minus Two: Some Limits on Our Capacity for Processing Information," *Psychological Review* 63, no 2 (March 1956): 81–97; and Herbert A. Simon, *Administrative Behavior,* 4th ed. (New York: the Free Press, 1997).

13. Peter Drucker, "Managing the Public Service Institution," *Public Interest,* no. 33 (Fall 1973), p. 58.

14. Arthur E. Bryson, Jr. and Yu-Chi Ho, *Applied Optimal Control: Optimization, Estimation, and Control* (Waltham, Mass.: Blaisdell Publishing Company, 1969). "Larry" Ho was my dissertation adviser.

15. For example, a group of scholars from the University of Houston created an experiment with five units at an Air Force Base, all with complex and interdependent tasks. In an effort to improve productivity, they introduced group-based feedback, then goal setting, and finally incentives. They concluded that "goal setting added somewhat to the feedback, but not a great deal, and that incentives did not add further"; the feedback, however, had

a "very strong effect." Robert D. Pritchard and others, "Effects of Group Feedback, Goal Setting, and Incentives on Organizational Productivity," *Journal of Applied Psychology* 73, no. 2 (May 1988): 353, 351.

16. Matthew D. Gallagher, "CitiStat: Bringing a New Level of Efficiency and Effectiveness to Baltimore City's Water Utility," in *Management Innovation in U.S. Public Water and Wastewater Systems,* edited by Paul Seidenstat and others (Hoboken, N.J.: John Wiley & Sons, 2005), p. 295.

17. Robert D. Behn, *Leadership Counts: Lessons for Public Managers* (Harvard University Press, 1991), p. 71; Robert D. Behn, "On the Motivational Impact of The List," *Bob Behn's Public Management Report* 1, no. 2 (October 2003).

18. A major proponent of the relevance of the "ego ideal" to management is Harry Levinson. See, for example, Harry Levinson, "Management by Whose Objectives?" *Harvard Business Review* 48, no. 4 (July–August, 1970): 125–34. This article has been reprinted in *Harvard Business Review* 81, no. 1 (January 2003):107–16 and in numerous anthologies, including Harry Levinson, *On the Psychology of Leadership* (Harvard Business Press, 2006), pp. 1–20.

19. William Bratton, *Turnaround: How America's Top Cop Reversed the Crime Epidemic* (New York: Random House, 1998), p. 237.

20. Dean Esserman, "How to Decentralize Control and Get Police Officers to Love Their Jobs," *Heritage Lectures,* no. 707 (June 1, 2001), p. 6. A lecture delivered at The Heritage Foundation on February 28, 2001.

21. For a discussion of the concept of "esteem opportunity," see Robert D. Behn, "On the Value of Creating Esteem Opportunities," *Bob Behn's Public Management Report* 1, no. 9 (May 2004); and Robert D. Behn, *Performance Leadership: 11 Better Practices That Can Ratchet Up Performance.* (Washington, D.C.: IBM Center for the Business of Government, 2004), pp.16–17.

22. A Google search for "relentless follow-up" generated over 3,400 hits. Many of these are about CompStat, CitiStat, and other PerformanceStats. Others emphasize the importance of "relentless follow-up" to those who work in sales and marketing.

23. W. Somerset Maugham, *Of Human Bondage* (New York: New American Library, 1991 [1915]), p. 264.

24. In an experiment on the effectiveness of feedback, one group of scholars found "that management in some cases seemed to focus much more on small amounts of negative productivity information rather than on the much larger amount of positive information," which "had the effect of making those meetings a somewhat punishing experience for unit members rather than a positive experience." Robert D. Pritchard and others, "Effects of Group Feedback," p. 354.

25. Barbara Levitt and James G. March, "Organizational Learning," *Annual Review of Sociology* 14 (1988), pp. 322–23. See also Daniel A. Levinthal and James G. March, "The Myopia of Learning," *Strategic Management Journal* 14 [special issue] (Winter 1993): 95–112; Weiping Liu, "Knowledge Exploitation, Knowledge Exploration, and

Competency Trap," *Knowledge and Process Management* 13, no. 3 (July-September 2006): 144–61; Nicolaj Siggelkow and Daniel A. Levinthal, "Escaping Real (Non-Benign) Competency Traps: Linking the Dynamics of Organizational Structure to the Dynamics of Search," *Strategic Organization* 3, no. 1 (February 2005): 85–115; and Pino G. Audia, Edwin. A. Locke, and Ken G. Smith, "The Paradox of Success: An Archival and Laboratory Study of Strategic Persistence Following a Radical Environmental Change," *Academy of Management Journal* 43, no. 5 (October 2000): 837–54.

26. Here's another, similar, definition: "Stretch targets are objectives that force organizations to significantly alter their processes in a way that often involves a whole new paradigm of operations." Kenneth R. Thompson, Wayne A. Hochwarter, and Nicholas J. Mathys, "Stretch Targets: What Makes Them Effective?" *Academy of Management Executive* 11, no. 3 (August 1997): 48.

27. For a discussion of the concept of the "binding constraint" (in both public management and economic growth), see Robert D. Behn, "On Why Public Executives Need to Fix Their Agency's Binding Constraints," *Bob Behn's Public Management Report* 4, no 10 (June 2007); Ricardo Hausmann, Dani Rodrik, and Andrés Velasco, "Getting the Diagnosis Right: A New Approach to Economic Reform," *Finance and Development* 43, no. 1 (March 2006): 12–15; Ricardo Hausmann, Dani Rodrik, and Andrés Velasco, "Growth Diagnostics," in *The Washington Consensus Reconsidered: Towards a New Global Governance,* edited by Narcis Serra and Joseph E. Stiglitz (Oxford University Press, 2008), pp. 324–54.

28. Or should the credit go to Bubber Miley or Irving Mills? Yes, Ellington wrote the music. But Irving Mills gets credit for the lyrics. Even before the song was published in 1932, however, James "Bubber" Miley, a trumpeter in the Ellington band in the 1920s, had coined and frequently used the phrase.

Chapter Twelve

1. Geoff Colvin, *Talent Is Overrated: What Really Separates World-Class Performers from Everybody Else* (New York: Penguin Group, 2008), p. 194.

2. W. Edwards Deming, *Out of the Crisis* (Center for Advanced Engineering Study, Massachusetts Institute of Technology, 1982, 1986), p. 71.

3. Robert D. Behn, "On Why All Public Executives Need to Cultivate the Skill and Habit of 'Short Division,'" *Bob Behn's Performance Leadership Report* 10, no. 1 (September 2012).

4. One study compiled a list of 55 managerial competences that other researchers had identified. Turo Virtanen, "Changing Competences of Public Managers: Tensions in Commitment," *International Journal of Public Sector Management* 13, no. 4 (2000): 333–41.

5. Marc D. Zegans, "The Dilemma of the Modern Public Manager: Satisfying the Virtues of Scientific and Innovative Management," in *Innovation in American Government:*

Challenges, Opportunities, and Dilemmas edited by Alan Altshuler and Robert D. Behn (Brookings, 1997), p. 105.

6. Too often, however, the phrase "competency management" has come to mean the appraisal and selection of individual employees for particular, desired competences (specifically individual attributes and personal characteristics) rather than the development of those organizational (as well as individual) competences necessary to achieve a jurisdiction's or agency's public purpose. For example, see David Farnham and Amanda Stevens, "Developing and Implementing Competence-Based Recruitment and Selection in a Social Services Department: A Case Study of West Sussex County Council," *International Journal of Public Sector Management* 13, no. 4 (2000): 369–82. Indeed, "competency management," wrote two scholars from Belgium, can "be seen as a shift away from performance management. While the focus of performance management is on results and output, the focus of competency management is on input: what do people bring into their job." Annie Hondeghem and Filip Vandermeulen, "Competency Management in the Flemish and Dutch Civil Service," *International Journal of Public Sector Management* 13, no. 4 (2000): 342–53.

7. Governor's Office of Crime Control and Prevention, "CompStat on Demand," September 2012 (www.goccp.maryland.gov/msac/documents/FactSheets/COMPSTAT-on-Demand.pdf).

8. Dean Esserman, "How to Decentralize Control and Get Police Officers to Love Their Jobs," *Heritage Lectures,* no. 707 (June 1, 2001). A lecture delivered at the Heritage Foundation on February 28, 2001, pp. 2, 4.

9. Robert J. Samuelson, "Why I Am Not a Manager," *Washington Post,* March 18, 1999, p. A21.

10. For a discussion of some of the pitfalls that confront the "technical expert" who is promoted to manager, see Andrew M. Dobo, "Do You Really Want to Be the Boss?" *Government Executive* 20, no. 12 (December 1988): 36–37.

11. These organizations have to promote from within. Even as a superstar vice president at General Electric can't jump to being a colonel in the U. S. Army. The Park Service, the Forest Service, and the Public Health Service have similar restrictions on their ability to hire middle managers from the outside, though this does not apply to political appointees who head these organizations (for example, the Secretary of the Army). This rule is true for most police and fire departments; a private-sector manager can't become a precinct commander.

12. The Federal Executive Institute (FEI) does not, however, have the depth and breadth of the courses offered by, for example, GE's John F. Welch Leadership Development Center at Crotonville, New York. And FEI's director does not have the status of GE's vice president for executive development.

13. Full disclosure: at the Kennedy School, I chair such an executive-education program: Driving Government Performance: Leadership Strategies That Produce Results.

14. Voltaire, *Candide, or Optimism,* edited and translated by Theo Cuffe (London: Penguin Books, 2005), chapter 23, p. 69.

15. Richard F. Elmore, "Leadership as the Practice of Improvement," in *Improving School Leadership, Volume 2: Case Studies in System Leadership,* edited by Beatriz Pont, Deborah Nusche, and David Hopkins (Paris: Organization for Economic Cooperation and Development, 2008), pp. 40, 41.

16. Ibid., p. 41.

17. Mark H. Moore, *Creating Public Value: Strategic Management in Government* (Harvard University Press, 1995), p. 71.

18. Deming, *Out of the Crisis,* p. 71.

19. Elmore, "Leadership as the Practice of Improvement," p. 39.

20. Michael Power, *The Audit Explosion* (London: Demos, 1994). See also, Michael Power, *The Audit Society: Rituals of Verification* (Oxford University Press, 1999). Power's account of the "audit explosion" concerns, primarily, what happened in the United Kingdom (and other Commonwealth countries) in the 1980s and early 1990, because, he argued, "it had already happened" in the United States "in the 1960s." Michael Power, "The Theory of the Audit Explosion," in *The Oxford Handbook of Public Management,* edited by Ewan Ferlie, Laurence E. Lynn, and Christopher Pollitt (Oxford University Press, 2005), pp. 326, 331.

21. "Auditee": I love the word. It makes perfect sense. For every "auditor," there must exist an "auditee." But you might expect me to love the word "auditee." After all, Power's division of the world is similar to my distinction between an "accountability holder" and an "accountability holdee." Robert D. Behn, *Rethinking Democratic Accountability* (Brookings, 2001), p. 1.

22. Power, *The Audit Explosion,* p. 40.

23. Power, "The Theory of the Audit Explosion," p. 335.

24. Alasdair Roberts, "Worrying about Misconduct: The Control Lobby and the PS 2000 Reforms," *Canadian Public Administration* 39, no. 4 (Winter 1997).

25. Power, *The Audit Explosion,* pp. 25, 28.

26. Power, "The Theory of the Audit Explosion," pp. 331, 335.

27. Ibid., p. 335.

28. Power, *The Audit Explosion,* pp. 25, 28, 31.

29. Ibid., p. 40.

30. Andrew Gray, Jane Broadbent, and Jean Hartley, "The State of Public Management—Improvement and Innovation," *Public Money and Management* 25, no. 1 (January 2005): 7.

31. Jean Hartley and John Benington, "Copy and Paste, or Graft and Transplant? Knowledge Sharing through Inter-Organizational Networks," *Public Money and Management* 26, no. 2 (April 2006): 102.

32. Donald F. Kettl, "The Global Revolution in Public Management: Driving Themes, Missing Links," *Journal of Policy Analysis and Management* 16, no. 3 (summer 1997): 447, 448. Also Kettl, *The Global Public Management Revolution: A Report on the Transformation of Governance* (Brookings, 2000).

33. Los Angeles County Department of Mental Health, "STATS: Introduction and Overview" (http://lacdmh.lacounty.gov/ToolsForAdministrators/stats.html).

34. James Q. Wilson, "The Bureaucracy Problem," *Public Interest* 6 (Winter 1967): 7.

35. In the United States at least, numerous observers have deplored the state—indeed, the decline—of the competence of government organizations. Forty years ago, Robert Wood argued that "the American government has relied heavily on the energies and the devotion of the organization amateur. . . . The country . . . cannot afford amateurs in administration any longer. . . . We must at long last take the problem of public management seriously." Robert Wood, "When Government Works," *Public Interest* 18 (Winter 1970): 51. Ten years later, James Sundquist criticized "the gradual deterioration of administrative capability" of the federal government: "at the top levels of the U.S. government, administrative capability has been allowed to decline, over a long period, with a resulting loss of capacity throughout the executive branch." As a result, he continued, "the performance of the government has fallen far short of what the people have expected and have a right to expect." James L. Sundquist, "The Crisis of Competence in Our National Government," *Political Science Quarterly* 95, no. 2 (Summer 1980): 190, 201,186. Fifteen years later, Sundquist repeated this critique: The U.S. "government has never established over the years a tradition and a structure that would ensure consistent attention by competent managers to the day-to-day operations of its departments and agencies." To illustrate this argument, he wrote, "It has been a century since we stopped putting uniforms on politicians and giving them command of army and navy units. Today, nobody would even think of making anyone other than a career military officer the chief of staff of the army." Yet, he continued, "we rarely look inside the career service to find leadership for civil departments." James L. Sundquist, "The Concept of Governmental Management: Or, What's Missing in the Gore Report," *Public Administration Review* 55, no. 4 (July/August 1995): 398, 399.

36. Quoted in James Lardner, "The C.E.O. Cop," *The New Yorker,* February 6, 1995, p. 51. Staying out of trouble is a common bureaucratic imperative. Two decades ago, one case study of the Coast Guard described "the risk-averse mentality bred by the Coast Guard's brutal promotion system." "You're not allowed many mistakes or your promotion days are over," observed one officer. "It's not considered a big mistake if you're out there trying to save someone and you bang up your boat. It's considered a big mistake if you piss somebody off." Susan Rosegrant, "The Coast Guard's Model Unit Program: Testing the Waters of Change (A)," Kennedy School of Government Case Program (C16-93-1194.0) (Harvard University, Cambridge, Mass.), p. 3.

37. Quoted in Chris Smith, "The NYPD Guru," *New York,* April 1, 1996, p. 34.

38. Jeffrey Pfeffer and Robert I. Sutton, *Hard Facts, Dangerous Half-Truths and Total Nonsense: Profiting from Evidence-Based Management* (Harvard Business School Press, 2006), pp 13, 14. Pfeffer and Sutton also have a website on evidence-based management (www.evidence-basedmanagement.com/).

39. Denise M. Rousseau, "Is There Such a Thing as 'Evidence-Based Management'?" *Academy of Management Review* 31, no. 2 (April, 2006): 261.

40. A study of the capacity of U.S. county governments to employ performance measurement concluded that it requires multiple people with multiple competences: "Capacity [to use performance measurement] requires that jurisdictions are able (1) to relate outputs to operations; (2) to collect timely data; (3) to have staff capable of analyzing performance data; (4) adequate information technology; and support from (5) department heads and (6) elected officials." The authors also found "that about one-third of counties use performance measurement and that about one-fifth of these have a high level of use." Moreover, "about one-third (31 percent–39 percent) of all counties which currently use performance measurement can be said to have adequate capacity for it." Evan Berman and XiaoHu Wang, "Performance Measurement in U.S. Counties: Capacity for Reform," *Public Administration Review* 60, no. 5 (September/October 2000): 417, 414. This study is over a decade old; nevertheless, it illustrates the challenges of developing adequate capacity for simply using performance *measures,* let alone for engaging in performance *leadership.*

41. New York City Administration for Children's Services, "Flash," November 2012 (www.nyc.gov/html/acs/downloads/pdf/stats_monthly_flash.pdf).

42. Erwin C. Hargrove and John C. Glidewell, *Impossible Jobs in Public Management* (University of Kansas Press, 1990): 133, 134.

43. In September 2011, Mattingly returned to the Foundation as a "Senior Associate."

44. ChildStat meeting of July 2, 2009.

45. Conversation with Heather Weston, December 28, 2012.

46. Henry Mintzberg, "The Manager's Job: Folklore or Fact," *Harvard Business Review* 53, no. 4 (July-August 1975): p. 54.

47. Ibid., p. 49.

48. Henri Fayol, *General and Industrial Management,* translated by Constance Storrs (London: Sir Isaac Pitman & Sons, 1949), p. 6.

49. Luther Gulick, "Notes on the Theory of Organization," in *Papers on the Science of Administration,* edited by Luther Gulick and L. Urwick (New York: Institute of Public Administration, 1937), p. 13.

50. Mintzberg, "The Manager's Job," p. 49. Other scholars, practitioners, and observers have created their own taxonomy of the roles of managers—some designed for the universe of managers, others for managers in specific fields such as health care, education, or human resources: Kristina L. Guo, "A Study of the Skills and Roles of Senior-Level Health Care Managers," *Health Care Manager* 22, no. 2 (April/May/June 2003):152–58; Steven T. Bossert, David C. Dwyer, Brian Rowan, and Ginny V. Lee, "The Instructional Management Role of the Principal," *Educational Administration Quarterly* 18, no. 3 (August 1982): 34–64; Raymond Caldwell, "The Changing Roles of Personnel Managers: Old Ambiguities, New Uncertainties," *Journal of Management Studies* 40, no. 4 (June 2003): 983–1004.

51. Malcolm Sparrow, *The Character of Harms: Operational Challenges in Control* (Cambridge University Press, 2008), pp. 8, 11.

52. For a few of these roles—such as negotiator or spokesperson—there are several formal and informal ways to learn the basics. Indeed, for those roles for which there exists some explicit knowledge, universities offer a variety of courses. For example, Harvard offers executive education courses on negotiation at its Business School, Law School, and Kennedy School of Government.

53. Barry Bozeman and Mary Feeney offered the following definition of mentoring: "a process for the informal transmission of knowledge, social capital, and psychosocial support perceived by the recipient as relevant to work, career, or professional development; mentoring entails informal communication, usually face-to-face and during a sustained period of time, between a person who is perceived to have greater relevant knowledge, wisdom, or experience (the mentor) and a person who is perceived to have less (the protégé)." Barry Bozeman and Mary K. Feeney, "Toward a Useful Theory of Mentoring: A Conceptual Analysis and Critique," *Administration & Society* 39, no. 6 (October 2007): 719–39.

54. Henry Mintzberg, *The Nature of Managerial Work* (New York: Harper & Row, 1973), pp. 190, 188.

55. Ibid., pp. 188, 190, 188.

56. Matthew D. Gallagher, "CitiStat: Bringing a New Level of Efficiency and Effectiveness to Baltimore City's Water Utility," in *Management Innovation in U.S. Public Water and Wastewater Systems,* edited by Paul Seidenstat and others (Hoboken, N.J.: John Wiley & Sons, 2005), p. 291.

57. Dimock observed that "feigned acquiescence is one of the indispensable tools of the career official," which involves "giving outward acquiescence and cooperation while actually slowing down the reform or killing it entirely." Marshall E. Dimock, "Bureaucracy Self-Examined," *Public Administration Review* 4 no. 3 (Summer 1944): 203.

58. Malicious compliance involves "blind compliance to procedures," wrote Carroll; the "workers know the right thing to do but also know that only rote compliance is safe from disciplinary action." John S. Carroll, "Organizational Learning Activities in High-Hazard Industries," *Journal of Management Studies* 35, no. 6 (November 1998): 713. Sutton described it as "following idiotic orders from on high exactly to the letter, thereby assuring the work will suck." Robert I. Sutton, *Good Boss, Bad Boss: How to Be the Best . . . and Learn from the Worst* (New York: Business Plus, 2010), p. 170.

59. P. David Elrod II and Donald D. Tippett, "The 'Death Valley' of Change," *Journal of Organizational Change Management* 15, no. 3 (2002): 273–91.

60. Jack Maple (with Chris Mitchell), *The Crime Fighter* (New York: Doubleday, 1999), pp. 246–47.

61. John F. Timoney, *Beat Cop to Top Cop: A Tale of Three Cities* (University of Pennsylvania Press, 2010), pp. 233, 234.

62. Kurt Lewin, "Frontiers in Group Dynamics: Concept, Method and Reality in Social Science; Social Equilibria and Social Change," *Human Relations* 1, no. 1 (June 1947): 34–35.

Chapter Thirteen

1. Robert I. Sutton, *Weird Ideas That Work: How to Build a Creative Company* (New York: Free Press, 2002), p. 22.

2. Howard Gardner, *The Disciplined Mind: What All Students Should Understand* (New York: Simon & Schuster, 1999), p. 119.

3. Susan Diesenhouse, "'Slumerville' No More," *Boston Globe,* April 6, 2005, p. D6.

4. Richard Florida, *The Rise of the Creative Class* (New York: Basic Books, 2002).

5. Beth Teitell, "Somerville Worries It's Growing Too Hip: Trendy Bustle Brings Uncertainty about City's Essence," *Boston Globe,* August 23, 2013, p. 1.

6. Interview with Curtatone, February 18, 2011.

7. Ibid.

8. "Learn about ResiStat" at www.somervillema.gov/spotlights/resistat.

9. ResiStat blog, http://somervilleresistat.blogspot.com/.

10. "Somerville SomerStat and ResiStat," Somerville Patch, http://somerville.patch.com/listings/somerville-somerstat-and-resistat.

11. "ResiStat—Your Wicked Awesome Somerville Resource," Life in the 'Ville, blog (http://lifeintheville.wordpress.com/2010/12/10/resistat-your-wicked-awesome-somerville-resource/).

12. Interview with Curtatone, September 24, 2009.

13. Thomas M. Keane, Jr., "The Model City," *Boston Globe Magazine,* May 14, 2006, p. 16.

14. Paul J. DiMaggio and Walter W. Powell, "The Iron Cage Revisited: Institutional Isomorphism and Collective Rationality in Organizational Fields," in *The New Institutionalism of Organizational Analysis,* edited by Powell and DiMaggio (The University of Chicago Press, 1991), pp. 63–82. This chapter is a revision of Paul J. DiMaggio and Walter W. Powell, "The Iron Cage Revisited: Institutional Isomorphism and Collective Rationality in Organizational Fields," *American Sociological Review* 48, no. 2 (April 1983):147, 160.

15. Eli B. Silverman, "Compstat's Innovation," in *Police Innovation: Contrasting Perspectives,* edited by David Weisburd and Anthony A. Braga (Cambridge University Press, 2006), pp. 268, 267, 275. Jack Maple, *The Crime Fighter* (New York: Doubleday, 1999), p. 93.

16. DiMaggio and Powell, "The Iron Cage Revisited," pp. 64, 66.

17. The Government Performance and Results Modernization Act of 2010 might be an example of coercive isomorphism; it requires all federal agencies to hold quarterly performance-review meetings. But it does not require (or even suggest) that agencies adopt a complete PerformanceStat strategy. It *requires* meetings and goals, but how a federal agency uses them is unspecified. The Office of Management and Budget's *Circular A-11* states that, in conducting a performance review, the agency head should, for example, "Hold goal leaders accountable" for a number of things, such as "knowing the quality of their data" and "identifying effective practices." And the agency head should "Agree on

follow-up actions." U.S. Office of Management and Budget, *Circular No. A-11, Preparation, Submission, and Execution of the Budget* (Washington, D.C.: Executive Office of the President, July 2013).

18. One exception is the Police Executive Research Forum, which has helped police departments learn about CompStat.

19. Describing a management innovation as a "best practice," Senge argued, "can do more harm than good, leading to piecemeal copying." Peter M. Senge, *The Fifth Discipline: The Art and Practice of the Learning Organization* (New York: Currency Doubleday, 1990), p. 11.

20. Robert D. Behn, *Performance Leadership: 11 Better Practices That Can Ratchet Up Performance* (Washington, D.C.: IBM Center for the Business of Government, 2004).

21. Eugene Bardach, *Getting Agencies to Work Together: The Practice and Theory of Managerial Craftsmanship* (Brookings, 1998), pp. 35-41.

22. Gardner, *The Disciplined Mind,* p. 119.

23. Quoted in Alden Whitman, "Mies van der Rohe Dies at 83: Leader of Modern Architecture. Expressed Industrial Spirit," *New York Times,* August 19, 1969 (www.nytimes.com/learning/general/onthisday/bday/0327.html?scp=3&sq=mies%20van%20de%20rohe&st=cse). Also quoted in Timothy J. Gilfoyle, "America's Heart," *Atlantic Monthly,* February 1999. www.theatlantic.com/past/docs/issues/99feb/gotham.htm.

24. Interview with Hirsch, February 15, 2011.

25. This heresy—to shun strategic planning and, instead, to "just start"—isn't just limited to government. As chief executive of Johnsonville Foods, Ralph Stayer employed it: "Just start," he learned. "Don't wait until you have all the answers." Why? "There were too many variables. I wasn't certain which systems to change, I just knew I had to change something in order to alter expectations and begin moving toward my goal." Ralph Stayer, "How I Learned to Let My Workers Lead," *Harvard Business Review* 68, no. 6 (November-December 1990): 74.

26. Robert D. Behn, *Leadership Counts: Lessons for Public Managers* (Harvard University Press, 1991), p. 127.

27. Robert D. Behn, "Management by Groping Along," *Journal of Policy Analysis and Management* 7, no. 4, (Fall 1988): 643–63; and Behn, *Leadership Counts,* Chapter Seven, "Management by Groping Along," pp. 127–50.

28. Thomas J. Peters and Robert H. Waterman, Jr., *In Search of Excellence: Lessons from America's Best-Run Companies* (New York: Harper & Row, 1982), pp. 119 & 155.

29. For more on "Aim, Fire, Ready," see Behn, "Management by Groping Along," p. 647; and Behn, *Leadership Counts,* p. 136.

30. Peters and Waterman do follow their admonition to "Ready. Fire. Aim." with the advice to "Learn from your tries." Ibid., p. 155. Still, an organization can only learn from its tries by comparing where it hit with where it was aiming.

31. Senge, *The Fifth Discipline,* pp. 68 and 7.

32. Ibid., p. 7.

33. Ibid., p. 8.

34. Ibid., p. 206.

35. Ibid., p. 236.

36. Ibid., pp. 14, 11.

37. For an application of Senge's five disciplines to the public sector, see: G. B. Reschenthaler and Fred Thompson, "Public Management and the Learning Organization," *International Public Management Journal* 1, no. 1 (1998), particularly pp. 82–95.

38. Senge, *The Fifth Discipline*, p. 15

39. Barry Sugarman, "Organizational Learning and Reform at the New York City Police Department," *Journal of Applied Behavioral Science* 46, no. 2 (June 2010): 164.

40. Ibid., p. 163.

41. Ibid., p. 173.

42. Dennis C. Smith, "Making Management Count: A Case for Theory-and-Evidence-Based Public Management," *Journal of Policy Analysis and Management* 28, No. 3 (Summer 2009): 500, 503.

43. Sugarman, "Organizational Learning and Reform," pp. 164, 162, 173–74 (emphasis in original).

44. Ibid., p. 162.

45. Ibid., p. 160 (emphasis in original).

46. Barbara Levitt and James G. March, "Organizational Learning," *Annual Review of Sociology* 14 (1988): 322–23; Daniel A. Levinthal and James G. March, "The Myopia of Learning," *Strategic Management Journal* 14 [Special Issue] (Winter 1993): 95–112; Weiping Liu, "Knowledge Exploitation, Knowledge Exploration, and Competency Trap," *Knowledge and Process Management* 13, no. 3 (July-September 2006): 144–61; Nicolaj Siggelkow and Daniel A. Levinthal, "Escaping Real (Non-Benign) Competency Traps: Linking the Dynamics of Organizational Structure to the Dynamics of Search," *Strategic Organization* 3, no. 1 (February 2005): 85–115; and Pino G. Audia, Edwin A. Locke, and Ken G. Smith, "The Paradox of Success: An Archival and Laboratory Study of Strategic Persistence Following a Radical Environmental Change," *Academy of Management Journal* 43, no. 5 (October 2000): 837–54.

47. Sugarman, "Organizational Learning and Reform," p. 158.

48. Sara J. Singer and Amy C. Edmondson, "When Learning and Performance Are at Odds: Confronting the Tensions," in *Learning and Performance Matter,* edited by Prem Kumar and Phil Ramsey (Singapore: World Scientific, 2008), pp. 39–40.

49. Amy C. Edmondson and Sara J. Singer, "Confronting the Tension between Learning and Performance," *Systems Thinker* 19, no. 1 (February 2008): 6, 7, 6. Edmondson and Singer focus on the private sector; their example is "mature markets, where solutions for getting a job done exist and are well understood" (p. 5)—a firm's equivalent of filling potholes.

50. Chris Argyris, "Double Loop Learning in Organizations," *Harvard Business Review* 55, no. 5 (September-October 1977): 115–25. Chris Argyris and Donald A. Schön, *Theory in Practice. Increasing Professional Effectiveness* (San Francisco: Jossey-Bass, 1974).

51. Senge made the same point, distinguishing between "adaptive learning" (or "survival learning") and "generative learning" which enhances the organization's "capacity to create" its shared vision. Senge, *The Fifth Discipline,* p. 14. Elsewhere, he wrote that "to be generative [is] to expand our capability." Thus, while adaptive learning "is about coping," generative learning "is about creating." Peter M. Senge, "The Leader's New Work: Building Learning Organizations," *Sloan Management Review* 32, no. 1 (Fall 1990): 8.

52. Senge, *The Fifth Discipline,* p. 10.

53. Amy C. Edmondson, "Learning from Mistakes Is Easier Said than Done: Group and Organizational Influences on the Detection and Correction of Human Error," *Journal of Applied Behavioral Science* 32, no. 1 (March 1996): 5–28.

54. Mark D. Cannon and Amy C. Edmondson, "Failing to Learn and Learning to Fail (Intelligently): How Great Organizations Put Failure to Work to Innovate and Improve," *Long Range Planning* 38, no. 3 (June 2005): 312–14.

55. Amy Edmondson, "Psychological Safety and Learning Behavior in Work Teams," *Administrative Science Quarterly* 44, no. 2 (June, 1999): 350, 354, 379, 375.

56. Cannon and Edmondson, "Failing to Learn and Learning to Fail (Intelligently)," pp. 312, 315.

57. Fiona Lee and others, "Effects of Inconsistency on Experimentation in Organizations," *Organization Science* 15, no. 3 (May–June 2004): 310.

58. See Chapter 15 for a discussion of the Yerkes-Dodson curve. The concept is straightforward: if performance is very low, increasing pressure for improvement will produce it. Eventually, however, increased pressure will reduce performance.

59. Kazuhiro Mishina, "Learning by New Experiences: Revisiting the Flying Fortress Learning Curve," in *Learning by Doing in Markets, Firms, and Countries,* edited by Naomi R. Lamoreaux, Daniel M. G. Raff, and Peter Temin (University of Chicago Press, 1999), p. 175.

60. Ibid., pp. 170, 175.

61. Ibid., p. 175.

62. Ibid., pp. 168, 174.

63. Sutton, *Weird Ideas That Work,* p. 22.

Chapter Fourteen

1. George Greenstein, *Portraits of Discovery: Profiles in Scientific Genius* (New York: John Wiley & Sons, 1998), p. 56.

2. Jon Elster, *Explaining Technical Change: A Case Study in the Philosophy of Science* (Cambridge University Press, 1983), p. 24. Elster notes: "Here the term 'mechanism' should be understood broadly, to cover intentional chains from a goal to an action as well as causal chains from an event to its effect." Later, Elster modified his concept of the mechanism, explaining: "In that work [his 1983 book], I advocated the search for

mechanisms as more or less synonymous with the reductionist strategy in science." Jon Elster, "A Plea for Mechanisms," in *Social Mechanisms: An Analytical Approach to Social Theory,* edited by Peter Hedström and Richard Swedberg (Cambridge University Press, 1998), p. 47.

3. Cathy Sharp, Jocelyn Jones, and Alison M. Smith, *What Do We Measure and Why? An Evaluation of the CitiStat Model of Performance Management and Its Applicability to the Scottish Public Sector* (Edinburgh: Scottish Executive Social Research, 2006).

4. In 2005–06, Scotland then created five experiments with CitiStat in the City of Edinburgh Council, the Aberdeen City Council, the National Health Service Tayside, the NHS Ayrshire, and the Arran Health Board.

5. A few don't. The most notable exception has been NYPD, which while Raymond Kelley was commissioner, did not permit visitors to its CompStat meetings.

6. Michael Polanyi, *The Tacit Dimension* (Garden City, N.Y.: Doubleday, 1966), p. 4.

7. John Lubbock, "Beauty in Nature," *Strand Magazine* 3 (January to June, 1892), p. 158.

8. John Lubbock, *The Beauties of Nature and the Wonders of the World We Live In* (London: Macmillan and Co., 1892; Boston: Adamant Media Corporation, 2005), p. 3.

9. Joseph A. Pechman and Michael P. Timpane, eds., *Work Incentives and Income Guarantees: The New Jersey Negative Income Tax Experiment* (Brookings, 1975); Robert A. Moffitt, "The Labor Supply Response in the Gary Experiment," *The Journal of Human Resources* 14, no. 4 (1979): 477–87.

10. Several observers have noted the absence of any theory to support particular management strategies. Drucker writes that one "explanation for the tendency of so much public administration today to commit itself to policies that can only result in nonperformance is the lack of concern with performance in public administration theory." Peter F. Drucker, "The Deadly Sins of Public Administration," *Public Administrative Review* 40, no. 2 (March/April 1980): 106. Talbot writes: "What is striking about most of the policy and practitioner, and even academic, literature is the absence of theoretical justification for particular models of performance proposed." Colin Talbot, "Performance Management," in *The Oxford Handbook of Public Management,* edited by Ewan Ferlie, Laurence E. Lynn, Jr., and Christopher Pollitt (Oxford University Press, 2005), p. 508. I am not reporting that anyone employing a PerformanceStat leadership strategy ever defined any of these 16 causal behaviors. Instead, the 16 are *my* effort to suggest (given what we know about human behavior in organizations) how the leadership behaviors that I have observed might help to foster (individually and collectively) improved organizational performance.

11. Pawson emphasizes that the standard "numerical meta-analysis" approach to evaluation "makes no effort to understand how programmes work." Ray Pawson, "Evidence-Based Policy: In Search of a Method," *Evaluation* 8, no. 2 (April 2002): 158.

12. Mario Bunge, "How Does It Work? The Search for Explanatory Mechanisms," *Philosophy of the Social Sciences* 34, no. 2 (2004): 182.

13. For many social policies, the mechanism is what Schelling calls the "rational, or at least purposive, individual" whose (often economic) behavior interacting with the behavior of other such motivated individuals creates the consequences. Thomas C. Schelling, "Social Mechanisms and Social Dynamics," in *Social Mechanisms,* edited by Hedström and Swedberg, p. 32. For examples of such mechanisms see: Thomas C. Schelling, *Micromotives and Macrobehavior* (New York: W. W. Norton & Company, 1978).

14. Yes, Newton's laws are approximations that happen to work very well, except approaching the speed of light, when scientists and engineers must use Einstein's equations. But many scientists and certainly most engineers never have to worry about this refinement.

15. Greenstein, *Portraits of Discovery,* pp. 56, 57.

16. Red Auerbach, who created the Boston Celtics' basketball dynasty, was a master at employing differential behaviors to motivate people. Below are two versions of Auerbach's approach. The first is from Bill Reynolds, *Cousy: His Life, Career, and the Birth of Big Time Basketball* (New York: Simon & Schuster, 2005), p. 174:

[Tommy] Heinsohn also came to know that Auerbach never motivated anybody the same way, that he intuitively understood which individual buttons to push. He knew never to criticize [Bob] Cousy or [Bill] Russell. He knew never to yell at [Bill] Sharman, who didn't take it well and might just retaliate by punching Red in the mouth. He rarely yelled at [Frank] Ramsey, who might take criticism to heart. Heinsohn was perfect. Auerbach could yell at him, and in doing so could get his message to the entire team. So it was Heinsohn who was too heavy, Heinsohn who wasn't playing defense intensely enough in practice, Heinsohn who wasn't running wind sprints hard enough, Heinsohn who was smoking too many cigarettes, Heinsohn who was always doing something wrong.

The second is from John Powers, "Auerbach's Legacy Remains Unflagging," *Boston Globe,* December 23, 1999:

If Auerbach wanted to chide Russell in the locker room, he did it by osmosis, by yelling at Heinsohn. "He'd say, 'Tommy you gotta do this, Tommy you gotta do that—and that goes for you, too, Russell,'" Heinsohn recalled.

17. Michael Polanyi, *Personal Knowledge: Towards a Post-Critical Philosophy* (University of Chicago Press, 1958), p. 87.

18. Peter Hedström and Petri Ylikoski, "Causal Mechanisms in the Social Sciences," *Annual Review of Sociology* 36 (2010): 64.

19. Peter Hedström and Richard Swedberg, "Social Mechanisms: An Introductory Essay," in *Social Mechanisms,* edited by Hedström and Swedberg, p. 13.

20. Hedström and Ylikoski, "Causal Mechanisms in the Social Sciences," pp. 50, 52.

21. Ibid., p. 54.

22. Bunge writes that "because most mechanisms are nonmechanical" (including both scientific and social mechanisms), "I prefer to call it *mechanismic*" [emphasis in the

original]. Bunge, "How Does It Work?" p. 203. Still, the use of "mechanisms"—complete with its cogs and wheels—to explain the observations of social science is well established. Hedström and Ylikoski conclude: "The basic idea of a mechanism-based explanation is quite simple: At its core, it implies that proper explanations should detail the cogs and wheels of the causal process through which the outcome to be explained was brought about." Hedström and Ylikoski, "Causal Mechanisms in the Social Sciences," p. 50.

23. Max Weber, *Economy and Society: An Outline of Interpretive Sociology* (Berkeley, Calif.: University of California Press, 1978), p. LIX.

24. For an introduction to complex adaptative systems, see Geert R. Teisman and Erik-Hans Klijn, "Complexity Theory and Public Management: An Introduction," *Public Management Review* 10, no. 3 (2008): 287–97; and M. Mitchell Waldrop, *Complexity: The Emerging Science at the Edge of Order and Chaos* (New York: Simon & Schuster, 1992).

25. Schelling, "Social Mechanisms and Social Dynamics," in *Social Mechanisms,* edited by Hedström and Swedberg , pp. 32–33.

26. Hedström and Swedberg, "Social Mechanisms: An Introductory Essay," p. 21.

27. Hedström and Ylikoski, "Causal Mechanisms in the Social Sciences," p. 61.

28. For example, these 16 plausible hypotheses focus on efforts to improve performance internally. They ignore leadership's need to build external support for any new undertaking. Thus, for example, another plausible hypothesis could be: Explaining the PerformanceStat strategy to key stakeholders can provide support necessary to sustain the initiative until it starts producing real results.

29. Hedström and Swedberg, "Social Mechanisms: An Introductory Essay," p. 15.

30. This raises a different "*How?*" question: Does the leadership team know *how* to implement these behaviors intelligently? This is Gilbert Ryle's "distinction . . . between *knowing that* something is the case and *knowing how* to do things" (emphasis added). Ryle argues: "When a person knows how to do things of a certain sort (e.g., cook omelettes, design dresses or persuade juries), his performance is in some way governed by principles, rules, canons, standards or criteria." Gilbert Ryle, "Knowing How and Knowing That: The Presidential Address," *Proceedings of the Aristotelian Society* 46 (1945–46): 4, 8. Or, I might add—when the thing being done is getting a public agency to produce results—the leadership team's own performance is in some way governed by its members' knowledge of important leadership behaviors.

31. Bunge, "How Does It Work?" pp. 207, 200, 186.

32. Eugene Bardach, *Getting Agencies to Work Together: The Practice and Theory of Managerial Craftsmanship* (Brookings, 1998), pp. 40–41, 56–57.

33. I could have collapsed the 16 behaviors into just two macro behaviors: Behavior I and Behavior M. Behavior I would focus on the approaches employed to identify and convey the Improvements to be made and would contain four subtheories: I1, I2, I3, and I4. Behavior M would focus on the Motivational strategies employed to achieve the improvements and would contain 12 subtheories: M1 . . . M12. I wanted, however, to emphasize the specific effects of each of the 16 behaviors.

34. Bunge, "How Does It Work?" p. 195.

35. This conclusion is consistent with the counterfactual standard of the causal-mechanism approach. Hedström and Ylikoski write: "A mechanism-based explanation describes the causal process selectively. It does not aim at an exhaustive account of all details but seeks to capture the crucial elements of the process by abstracting away the irrelevant details. The relevance of entities, their properties, and their interactions is determined by their ability to make a relevant difference to the outcome of interest. If the presence of an entity or of changes in its properties or activities truly does not make any difference to the effect to be explained, it can be ignored. This counterfactual criterion of relevance implies that mechanism-based explanations involve counterfactual reasoning about possible changes and their consequences." Hedström and Ylikoski, "Causal Mechanisms in the Social Sciences," p. 53.

Chapter Fifteen

1. Interview with Hirsch, February 15, 2011.

2. Kurt Lewin, *Field Theory in Social Science; Selected Theoretical Papers,* edited by Dorwin Cartwright (New York: Harper & Brothers Publishers, 1951), p. 169.

3. Luther Gulick, "Notes on the Theory of Organization," in *Papers on the Science of Administration,* edited by Luther Gulick and L. Urwick (New York: Institute of Public Administration, 1936), p. 13.

4. J. Richard Hackman, "The Psychology of Self-Management in Organizations," in *Psychology and Work: Productivity, Change, and Employment,* edited by Michael S. Pallack and Robert O. Perloff (American Psychological Association, 1986), p. 102.

5. The research on the motivational impact of goals is long and significant. Here are just a few publications: Gary P. Latham and Edwin A. Locke, "Self Regulation through Goal Setting," *Organizational Behavior and Human Decision Processes* 50, no. 2 (1991): 212–47; Gary P. Latham and Craig C. Pinder, "Work Motivation Theory and Research at the Dawn of the Twenty-First Century," *Annual Review of Psychology* 56 (2005): 485–516; Edwin A. Locke and Gary P. Latham, *Goal Setting: A Motivational Technique That Works* (Englewood Cliffs, N.J.: Prentice Hall, 1984); Edwin A. Locke and Gary P. Latham, *A Theory of Goal Setting and Task Performance* (Englewood Cliffs, N.J.: Prentice-Hall, 1990); Edwin A. Locke and Gary P. Latham, "Building a Practically Useful Theory of Goal Setting and Task Motivation: A 35-Year Odyssey," *American Psychologist* 57, no. 9 (2002): 705–17; Edwin A. Locke and Gary P. Latham, "What Should We Do about Motivation Theory," *Academy of Management Review* 29, no. 3 (2004): 388–403; Terence R. Mitchell and Denise Daniels, "Motivation," in *Handbook of Psychology,* vol. 12, *Industrial and Organizational Psychology,* edited by Walter C. Borman, Daniel R. Ilgen, and Richard J. Klimoski (New York: John Wiley and Sons, 2003), pp. 225–54; Robert Rodgers and John E. Hunter, "Impact of Management by Objectives on Organizational Productivity," *Journal of Applied Psychology* 76, no. 2 (1991): 322–36.

6. Christopher Pollitt, "Performance Management in Practice: A Comparative Study of Executive Agencies," *Journal of Public Administration Research and Theory* 16, no. 1 (2006): 35.

7. Stephen G. Harkins and Richard E. Petty, "Effects of Task Difficulty and Task Uniqueness on Social Loafing," *Journal of Personality and Social Psychology* 43, no. 6 (1982):1214–229.

8. Most of the research in social and personal psychology is based on laboratory experiments with undergraduates. For such experiments, the consequence to the student subject is almost always trivial, of much less consequence for the subjects (or for anyone else) than any course quiz. Sometimes these undergraduate subjects are tricked; the formal task that they have been given is not the behavior that the laboratory experiment is attempting to examine. See, for example, John M. Darley and Bibb Latané, "Bystander Intervention in Emergencies: Diffusion of Responsibility," *Journal of Personality and Social Psychology* 8, no. 4 (1968): 377–83; Bibb Latané and John M. Darley, "Group Inhibition of Bystander Intervention in Emergencies," *Journal of Personality and Social Psychology* 10, no. 3 (1968): 215–21. A significant exception to the tradition of the undergraduate psychology lab, and thus to the external validity of the conclusions, is the research of Adam Grant: Adam M. Grant, "Relational Job Design and the Motivation to Make a Prosocial Difference," *Academy of Management Review* 32, no. 2 (2007): 393–417; Adam M. Grant, Jane E. Dutton and Brent D. Rosso, "Giving Commitment: Employee Support Programs and the Prosocial Sensemaking Process," *Academy of Management Journal* 51, no. 5 (October 2008): 898–918; Adam M. Grant and Kimberly A. Wade-Benzoni, "The Hot and Cool of Death Awareness at Work: Mortality Cues, Aging, and Self-Protective and Prosocial Motivations," *Academy of Management Review* 34, no. 4 (2009): 600–22.

9. On June 14, 2006, in preparation for the next day's CitiStat session, Jay Sakai, director of Baltimore's Bureau of Water and Wastewater, met with his staff. Sakai knew that, because his bureau was doing a good job on several of its priority performance targets, the mayor's team would want some further improvements. Thus, Sakai asked his staff what they should suggest. After all, he pointed out, if they did not offer some new and reasonable targets, the mayor's office might impose some unreasonable ones.

10. Pollitt, "Performance Management in Practice," pp. 25–44.

11. Washington Traffic Safety Commission, *Washington State Strategic Highway Safety Plan 2013* (targetzero.com/PDF/TargetZeroPlan.pdf).

12. Richard P. Nathan, *The Administrative Presidency* (New York: John Wiley & Sons, 1983), p. 30.

13. Alfred Tat-Kei Ho, "Accounting for the Value of Performance Measurement from the Perspective of Midwestern Mayors," *Journal of Public Administration Research and Theory* 16, no. 2 (2006): 219.

14. Ho assessed the interest of Midwestern mayors in performance measurement and observed: "mayors of larger cities were less likely to take personal initiatives to launch performance management reforms." Yet in Baltimore, which is larger than any city Ho

surveyed, three mayors did make performance measurement—and *performance leadership*—a personal initiative. Ibid., p. 224.

15. Anthony Downs, *Inside Bureaucracy* (Brookings, 1967), p. 145.

16. Robert D. Behn, "On Why Public Executives Need to Avoid Dashboards as Data Dumps," *Bob Behn's Public Management Report* 5, no. 11 (July 2008).

17. Pollitt, "Performance Management in Practice," p. 34.

18. Kipling Williams, Stephen Harkins, and Bibb Latané, "Identifiability as a Deterrent to Social Loafing: Two Cheering Experiments," *Journal of Personality and Social Psychology* 40, no. 2 (1981): 303, 311. See also: Kipling D. Williams, Steve A. Nida, Lawrence D. Baca, and Bibb Latané, "Social Loafing and Swimming: Effects of Identifiability on Individual and Relay Performance of Intercollegiate Swimmers," *Basic and Applied Social Psychology* 10, no. 1 (1989): 73–81.

19. Downs observes that the creation of "a separate monitoring agency" (which a PerformanceStat office certainly is) "tends to increase the rigidity of the operating bureau" because (a) the monitoring agency "imposes ever more complex and ever more restrictive regulations," (b) the operating agency must devote "more and more of its resources to satisfy the increasing demands of the monitors for information and written reports," and (c) the operating agency "tends to devote ever more resources to figuring out ways of evading or counteracting the monitors' additional regulations." *Inside Bureaucracy,* pp. 158–59.

For PerformanceStat, the first of these three behaviors doesn't (quite) apply. Instead of regulations, PerformanceStat imposes targets and assignments, which can certainly become more complex and more demanding. Downs's second argument does indeed hold; the leaders of each subunit must show up for their regular meetings and devote time and other resources to preparing for them. Over time, however, the chief executive's leadership team can reduce significantly the effort that subunit managers devote to evasive tactics, if only by replacing agency heads who engage in them. But they may not have the same success in reducing the evasive behavior of front-line supervisors and workers.

20. Jeffrey Pfeffer, "Organizations and Organization Theory," in *The Handbook of Social Psychology,* 3rd ed., vol. I, *Theory and Method,* edited by Gardner Lindzey and Elliot Aronson (New York: Random House, 1985), p. 390. See also Clive Seligman and John M. Darley, "Feedback as a Means of Decreasing Residential Energy Consumption," *Journal of Applied Psychology* 62, no. 4 (1997): 363–68; Edward L. Thorndike, "The Law of Effect," *American Journal of Psychology* 39, no. 1/4 (December 1927): 212–22.

21. Obviously, this leadership behavior cannot be employed in organizations that are not large enough to have multiple subunits whose performance data can be compared.

22. Carla O'Dell and C. Jackson Grayson, "If Only We Knew What We Know: Identification and Transfer of Internal Best Practices," *California Management Review* 40, no. 3 (Spring 1998): 154–74.

23. At the Maryland Stat Summit, September 10, 2008.

24. See Robert D. Behn, *Leadership Counts: Lessons for Public Managers* (Harvard University Press, 1991), pp. 104–26.

25. Interview with O'Malley, April 22, 2008.

26. For a discussion of when naming and shaming might work, see: Ray Pawson, "Evidence and Policy and Naming and Shaming," *Policy Studies* 23, no. 3/4 (2002): 211–30.

27. James Lincoln and Didier Guillot, "A Durkheimian View of Organizational Culture," in *Social Theory at Work,* edited by Marek Korczynski, Randy Hodson, and Paul K. Edwards (University of Oxford Press, 2006), p. 105.

28. John Aloysius Farrell, "Officials' Anti-Church Bias Alleged," *Boston Globe,* August 17, 2001, p. A2. See also: Brookings, "A Governance Studies Event: White House Issues Report on Barriers to Faith-Based Organizations," August 16, 2001 (www.brookings.edu/events/2001/0816faith-based-initiatives.aspx).

29. Edgar H. Schein, *Organizational Culture and Leadership,* 2nd ed. (San Francisco: Jossey-Bass, 1992), p. 12.

30. Robert D. Behn, *Rethinking Democratic Accountability* (Brookings, 2001), particularly chapter 1.

31. Caren Siehl and Joanne Martin, "The Role of Symbolic Management: How Can Managers Effectively Transmit Organizational Culture?" *Leaders and Managers: International Perspectives on Managerial Behavior and Leadership,* edited by James G. Hunt, Dian-Marie Hosking, Chester A. Schriesheim, and Rosemary Stewart, vol. 7 (Elmsford, N.Y.: Pergamon Press, 1984), pp. 227, 228.

32. Anne M. Khademian, *Working with Culture: How the Job Gets Done in Public Programs* (Washington: CQ Press, 2002), p. 3.

33. Philip Selznick, *Leadership in Administration: A Sociological Interpretation* (New York: Harper & Row, 1957), p.151. For more on the role of stories in creating an organizational culture, see: Joanne Martin and Melanie E. Powers, "Truth or Corporate Propaganda: The Value of a Good War Story," in *Organizational Symbolism,* edited by Louis R. Pondy and others (Greenwich, Conn.: JAI Press, 1983), pp. 93–107); Ian I. Mitroff and Ralph H. Kilmann, "Stories Managers Tell: A New Tool for Organizational Problem Solving," *Management Review* 64, no. 7 (1975): 18–28; Schein, *Organizational Culture and Leadership,* pp. 89–92, 182–84, 25; Alan L. Wilkins, "The Creation of Company Cultures: The Role of Stories and Human Resource Systems," *Human Resource Management* 23, no. 1 (1984): 41–60.

34. The potential for evaluation can have conflicting effects, facilitating the performance of simple or well-learned tasks, while inhibiting the performance of complex or novel tasks. Stephen G. Harkins, "Social Loafing and Social Facilitation," *Journal of Experimental Social Psychology* 23, no. 1 (1987): 1–18.

35. Ibid.

36. Robert M. Yerkes and John D. Dodson, "The Relation of Strength of Stimulus to Rapidity of Habit-Formation," *Journal of Comparative Neurology and Psychology* 18 (1908): 459–82.

37. Yaniv Hanoch and Oliver Vitouch, "When Less Is More: Information, Emotional Arousal and the Ecological Reframing of the Yerkes-Dodson Law," *Theory and Psychology* 14, no. 4 (2004): 427–52.

38. Charles A. O'Reilly, III, and Barton A. Weitz, "Managing Marginal Employees: The Use of Warnings and Dismissals," *Administrative Science Quarterly* 25, no. 3 (1980): 467.

39. I am referring not to a literal hammer but to the much more famous metaphorical one: "If all you have is a hammer, everything looks like a nail." There are multiple sources for this saying including these two. The philosopher Abraham Kaplan called it "the law of the instrument": "Give a small boy a hammer, and he will find that everything he encounters needs pounding." Abraham Kaplan, *The Conduct of Inquiry: Methodology for Behavioral Science* (San Francisco: Chandler Publishing, 1964), p. 28. The psychologist Abraham Maslow put it slightly differently: "I suppose it is tempting, if the only tool you have is a hammer, to treat everything as if it were a nail." Abraham H. Maslow, *The Psychology of Science: A Reconnaissance* (New York: Harper and Row, 1966), p. 15.

40. Abraham Lincoln, "Address before the Wisconsin State Agricultural Society, Milwaukee, Wisconsin" (September 30, 1859), quoted in Roy P. Basler, ed., *The Collected Works of Abraham Lincoln,* vol. III (Rutgers University Press, 1953), pp. 481–82. The more complete quotation is: "It is said an Eastern monarch once charged his wise men to invent him a sentence, to be ever in view, and which should be true and appropriate in all times and situations. They presented him the words: 'And this, too, shall pass away.' How much it expresses! How chastening in the hour of pride! How consoling in the depths of affliction!"

41. Interview with Hirsch, February 15, 2011.

Chapter Sixteen

1. Theodore Levitt, "Management and the 'Post-Industrial' Society," *Public Interest,* no. 44 (Summer 1976): 77.

2. Niccolò Machiavelli, *The Prince,* translated by Peter Bondanella and Mark Musa (Oxford University Press, 1984 [1532]), p. 21.

3. Government Performance and Results Act of 1993, P. L.103–62.

4. GPRA Modernization Act of 2010, P. L.111–352.

5. Traditionally, we associate leadership with hierarchical authority. Heifetz, however, made a clear distinction between a formal position of authority and the actual exercise of leadership. He tends "to avoid the term leader because it generally connotes an authority figure." Instead, he prefers "to use the active phrase, 'exercising leadership.'" He wants to "focus on the activity of leadership and not on the role of authority or the intrinsic qualities of any person." And this "activity of leadership" can come from anyone, anywhere in the organization. Ronald A. Heifetz, *Leadership without Easy Answers* (Harvard University Press, 1994), p. 326.

What official status would an individual or team need to be able to exploit the PerformanceStat potential? I think only three capabilities are essential: the ability to collect data that are relevant to their purpose; the ability to call a meeting that others feel obliged to attend; and the ability to (re)allocate some resources. None of the other key operational components depend on anyone's formal status (though hierarchical ranking does help).

6. Charles A. Kiesler and Sara B. Kiesler, *Conformity* (Reading, Mass.: Addison-Wesley, 1990).

7. Machiavelli, *The Prince*, p. 21. For a more detailed and contemporary examination of Machiavelli's point, see Luke Novelli, Bradley L. Kirkman, and Debra L Shapiro, "Effective Implementation of Organizational Change: An Organizational Justice Perspective," in *Trends in Organizational Behavior*, edited by Cary L. Cooper and Denise M. Rousseau, vol. 2 (Chichester, U.K.: John Wiley and Sons, 1995), pp. 15–36.

8. Jonathan Alter, *The Defining Moment: FDR's Hundred Days and the Triumph of Hope* (New York: Simon & Schuster, 2006), p. 292.

9. Ibid., pp. 293, 204.

10. Robert Fechner, *Objectives and Results of the Civilian Conservation Corps Program* (Washington: Civilian Conservation Corps, 1938), pp. 6, 9 (http://digilab.browardlibrary.org/cdm4/document.php?CISOROOT=/ccc&CISOPTR=691&REC=11).

11. George Bernard Shaw, *Man and Superman: A Comedy and a Philosophy* (New York: Brentano's, 1914), p. 238.

12. Woodrow Wilson, "The Study of Administration," *Political Science Quarterly* 2, no. 2 (June 1887): 220, 218, 202.

13. Tony Bovaird and Elke Löffler, "Lessons from Europe: Innovations in Rural Service Delivery," Proceedings of the 2005 National Rural Affairs Conference, Castle Green, Hotel Kendal, February 24, 2005.

14. George Bernard Shaw, L. W. Conolly, eds., *Mrs. Warren's Profession* (Peterborough, Ont.: Broadview Press, 2005, 1893), Act II, p. 121.

15. Jack Maple, *Crime Fighter: How You Can Make Your Community Crime-Free* (New York: Doubleday, 1999), p. 93.

16. Jeffrey Pfeffer and Robert I. Sutton, *Hard Facts, Dangerous Half-Truths, and Total Nonsense: Profiting from Evidence-Based Management* (Harvard Business School Press, 2006), pp. 176, 177.

17. Ibid., pp. 178–85.

18. Karl E. Weick, "Small Wins: Redefining the Scale of Social Problems," *American Psychologist* 39, no. 1 (January 1984): 40, 43.

19. Ibid., pp. 43, 41.

20. "Vacants to Value," Baltimore Housing website, www.baltimorehousing.org/vacants_to_value.aspx.

21. Robert D. Behn, "Collaborating for Performance: Or Can There Exist Such a Thing as CollaborationStat?" *International Public Management Journal* 13, no. 4 (December 2010): 429–70.

22. Anthony Downs, *Inside Bureaucracy* (Brookings, 1967), p. 198.

23. Malcolm K. Sparrow, Mark H. Moore, and David M. Kennedy, *Beyond 911: A New Era for Policing* (New York: Basic Books 1990).

24. Downs, *Inside Bureaucracy*, p. 204.

25. Herbert A. Simon, "Decision-Making and Administrative Organization," *Public Administration Review* 4, no. 1 (1944): 16; Herbert A. Simon, *Administrative Behavior: A Study of Decision-Making Processes in Administrative Organizations*, 4th ed. (New York: The Free Press, 1997), p. 2.

26. In 1969, Roy Ash, President Nixon's first budget director, converted the old Bureau of the Budget into the Office of Management and Budget. Over four decades later, the Executive Office of the President and OMB are still trying to figure out how to make the M effective.

27. The bases for criticism include:

—Was the right kind of target chosen? Did the public executive choose to focus on a performance deficit that is truly relevant?

—Was the target significant enough? Did the public executive choose a performance target that is clearly consequential?

—Was the time frame fast enough? Did the public executive choose to achieve this higher level of performance quickly enough to make the result meaningful?

28. Robert D. Behn, *Rethinking Democratic Accountability* (Brookings, 2001), p. 15.

29. Dennis C. Smith, "Making Management Count: A Case for Theory-and-Evidence-Based Public Management," *Journal of Policy Analysis and Management* 28, no. 1 (Summer 2009): 500.

30. Gregg G. Van Ryzin, "Expectations, Performance, and Citizen Satisfaction with Urban Services," *Journal of Policy Analysis and Management* 23, no. 3 (Summer 2004): 445–46. A similar result was found for customer satisfaction with consumer products. See Richard L. Ullvei, *Satisfaction: A Behavioral Perspective on the Consumer*, 2nd ed. (Armonk, N.Y.: M. E. Sharpe, 2009).

31. Van Ryzin, "Expectations, Performance, and Citizen Satisfaction with Urban Services," pp. 446, 433.

32. IESE is Instituto de Estudios Superiores de la Empresa.

33. Pankaj Ghemawat, *Commitment: The Dynamic of Strategy* (New York: The Free Press, 1991), pp. 25, 26.

34. Denise M. Rousseau, "Organizational Behavior in the New Organizational Era," *Annual Review of Psychology* 48 (1997): 526.

35. Robert Rodgers and John E. Hunter, "Impact of Management by Objectives on Organizational Productivity," *Journal of Applied Psychology* 76, no. 2 (April 1991): 322. See also Robert Rodgers, John E. Hunter, and Deborah L. Rodgers, "Influence of Top Management Commitment on Management Program Success," *Journal of Applied Psychology* 78, no. 1 (February 1993): 151–55.

36. André A. de Wall and Harold Counet, "Lessons Learned from Performance Management Systems Implementations," *International Journal of Productivity and Performance Management* 58, no. 4 (2009): 367, 381.

37. Ghemawat, *Commitment*, pp. 14, 15.

38. Ibid., p. 16.

Appendix A

1. These eight are not the only nonpolicing explanations. Rick Nevin argued that the decline in children's exposure to lead (in gasoline and paint) in the 1970s and 1980s was a contributing cause. See Rick Nevin, "How Lead Exposure Relates to Temporal Changes in IQ, Violent Crime, and Unwed Pregnancy," *Environmental Research* 83, no. 1 (May 2000): 1–22; Rick Nevin, "Understanding International Crime Ttrends: The Legacy of Preschool Lead Exposure," *Environmental Research* 104, no. 3 (July 2007): 315–36; Rick Nevin, "Why Is the Murder Rate Lower in New York City?" May 29, 2013 (www.ricknevin.com/uploads/Why_is_the_Murder_Rate_Lower_in_NYC.pdf). Eric Baumer and Kevin Wolff offer a list of "the major explanations for contemporary crime declines," which include (in addition to the usual suspects) increased video gaming, reduced alcohol consumption, and increased use of psychiatric pharmaceutical therapies. See Eric P. Baumer and Kevin T. Wolff, "Evaluating Contemporary Crime Drop(s) in America, New York City, and Many Other Places," *Justice Quarterly* (forthcoming).

2. People can, of course, make precisely the opposite assumption. "Scholars and senior decision-makers will," observed Zimring, "be chronically tempted to assume human causes for good news." He calls this "the euphoric fallacy." Franklin E. Zimring, *The Great American Crime Decline* (Oxford University Press, 2007), p. 42.

3. Alfred Blumstein, "Disaggregating the Violence Trends," in *The Crime Drop in America,* edited by Blumstein and Joel Wallman, 2nd ed. (Cambridge University Press, 2005) p. 19.

4. John J. Donohue, "Understanding the Time Path of Crime," *Journal of Criminal Law & Criminology* 88, no. 4 (Summer 1998), p. 1423.

5. This explanation is mentioned in Benjamin Bowling, "The Rise and Fall of New York Murder: Zero Tolerance or Crack's Decline?" *British Journal of Criminology* 39, no. 4 (Autumn 1999), p. 539. For a concise explanation of regression toward the mean, see J. Martin Bland and Douglas G. Altman, "Statistical Notes: Regression towards the Mean," *British Medical Journal* 308, no. 6942 (June 4, 1994): 1499.

6. U.S. Bureau of Justice Statistics (http://bjsdata.ojp.usdoj.gov/ucrdata). The U.S. violent crime rate peaked at 864 in 1995; by 2010, it was down to 405 (though still more than double the 1960 rate).

7. For an example of how "regression toward the mean" can help explain what happens after a policy intervention, see Donald T. Campbell and H. Laurence Ross, "The Connecticut Crackdown on Speeding: Time-Series Data in Quasi-Experimental Analysis," *Law & Society Review* 3, no. 1 (August 1968), pp. 33–53. In 1955, deaths from highway accidents in Connecticut jumped; so the state's governor implemented a crackdown on speeding, and—surprise?—deaths from highway accidents went down.

8. Donohue, "Understanding the Time Path of Crime," p. 1423.

9. Ibid., pp. 1426, 1449.

10. Steven D. Levitt, "Understanding Why Crime Fell in the 1990s: Four Factors That Explain the Decline and Six That Do Not," *Journal of Economic Perspectives* 18, no. 1 (Winter 2004): 182.

11. Ted Joyce, "Did Legalized Abortion Lower Crime?" *Journal of Human Resources* 39, no. 1 (Winter 2004), pp. 1–28.

12. Steven D. Levitt and Stephen J. Dubner, *Freakonomics: A Rogue Economist Explores the Hidden Side of Everything* (New York: Harper Perennial, 2009), p. 12.

13. Levitt, "Understanding Why Crime Fell in the 1990s," p. 173. For additional analysis by Levitt and Donohue on the connection between abortion and crime, see John J. Donohue, III and Steven D. Levitt, "The Impact of Legalized Abortion on Crime," *Quarterly Journal of Economics* 116, no. 2 (May 2001): 379–420; John J. Donohue III and Steven D. Levitt, "Further Evidence That Legalized Abortion Lowered Crime: A Reply to Joyce," *Journal of Human Resources* 39, no. 1 (Winter 2004): 29–49.

14. Zimring, *The Great American Crime Decline,* pp. 148–49.

15. Levitt, "Understanding Why Crime Fell in the 1990s," p. 184.

16. Steven D. Levitt, "The Effect of Prison Population Size on Crime Rates: Evidence from Prison Overcrowding Litigation," *Quarterly Journal of Economics* 111, no. 2 (May 1996): 348. "An uncertain estimate of 16 to 25 index crimes averted per year per each additional prisoner"—can be found in Thomas B. Marvell and Carlisle E. Moody, Jr., "Prison Population Growth and Crime Reduction," *Journal of Quantitative Criminology* 10, no. 2 (June 1994): 109–40. They also estimated that "a 10% increase in prison population is associated with roughly 13% fewer homicides." Thomas B. Marvell and Carlisle E. Moody Jr., "The Impact of Prison Growth on Homicide," *Homicide Studies* 1, no. 3 (August 1997): 205.

17. Franklin E. Zimring and Gordon Hawkins, *Incapacitation: Penal Confinement and the Restraint of Crime* (Oxford University Press, 1995), pp. 100–01.

18. William Spelman, "The Limited Importance of Prison Expansion," in *The Crime Drop in America,* edited by Blumstein and Wallman, pp. 123, 125, 114, 125.

19. Brian R. Edlin, Kathleen L. Irwin, Sairus Faruque, Clyde B. McCoy, Carl Word, Yolanda Serrano, James A. Inciardi, Benjamin P. Bowser, Robert F. Schilling, and Scott D. Holmberg, for The Multicenter Crack Cocaine and HIV Infection Study Team, "Intersecting Epidemics—Crack Cocaine Use and HIV Infection among Inner-City Young Adults," *New England Journal of Medicine* 33, no. 21 (November 24, 1994):1422–427. James W. Cornish and Charles P. O'Brien, "Crack Cocaine Abuse: An Epidemic with Many Public Health Consequences," *Annual Review of Public Health* 17 (1996): 259–73.

20. National Institute on Drug Abuse, *National Household Survey on Drug Abuse: Population Estimates, 1991* (Rockville, Md.: U.S. Department of Health and Human Services, Public Health Service, Alcohol, Drug Abuse, and Mental Health Administration, 1991), DHHS Publication (ADM) 92-1887, p. 37.

21. Blumstein offered several reasons: Juveniles were a "natural source" of labor, were "willing to work more cheaply than adults," were "less vulnerable to punishments," were more "willing to take risks," and had few other employment opportunities. Alfred Blumstein, "Youth Violence, Guns, and the Illicit-Drug Industry," *Journal of Criminal Law and Criminology* 86, no. 1 (Autumn 1995): 30.

22. Ibid., pp. 30, 10, 27.

23. Bowling, "The Rise and Fall of New York Murder," p. 551. For additional analyses of the link between trends in crack use and trends in crime in the 1980s and the 1990s, see Eric Baumer, Janet L. Lauritsen, Richard Rosenfeld, and Richard Wright, "The Influence of Crack Cocaine on Robbery, Burglary, and Homicide Rates: A Cross-City, Longitudinal Analysis," *Journal of Research in Crime and Delinquency* 35, no. 3 (August 1998): 316–40; Bruce D. Johnson, Andrew Golub, and Eloise Dunlap, "The Rise and Decline of Hard Drugs, Drug Markets, and Violence in Inner-City New York City," in *The Crime Drop in America,* edited by Blumstein and Wallman, pp. 164–206; John E. Conklin, *Why Crime Rates Fell* (Boston, Mass.: Allyn and Bacon, 2003), chapter 6, pp. 99–120.

24. Zimring, *The Great American Crime Decline,* pp. 81–85; Andrew Karmen, *New York Murder Mystery: The True Story behind the Crime Crash of the 1990s* (New York University Press, 2000), pp. 166–84.

25. Jeff Grogger, "Market Wages and Youth Crime," *Journal of Labor Economics* 16, no. 4 (October 1998): 787, 757, 756.

26. Unemployment Rate, 16 to 19 years, Series LNS14000012, Labor Force Statistics from the Current Population Survey, Bureau of Labor Statistics, U.S. Department of Labor (http://data.bls.gov/PDQ/servlet/SurveyOutputServlet).

27. Jeff Grogger, "An Economic Model of Recent Trends in Violence," in *The Crime Drop in America,* edited by Blumstein and Wallman, pp. 281–82.

28. Zimring, *The Great American Crime Decline,* p. 68.

29. Laura Dugan, Daniel Nagin, and Richard Rosenfeld, "Exposure Reduction or Retaliation? The Effects of Domestic Violence Resources on Intimate Partner Homicide," *Law & Society Review* 37, no. 1 (March 2003): 169, 172, 171. See also Laura Dugan, Daniel S. Nagin, and Richard Rosenfeld, "The Effects of State and Local Domestic Violence Policy on Intimate Partner Homicide," in *Violence against Women and Family Violence: Developments in Research, Practice, and Policy,* edited by Bonnie S. Fisher (Washington: National Institute of Justice, 2004), pp. II-6-1 to II-6-10; Laura Dugan, Daniel Nagin, and Richard Rosenfeld, "Do Domestic Violence Services Save Lives?" *NIJ Journal,* no. 250 (November 2003): 20–25; Laura Dugan, Daniel Nagin, and Richard Rosenfeld, "Explaining the Decline in Intimate Partner Homicide: The Effects of Changing Domesticity, Women's Status, and Domestic Violence Resources," *Homicide Studies* 3, no. 3 (August 1999): 187–214.

30. Rosenfeld, "Crime Decline in Context," p. 28.

31. Friedman, "Volunteerism and the Decline of Violent Crime," pp. 1456, 1458, 1456, 1457.

32. Robert J. Sampson, *Great American City: Chicago and the Enduring Neighborhood Effect* (University of Chicago Press, 2012), p. 150.

33. Sampson, *Great American City,* pp. 27, 127, 152. See also: Robert J. Sampson, Stephen W. Raudenbush, and Felton Earls, "Neighborhoods and Violent Crime: A Multilevel Study of Collective Efficacy," *Science* 277, no. 5328 (August 15, 1997): 918–24;

Robert J. Sampson, Jeffrey D. Morenoff, and Felton Earls, "Beyond Social Capital: Spatial Dynamics of Collective Efficacy for Children," *American Sociological Review* 64, no. 5 (October 1999): 633–60; Robert J. Sampson and Stephen W. Raudenbush, "Systematic Social Observation of Public Spaces: A New Look at Disorder in Urban Neighborhoods," *American Journal of Sociology* 105, no. 3 (November 1999): 603–51.

34. Sampson and others, "Neighborhoods and Violent Crime," p. 918.

35. Friedman, "Volunteerism and the Decline of Violent Crime," p. 1453.

36. Peter K. B. St. Jean, *Pockets of Crime: Broken Windows, Collective Efficacy, and the Criminal Point of View* (University of Chicago Press, 2007), p. 249. Note: police, by helping to create neighborhood watch groups and engaging in broken-windows policing, could foster a neighborhood's collective efficacy.

37. LaFree, "Social Institutions and the Crime 'Bust' of the 1990s," p. 1349. Several years before, I staked out a different view: "After language and fire, the most important human invention is the deadline." Robert D. Behn, *Leadership Counts: Lessons for Public Managers* (Harvard University Press, 1991), p. 27.

38. Gary LaFree, *Losing Legitimacy: Street Crime and the Decline of Social Institutions in America* (Boulder, Colo.: Westview Press, 1998), p. 70.

39. LaFree, "Social Institutions and the Crime 'Bust' of the 1990s," pp. 1325, 1368.

40. Ibid., pp. 1354, 1367, 1354, 1355, 1326, 1350.

Appendix B

1. "Commissioner Gilmore, ..." STARS meeting, June 24, 2005. "Commissioner Grey, ..."STARS meeting, December 5, 2008.

2. STARS meeting, July 27, 2007.

Appendix C

1. Leon Festinger, "A Theory of Social Comparison Processes," *Human Relations* 7, no. 2 (1954): 117–40.

2. Tamao Matsui, Takashi Kakuyama, and Mary Lou U. Onglatco, "Effects of Goals and Feedback on Performance in Groups," *Journal of Applied Psychology* 72, no. 3 (1987): 407–15.

3. Edward E. Lawler, III, and John Grant Rhode, *Information and Control in Organizations* (Santa Monica, Calif.: Goodyear Publishing, 1976).

4. Wolfgang Stroebe, Michael Diehl, and Georgios Abakoumkin, "Social Compensation and the Köhler Effect: Toward a Theoretical Explanation of Motivation Gains in Group Behavior," in *Understanding Group Behavior: Small Group Processes and*

Interpersonal Relations, edited by Erich H. Witte and James H. Davis (Mahwah, N.J.: Erlbaum, 1996), pp. 37–65.

5. Yan Chen, F. Maxwell Harper, Joseph Konstan, and Sherry X. Li, "Social Comparisons and Contributions to Online Communities: A Field Experiment on MovieLens," *American Economic Review* 100, no. 4 (September 2010): 1358–1398.

6. Remus Illies and Timothy A. Judge, "Goal Regulation across Time: The Effects of Feedback and Affect," *Journal of Applied Psychology* 90, no 3 (2005): 453–67.

7. Jerry Suls, René Martin, and Ladd Wheeler, "Social Comparison: Why, With Whom, and With What Effect," *Current Directions in Psychological Science* 11, no. 5 (2002): 162.

8. Joanne V. Wood, "Theory and Research Concerning Social Comparisons of Personal Atrributes," *Psychological Bulletin* 106, no. 2 (September 1989): 239.

9. Kevin J. Williams, John J. Donovan, and Tonya L. Dodge, "Self-Regulation of Performance: Goal Establishment and Goal Revision Processes in Athletes," *Human Performance* 13, no. 2 (2000): 159–80; John J. Donovan and Kevin J. Williams, "Missing the Mark: Effect of Time and Causal Attributions on Goal Revision in Response to Goal-Performance Discrepancies," *Journal of Applied Psychology* 88, no. 3 (2002): 379–90.

10. For a discussion of "friendly competition," see Robert D. Behn, "On the Characteristics of Friendly Competition," *Bob Behn's Public Management Report* 1, no. 3 (November 2003); and Robert D. Behn, *Performance Leadership: 11 Better Practices That Can Ratchet Up Performance* (Washington, D.C.: IBM Center for the Business of Government, 2004): 16–17.

11. Behn, *Leadership Counts,* pp. 80–81.

Appendix D

1. Most professional graduate school programs do offer courses in data analysis. Students may be exposed to a variety of analytical techniques (though some escape, taking only the minimal requirement).

2. The first human skunkworks, formed by Lockheed Aircraft Corporation during World War II, was a small creative operation that, released from the usual corporate and government constraints, produced the P-80, the first U.S. jet fighter, in just 143 days—37 ahead of schedule. The name, however, came from Al Capp's comic strip Li'l Abner, in which the Skonk Works was a secret, smelly still, run by Big Barnsmell, that produced an illicit moonshine called "Kickapoo Joy Juice" from dead skunks, old shoes, and whatever else was available. Because the Lockheed team was secret, used whatever was available to produce its planes, and was located next to a very smelly plastics factory, it adopted the name.

3. One iconic textbook in accounting—now in its 12th edition—is titled simply *Management Control Systems.* Indeed, from a collection of the standard textbook titles,

it appears that accounting *is* control. Robert Anthony and Vijay Govindarajan, *Management Control Systems* (New York: McGraw-Hill/Irwin, 2006); Eddy Vaassen, Roger Meuwissen, and Caren Schelleman, *Accounting Information Systems and Internal Control* (Hoboken, N.J.: Wiley, 2009); Leslie Turner and Andrea Weickgenannt, *Accounting for Information Systems: Controls and Processes* (Hoboken, N.J.: Wiley, 2008); Jerold Zimmerman, *Accounting for Decision Making and Control* (New York: McGraw-Hill/Irwin, 2010); Steven M. Bragg, *Accounting Control Best Practices* (Hoboken, N.J.: Wiley, 2009); Rose Hightower, *Internal Controls Policies and Procedures* (Hoboken, N.J.: John Wiley & Sons, 2009).

4. A Google search for the phrase "organization-wide consistency" produced over 7,000 results, most of which were about consistency in the private sector, and most of which advocated it. For example, Microsoft advertises that its "Office Enterprise Project Management Solution" will "implement standards and best practices for organization-wide consistency and compliance" (www.msproject.com/documents/EPMSolution-Datasheet.pdf). In Accenture's journal, two partners write, "The challenge of improving job performance becomes even greater in tough economic times." Thus they advocate improvements in a firm's "mission-critical workforce," which (among other things) had produced such "measurable business results" as "increased organization-wide consistency by 30–50%." Dorothy V. Von Kette and Patrick Mosher, "Mission Critical" (www.accenture.com/NR/rdonlyres/B4E203E3-E3CA-418B-95A0-BED0C46AD4BA/0/Mission_Critical.pdf).

Index

About the Author

Robert Behn is a lecturer at Harvard's Kennedy School of Government, where he is faculty chair of the executive education program "Driving Government Performance: Leadership Strategies that Produce Results." He is the author of *Rethinking Democratic Accountability* (Brookings) and writes the online monthly Bob Behn's Performance Leadership Report.

CPSIA information can be obtained at www.ICGtesting.com
Printed in the USA
BVOW04s0841041114

373559BV00003B/5/P